D1553886

PIONEERS OF PROMOTION

The William F. Cody
Series on the History and
Culture of the American West

To the four doctors who ignited my love for history:
the late Marc Ross, Ph.D., during high school;
the late John L. Thomas, Ph.D., during college;
Howard R. Lamar, Ph.D., during and after graduate school;
and Alan Dobrow, M.D., every day of my life

PIONEERS OF PROMOTION

How Press Agents for Buffalo Bill, P. T. Barnum, and the World's Columbian Exposition Created Modern Marketing

JOE DOBROW

UNIVERSITY OF OKLAHOMA PRESS : NORMAN

Also by Joe Dobrow

Natural Prophets: From Health Foods to Whole Foods—How the Pioneers of the Industry Changed the Way We Eat and Reshaped American Business (Emmaus, Penn., 2014)

BUFFALO BILL
CENTER
OF THE WEST

Buffalo Bill Center of the West sponsorship of The William F. Cody Series on the History and Culture of the American West is generously funded by the Geraldine W. & Robert J. Dellenback Foundation, Inc.

LIBRARY OF CONGRESS CATALOGING-IN-PUBLICATION DATA

Name: Dobrow, Joe, author.
Title: Pioneers of promotion : how press agents for Buffalo Bill, P. T. Barnum, and the World's Columbian Exposition created modern marketing / Joe Dobrow.
Description: First Edition. | University of Oklahoma Press : Norman, OK [2018] | Includes bibliographical references and index.
Identifiers: LCCN 2017055309 | ISBN 978-0-8061-6010-8 (hardcover : alk. paper)
Subjects: LCSH: Marketing—United States—History—19th century. | Advertising—United States—History—19th century. | Burke, John M., –1917. | Barnum, P. T. (Phineas Taylor), 1810–1891. | Handy, Moses P. (Moses Purnell), 1847–1898.
Classification: LCC HF5415.1 .D593 2018 | DDC 381.0973—dc23
LC record available at https://lccn.loc.gov/2017055309

Pioneers of Promotion: How Press Agents for Buffalo Bill, P. T. Barnum, and the World's Columbian Exposition Created Modern Marketing is Volume 5 in The William F. Cody Series on the History and Culture of the American West.

The paper in this book meets the guidelines for permanence and durability of the Committee on Production Guidelines for Book Longevity of the Council on Library Resources, Inc. ∞

1 2 3 4 5 6 7 8 9 10

CONTENTS

ILLUSTRATIONS

PLATES

FIGURES

SERIES EDITORS' PREFACE

Many are familiar with Buffalo Bill's Wild West, the Columbian Exposition, and the Barnum and Bailey Circus, yet the names of promoters John Burke, Moses Handy, and Tody Hamilton remain relatively obscure. Readers may even wonder why an internationally renowned Wild West show, a world's fair, and a circus needed any advertising whatsoever. Joe Dobrow's *Pioneers of Promotion* not only examines the efforts of Burke, Handy, and Hamilton to shape modern marketing techniques; it also asks us to consider how the nascent techniques of mass advertising secured the historical memory embedded in these specific forms of entertainment.

Before John M. Burke, most "promotion" consisted of simple advertisements that briefly described the event or the product (with the notable exception of the famed showman P. T. Barnum). But Burke was visionary and innovative; without the taint of Barnum's humbuggery, he introduced modes of promotion that have now become part of the stock in trade of modern marketing—the celebrity endorsement, the press kit, the press junket, the op-ed, mobile billboards, and licensing deals—all techniques that students such as Handy and Hamilton adopted in their own marketing strategies. The combined legacy of Burke, Handy, and Hamilton, three pioneers of promotion, remains notable in today's consumption-driven economy. Focusing on three individuals who worked in the realm of entertainment, Dobrow reveals an overlooked dimension of the history of marketing and demonstrates the influence of the entertainment industry on modern promotion practices.

Pioneers of Promotion brings to the forefront three critical figures often relegated to the background of the successful businesses they helped create. Burke, Handy, and Hamilton, usually footnotes in studies of Buffalo Bill's Wild West, the Columbian Exposition, and the Barnum and Bailey Circus, demonstrate how emerging technologies enabled new forms of public relations that shaped how culture gets sold and fostered many marketing techniques still in use today. The William F. Cody Series on the History and Culture of the American West is pleased to include this study of the heretofore-unheralded men who experimented with the interplay of spectacle and marketing to make mass entertainment like Buffalo Bill's Wild West visible to the masses.

Jeremy Johnston
Frank Christianson
Douglas Seefeldt

AUTHOR'S NOTE

In theory, writing about some of the biggest events and most famous people of the Gilded Age should not be hard.

This was a time, after all, in which the publication of newspapers and magazines in America exploded and helped nurture the principle of independent journalism, so there is a tremendous amount of documentation. This was also the first period in human history in which photography, motion pictures, and audio recordings were available to capture the dimensionality of life. With all those increasingly objective words being printed, and all those pictures-worth-a-thousand-words being snapped, the major events of the day were well chronicled. A lot of that material was lost to us for a long time, but the ongoing digitization of hundreds of periodicals and materials, even obscure ones, is now reopening opportunities for the researcher to peer back into the minutiae of daily life.

In practice, though, re-creating history is never an easy business.

First, the "soft" stuff of people's lives—motivations, emotions, causality—usually remains cloaked in darkness, unless we are so fortunate as to find surviving diaries or other first-person narratives.

In *Pioneers of Promotion,* I have attempted to document the lives and accomplishments of several individuals who were well known, and in some cases quite famous, during their lifetimes, but who have been largely forgotten by history. This includes the press agents Tody Hamilton of the Barnum & Bailey Circus, John M. Burke of Buffalo Bill's Wild West, and Moses P. Handy of the World's Columbian Exposition. Of these, only Handy left behind a significant paper trail, in the form of dozens of boxes of papers and ephemera that are now part of the Handy Family Papers at the William L. Clements Library, University of Michigan; but even there, sifting through his spare diaries, personal and official correspondence, and canceled checks does not allow for a thorough reconstruction of his life. The major components of his body of work are there, but the connective tissue is missing and must be inferred.

Burke and Hamilton left no similar caches of personal documentation. Fortunately, during the primes of their lives, both men were in the public eye and hence were frequently featured and quoted in print. Yet the reflected glow does not always provide the sharpest resolution.

Second, the credibility of certain sources presents a challenge. In total, I used nearly 1,500 sources in writing this book. Most were primary materials, especially newspaper articles. But newspapers in this era frequently contained misspellings, factual errors, or stories printed as news that were little more than rumors; and they were often imbued with distinct political or editorial points of view. That can be problematic for the researcher. I found many instances of perplexing reportage, such as the existence of newspaper articles authoritatively stating that Burke was born in New York, Philadelphia, Delaware, and Maryland.

Hence, individually, the newspapers provide illuminating if sometimes contradictory facts about (and great quotations from) the people I have featured; collectively, newspapers offer the ability to triangulate the details and sequence of major events in these figures' lives, and to piece back together their promotional strategies and tactics.

Also problematic is that none of the men featured in this book were solo actors. For example, Burke was general manager of the Wild West and for a long time its primary press agent, or advance man, but he was often surrounded by a talented team, including Prentiss Ingraham, William Gardner, Louis Cooke, George Starr, Lew Parker, Carter Couturier, Harvey Watkins, Charles Wells, Frank Small, Frank Winch, Willard Coxey, and Dexter Fellows. He also interacted constantly and in diverse ways with the Wild West partners, William F. Cody and Nate Salsbury. How their labors were divided, and who reported to whom, is not always apparent from the historical record, although Burke was clearly the one who created the promotional tone and strategy for the Wild West and was always its spiritual north star. Nevertheless, in most cases, articles had no bylines, print ad authors were uncredited, and newspaper stories made no mention of *which* press agent was speaking to the reporter, so I occasionally refer to the work done by "the team" and in other cases deduce that Burke (or Handy or Hamilton for their organizations) was the responsible party based on the language or timing or circumstances. The lack of absolute attribution in these limited instances in no way diminishes the achievements of the primary actors featured here, for they were widely recognized as the dominant promotional leaders of their respective organizations and undoubtedly had a hand in nearly all the work of their departments.

A fourth complicating factor in the re-creation of nineteenth-century marketing is our twenty-first-century use of terminology.

In our world, *advertising* is a straightforward and neutral pay-for-space proposition and is viewed as a parallel or complementary activity to *public relations* (PR), or *publicity* (which both have taken on a pejorative sensibility, often derided as "spin" or "publicity stunts") and *promotion* (which connotes either an attention-seeking special event or a sale, as in a BOGO—buy one, get one—promotion). Nowadays, these tactics all ladder up to the term *marketing,* which has evolved beyond its academic research roots to become a rather generic mainstream word. For example, most companies today have a marketing department and a vice president of marketing, part of whose function it is to implement advertising, PR, and promotional work.

But in the nineteenth century, as these functions were just beginning to take shape, the nomenclature and taxonomy were quite different. *Advertising* was used much as it is today, albeit more broadly. But *marketing* still meant simply "shopping at the market," and PR had not entered the lexicon at all; the function of what we might now think of as media relations was then called *press agentry* or *indirect advertising.*

Moreover, while some people like Handy made a sharp distinction between *promotion* (which was the art of "arousing interest," essentially lobbying) and *publicity* (which involved printing presses), those terms were more commonly used generically and interchangeably, akin to our modern usage of *marketing,* and were sometimes even used as synonyms for *advertising* (as in the famous 1897 advertising textbook *Fowler's Publicity*).

Confusing, to say the least.

For authenticity, I use some of the archaic terminology—where necessary, comparing it to its modern counterpart for ease of understanding—but for the purposes of flow, I adopt a hierarchy in which the overarching industry, the "tent" that I metaphorically invoke throughout the text, is referred to equally in the nineteenth-century (*promotion*) and twenty-first-century (*marketing*) manners.

Caveats aside, the result of this style of research and writing is a large and intricate mosaic, comprising thousands of small pieces that, viewed from a distance, present a novel perspective on the early development of an industry we know well—and on its architects, whom we do not know at all.

Of course, many insightful historians and cultural commentators have written about P. T. Barnum, William F. Cody, the Barnum & Bailey Circus, Buffalo Bill's Wild West, and the World's Columbian Exposition as exemplars of the new American popular culture . . . or the cult of celebrity . . .

or the growth of the entertainment business . . . or shifting geopolitics . . . or evolving views of race, ethnology, classism, and imperialism . . . or any number of other historical and sociological perspectives.

This study has a very different take. As a longtime practitioner of marketing, I necessarily view these people and spectacles (and their pioneering press agents) primarily through *that* lens. This yields a picture of them as seminal forces in the surprisingly early development of an industry that most scholars have heretofore regarded as a product (or cultural byproduct) of the twentieth century.

Moreover, as a native easterner transplanted in the West, I am keenly aware of the symbiosis between the frontier and the nascent industry of marketing. The former could not have fully "vanished" without the latter, and the latter could not have fully appeared without the former. So the West—and particularly the pervasive myth of the Old West—emerges as a sort of shadow character in this book, and Burke and some of the other press agents as pathfinders in our nation's long psychological westering movement.

Ultimately, then, this is a history of the pioneers of promotion, and of the promotion of pioneers. At its core is a tale not just of marketing, but of marketers—men and women of insight, genius, charisma, and the tremendous energy that was characteristic of the late nineteenth century. They have been almost entirely forgotten, but their influence is still woven into the very fabric of our modern marketing centrism and enduring aspirational westernness. The likes of Handy, Burke, and Hamilton would feel comfortable here. They would recognize many twenty-first-century marketing challenges, and would be able to suggest reasonable and probably very clever solutions.

This is their story.

PIONEERS OF PROMOTION

When in time every nook and corner of the world is peopled, when every point is accessible by water, rail or aeroplane, when science makes easy communication by mail, telegraph, phone or wireless, then will the student of world history reveal, as it were, in romance when reading of the discovery, the investment and the conquering of once isolated sections.

Then only will the work of the American pioneer, the settler and their advance guard, the army and its guide—the American scout—assume an importance in history that will clothe many names with enduring fame, such as now attaches, for instance, to Boone, Carson, Crockett, Bridger, and later Cody, better known as Buffalo Bill.

"Buffalo Bill Is Survivor of an Era of Romance,"
Denver Times (August 20, 1911)

1

BURYING A LEGEND

John Burke's body lies a'mouldering in the grave

For a small town, Golden, Colorado, is certainly a place of large contrasts.

Neatly tucked in a valley between North Table Mountain and South Table Mountain, about twelve miles west of Denver, Golden sits where the high plains abruptly end their eight hundred-mile run at the foot of the soaring Rockies. Home to only twenty thousand people, it is nevertheless known by millions because of its recurring cameo in the ad campaigns of its largest employer, the Adolph Coors Brewing Company. And although Golden was founded during the Pike's Peak gold rush of 1859 and is still home to the Colorado School of Mines, it actually derives its euphonious name not from a metal but from a man—Thomas L. Golden, a Georgian who came west in search of treasure and then left. (What's more, the most important metal in town is not gold, but aluminum, courtesy of the Rocky Mountain Metal Container facility, the largest aluminum can production center in the world.)

And then there is Golden's best-known resident: William Frederick Cody (Buffalo Bill), probably the most famous American of his era, who helped settle the rugged frontier, entertained more than 50 million people with his Wild West show, and was the subject of more than 550 dime novels . . . but who is buried there in relative obscurity high atop Lookout Mountain.[1]

To reach the Buffalo Bill Museum and Grave from the center of Golden, you turn onto 19th Street just south of where Clear Creek crosses under Highway 6 on its long amble to the South Platte River. From there it is a short though rugged drive up Lookout Mountain Road, through some forty-two turns, many of them hairpins, up, up, up, climbing 1,700 feet in less than five miles, squeezing past the inevitable thrill-seeking cyclists. (For a major attraction, the museum is in a relatively inaccessible location: annual attendance averages seventy thousand, but on days of inclement weather, it sometimes attracts only twenty visitors, maybe fewer.) Each turn reveals a new and more magnificent vista: the snowcapped peaks to the west, the skyline of Denver floating ethereally in the distant clouds to the east, and the evergreens standing tall and proud against the backdrop of tawny rocks and hayfields below.

Why Lookout Mountain became Cody's final resting place is a matter of considerable controversy. Born in Iowa and raised in Kansas, Cody would later call many places home, including Rochester, New York; North Platte, Nebraska; and the town he founded, Cody, Wyoming. All of them could lay claim to a more important role in his life than could Denver (or Golden), which happened to be where his sister May lived, where he died, and where Harry Tammen, the owner of the *Denver Post* and a persistent creditor late in Cody's life, wielded great influence—perhaps, some people at the time said, including a payment to Cody's widow, Louisa, to keep the body there. Indeed, Cody himself had at one time selected a burial spot on Cedar Mountain in Wyoming, overlooking the town of Cody, and had marked it with some rocks; he even drew up a will in New York in 1906 specifying Cedar Mountain for his grave and allocating ten thousand dollars to his executors to erect a monument there. Yet anecdotes also describe Cody's love for the majestic views from Lookout Mountain, his desire to be buried *there*, and a later will, dated February 19, 1913, ceding control over such decisions to Louisa as executor of the estate.

Regardless, here he has lain ever since the day in June 1917 when some twenty thousand people wended their way up the mountain to pay final respects, just one manifestation of an outpouring of grief and respect that had not been experienced in America since the death of Abraham Lincoln.

Today, the colorful and well-thought-out displays at the small museum offer some wonderful insights into Cody's amazing life. A few steps away is a rustic-looking wood-and-stone structure, the original museum building from 1921, called the Pahaska Tepee, which now houses a café and a gift shop densely packed with Buffalo Bill–themed key chains, magnets, t-shirts, mugs, postcards, books, posters, license plate frames, Stetsons, souvenir rugs, and one of those machines that stamps an image on a penny. Sitting atop spinning racks of postcards are signs created on a printer that was low in ink: "Buffalo Bill Says Half Off On Fudge." On the outside of the building is a wooden sign plugging Duffy's Rowdy Root Beer.

From the Pahaska Tepee you can walk along a pathway, to which patches of snow and ice cling persistently into springtime, past the inevitable silver triangular coin-operated binoculars, up to the grave.

It is a solemn and modest place—a small stone column with an inset plaque, surrounded by a wrought-iron picket fence—but the views are impressive. From here, on a good day, you can see beyond eastern Colorado all the way to Kansas, Nebraska, and Wyoming. If you look hard enough, perhaps you can also see back in time, with the jagged mountains, open plains, smokestack plumes, and seemingly Lilliputian metropolis all suggesting important passages in western history that brought us to this point, this place, this very moment.

But the reverie does not last long, for looming above it all is the enormous red-and-white Lake Cedar Group television antenna, part of a cluster of towers, antennae, and microwave-relay dishes that punctuate the view like asterisks as you stand by Cody's grave. The antenna, erected in 2009 to replace the even larger KCNC-TV tower and predecessor radio and TV towers on Lookout Mountain dating all the way back to 1952, is today shared by Denver television stations 4, 7, 9, and 20, beaming high-definition news and episodes of *The Big Bang Theory* and *Grey's Anatomy* to the good people of greater Denver. At 730 feet, it is large, but all the more so because it is built on the side of a steep mountain that itself sits on top of a mile-high plain. "Nothing special in the United States," said Don Perez, a veteran television engineer who worked on the project, of the tower's size. "We just happened to have a big rock to park our antenna on."[2]

Thus, controversy aside, it is hard to imagine a more fitting resting place than this big rock for a man whose dashing career of scouting, fighting Indians, and hunting buffalo helped win the West, and whose re-creation of all those events on stage and in arenas helped fixate the western myth and transform the world of marketing and communications. In his life Cody was a bridge between Old World and New, and so he is in his death. The vastness, the fresh air, the endless prairie, the vistas, the heretical challenge to Mother Nature's dominion, the encroach of industry, the tourist tchotchkes, the towering communications beacons—all are as they should be.

And yet there is something wrong, something important, something out of balance in this world. There is a spirit missing. Because Cody's story, Cody's legend, would never have come to pass without the trailblazing promotional efforts of John M. Burke—for forty-five years Cody's press agent, publicist, advance man, general manager, mythmaker, impresario, apologist, storyteller, and friend.

As early as 1869, Major Burke, as he was widely known, recognized Cody's heroic nature and the powerful symbolism of the fading West, and he gradually fused them together. Looking back at that first encounter with Cody, Burke wrote (with his typical hyperbole and tortured syntax) that the scout "seemed surcharged with youth, life, blood, graceful, dignified poise, while the fact of his daily duty being to defy savage death surrounded him with a tragic atmosphere investing him with a halo of glory, in the actual, equaling that with which sacred history adorns its martyrs and militant heroes, since the days of Charlemagne and the Crusaders. Oh, for the photo color film then!"[3]

Burke befriended newspaper editors everywhere, regaled them with western stories both apocryphal and apothegmatic, exaggerated or invented tales of Cody's (and his own) legendary career, mastered the use of photography and lithography with iconic images he plucked from the West, aggrandized Cody's heroic deeds, kept them in front of the public, and in so doing generated a blizzard of advance publicity for the Wild West everywhere it traveled, year after year. "Even when editors doubted his embellished tales of Cody's heroism, they printed them," wrote historian Scott Cutlip.[4] As a result, Burke kept the crowds coming and made what he called the "mimic arena" into one of the most popular attractions of the era, one that toured small towns and large cities for more than three decades and played in front of most of the crowned heads of Europe and military and entertainment heroes of the day.

Thus, Burke may not have *invented* Buffalo Bill, the Wild West, or the modern concept of celebrity; he just buffed them to a blinding sheen. And he did all of this in an era when the functions of "promotion" and "marketing" were so new, so undeveloped, that they hadn't even entered the lexicon, let alone the public consciousness. There truly was no marketing industry yet and wouldn't be for another two or three decades. Yet without broadcast technology, without mass media, without any obvious means for large-scale promotion, Burke somehow built William F. Cody into the nation's first great marketing pitchman.

Burke was an easterner who adopted the look and outlook of a pioneer, complete with flowing locks, sombrero, and boots. He had followed Cody all over the world (or more properly, Cody had followed him, since Burke was the advance agent for the Wild West, traveling ahead of the show by a week or two)—even to Wyoming's Big Horn Basin, where, close to Cody's once-chosen burial place of Cedar Mountain, Burke found one of his own.[5] In an article in the *New York Times* in May 1902, Burke described a giant spur of McCullough Peak, officially designated on maps as Burke's Bluff, Wyoming, fifteen thousand feet up. "I will have it all to myself," Burke told the reporter. "My solitary tomb up among the clouds will dominate the finest valley on God's footstool. I will be lonelier but safer there than in any cemetery, and I will have only the stars and the eagles for companions."[6] Burke informed another reporter that he had even changed his life insurance policy to ensure that his wishes to be buried in the Big Horn Basin were carried out.[7]

Burke died on April 12, 1917, just ninety-two days after Cody—of, as some historians later speculated, a broken heart.[8]

But for all his grandiose plans, Burke did *not* end up in a tomb among the clouds, or anywhere near Cody or the stars or the eagles, for that matter. He was buried 2,001 miles away from McCullough Peak, Wyoming, and 1,684 miles away from Lookout Mountain, Colorado, in an unmarked grave in Mount Olivet Cemetery, on the somewhat gritty northeast side of Washington, D.C. Burke's plot is in section 53, home to 1,400 gravesites (and as many as 2,800 graves, since interment often happened in double-decker fashion) in an eighty-six-acre cemetery, which is shoehorned into a neighborhood now surrounded by auto body shops, cab dispatchers, public storage units, craft breweries, Gallaudet University, and the city's Department of Public Works Fleet Management yards. It was an unfitting end to a man who idolized Cody, shadowed and protected Cody, loved the West, lived the West, and more than almost any other person of his era, understood the marketing power of symbols and images.

Like many red-blooded American boys growing up in the second half of the twentieth century, Jim Fuqua had a certain fascination with the Old West.

Born in 1948 and raised in Delaware, he was far removed from the substance of the actual West. But this was literally prime time for the mythic West, with television shows such as *Gunsmoke*, *Bonanza*, *Have Gun—Will Travel*, *The Lone Ranger*, *Death Valley Days*, *Sky King*, *Wagon Train*, *Maverick*, *Rawhide*, and *The Rifleman*. They were accompanied by a flood of Hollywood westerns (on average, one was released every single week of the 1950s), various other productions of Broadway (*Annie Get Your Gun, Oklahoma!*) and Madison Avenue (the Marlboro Man), and a boom in what historian Robert Athearn called the "hardiest weed that ever grew on the literary landscape"—western paperbacks, with some 35 million copies sold each year.[9] Fuqua, with his cowboy hat and Mattel Fanner 50 cap pistol (complete with real leather junior holster!), would often go off to play a sort of faux western ring-a-levio in the woods near his home in the new tract housing suburb of Elsmere, south of Wilmington.

Indeed, inculcated with a heavy dose of gunslingers and pioneers, many boys of Fuqua's generation routinely invoked the legends of Daniel Boone, Wyatt Earp, George Armstrong Custer, Sitting Bull, and Billy the Kid. They also had some awareness of the name Buffalo Bill, a man connected with a vague notion of western heroism but whose actual achievements were lesser known.

"Yeah, I knew who Buffalo Bill was," recalls Fuqua with a laugh. "He was the famous Western guy. He did a lot of *stuff.*"[10]

An image was there—a long-haired, rifle-toting, white-hatted "good guy" Indian fighter—though specifics were badly lacking. Was he a figure from history or a character from a book? Was he the same as Wild Bill? Buffalo Bill Cody had simply become part of an inherited body of knowledge, the stories, myths, and legends that had seeped into the consciousness of children, especially boys, for many generations—and that was sufficient to elevate him into the tabernacle of Jim Fuqua's childhood heroes. The real Buffalo Bill had died when Jim's father was just a small boy himself, but the mythical one lived on, in the collective consciousness as well as in literature and celluloid.

Yet unlike his cowboys-and-Indians playmates, who on any given Saturday in 1959 might have headed to the bijou theater in Wilmington to see the double feature of *Good Day for a Hanging* and *Rio Bravo*, Jim Fuqua had a special interest in Buffalo Bill. That's because on Sundays, when his aunts and uncles would often come over for dinner, he listened intently to their stories about their mother, Katie Burke, who had died in 1918 at the age of forty-eight, and about *her* father, Thomas A. Burke, brother of John M. Burke, the man the newspapers had called "Buffalo Bill's Bosom Friend." Someone in the family had clipped a 1946 article from the *Reader's Digest* about Burke and Cody ("How the power of publicity turned a simple prairie scout into an immortal symbol of our western frontier"), and other scattered pieces of Burke memorabilia in the Fuqua household tied them back to the days of the Wild West—an old photograph, a baptismal certificate, a piece of embroidery dated 1914. It wasn't much, but when you are a boy, any connection to a legend like Buffalo Bill Cody, however tenuous, is to be treasured.

What Fuqua did *not* know was that his great-granduncle had already been measured by several historians and for the most part found wanting—an oversight that has continued to the present day. Some of Cody's biographers have dismissed Burke as a Barnumesque charlatan, a master snake oil salesman and self-promoter who never saw a sentence he couldn't butcher. Others saw him as a somewhat more important figure, a shaper of Cody's legacy and one of the pillars of the Wild West's long and successful run. Either way, to the extent that Burke appeared at all, it was usually just a historical footnote to Cody, and never in any serious studies of the history of marketing. He *was* depicted in the 1976 Robert Altman movie *Buffalo Bill and the Indians*, starring Paul Newman as Cody, but Kevin McCarthy's Burke came off as a fat blowhard in a fur coat. Introducing a singer to Cody, McCarthy/Burke proclaims, "Bill, Buffalo Bill, Monarch of the West, it delights me to present this compellingly cornucopious canary, this curvaceous cadenza in the compendium of classical soupçon. This collagen of champagne and columbine. This cultivated coloratura of Colorado. Words fail me. Lucille DuCharme." That was McCarthy/Burke's only major line in the film.

But what the historians heretofore have missed is the profound role Burke played not just in establishing the legend of Buffalo Bill and promoting the Wild West, but in laying the very cornerstones of the marketing industry itself. He had an innate talent for communications and a remarkably sophisticated grasp of how imagery and celebrity could (and would) be used for persuasion, especially when linked to the allegorical American West. He understood what kinds of messages resonated emotionally with consumers, and how to use the press to convey them. He also had an almost preternatural sense of history—predicting, among other things, that the volatile Alsace-Lorraine region of Europe would become the seat of world war, and even anticipating that the day would come when the United States would elect a member of the minority as president. Little wonder, then, that he was so far ahead of everyone else in anticipating the power of marketing.

Burke's charisma and joie de vivre were readily apparent to all who knew him—and there were many who did, as evidenced by the more than four hundred names of friends and acquaintances he dropped in a single astonishing 4,700-word career retrospective article for the *New York Clipper* in 1916. Observant researchers can even see him winking from the grave once or twice, as, for example, when we study the printed programs of the Wild West and realize that in 1895, the classic front-cover image of the cowboy, which had been in place for a while, was suddenly replaced mid-season by the heroic visage of the then-fifty-three-year-old John M. Burke, complete with flowing locks and sombrero.

Now, a century after his death, the trail of Burke's stunningly effective marketing has suddenly started to become visible, like images ghosting onto photographic paper in a darkroom fixer bath, as more and more small publications from the nineteenth century are digitized. The man traveled widely, had friends in seemingly every newspaper office, and utilized many different strategies and techniques to keep Cody and the Wild West in the public eye. To research the life and accomplishments of John M. Burke today is to take a trip back to the very headwaters of the marketing industry.

And as the newspaper record makes clear, Burke became increasingly famous himself. "Picturesque," the papers often called him. "Beau ideal of a Westerner." "Dean of boomers." "Prince of press agents." "Hot air and kind words dispenser." "Genial," "jovial," "jolly," "majordomo," "right bower." The headlines often heralded his arrival in town. In 1906, the *New York Sun* noted that he was "scarcely less known" than Buffalo Bill himself.[11]

A colorful character. A visionary. A pioneer. A celebrity. How, then, is it possible that Jim Fuqua's great-granduncle met with such an anonymous fate—buried in an unmarked grave two thousand miles from the lofty perch he had earmarked for his final resting place? Or that his role as a founding father of the marketing industry has been so completely eroded by the sands of time?

2

THE BIG TENT OF P. T. BARNUM AND TODY HAMILTON

"A blazing kaleidoscopic vision"

It's a Barnum and Bailey world,
Just as phony as it can be.
But it wouldn't be make believe
If you believed in me.

"It's Only a Paper Moon" (1933)
Music by Harold Arlen, lyrics by E. Y. "Yip" Harburg and Billy Rose

In 1888, a fairly obscure thirty-eight-year-old writer from Chicopee Falls, Massachusetts, named Edward Bellamy suddenly gained a large measure of fame with the publication of his book *Looking Backward: 2000–1887.*

In it, he told the story of Julian West, a young man from Boston who is hypnotized by a "Professor of Animal Magnetism" and wakes up in the year 2000. West meets Dr. Leete and his daughter, Edith, who proceed to serve as his tour guides through a recognizable but distinctly socialist America, an orderly world with central dining halls and public laundries, where wealth has ceased to matter. Bellamy's Boston was a cooperative utopia, but also one with some amazing new technologies such as music that is piped into the home through telephones, and credit cards that can be used to purchase goods from warehouse stores that move products around through pneumatic tubes. Although the book's purpose was to lay out a collectivist vision of a political movement that would come to be known as nationalism, it was also a remarkable bit of futuristic soothsaying, especially since, as Bellamy himself wrote, "One can look back a thousand years easier than forward fifty."[1]

Looking Backward was a huge commercial success, the third-best-selling work of its era, behind only *Uncle Tom's Cabin* and *Ben-Hur*. An estimated half-million copies were sold in the United States in the first two decades after its release, and perhaps five or six times that number through international editions in countries from Europe to Russia to New Zealand.[2] It spawned dozens of sequels, satires, and responses, and more or less inaugurated the literary time-travel genre that for more than a century would find expression in the highbrow (H. G. Wells's 1895 book *The Time Machine*, Fritz Lang's 1927 movie *Metropolis*) and the low (Matt Groening's animated series *Futurama*, director Steve Pink's 2010 cinematic dreck *Hot Tub Time Machine*, and its even more inexplicable 2015 sequel).

Curiously, though, there seems to have been an expiration date on *Looking Backward*'s influence. It is still in print today but is not terribly well known; and Bellamy, whose name had once been so familiar that enthusiastic supporters known as Bellamyites ran more than 165 Bellamy Nationalist Clubs in the United States, has been largely forgotten.

That was the fate of many great cultural icons of the nineteenth century, which burst forth like red-hot magma into a rapidly changing societal landscape and then eventually cooled into igneous anonymity. Among them were *The Wide, Wide World*, by Elizabeth Wetherell (pseudonym of Susan Warner), one of America's earliest best sellers, which went through fourteen editions in two years after its publication in 1850; Henriette Sontag, the mesmerizing German soprano whose voice composer Hector Berlioz once described as "sweetness never surpassed, agility almost fabulous," who captivated Europe in the 1820s and America thirty years later; Martin Beck, whose expansive Orpheum Circuit encompassed forty-five vaudeville theaters in dozens of cities across the United States and Canada; Donald Dinnie, the Scottish strongman and "greatest athlete in the world," whose career spanned fifty years and whose name was appropriated during World War I to describe heavy artillery shells; and Childs Restaurants, which began in 1888 and would grow to become the largest restaurant chain in America, serving 50 million people a year.[3] All were once front-page news and everyday topics of parlor discussion. All are long forgotten.

Indeed, it is fascinating to speculate about which of *today's* icons will still have any cultural currency in the twenty-second century. The books of Anne Tyler? The voice of Renée Fleming? TED talks? Andy Murray? Taco Bell? People in all eras have tended to exhibit what might be called an Ozymandian bias, believing that the fixtures of their society, such as grand edifices, complex transportation systems, world-famous celebrities, and venerable brands, would be around forever—only to be left, like the wrecked colossus of Shelley's poem, as "vast and trunkless legs of stone."

Our era is no different, although the proliferation of media outlets and the very notion of "cloud storage" might fool us into believing in cultural immortality. Then again, we now live in a world in which deeply embedded and ubiquitous brands (Circuit City, MCI, General Foods) have quickly disappeared; century-old institutions that were "too big to fail" (Lehman Brothers, Bear Stearns) have vaporized in a matter of days; and even epochal processes like global warming have been compressed into frighteningly short spans seemingly playing out before our eyes with super-storms, historic droughts, and Greenland glaciers calving off chunks the size of Manhattan. So who is to say how fast history will erode the more ephemeral cultural landmarks of our times?

Of course, some products of popular culture prove more durable than others. While the most recent paperback version of *The Wide, Wide World* languishes well beyond the top million on Amazon.com's ranking, new editions of *Ben-Hur* are published nearly every year. No one recalls much about Henriette Sontag's tour of the United States in 1852, but the tour of Jenny Lind, "The Swedish Nightingale," two years earlier is still remembered as a sensation, commemorated in song, story, and candy. And while showmen like Martin Beck and the wrestler Dinnie never even made it into the anteroom of history, their contemporary, William F. Cody (Buffalo Bill), still occupies his own wing.

What is it that ultimately distinguishes eternal eminence from digital detritus? Luck, certainly, and timing, and on rare occasions extraordinary innate talent, as well as a host of factors beyond one's control; but also that curious type of historical distention that comes from exceptionally good marketing. When the "branding" or "positioning" or "messaging" attached to a certain product or person or idea works—truly *works*, connecting with people at the most emotional level, fulfilling not just their needs but their desires and aspirations—then it is not constrained by mere temporal boundaries. Fame may indeed be fleeting, but great marketing can live on for generations.

Let's travel backward in time.

Here in our own era, technology is usually hailed as the consummate symbol of progress. The Internet, for example, has been a great democratizing force, opening up the whole storehouse of accumulated human knowledge, connecting it in ingenious ways, disaggregating it into binary code, and somehow projecting it across vast networks to make raw information accessible to billions of people in remote locations. Similarly, Global Positioning System (GPS) technology has enabled *Homo sapiens*, with our limited scope of sight, to be able to see the world in entirely new ways—from twenty-two thousand miles up but in nearly infinite detail—so that our understanding of place, movement, speed, direction, and connectedness has changed forever. Google has supplanted the Dewey Decimal System and, to a certain extent, libraries themselves. Voicemail and texting have replaced the busy signal and the operator. Technology is the standard by which modern humans measure our worth, the Darwinian yardstick that gauges our increasing distance from the Dark Ages, the Paleolithic period, and the very brief era when CompuServe was cutting edge.

But that was also true in our parents' and grandparents' eras, when television, radio, the airplane, and the automobile played transformative roles in people's daily lives. And it was true even in the nineteenth century, when the breathtakingly rapid transition from a preindustrial society to a technology-driven industrial one probably forced more changes in the expansiveness of Americans' thinking than in any other period, prior or subsequent.

Consider that as late as the 1830s, most Americans still lived in a world without electricity, railroads, the telephone, the telegraph, or even the camera. Messages could only be transmitted from city to city by handwritten letters, their speed limited by the primary mode of transport: horse. Human activity followed natural circadian cycles, ending when the sun went down, save for that which could be accomplished with the limited illumination afforded by gas lamps, whale oil lanterns, or candles. Mirrors enabled people to see their reflections, but images could only be reproduced by painters and illustrators.

All of that began to change midcentury. The first commercial telegraph line, between New York and Washington, began operating in spring 1846, and within five years seventy-five telegraph companies were doing business in the United States, conveying messages (and soon money) at the speed of light. The transcontinental railroad was completed in 1869, making travel, migration, and commerce over much greater distances infinitely easier. Alexander Graham Bell told Watson to "come here" with his first primitive telephone in 1876, but just fourteen years later, the U.S. Census Bureau reported 467,000 telephones already in service in the country, and 453 million conversations; distances seemed to shorten, and separation began to take on a different meaning. Daguerreotypes and cartes de visite enabled people to "stop time" and share images of distant places and people, and soon thereafter (1880), the halftone process was developed to reproduce photographs in newspapers. Edison started providing electric lighting to residential homes in 1882, turning nighttime into day, and then electrical energy was harnessed to power motors large and small, fueling the industrial revolution.

It was, in essence, a new world of analogs, in which, for the first time in history, a person did not need to be present to have a presence. One's voice, words, work, and picture could be in two places at the same time, or transported quickly—sometimes instantaneously—from one location to another.

And all this happened within the span of a single human lifetime.

The effect on the eternal sense of order was so profound that it is hard for us technology-addled, cocksure moderns to even imagine. Perhaps a reasonable analogy is the sense of discombobulation we would feel if, having only now grown accustomed to the speed of bullet trains and supersonic airplanes, we suddenly saw the *Star Trek* "transporter" become a reality.

But it was not just the transmission or replication of ideas and images that was so transformative to mid-nineteenth-century society; soon, it was their *manipulation*, too. For right on the heels of all these highly visible technological innovations came another transcendent development, this one cloaked in layers of subtlety and hidden from view, but in many ways even more powerful: the ability to define and refine the flow of information, and to use that to persuade, shape perceptions, and change behaviors. Today, we call it promotion, or spin, or advertising—collectively, marketing. Back then, it was an entirely new and as-yet unnamed science. But it would quickly emerge as a potent force, capable of creating eternal heroes and celebrities, attracting enormous audiences, stimulating demand and desire, influencing policymakers, shaping public opinion, steering behavior (for good and evil), and establishing brand empires.

Advertising is certainly not a new trade. A three-thousand-year-old piece of papyrus discovered in the ruins of the ancient city of Thebes put that notion to rest. On it, written in hieroglyphics, was an offer for the return of a lost slave named Shem, "five feet two inches, of ruddy complex, with brown eyes." It read: "For news of his whereabouts, half a gold coin is offered. And for his return to the shop of Hapu the Weaver, where the best cloth is woven to your desires, a whole coin is offered."[4] History does not record whether Shem was ever found, nor whether Hapu's business suddenly began to surge.

Before the printing press was invented, in the fifteenth century, handwritten public notices like the Thebes papyrus were the closest thing to a mass information vehicle, so it is not surprising that they were used in many societies by those with goods or services to promote. In Rome, handwritten *acta* were commonly tacked up in the Forum; in China, during the Han Dynasty, information sheets called *tipao* were circulated among bureaucrats and sometimes posted in public places. The handbills and posters of early American society may have inverted the ratio of advertisement-to-news, but they were clear lineal descendants of the ancient information sheets.

Printed advertisements began appearing in British periodicals around 1624, and in American newspapers by 1704. Some of the earliest publications of Benjamin Franklin, such as his 1729 *Pennsylvania Gazette* and 1742 *General Magazine*, featured several pages of "new advertisements"—things like "super fine crown soap," lampblack, Antigua rum, and "a Plantation containing 300 Acres of good Land, 30 cleared."[5] All these early ads were simplistic: little more than a few lines of tiny agate (5.5-point) type laid out in a single column, without any images or white space or persuasive wordplay, and with only the simplest of headlines, if any. They typically announced the *availability* of products, not their attributes. "September 1836. Fall Goods at the Variety-shop" read one of the more robust ads in the *Burlington Free Press*, placed by the merchants Amos Pangborn and James Brinsmaid, who had a store on Church Street. "We are getting in our Fall

TYPICAL MID-NINETEENTH-CENTURY ADVERTISEMENTS.

Harper's Weekly, like many magazines and newspapers, had a page full of "reading notices," including several for patent medicines. *Harper's Weekly*, December 4, 1858, Archive.org, The Lincoln Financial Foundation Collection.

Goods, all things necessary to keep our assortment in good order; Watches, Clocks, perfumery, Tea-pots, Military Goods, Castors, Jewelry, Stocks, Collars, linen and satin Bosoms, Lamp wicks, Toys, and an endless variety of Fancy articles. All persons are invited to call and look at them at the Variety Shop."[6] That was state-of-the-art advertising in the Jacksonian Era.

In part, that's because there was not much need for creativity. America in 1840 was still a young country of 17 million people, spread out over vast territory, growing fast but closer in character to the colonies than to the United States. Towns were separated from each other by miles and days, with few railroads and no telegraphs to connect them. There were no large markets; all commerce was local. Consequently, there were not many branded goods, nor much competition between products or merchants, and hence no imperative to advertise. Indeed, it has been estimated that until 1840, more goods were produced in American homes than in factories.[7]

There were also no forms of mass entertainment. Thoroughbred racing, boxing, cricket, and cockfighting could attract a crowd, but no organized leagues of spectator sports existed. Books were probably the closest thing to a national good, with the same product being distributed in all the states, so they were one of the focal points (along with patent medicines) of what advertising there was—accounting for many ads in newspapers, and frequently containing pages of advertisements themselves.

Moreover, society was overwhelmingly agricultural rather than consumerist—farmers made up 69 percent of the workforce—so there was little disposable income to spend on goods, services, or entertainment, and frequently no ability to read the ads, anyway.[8] Per capita annual income was still below one hundred dollars by midcentury, and roughly one-third of the population in 1840 was illiterate.[9]

Another reason advertising remained understated for so long was the dearth of outlets for it. In 1800, only about two hundred newspapers were published in America, and thirteen magazines—all with circulations that were probably less than one thousand.[10] Numerous technological constraints stood in the way of expansion. Printing presses, for example, were run by hand and could produce no more than two or three hundred sheets per hour. Every step was manual and exhausting, from compositing the type to inking the plates to stacking the sheets. Moreover, paper was made of cotton or sometimes flax fiber derived from rags, which were in short supply and had to be imported from Europe. In 1850, almost 21 million pounds of rags were shipped over, and it became so expensive that soon there were experiments and proposals to make paper out of just about anything else: bananas, fish, marshmallows, spider webs . . . even Egyptian mummies, of which, it was estimated, some 500 million might be available.[11]

The upshot was that until the process of turning wood pulp into paper was perfected around 1870, printed publications were generally more expensive than the public could afford, and thus publishers continued to keep their papers short, densely laid out, free of illustrations, and not particularly conducive to advertising. In short, through the first three or four decades of the nineteenth century, a "culture of promotion" did not exist because there was almost nothing big to promote and little means for doing so, anyway.

But this was a century of almost incomprehensibly rapid growth, and things were already changing. Demographic and geographic shifts in the population created larger metropolitan centers, as well as improvements in income, literacy, and commerce. The total population increased 33 percent between 1830 and 1840, and another 36 percent between 1840 and 1850. By 1840 there were five big cities in the country: New York had more than three hundred thousand residents, Baltimore and New Orleans more than one hundred thousand, and Philadelphia and Boston more than ninety-three thousand. Three thousand miles of railroad lines had been laid, mostly up and down the Atlantic seaboard, and within a decade, the railroad would reach the Great Lakes, too.[12] The Erie Canal and the Delaware and Raritan Canal were both open, and regular transatlantic cargo and passenger steamship service also began around this same time. And although the Panic of 1837 triggered an economic depression that lasted for several years, gross domestic product rose 16 percent from 1839 to 1843.[13]

With the development of large markets, significantly enhanced transit of goods, and higher per capita income, the mercantile economy took off. Those who had always been mere "customers," engaging in spiritless transactions, were suddenly flooded with choice and variety from mail order catalogs, overseas trading companies, and new retail formats—and the consumer mentality began to take hold. There was no more potent symbol of this than the building that soon arose at 280 Broadway in New York: the Marble Palace, home of A. T. Stewart Dry Goods, the first great department store in the country. It was a huge Italianate building made of

Tuckahoe marble, with picture windows on the ground floor; the building still stands.[14] Stewart offered shawls, calicoes, gloves, hosiery, "yankee notions," carpets, and more. The Marble Palace was the country's center of inchoate consumerism, "the most splendid fancy store in America—perhaps the world," wrote the *Vermont Phoenix* in 1847, a great bazaar where "the lady of family and education, the parvenu, the cheap purchaser of gloves and ribbons, the spoilt miss, the extravagant wife, and the frugal companion" were "all shuffled together . . . like a pack of cards."[15]

Stewart amassed a fortune and in 1862 would go on to build an even larger department store, the six-story $2.75 million Iron Palace, at Broadway and 10th Street—a building that would eventually be bought by department store magnate John Wanamaker and converted into his New York flagship store, one of the century's crowning commercial achievements.

Meanwhile, the printing industry unleashed one innovation after another. Steam-powered presses using revolving impression cylinders increased printing efficiency fourfold, producing up to eleven hundred sheets per hour. Then in 1846, Richard Hoe patented his type-revolving rotary press, which led to production runs of up to twenty thousand single-sided sheets per hour.[16] Soon thereafter, the rotary press was combined with a paper web (roll of paper), enabling printers to achieve their long-desired goal of printing on *both* sides of the paper simultaneously. High speed inline folding machines were invented to keep pace.

Heretofore, newspaper publishing had always been an aristocratic business, run by and for the upper class. But these gains in productivity now made it possible for publishers to lower the cost of newspapers from the standard six cents to one, inaugurating the era of the so-called penny press, when newspapers became accessible and ubiquitous, the tool of the common man. As historian LeRoy Ashby showed, eight of the first ten publishers of penny press dailies had modest working-man roots as printers or cabinetmakers. One of them, Benjamin Day, who launched the *New York Sun* as a populist penny newspaper in 1833, said he was not targeting "the rich aristocrat who lolls in his carriage" but "the humble laborer who wields a broom in the streets."[17]

Circulations skyrocketed, and so did the number of publications and their size (typically from four columns to six, and from four pages to eight or more). The *Sun* amassed a circulation of eight thousand within six months; within three years, it had jumped to thirty thousand, one of the largest in the world. (Interestingly, its prospectus justified its existence on more than just journalistic grounds: "The object of this paper is to lay before the public, at a price within the means of everyone, ALL THE NEWS OF THE DAY, and at the same time afford an advantageous medium for advertising." By 1839, two-thirds of the *Sun* was filled with advertising.[18]) James Gordon Bennett began publishing the *New York Herald* in 1835 and declared, "This is the age of the Daily Press." By 1838, New York alone had thirty-five penny newspapers.

Overall, the number of daily newspapers in America jumped from 512 in 1820 to 3,000 by the start of the Civil War in 1861, and the circulation went from 300,000 to 1.5 million—increases of more than 400 percent during a period in which the overall population grew 226 percent.[19]

Alexis de Tocqueville noted during his tour of America in 1831–1832, and wrote in his subsequent book *Democracy in America*, that because American law did not require a license to publish, "The number of periodical and occasional publications which appears in the United States actually surpasses belief. . . . In America there is scarcely a hamlet that has not its newspaper."[20]

But the explosion in newspaper and magazines had another profound impact, one that even the prescient de Tocqueville was unable to see: it created, for the first time in history, a vehicle for connecting to, and ultimately influencing, a mass audience.

Advertising was the most obvious way to do that, and it quickly emerged as a tertiary source of revenue for publishers who had traditionally only made money through subscriptions and newsstand sales; an estimated 11 million ads appeared in the country's two thousand newspapers in 1847.[21] Advertising would soon grow to become the newspapers' primary revenue stream.

For now, all these efforts were rather modest. Madison Avenue in New York was still just farmland. When the first advertising agent in the country, Volney Palmer, hung out his shingle in 1842, he did little more than purchase and broker space in newspapers for "the enterprising business portion of the community . . . to learn the terms of subscription and advertising . . . without the trouble and perplexity of fruitless inquiries."[22] But now that there was a way to reach the masses, more or less all at once and with the same information, it meant there was also a way to control, influence, and ultimately manipulate the messages that people were receiving—and that opened the door to a new era in advertising. It just needed a spark to kindle the fire.

Then, in one of those odd historical confluences of man and moment, onto the national stage leaped Phineas Taylor Barnum—showman, show-off, progenitor of a unique form of exhibition fakery called the humbug, proprietor of entertainment both lowbrow and highfalutin, possessor of a unique quality known at the time as "Yankee push."

Barnum had spent his early years as a newspaperman, and perhaps that helped him to see what almost no one else yet had: the power of the press not just for advertising a good but for *persuading* people to buy it. Because, after all, the expanded pages of editorial copy now in circulation—everything from local news stories to press exchange items to letters from correspondents—offered untold opportunities to cozy up to (or hire) reporters, or to supply one's own messages. "Indirect advertising" it was called; and in appropriating the "news" part of the newspaper, Barnum was essentially erecting a second tent pole, alongside traditional advertising, underneath what he instinctively knew was a much larger promotional canvas. "I thoroughly understand the art of advertising, not merely by means of printers' ink, which I have always used freely, and to which I confess myself so much indebted for my success, but by turning every possible circumstance to my account," he wrote in his autobiography.[23]

Through his highly creative efforts to draw crowds and curiosity seekers to see his exhibitions, performers, and many other oddities, Barnum quickly emerged as the master promoter of the era. He became an expert in the use of advertising, both direct and indirect, and in many other facets of what we would now consider marketing, including photography, vanity publishing, staged events, bold signage, and the fine art of color lithography for his circus bill posting. In fact, as historian Bluford Adams wrote, "Barnum . . . stood for advertising in the minds of many Americans. By the 1850s, the latest innovations in marketing were commonly known as Barnumisms."[24]

And that was still two decades before he came to the enterprise that would create his most enduring legacy: the circus, to which his name was attached for 146 years, right up until its closure in 2017, even though its ownership and management changed hands many times after his death in 1891. (Indeed, that legacy has hardly waned at all. Barnum was the subject of numerous movies, biographies, and a Broadway show in the late twentieth century, and Barnum productions continue to roll off the presses and the back lots of Hollywood today.)

Barnum had an unprecedented ability to discover and develop spectacles that could attract the curious multitudes and separate them from their money, all slickly wrapped in a putative framework of moral education—a formula that proved very popular with all classes of people.

Yet the reason his fame has endured long beyond the spectacles themselves is because of his sense of showmanship, essentially a blend of personal charisma and persuasive marketing that in our era has become a fixture of modern American culture. Time after time, P. T. Barnum found ways to repurpose the tools of his world to generate inspired promotions and magnificent publicity campaigns for his exhibitions. And this is what separated him from all the other contemporary cultural wonders. The Henriette Sontags and Donald Dinnies and Childs Restaurants—they were products of their times; but Barnum was a prodigy of another time, the marketing-driven twentieth-century world of entertainment, celebrity, popular culture, and "massification," to which the country was headlong, if unwittingly, driving.

Born in Connecticut in 1810, Barnum was enterprising right from the start. His father was an innkeeper and a merchant whose entrepreneurial DNA was clearly passed along to his son—a good thing, since Philo Barnum died insolvent when Phineas was just fifteen. By the time he reached his early twenties, P. T. had already been involved with numerous businesses including fruit-and-confectionery sales, hardware, crockery retailing, real estate speculating, auctioning used books, a weekly newspaper called the *Herald of Freedom*, and state lotteries—which he advertised with extravagant rhymes on handbills, circulars, and posters.

Barnum also received an education in hawking the one type of product that demanded (and permitted) creative promotion in the nineteenth century: patent medicines—the overhyped balms, elixirs, tinctures, and tonics that many people relied on in an age before professional pharmacology gained currency.

While most other consumer goods were in short supply and high demand, the situation was exactly reversed in the nostrum business. This led to ever-more hyperbolic efforts to attract attention and win market share. In Barnum's time newspaper ads for patent medicines were commonplace, such as this notice that appeared in 1837:

> LIFE! LIFE! LIFE.
> DR. JONA. MOORE'S
> *Essence of Life.*
> 40 CENTS PER BOTTLE
>
> The most highly esteemed medicine that has ever been discovered for curing Coughs, Colds and whooping cough, which, if taken at the commencement of the disease, may be cured in a short time.[25]

This was followed by testimonials from five ministers of the Gospel from Windham County, Vermont, and six physicians.

The same four-page newspaper contained text advertisements for Dr. Brandreth's Vegetable Universal Pills; Russell's Itch Ointment, Salt Rheum Ointment, Vegetable Billious Pills, and Stomach Bitters ("composed purely of vegetables of the most innocent yet specific virtues"); N. H. Down's Vegetable Balsamic Elixir; West's Patent Chlorine Cosmetic and Pills; Kreosote Tooth-Ache Drops; Albion's Corn Plaster; and Dr. Relfe's Aromatic Pills for Females ("The Pills are an approved general remedy in cases of Obstructions; Debility; Hypochondria; Green Sickness; Giddiness; Palpitations of the Heart; bad Digestion; Loathing of Food; Pain of the Stomach; Shortness of Breath upon every little motion; Sinking of the Spirits, and its consequences, a dejected countenance; and dislike for exercise and conversation").[26]

To some, patent medicine advertising was detestable, a stain on the cultural landscape, similar to how many people today regard website pop-up ads and penile enhancement e-mail spam. Samuel Clemens (Mark Twain), for one, frequently lambasted patent medicines in his late-century books, and as early as 1865 he wrote a piece for the *San Francisco Chronicle* in which he decried banjo music to be so foul that it would "suffuse your system like strychnine whisky [and] go right through you like Brandreth's pills." (Later in life, Twain would have a change of heart, inventing his own patent medicine to address the problem of "chilblains"—swollen hands—and singing the praises of another remedy that relieved his hemorrhoids.[27])

Barnum, however, had grown up in a household in which salesmanship was the family business. "The customers cheated us in their fabrics: we cheated the customers with our goods," he wrote. "Each party expected to be cheated, if it was possible. Our eyes, not our ears, had to be our masters. We must believe little that we saw, and less that we heard."[28]

Moreover, he had a maternal grandfather who was an inveterate practical jokester. So the balderdash of patent medicine advertising apparently amused him greatly and brought out some of his best work. According to Charles Goodrum and Helen Dalrymple, in their book *Advertising in America: The First 200 Years,* Barnum produced handbills and posters "shouting the benefits of his concoctions by the use of wild, typographic displays to attract attention," and used "agonizing testimonials" and even endorsements from members of the U.S. Senate to promote patent medicines.[29] It would be good training for what was to come.

In 1835, Barnum stumbled into his true calling: showmanship, "that insatiate want of human nature—the love of amusement."[30] Appropriately enough, it happened through an ad: a notice in the *Pennsylvania Inquirer* of July 15, 1835, promoting the appearance of Joice Heth, a "negress" who was supposedly 161 years old and formerly belonged to the father of George Washington. Barnum traveled to Philadelphia and later wrote:

> Joice Heth was certainly a remarkable curiosity, and she looked as if she might have been far older than her age as advertised. She was apparently in good health and spirits, but from age or disease, or both, was unable to change her position; she could move one arm at will, but her lower limbs could not be straightened; . . . she was toothless and totally blind and her eyes had sunk so deeply in the sockets as to have disappeared altogether.
>
> Nevertheless she was pert and sociable, and would talk as long as people would converse with her. She was quite garrulous about her protégé "dear little George," at whose birth she declared she was present, having been at the time a slave of Elizabeth Atwood, a half-sister of Augustine Washington, the father of George Washington.[31]

Barnum sold his grocery business, paid one thousand dollars to purchase Joice Heth (a practice that was of course still common while the law of the land allowed slavery), and proceeded to take her on tour as part of what he called Barnum's Grand Scientific and Musical Theater. He claimed in his 1869 autobiography to have genuinely believed Joice Heth's story, right up until the public autopsy he commissioned after her death in 1836 (and charged 1,500 people fifty cents each to witness) revealed her true age to be about eighty. Yet so much of what he did throughout his life was with a hoodwink and a nod that one cannot be sure he wasn't *still* playing a prescribed part even in his autobiography.

Certainly he was not the *creator* of this unusual spectacle, nor for that matter of many of the bizarre acts he would exhibit in the coming decades. But he was the originator of the promotional frenzy that soon accompanied Joice Heth at every stop on the tour. Barnum was just doing what came naturally to him. He plastered New York with posters. He placed ads that read, "Joice Heth is unquestionably the most astonishing and interesting curiosity in the World!"[32] One lengthy ad he wrote appeared in the *New-York Evening Journal*:

> She weighs but forty-six pounds, and yet is very cheerful and interesting. She retains her faculties in an eminent degree, converses freely, sings numerous hymns, relates many interesting anecdotes of Gen. Washington, the red coats, &c, and often laughs heartily at her own remarks, or those of the spectators. . . . The appearance of this marvellous relick of antiquity strikes the beholder with amazement, and convinces him that his eyes are resting on the oldest specimen of mortality they ever before beheld. Original, authentick, and indisputable documents prove that however astonishing the fact may appear, JOICE HETH is in every respect the person she is represented.[33]

How persuasive Barnum's ads must have seemed, with all the convincing detail and confident tone! He was attuned to the consumer's mind in a way no one else was. Moreover, his distaste for what he had once called the "codfish aristocracy" made the penny press the perfect vehicle, and its great unwashed mass of readers the perfect targets. Although he had virtually no precedents on which to model his campaign—save, perhaps, for some of the patent medicines he had promoted in his early hornswoggling—he knew exactly what to do. "I saw that everything depended upon getting people to think, and talk, and become curious and excited over and about the 'rare spectacle.' Accordingly, posters, transparencies, advertisements, newspaper paragraphs—all calculated to extort attention—were employed, regardless of expense."

Barnum used some exceptionally creative tactics.

One was to write anonymous letters to the editors denouncing Joice Heth as "a humbug, a deception cleverly made of India rubber, whalebone, and hidden springs."[34] (He further obscured her true identity by publishing a short biography of her, *The Life of Joice Heth, the Nurse of George Washington*, and by having his advance man, Levi Lyman, meet with ministers to display Heth's baptismal documents, which he had forged.) Barnum was stirring his own pot, for he knew that controversy would be good for the gate; this was, perhaps, one of the first instances of the common twentieth-century maxim that "no publicity is bad publicity."

Another tactic was to use indirect advertising, by convincing newspapers to write their own feature stories about Joice Heth. In a series of articles Barnum wrote for the *New York Atlas* in 1841 under the pseudonym Barnaby Diddleum, he smugly described some of the editorial coverage he had been able to generate, including this quotation from the *Providence Herald:*

> To say we were astonished would be but a feeble expression of our feelings. We look on this extraordinary specimen of humanity, with something bordering on awe and veneration, and when we heard her converse on subject or circumstance which must have occurred more than a century, since, and especially those connected with the birth—the infancy, and childhood of the immortal Washington—the mind was carried away by an intensity of interest, which no other object of curiosity has ever created in our breast. Before having seen this woman, a person may be inclined to be incredulous as to the story of her very great age. He may think of demanding documentary evidence in proof. But the first glance at the original before him will banish all scepticism [*sic*] on the subject, and on examination, he will find evidence estamped upon it by the hand of nature, too plain and forcible to require corroboration.[35]

In another article, Barnum/Diddleum told a rival why his exhibitions always attracted a crowd, in the process describing his own indirect advertising methodology:

> By and by, it wouldn't be a bad plan on entering a town where you play to call on the principal paper or papers, if there are two, and say you want a card [advertisement] for your benefit published, and this you must be sure to pay for in advance. . . . At all events the card business can do no harm, and may do much good. I would as soon travel throughout the country without grease to the wheels of my

> wagon as to neglect it. Well, having got this notice you must take a dozen or twenty papers. . . . One, of course, you'll reserve for your scrap book for your own amusement in showing it to your friends. The others you will send, of course, to the editors, or the principal editors in the chief cities, especially where you are likely to perform. You must mark the paragraph round with ink, and write on the margin 'please notice.'[36]

This was certainly one of the first times in history that such techniques had ever been used—anticipating everything from the press kit to the wire services to the highlight marker. And the combined effect of Barnum's efforts was clear to see: he whipped up curiosity about the Joice Heth exhibition, drew sellout crowds, and raked in profits of $1,500 a week, a small fortune for that era.

These types of humbugs, or elaborate hoaxes, became Barnum's chief line of business; later, they would evolve, slightly, and take the form of the "freak show." They brought him notoriety, as well as credit for a great line ("There's a sucker born every minute") that he never actually uttered, although he ultimately looked back upon the humbugs as "the least deserving of all my efforts in the show line."[37] Still, his success in bamboozling showed that he had a sort of extrasensory perception of the ethos of his chaotic times (which historian LeRoy Ashby memorably called "a jamboree of exaggeration, chicanery, flimflam, and bunkum") and frequently tapped into this to draw a crowd.[38] For him, the humbug was not some kind of shell game to defraud people but a playful challenge, a magician's invocation to see if they had the intellect and the perceptiveness to discern the real from the fake. "Now and then some one would cry out 'humbug' and 'charlatan,' but so much the better for me," Barnum wrote. "It helped to advertise me, and I was willing to bear the reputation."[39]

Everything Barnum did, every enterprise in which he engaged, was predicated on its marketability.

In 1841, Barnum purchased Scudder's American Museum on Ann Street in New York for fifteen thousand dollars and rebranded it Barnum's American Museum. It quickly became the most popular attraction in New York, in part because of the bizarre eclecticism of its thirty thousand exhibits (waxworks, flea circus, rifle range, glassblowers, rope dancers, a dog that supposedly worked a weaving loom, an oyster bar cut from the Chesapeake coast, the bearded woman, the thin man, albinos, Gypsies, Indians, jugglers, Siamese twins, live giraffes, crocodiles, sloths, a whale, etc.), but also because of the bold and creative ways in which it was promoted. Barnum opened the museum at sunrise; built a giant "BARNUM" sign on the outside with gas lights, which reflected in the windows of the venerable St. Paul's Chapel across the street; used powerful Drummond lights on the roof, which "in the darkest night, threw a flood of light up and down Broadway"; offered balloon rides from his roof garden; flew colorful flags and banners; published an illustrated museum magazine, in which he declared that he had, "with justice, been designated the NAPOLEON of his profession"; hired a man to mysteriously move bricks from street corner to street corner throughout Lower Manhattan, attracting five hundred curious onlookers whom he led right into the museum (only for them to learn that it was a pointless stunt); paraded one of his newly acquired museum elephants back and forth near his Bridgeport home as if it were plowing the fields, in plain view of the curious onlookers aboard the New York and New Haven Railroad trains; and even paid bad musicians to play from the museum balconies, hoping that their discordant cacophony would drive people inside.[40] Between its opening and its final demise after a second huge fire in 1865, the museum was visited by an estimated 38 million people.[41]

One of the most famous of the museum's exhibits was the Feejee Mermaid (in reality, a monkey's head and torso cleverly sewn onto the tail of a large fish), unveiled in 1842, which proved to be so popular that it tripled the museum's receipts in four weeks and was eventually sent on tour. Barnum again utilized some clever artifice, dispatching his advance agent Lyman—a name so phonetically suited to the task that one wonders if P. T. somehow handled the christening himself—to pose as Dr. Griffin, the purported man of letters who had purchased the mermaid in China on behalf of the Lyceum of Natural History in London. Barnum also sent out notices about the Feejee Mermaid, similar to our modern-day press releases, and watched as the newspapers ran his stories verbatim. "Thus was the fame of the Museum, as well as the mermaid, wafted from end of the land to the others," he chortled. "I was careful to keep up the excitement, for I knew that every dollar sown in advertising would return in tens, and perhaps hundreds, in a future harvest."[42]

Attacking the promotional effort with both sophistication and tenacity, Barnum typically supplemented his advertising and indirect advertising with posters, lithographs, souvenir photographs—taking full advantage of the new graphic arts to stimulate viewers' imaginations—and sometimes publishing multiple pamphlets for the same exhibition.[43]

He also continued to use the newspapers as his multifaceted tool and sounding board.

> I was prodigal in my outlays to arrest or arouse public attention. . . . I printed whole columns in the papers, setting forth the wonders of my establishment. Old "fogies" opened their eyes in amazement at a man who could expend hundreds of dollars in announcing a show of "stuffed monkey skins"; but these same old fogies paid their quarters, nevertheless, and when they saw the curiosities and novelties in the Museum halls, they, like all other visitors, were astonished as well as pleased, and went home and told their friends and neighbors and thus assisted in advertising my business.[44]

When he put his distant cousin, the then-twenty-five-inch-tall Charles Stratton (General Tom Thumb), on exhibition, he distributed enough biographies and lithographs to newspaper editors to generate enormous advance publicity; almost one hundred thousand people paid to see him during his thirteen months at the American Museum. Then, before Barnum took Tom Thumb on a tour of Europe in 1844, he prepared by reading every London newspaper he could find and sending out "letters of introduction" to the editors. The coverage he received was unprecedented, and the three-year tour went on to play before Queen Victoria, the czar of Russia, other dignitaries, and 5 million common folk in France, Spain, Belgium, and elsewhere. It generated profits of $1 million.[45]

The power of the press also helped launch Barnum's spectacular tour of soprano Jenny Lind, the "Swedish Nightingale," in 1850. Barnum mortgaged his home and museum to obtain the $187,500 needed to pay her in advance and to ensure that her concerts sold out. Lind had been a sensation in Europe, but according to Barnum, she was "comparatively unknown on this side of the water . . . millions had merely read her name, but had no distinct idea of who or what she was."[46] But with Barnum's penchant for promotion, those mortgages were a sucker's bet.

He began writing letters to newspaper editors touting the tour more than six months in advance. Later, he announced a contest through the newspapers to pay one hundred dollars for the writing of a "national song" for Lind to sing in America (seven hundred people entered) and sent out

BARNUM'S REPUTATION AS A PROMOTER was already well enough established by 1850 to be worthy of satire. This sketch, spoofing the showman's presentation of Jenny Lind, features the use of a giant poster, handbills flung into the crowd, the manipulation of newspapers (playing wind instruments), and Barnum himself watching from inside the ticket office. William Schaus, artist, *Panorama of Humbug No. 1*, 1850, Library of Congress, Prints and Photographs Division; http://hdl.loc.gov/loc.pnp/cph.3a05239.

previews of Lind's tour that included this thunderstruck endorsement from the esteemed German composer Jules Benedict:

> SCHLAGENBAD, Wednesday, July 24.
>
> My dear sir—I have just heard Mlle. Jenny Lind, whose voice has acquired—*if that were possible*—even additional power and effect, by a timely and well chosen repose.—Mr. Wilson will bring you the programme for the first concert, which cannot fail to produce the most thrilling sensation in your noble metropolis. You may depend on it, that such a thrilling performance as her's [*sic*]—in the finest pieces of her repertoire—must warrant an unprecedented excitement, and justify all the expectations.[47]

The letter originally ran in the *New York Daily Tribune* and was picked up in papers like the *Evansville Daily Journal*, which ran it nine days before Lind reached American shores. Evansville was 165 miles away from the nearest Lind concert location in St. Louis.

Left unsaid was the fact that Barnum had paid Benedict £5,000 sterling to serve as Lind's accompanist and musical director on the tour—and that the letter was actually written by Barnum himself.[48]

When Lind's ship, the *Atlantic,* arrived in New York from Liverpool on September 1, it was greeted by forty thousand people; twenty thousand more waited at the Irving House hotel, lingering there well into the evening hoping to catch a glimpse of her. The *New York Daily Tribune* devoted four of its six front-page columns the next day to Jenny Lind; a fifth column featured a long poem dedicated to her that was so arcane ("Frigga's queenly care extending / Joins with Saga's runic lore; / Gaijon, maiden never ending, / Gold-teared Freya, still heart-sore") that it required fifty-two footnotes of explanation.[49]

Barnum next arranged an auction of tickets for the first Jenny Lind concert. "I clearly foresaw what effect this auction sale of Jenny Lind tickets would necessarily have in the existing excited state of the public mind," Barnum later wrote in the *Cosmopolitan,* "and that the higher the prices obtained, the more would the frenzy be increased."[50] Three-thousand people came to the Castle Garden Theatre for the ticket auction event (even though they all had to pay 12 ½ cents admission), and in an ironic nod to his roots, Barnum arranged for one of the final bidders to be a representative of none other than Dr. Benjamin Brandreth, the patent medicine king.

Soon, "Lindmania" swept across the country, fueled in part by twenty-six reporters Barnum hired to pump out feature stories about the singer. There was Jenny Lind sheet music and Jenny Lind merchandise—gloves, bonnets, hats, shawls, cigars, even sofas and chairs. It was a layered, nuanced, and remarkably sophisticated campaign, and it resulted in one of the most triumphant moments in American culture in the first half of the nineteenth century, not to mention one of the most profitable: Barnum netted five hundred thousand dollars from the tour, even though Lind ended it early to go out on her own.

The ensuing period was not always easy for Barnum. He squandered much of his fortune through bad investments, and then lost his lavish Connecticut mansion, Iranistan, and separately, the American Museum, to fire. Barnum went on the lecture circuit, then dabbled in politics for a while; he was twice elected to the Connecticut State Legislature and once to the mayoralty of Bridgeport, but in 1867 he lost a bid for the U.S. House.

Yet the impresario in him could never be suppressed, and in 1871 he opened P. T. Barnum's Great Travelling Museum, Menagerie, Caravan & Hippodrome, a "magic city" of circus acts in giant tents covering six acres, which could accommodate ten thousand spectators at a time. Within about a year it had metamorphosed into P. T. Barnum Great Travelling World's Fair and Greatest Show on Earth. An 1872 ad boasted that it featured "seven superior exhibitions in six separate colossal tents, which, at a challenge of $100,000, is ten times larger than any other show ever seen on Earth."[51] In 1881, he joined with James Anthony Bailey, manager of the Cooper and Bailey Circus, and formed the euphonious, syncopated, alliterative combination that, after some starts and stops, endured for more than 130 years: Barnum & Bailey.

It is difficult for a twenty-first century American to appreciate the importance of the circus in the Gilded Age. These days, the circus has lost much of its spangle. We have professional sports that attract tens of millions of spectators each year. We have curiosities and freaks "going viral" every day on YouTube. We have Nik Wallenda walking a tightrope between two Chicago skyscrapers without a net, broadcast live on TV while we sip chai from the comfort of our living rooms and absentmindedly scroll through our Facebook feeds. Variety shows like Blue Man Group and Cirque du Soleil have carved out their niches, but the *circus?* Elephants, clowns, and the lady shot out of the cannon? It's mostly a vestige, an idyll, a pink-cotton-candy memory of another time.

In the nineteenth century, however, the circus was an epic form of entertainment. Factories, schools, and businesses closed their doors on the day the circus arrived, and as historian Janet Davis wrote, "Thousands of 'strangers' from around a county streamed into town. Big cities overflowed. Provincial communities became temporary cities, complete with anonymous, pushing crowds."[52]

Barnum responded in the way he knew best: unapologetic, unrelenting promotional ardor. In a typical year, nearly one-third of the circus's entire expenses, more than one hundred thousand dollars, were spent on publicity and advertising. He introduced a live promotion, the precircus parade, or "caravan," which became a staple of the circus for decades. He commissioned painters and illustrators to produce beautiful artwork to promote the show, and incorporated these into huge lithographs that were plastered everywhere by industrious crews who rode the rails ahead of the show in a specially designed sixty-four-foot steel advertising coach. (In 1879, Barnum arranged for seventy lithographs to be hung together to cover the side of a large building in Newport, Rhode Island, a three-thousand-dollar stunt he called "the biggest and best show bill in the world."[53]) The railcar itself featured Barnum's portrait on the outside, along with intricately painted circus scenes and animals, and a work area inside for the press agents and twelve-member "paste brigade."[54]

In time, multiple ad cars would work in tandem, and the "billers" might hang between six and ten thousand posters in a single day on barn doors, store windows, sheds, fences, and hastily constructed billboards. The cars were often outfitted with upright boilers that produced steam for making the poster paste (using cooking flour), and occasionally that steam was also used to power a calliope, which itself was a major attraction in the quiet, dusty outposts in which the circus often played.[55]

The scale of the bill-posting operation exceeded anything we would know in modern times. Three different specially equipped railroad advertising cars, each with its own crew and supply of lithographs, photographs, and other promotional materials, could be readily attached to local trains so that they could "leapfrog" past each other and perform designated functions. Barnum & Bailey would document this in 1894, when their teams worked to promote eighteen one-day stands in as many days on the route between Indianapolis and LaPorte, Indiana. The crew from Car Two reached 434 towns and posted more than 60,000 sheets of paper as they fanned out in cities and along wagon routes. Car Four's crew handled the railroad routes, reaching 588 territorial towns with 38,792 sheets. Then Car Six came back through two weeks after Car Two to replace nearly half the posters that had originally been installed, and which may have been damaged or papered over by rivals.[56]

It was an impressive enterprise. But of course, Barnum's circus itself was impressive. It expanded to three rings, and soon there were oddities and exhibits from exotic ports of call—Bengal tigers, racing dromedaries driven by rajahs, Highland bagpipers, Roman knife throwers, Moorish warriors, Bruno the Clown Bear, Madam Yucca the Champion American

Female Hercules, re-creations of the fall of Babylon and of battleship fights, and so on.

On posters and ads, he alternately referred to it as a "great ethnological congress" and "veritable pandemonium," because as all great marketers do, Barnum truly understood his audience—both the Brahmins and the Boweryites. He knew what appealed to the blue-blooded aristocratic Americans—sensed their thirst for learning and penchant for acquiring the trappings of European culture—because he had become one of them. But Barnum also related to the common folk and clearly understood their desire to see more of the world and to begin to decipher the inexplicable forces of science and nature. "I desire to elevate the morals and refine the tastes of my patrons," he said.[57] This was, after all, a new age of wonder, of vast possibilities and unknowns drawing ever nearer through modern travel and communications; a day at the circus could be very enlightening. This seemingly contradictory ability to both dazzle and edify was the beating heart of Barnum's genius.

Barnum turned seventy in 1880 and no longer had the energy to travel with the show. He also had no (male) heirs and no (promotional) heirs apparent. But he effectively found both with the hiring in 1881 of a tall, thin, dapper, downswept-mustachioed press agent by the name of Richard Francis "Tody" Hamilton (the nickname conferred when he was very young, because of his tendency to hop around like a toad) and his prolific fountain pen. Barnum knew that Hamilton would carry the torch forward into the new century, igniting a promotional pyre whose embers would glow for a long, long time.

Working together for the final ten years of Barnum's life, they would sensationalize the circus, but also legitimize and professionalize the field of promotion. Barnum paid Hamilton what one newspaper deemed "enormous" sums of money from time to time instead of the standard press agent's salary of five thousand dollars a year, and on one occasion, when the famously teetotaling Barnum caught a glimpse of Hamilton sipping champagne at a banquet, he said, "There is not a man connected with my show who drinks . . . except 'Tody' Hamilton, and he does as he pleases."[58] Never one to share much of the spotlight, Barnum nevertheless said he owed more of his success to Tody than to any other man.[59]

Who was Tody Hamilton?

Born in Manhattan on June 23, 1847, he was a precocious child. He attended school at Fordham College in New York at the age of eight, and at twelve he took to the sea, sailing for Panama and San Francisco. Then, like all great promoters of the nineteenth century, he devoted part of his early career to journalism. At fourteen, Hamilton followed his father and grandfather into the newspaper business, writing for the *New York Sun* during the Civil War, and a bit later for James Gordon Bennett's *New York Herald.* It was a peripatetic upbringing, but one well suited to his active mind. "We're pretty much all misfits in this life," he later mused. "Circumstances put us into one place and, perhaps, we make a fair success there. But we've always got a yearning eye on some other niche."[60]

In 1868, at the age of twenty-one, Hamilton made five hundred thousand dollars speculating in real estate and on Wall Street, and then lost it all. He started three esoteric trade magazines, *Hairdresser, Railroad Age,* and *Steamship Gazette,* and around 1880 launched a Sunday evening newspaper (published at 3 P.M.) called the *Evening Journal,* which lasted for only nine weeks.

Because his father's newspaper office had been located right across from Barnum's American Museum at Broadway and Ann Streets, Tody had visited often and developed an obsession that never quite went away. Thus, time and time again, he found himself returning to the novelty entertainment business. Beginning in 1875, he was the business manager for the Great New York Aquarium at 35th Street and Broadway. After that, he promoted a six-day roller-skating contest.

When he came to work for P. T. Barnum as advertising and press agent, at the age of thirty-four, Hamilton's job at first was to keep news *out* of the papers, "to see that the bloom on the show's reputation was not disturbed by the rude hand of criticism."[61] Barnum, after all, was known as the Prince of Humbugs and was a controversial figure.

But in that same year, 1881, the great showman first teamed up with James Bailey to launch the new traveling circus that would eventually become known as Barnum & Bailey's Greatest Show on Earth, and expanded it to three rings full of exotic entertainment. This was precisely the same time newspapers were becoming more discerning, more professional, and hiring more reporters to go out and gather the news. For all these reasons, Hamilton's mandate quickly shifted. Instead of the old

TODY HAMILTON, "Barnum's cyclone press agent," was such a masterful promoter of the circus that one newspaper referred to him as the "world-renowned Editor-Tamer." Circus World Museum, Baraboo, Wisconsin.

job of distributing reading notices, he now had to fight for space in the newspapers. He was no longer just a disseminator but an originator, and he became involved in the new form of press agentry, which the *Christian Science Monitor* called "a contest between watchful journalism and wakeful invention."[62] As the *National Police Gazette* noted, the role of the press agent was now "to work up a fancy sensation, to create a stir, to warm a dying idea into fitful brilliancy."[63]

Hamilton would go on to become the key promotional strategist for the circus, the lightning rod that would conduct Barnum's high-wire electricity down to the ground and send a jolt through the media and the public. Instead of shying away from publicity, he pursued it aggressively. In so doing, Tody Hamilton became the model for the Gilded Age press agent, which in turn became the model for the modern public relations manager.

Hamilton brought to the new job a charming smile, a raconteur's wit, and one of the world's more creative and impressive vocabularies. He was said to have memorized more adjectives than any man on earth and invented 10 percent of them. In his journalism days, he had seen the power of persuasive words. "To state a fact in ordinary language," he once said, "is to permit a doubt concerning the statement."[64]

There was never any doubt about Tody Hamilton, for none of his language was ordinary. In the course of writing ads and posters and cranking out 2 million words of copy a year for Barnum & Bailey, Hamilton quickly acquired a reputation for his imaginative use of alliteration and unexpected word combinations. "Another Awful, Appalling Aerial Automobile Somersaulting Act by a Young and Fameless French Lady" read one of his headlines.[65] "Marvelous Miracles of Monstrous Moment" read another. "Fabulous Fat Fanny Feeding Ferociously on Farinaceous Foods," a third.[66] He described the trapeze artists' "turning, twisting, tossing, tilting, transposition in midair," and called their act "the most daring and desperate aerial duel with death ever ventured by mortal man."[67] He deemed a circus act called Le Autobolide "the thrilling dip of death, an absolutely unparalleled deed of daring, just as illustrated and costing nearly $2,000 a minute; the sensation of all sensations, which may be aptly termed a fearful frolic with fate;" an act called The Limit was "the most fearless and reckless exploit ever successfully performed—a thrilling, turning, tumbling, twisting, twirling, tilting automobile in mid-air."[68] He called C. M. Robinson, champion bareback rider of the world, the "teetotal topmost tallest" man in the universe.[69] Among the animals there was La Paloma, "the peerless pedestrian puma," and an elephant whose "ebullitions of athletic elephantine power are sometimes stupendous."[70] In 1898, the magazine *Current Literature* gushed, "His sustained use of adjective after adjective, each seemingly the strongest in the language and each succeeded by a much stronger, calls into play the utmost skill. As Barnum was the greatest of all Americans, so is Tody Hamilton, his one and only prophet, the greatest of our poets and writers of fiction."[71]

To the modern sensibility, it all sounds like a bunch of cornball buffoonery, the linguistic equivalent of the very clown shenanigans and sideshow skylarking that made up the less savory parts of the show Hamilton was promoting. But to the ear of a Gilded Age American, accustomed to the starchy language of most newspaper pages and all officialdom, it was truly a sensation—one that lent excitement and legitimacy to Barnum's new effort and that managed to land one circus feature story after another in the newspapers, often on the front page.

(Interestingly, Barnum himself favored statistics—especially those with dollar signs in front of them—over words. Included in the program for the circus's debut in London on November 11, 1889, was a letter from Barnum that read in part:

> Plain, honest words accord best with great deeds. Bombast or exaggeration, unjustifiable at all times, would be sadly out of place in setting forth the unparalleled magnitude and daring novelty of an exhibition enterprise which involves a capital of $3,000,000, the cost of transportation six thousand miles, and a daily expenditure of $6,800. Added to this are the labors of 1,200 men and women, 380 horses, and the care and feeding of hundreds of the rarest wild animals, many of which are trained to do almost everything but speak.

Of course, the very same program contained a Hamiltonian headline that was chock full of bombast: "AMERICA'S TRUTHFUL, MORAL, INSTRUCTIVE, GRANDEST AND BEST, LARGEST AMUSEMENT INSTITUTION."[72])

Hamilton's linguistic gymnastics were nothing but puffery, of course, but they also spewed so naturally and extemporaneously from his fertile mind that they made everyone smile; the late actor/comedian Robin Williams comes to mind as a modern counterpart. In an off-the-cuff interview with the *New York Times* in 1903, Hamilton declared,

> This, the greatest show on earth, is a most supremely satisfying, enobling [*sic*], gratifying, superb, spectacular affair, teeming with life and vivid color, inspiring admiration and abundantly complete with gorgeous sights and the truthfully illustrated art of athletics, the whole forming a blazing kaleidoscopic vision of animated and iridescent splendor that has astonished the crowned heads of Europe and the high officers of the Republic of France.[73]

(The *Times* then noted sardonically that the stenographer ran out of ink in the fountain pen's reservoir.)

The fact that Tody Hamilton played the English language so artfully earned him unstinting praise from reporters and editors—not to mention lots of coverage. "Octosyllabic artist," they called him. "Master of the coruscating, incandescent, and unparalleled adjective."[74] "Boss hustler of the United States" who "writes everything in royal octavo style."[75] "Barnum's cyclone press agent and descriptive epigrammist. America's representative word-smith! A wild, whirling tornado of breathless adjective!! An inexhaustible mine of glittering epithet!!!"[76] The *New York Sun* praised "the polysyllable magnificence of Tody Hamilton's advertisements."[77] Another publication commended the "wonderful ingenuity he shows in exalting the common English speech to powers unknown and unsuspected by others. He has managed to get our mother tongue on the highest pair of stilts ever known."[78] The humorist Irwin S. Cobb once wrote, "When Tody started in to write about the elephant quadrille you had to turn over to the next page to find the verb."[79]

Many a person wore out his *Roget's Thesaurus* trying to imitate Hamilton's style. Wrote one, in tribute to Hamilton: "'Tis his transmutation transmitted and translated into tens of tongues that tell thrilling and titillating tales to towns that teem with thousands and that transform things trite and thin into tremendously think and telling truths that terrify timorous teachers, transfigure terms and take a thundering tough trip to the threshold of trembling tautology."[80]

Hamilton was so renowned for his adjectival stylings that he even became fodder for the most famous humor magazine of the era, *Puck*, in a parody song they published called "The Circus Placard (as sung by 'Tody' Hamilton)":

If you want a receipt for that edict oracular
Known to the world as a circus placard,
Take all the long adjectives in the vernacular—
Words that have only one syllable barred: —

Astounding, incredible, startling, sensational.
Fabulous, famous, enormous, unclassed.
Wonderful, elephantine, aggregational.
Glittering, gorgeous, outre, unsurpassed.

Radiant, ravishing, lustrous, quotidian.
Fulgent, prodigious, colossal, bizarre.
Enchanting, astonishing, Afric, Numidian.
Shimmering, glimmering spectacular.

Gargantuan, Gog and Magog, Brobdingnagian.
Magical, marvellous, mystical, Magian.
Only live specimen born in a cage ian.
Novel, eccentric, abnormal, unique.
Loop looping, death flouting, killed every week—

Take of these adjectives all that are usable.
Set them in order so they'll be perusable.
Print on pink paper, and paste by the yard.
And the happy result is a circus placard.[81]

Long after Tody Hamilton's death in 1916, his name would be used as a sort of shorthand code for fustian writing and hyperbole by literati like Christopher Morley and H. L. Mencken.

But there was more to him. He was also expressive, smart, clever, and reliable, and he remembered reporters' and editors' names from year to year. "That famous press agent and thoroughly good fellow, in and out of business," one newspaper called him.[82] "[The] advance agent of happiness... a singular blend of dignity and geniality," wrote another.[83] "A genuine cosmopolitan and as a good fellow the grand ultimate," reported yet another.[84] The *Salt Lake Tribune* said, "There is hardly a village in the land from ocean to ocean or from the lakes to the gulf where the noted advance agent of the greatest show on earth has not personal friends who will always be interested in him."[85]

There was still another aspect of Hamilton's promotional work that was even more dynamic than his language and his affability, one that would have a lasting impact on the industry: he *manufactured* news.

By the time Hamilton had reached his periphrastic prime, there was already a long tradition of hoaxes being used to gin up publicity, especially in America. In 1835, the *New York Sun* famously ran a series of articles that described the purported discovery by the well-known astronomer "Sir John Herschel, L.L.D., F.R.S. &c," of life on the moon: herds of shaggy brown quadrupeds, goatlike monsters of bluish lead color, and four-foot-high winged humanoids. In 1869, a New York tobacconist named George Hull created the so-called Cardiff Giant, a ten-foot sculpture that was stained and weathered to appear like a petrified human being, and charged admission to see it. (Of course, no one had been more successful at such fakery than Barnum himself—from Joice Heth to the Feejee Mermaid—and indeed, after his offer of fifty thousand dollars for the Cardiff Giant was rebuffed, he created his own version and charged the fake with being a fake.)

But what Tody Hamilton did under Barnum's watchful eye was different: not hoaxes, not humbugs that strained the common man's credulity, but events that seemed legitimate or even educational, though contrived—publicity stunts, as they are known today. And no one was better at them than Tody Hamilton.

The first and most famous of these was the purchase of Jumbo, the giant African elephant, from the London Zoological Gardens in 1882. Some accounts say that it was Hamilton who suggested the idea to Barnum, but regardless of Tody's role at the beginning of this affair, he was a major architect of its middle, end, and afterlife.[86]

Barnum's purchase, for ten thousand dollars, caused an outcry from the British, who, after sixteen years of taking rides on the elephant's back, had come to think of Jumbo as a national treasure (though he had already lived in Africa, Germany, and France before coming to England). Children wrote letters to the zoo, and to Barnum, and to Queen Victoria, begging them to reconsider—all of which, with Hamilton's guidance, led to lots of press coverage.[87] An injunctive lawsuit was filed to try to keep the elephant in London—more press.

Hamilton also worked to generate extensive newspaper coverage of the Herculean logistics needed to transport Jumbo from the zoo to the docks. The elephant at first refused to move and lay down in the street for a week; Barnum reportedly commented, "Let him lie there as long as he wants to. The publicity is worth it."[88] His handlers did eventually get the elephant on the *Assyrian Monarch* to New York, where, spurred by the Hamilton-generated media coverage, thousands of onlookers awaited in a scene reminiscent of Barnum's earlier European import, Jenny Lind, decades earlier. And as with Lind, a merchandising and media phenomenon soon swept across the United States—"Jumbomania."

Jumbo debuted at the Greatest Show on Earth on Easter Sunday, 1882, at Madison Square Garden, and in the months that followed, he was the central focus of Hamilton's advertising and press agentry. "'JUMBO,' the Gigantic Elephantine Monster," heralded one of the ads with an illustration of the elephant straining at his harness and chains. "HIS ENORMOUSLY DEVELOPED STATURE. . . . FORTY STRONG DRAUGHT HORSES HAULED HIM TO THE SHIP. . . . This Miraculous Moving Mountain of Flesh, This Most Prodigious Towering Animate Wonder" (see plate 1).[89]

In 1883, Barnum and Hamilton tried to mount a stunt to capture the attention of New Yorkers: moving Jumbo and the circus from Madison Square Garden to Brooklyn by a parade across the imposing new Brooklyn Bridge (which had not yet opened to the public) at 10 P.M. "I have often wished to test the strength of the structure," Barnum told reporters, "and it would be a capital idea to try it. Anyway, I'm ready to risk Jumbo on the strength and durability of American enterprise, and we will have to arrange for electric lights, so that the public will have a chance to see the elephant on a higher elevation than has been attempted by any elephant in the world."[90]

The idea, and Barnum's offer of five thousand dollars, was declined, but the duo successfully pulled it off the following year, with Hamilton leading the parade on a gray charger, followed by Jumbo, twenty other elephants, and seventeen camels, among others; a crowd of two thousand gathered to watch.[91] "What do you charge for 'helephants?" Hamilton asked the puzzled toll-taker.[92]

The parade of animals would become a mainstay in the Barnum-Hamilton promotional playbook and nearly always preceded the opening of the circus in a new town. The *New York Times* provided a vivid description of one such parade in 1883:

> There was a sound of a hundred musical instruments—the psalter, the fife, the drum, the bassoon, the calliope, the hand-organ, the jews-harp, the viol, the French horn, the flute, the tin whistle, the harmonicom, the accordion, and every other instrument of torture known to science or religion, accompanied by a glare of electric light, blue, green, yellow, pink, red and purple fire, Roman candles, rockets, pinwheels, gunpowder, dynamite, nitroglycerine, and other explosives as the mighty procession loomed up in the dim distance. Nearer they came; louder sounded the music; more gloriously flared the pyrotechnics; more fiercely growled the lions; bass-profundo

> chorused the tigers; more merrily jogged the elephants; blithely bobbed the camels; grandly rolled the chariots, and the multitude burst into a roar of applause, which almost shook the City to its foundations, and caused the cobblestones to grind against each other in the streets. First a number of gorgeously caparisoned heralds mounted upon prancing steeds, winding flashing trumpets; . . . a quartet of beautiful women on horseback cavorted gayly after, followed by a score of mounted wariors [*sic*] in armor; wagons inclosing raging tigers, lions, hyenas, leopards, panthers, bears, and numerous other beasts next rolled by. Knights in armor, ladies in flashing tinsel and glittering spangles, the old woman who lived in a shoe, Santa Claus, and other allegorical figures burst upon the spectators. Wagons drawn by every species of quadruped from giraffes to zebras, racing elephants, chariots and horsemen, wheeled past in a blaze of fire and glory."[93]

Manufactured news generated a great deal of manufactured news coverage. Little wonder that Barnum's circuses often sold eight to nine thousand tickets in less than an hour.[94] By 1888, the shows were attracting more than one hundred thousand patrons each week, and the "street pageants" more than three hundred thousand.[95]

Over the next three years, Tody Hamilton featured Jumbo, the "mastodonic marvel," as the centerpiece of most of his promotional posters, press releases, and stories.[96] But on September 15, 1885, while crossing some railroad tracks near the circus grounds in Ontario, Jumbo was struck and killed by an oncoming locomotive. Ironically, this tragic event may have generated more newspaper coverage than anything Hamilton and Jumbo had ever done together. Telegraphs spread the word instantly, and there was an outpouring of grief around the world. "The friend of youth, the admired of all, the boast and wonder of the age, is no more," wrote the *Washington Evening Star* in a typical editorial, "and what remains to us is to bear our loss with resignation and to extract from the sad event its moral lessons."[97]

Barnum tried to turn his loss into a promotional gain, concocting a story about how Jumbo had died trying to save another elephant and his trainer. But Hamilton seems to have been behind the even more manipulative (albeit clever) effort that resulted in stuffing Jumbo's skin and mounting his bones so he could continue touring as part of the Greatest

Show on Earth.[98] And the following year, when Barnum arranged to bring Jumbo's "widow," Alice the elephant, to the United States, Hamilton was there with a passel of reporters to greet her at the dock. "The recognition between Alice and 'Tody' was instantaneous," wrote the *New York Times*, in a lengthy article on page two,

> and she seemed to read in his eyes the awful intelligence that her dear old Jumbo was no more. She burst into a flood of tears, and throwing her trunk around "Tody's" neck, seemed to whisper in his ear between her sobs, "I know you were my husband's friend. . . ." Mr. Hamilton discussed the advisability of taking Alice at once to the Madison-Square Garden, and finally decided that it would not do to take her through the streets of New-York in the daytime. He knows enough about elephants to know that when angered the female is more to be feared than the male, and he thought of the terrible destruction of property which might follow if Alice should get on the rampage in the streets of this city.[99]

Hamilton was also well known for manufacturing news stories about animals that had supposedly escaped from their enclosures—possibly into the streets of Manhattan!—or gone missing. On another occasion he earned some ink by having Marie Bayrooty, the dancing dervish from Beirut, set a record as a human top by spinning for thirty-two straight minutes at Madison Square Garden. He apparently also offered Admiral George Dewey, hero of the Battle of Manila, one hundred thousand dollars a week to appear in the show.[100]

Was any of it true? Some. As the *New York Sun* wrote of him, "Telling the truth is an ungovernable passion. . . . Sometimes he rolls it in adjectives till it's as big as a three ring tent; but there's always a kernel of truth inside."[101] Like his mentor Barnum, he knew that there had to be implicit trust between the press corps and the promoter. In 1904, Hamilton took stock of the transformations in the role of the press agent in an article in the *Fourth Estate* (a trade magazine about and for the press, whose very existence indicated how much things had changed since Tody's early days in journalism), decrying the "detestable methods" of using fake information to create "temporary notoriety" in the newspapers: "The better press agents rarely resort to [that]. . . . On the contrary, the press agent who deals only in facts that will stand investigation, and that can be printed without question, is a much sought after individual and a welcome visitor everywhere."[102] He was, effectively, marking the evolution of the press agent into the public relations professional.

Nevertheless, he always had a twinkle in his eye, and late in life he admitted to his newspaper friends, "Why, if I had written only truth for the past twenty-five years I never could have held my job six months. And think what the New York papers would have missed!"[103]

3

BOOM OR BOOST: PROMOTING THE WEST

"We have watched the flow of immigration . . . obliterating every vestige of the pioneer trails"

> The *untransacted* destiny of the American people is to subdue the continent—to rush over this vast field to the Pacific Ocean . . .—to change darkness into light—to stir up the sleep of a hundred centuries—to teach old nations a new civilization . . .—to emblazon history with the conquest of peace—to shed a new and resplendent glory upon mankind.

William Gilpin, *Report to the U.S. Senate* (1846)

P. T. Barnum was certainly the most important promotional force of midcentury America. He had entered his career with only one primitive promotional tool at his disposal: the print ad. By the time he was done, he had introduced and all but perfected many others, including indirect advertising, bill posting, the publicity stunt, and manufactured news—all of them new "tent poles" supporting a marketing canvas bigger than even his big top.

So, given his unprecedented success—brilliantly magnified and carried forward by the "octosyllabic artist" Tody Hamilton—it would have been reasonable to expect that the course of the new industry would conform rather closely to his, and that others would follow in the oversize footprints he had left behind in the fairground sawdust and mud.

That is not what happened.

Certainly, many of the Barnum-Hamilton pioneering methods were widely copied and still are to this day. They had hacked out a path that press agents and publicists might follow. But it was only one path—as it turned out, a flawed one—and even in their lifetimes, it would start to be supplanted by others. Indeed, this would be the pattern that marketing *always* repeats: new technologies for communication are invented, new techniques for persuasion are developed, but the more widely they are adopted, the more inured to them consumers become, and soon the search is on for a better marketing mousetrap. After all, there was also a time when the [newspaper classified] [magazine ad] [press release] [Burma Shave sign] [radio spot] [TV jingle] [celebrity endorsement] [video news release] [mailed AOL floppy disk] [website banner ad] [QR code] [search engine marketing campaign] [geo-fenced text message beacon] was considered to be the paramount achievement in promotion, the sophisticated end to which all the means of all previous advertising had pointed; that time always passed.

But there were also inherent problems in the Barnum-Hamilton style that limited its effectiveness.

First, there was Barnum's towering ego, which, in an era of modesty and sublimity, did not sit well with everyone. Self-promotion was an important but inimitable part of his marketing formula. He knew, in a way that Donald Trump does in modern times, that his own celebrity would help sell tickets and that his name was larger and more powerful than his edifices and promotions. As he himself wrote in the *New York Atlas* in 1845, "Barnum is possessed of an enterprise that is *indomitable.* He has a spirit of perseverance seldom equaled; but the grand secret of his success is, that he has a *genius* corresponding with his high aspirations."[1] In 1853, he launched his own newspaper, the *Illustrated News,* as a means for promoting himself and his many endeavors; he would resurrect this tactic in the 1870s with *P. T. Barnum's Advance Courier,* an illustrated twenty-four-page publication, written largely by Barnum himself, five hundred thousand copies of which were distributed for free in towns the circus was about to visit. He exhibited a similar lack of humility during an excursion to the top of New Hampshire's imposing Mount Washington, when Barnum telegraphed from the summit that it was, perhaps, the second greatest show on earth.

But he could never quite escape his own imposing shadow, which often led to withering criticisms like that of the *Grand River (Mich.) Times,* which said, "That fellow would exhibit the corpse of his mother, if there was anything peculiar to attract the attention of the curious, and thereby a few dollars more accrue to his already abundant treasury"; or the *Wilmington*

P. T. BARNUM'S ADVANCE COURIER.

P. T. BARNUM, Editor. 1871. Circulation 800,000.

P. T. BARNUM TO THE PUBLIC.

AFTER thirty years' active career in the Museum and Show Business, I undertook, at the end of two disastrous conflagrations, to retire permanently from business cares, and, taking Horace Greeley's characteristic advice, "Go a Fishing" for the balance of my days.

But neither ease nor fortune of itself furnishes a comfortable content; and being stimulated by energies that will not abate, by a constitution unimpaired, and by a desire once more to gratify the demands of an anxious public, I have absolutely become "restive" under "rest."

A custom now prevails in the Spectacular world, after having astonished a gazing multitude with a succession of gorgeous scenes, to crown all—just before the curtain comes down for the last time—with one picture of wonders, into which money and pains have been put with almost a lavish recklessness, that the entertainment may close with startling *éclat*. Being inspired by a like ambition, I am therefore prompted to undertake a new Mammoth Enterprise, by collecting, equipping, and putting in actual operation a great NATIONAL MUSEUM, MENAGERIE, CARAVAN, and HIPPODROME combined—an Exhibition which I purpose to make as absolutely NOVEL, COLOSSAL, EXHAUSTIVE, AND BEWILDERINGLY VARIOUS as money and experience can make it; and which I can transport, by means of 500 MEN AND HORSES, to every important neighborhood, township, and city of my own native land.

I intend it to constitute in the aggregate, when put on the road, the LARGEST GROUP OF WONDERS EVER KNOWN; while the admission to the entire series of attractions will be that of ordinary travelling exhibitions, viz., 50 cents; children under 9 half-price.

My facilities and experience were never so good as at present. I could never so well as now bring into requisition and summon to my service "the uttermost parts of the earth," nor find men so able and willing to carry out my long matured plans.

This Enterprise will combine—as all my shows have aimed to do

PHINEAS T. BARNUM.

THE COURIER, such as this magazine-like version from Barnum's first year in the circus business, 1871, was a staple of nineteenth-century promotion. Hundreds of thousands of copies were distributed to mailboxes, businesses, and gathering places, often with the date and location of the coming performance overprinted in red at the bottom. Courtesy of Chris Berry.

(N.C.) Journal, which in 1857 simply called him the "contemptible showman."[2]

Second, the name Barnum had become synonymous with hucksterism, and this would sully the entire nascent industry, turning it into a parody of itself, not unlike the used car industry of today.

For example, his first autobiography, 1854's *The Life of P. T. Barnum*, stirred great controversy because it revealed how often he had deceived the public. In its review of the book, the *Cincinnati Enquirer* concluded that the author was a "shameless liar and systematic swindler" who "should be sent to the pillory at least one week in every month."[3] (Of course, this didn't bother him. He would sell it cheaply at his shows and rework it repeatedly; in time, it sold more copies in America than any other book except the New Testament.[4])

Similarly, a Vermont newspaper wrote in 1859,

> The appearance of that arch humbug, P. T. Barnum . . . was the signal for a grand rally of all the humbugs. . . . With Barnum's downfall we had hoped that the world would have learned a lesson, and that our eyes and ears would be rid of the show bills, placards and advertisements of wonderful feats, cures, and ways to be rich. . . . The last we hear of Barnum is that he meets with faint applause and very indifferent success.[5]

And the *New York Mercury* noted in 1860 that despite his notoriety, "the spirit of envy and spleen . . . would perpetually connect the odor of humbug with the name of Barnum."[6]

Of course, that was all before the Greatest Show on Earth. Barnum's irrepressible, irreplaceable personality and success with the circus at least partially neutralized that "odor." Hence, for many years after his death in 1891, his familiar visage would continue to adorn the circus posters; and because of Hamilton's linguistic aerobatics—the lexical embodiment of Barnum—his spirit would be there, too.

Nevertheless, in 1910 the trade paper *Printers' Ink* would comment in an editorial marking the centennial of the showman's birth that Barnum had "exhausted the sensation power of advertising" and that the marketing industry had moved away from his "lamentably gross and misrepresentative" techniques because "there are not so many people who want to see men eat glass and nails or swallow snakes as there used to be."[7]

There was one other critical limitation to Barnum's influence on the future direction of the promotional industry.

Both he and Hamilton were easterners who viewed civilization as beginning in Europe and finding its ultimate expression on the U.S. Atlantic seaboard. Like the people around them, including most of the patrons of their circus, they turned to England and the Continent for legitimacy, and increasingly to Asia and Africa for intrigue.

But for America after the Civil War, East was no longer the axis of the future. The West was the rising star.

Even while Barnum had been enthralling people at his New York museum, throughout the exhibition halls of Europe, and on fairgrounds from Worcester to Williamsport, America had begun to shift its gaze westward—to the frontier, where man's struggle to subdue the elements and prove the evolutionary worth of a cerebrum were beginning to fulfill the inevitable mandate of populating the continent from sea to sea.

It had begun with Jefferson, or even earlier, but it took a more promotional turn with the enthusiastic expansionism of cantankerous Senator Thomas Hart Benton of Missouri. In the wake of the Lewis and Clark Expedition of 1804–1806, Benton had begun railing for policies and programs that would pave the way for settlement of the West, and he kept it up for forty years—not just in the halls of Congress, but in newspapers and pamphlets. He eventually secured legislation in the 1840s authorizing his son-in-law, John C. Frémont, to begin mapping the trail to Oregon in explorations "whose sole purpose was to advertise the Oregon country," according to historian Bernard DeVoto, in his book *The Year of Decision: 1846*. DeVoto noted that Frémont's reports, written with the help of his wife, Benton's daughter Jessie, were highly influential: "The westering nation read them hungrily . . . here was a spectacle that fed the nation's deepest need. They were adventure books, they were charters of Manifest Destiny, they were texts of navigation for the uncharted sea so many dreamed of crossing, they were a pageant of daring, endurance, and high endeavor in the country of peaks and unknown rivers."[8]

Many other public figures began to sing the song of the West as well, and with that, a whole new generation of promoters rose up. "Boomers" and "boosters," they were called, and with all the golden-tonsiled rhetoric they could muster, they lustily promoted Benton-like settlement, development, and railroad expansion in imagined western metropolises that at present were often no more than stakes hammered into the desiccated soil of desolate windswept plains.

Benton was often deemed a "humbugger," linking him to Barnum, but the contrasts were dramatic. While Barnum had succeeded in moving the coverage of his shows out of the "amusements" section and onto the front page, they were still just eastern amusements (and, perhaps not coincidentally, the Greatest Show on Earth would not even visit the Great Plains and beyond until 1880); *this*, the West, the nation's destiny, was a topic as big as all outdoors, and it would require a larger and more profound promotional effort than had ever been seen before.

In the second half of the nineteenth century, with speeches and pamphlets and ads, the boosters appealed to immigrants, down-on-their-luck easterners, adventurers, and fortune seekers alike. Their promotional pitches rhapsodized about lands of limitless natural resources, sprawling cities that were just a railroad spur line away, and drought-stricken homesteads west of the hundredth meridian that would be magically transformed into arable wonderlands because after all, as they assured the gullible, "rain follows the plow." They spoke in the oak-paneled social clubs of the East, and atop wooden crates on the backs of stagecoaches in jumping-off towns like Independence, Missouri, and Olathe, Kansas. They produced slick brochures—often mailed to Europe—peppered with convincing data and statistics, and propaganda pieces cleverly disguised as land guides and travel books. They advertised stock offerings and acreage in the agate-type ads, and glories-to-behold in what were essentially huge newspaper advertorials—including one that lyrically described Sheridan, Wyoming, where "prosperity and civilization have taken the place of rapine, murder and savagery" and "the Big Horn mountains now cast a shadow of peace over a valley flowing with milk and honey, as the last rays of a setting sun turn the silver sheen of Cloud's peak to the golden mellow of eventide."[9]

The boosters also produced (and reproduced, thanks to Currier & Ives) majestic landscape artwork—which, wrote historian Bill Cronon, often featured an "exaggerated bounty" or "exotic richness [that] confirmed its prophetic narrative role as the land of heart's desire."[10] A prime example was Fanny Palmer's 1868 painting *Across the Continent: "Westward the Course of Empire Takes Its Way"* (see plate 2), which depicted an idyllic frontier town at the base of mountains and a river, from which wagon trains still head west but through which the railroad is quickly and happily making its way. Men industriously clear the land, children play in front of the log cabin schoolhouse, Indians are isolated on the other side of the tracks, buffalo retreat into the distance, and telegraph poles are being erected out to the horizon. It was a powerful piece of imagery.

There was occasionally some Barnumesque flimflammery to the

boosters' methods; the West, being big and wide open and *out there,* has always attracted more than its fair share of schemers and scammers, from prospectors' reports of the mother lode, to the bunko man Soapy Smith, to Rio Rancho—the barren development in New Mexico that attracted so many eastern investors in the 1970s, sight unseen. But their marketing was largely straightforward, if a bit overripe.

The boosters' message was frequently about opportunity—cheap land, valuable mineral resources, swelling populations in need of goods—but also about escape. With the expansion of the railroads, the West began to emerge as an alternative leisure destination to Europe, and as a refuge for the unwell and infirm. Starting in the 1880s, the Southern Pacific Railroad began to promote the dry climate and sunshine of California as an antidote to consumption (tuberculosis); in 1890, the city of Santa Fe published a booklet entitled *Santa Fe as a Health Resort,* which noted that while consumption had been responsible for 25 percent of the deaths in New England the previous year, the death rate was less than 3 percent in New Mexico.[11]

The western boosters also copied the techniques of the press agents, writing letters to the newspapers for publication and persuading magazine editors to join their noble mission. In December 1882, for example, the *Century* magazine responded to a letter to the editor by noting a renewed "Western furore":

> It is hardly an exaggerated estimate to say that a million of people [*sic*] have transferred themselves, during the past eight months . . . to the prairies of Dakota, Nebraska, Kansas, and Texas, the valleys of the Rocky Mountain system, and to the farther regions of the Pacific slope. So rapidly have the vacant spaces in the center of the continent and on its western shore filled up in recent years, that there is no longer a frontier. . . .
>
> No doubt the question, "Shall I go West?" is the uppermost problem in the minds of thousands of the young men of the East, who have still their careers to make, and have not yet gained a secure and promising footing in the business world. . . . [T]he chances for a young man of average pluck and energy are unquestionably much better in the West than in the East. He shares the advantages of being among the first to open a fresh store-house of natural wealth. He gets the first dividend on the increase of value resulting from bringing

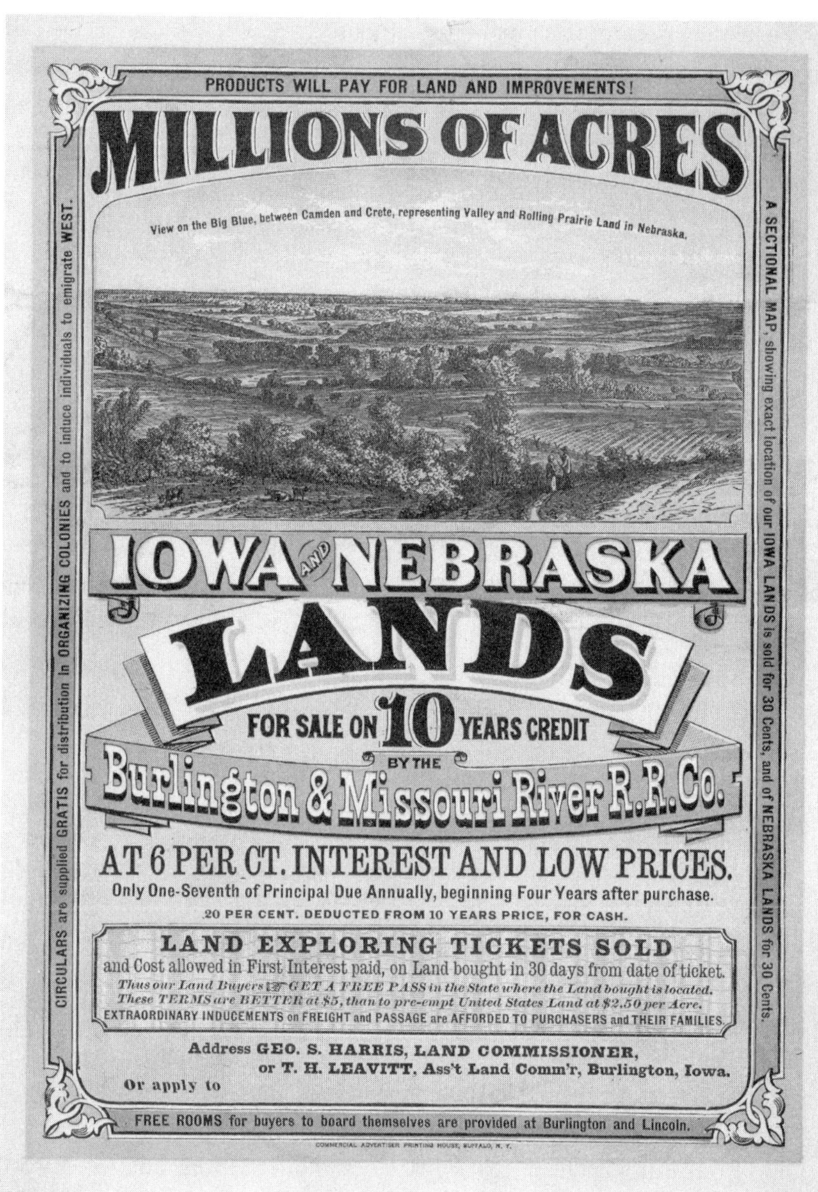

RAILROAD PROMOTIONS like this 1872 circular from the Burlington & Missouri River Railroad Company sang the booming song of the West, offering cheap land and free rooms and depicting an illimitable future. Library of Congress, Printed Ephemera Collection; http://hdl.loc.gov/loc.rbc/rbpe.13401300.

> population upon the soil. The land he buys for three or four dollars an acre, or gets for nothing by homestead settlement, soon becomes worth ten or fifteen. If he embarks in trade or in any mechanical pursuit, his wares or his services are in brisk demand, because all the new-comers around him require goods and implements. Then there is a certain stimulus in the moral atmosphere caused by the ambitions and energies of a new community full of hope and activity, which makes hardships easy to bear and causes buoyancy of spirits.[12]

The West became the largest "product" that anyone had ever tried to sell, and this had a profound influence on the promotional industry—for the first time in history, marketers began to go beyond attributes. More than plats, its pitchmen were selling dreams and opportunity.

No one embodied this fervid spirit more than William Gilpin, a founding father of western boosting, who was so eager to promote the region that he positively hyperventilated manifest destiny.

"What an immense geography has been revealed!" said Gilpin, the former Colorado territorial governor, to a Fourth of July gathering in 1868. "What infinite hives of population and laboratories of industry have been electrified and set in motion!"[13]

Gilpin hailed from the Brandywine River Valley near the Delaware, Pennsylvania, New Jersey, and Maryland borders, part of a wealthy and privileged family that counted Andrew Jackson as one of its many friends; but by the time of that speech, he was as western in his outlook as any buckskin-wearing homesteader with a Springfield rifle and had already been pegging away at western expansion for a quarter century.

Early in his life Gilpin had traveled to England, attended West Point and the University of Pennsylvania, fought in the Seminole War, and slotted himself into many of the customary roles that the wealthy and cultivated men of his generation usually filled: scholar, farmer, soldier, lawyer, newspaper editor, land speculator. But from his adopted home of Independence, Missouri, he watched the pioneers head westward and longed to do the same.

Soon, he did—and in 1843 joined up with Frémont on his second Oregon expedition. This was the first in a series of western adventures for Gilpin (military campaigns into New Mexico; battles with the Comanche and Pawnee Indians) that inculcated in him the spirit of the frontier, and no small amount of practical knowledge of it, too. In 1846, he addressed lawmakers with the recommendation, among other things, of expansion of mail service to the West, in a letter that Bernard DeVoto described as "a document in nationalism, a compendium of the intoxicating dreams of the 1840s—that mixed, turbulent, intense decade when there seemed to be no limit to American achievement and no necessary bound to American hope."[14] Gilpin was riding point in the vanguard of those who, in DeVoto's words, were "learning to think continentally," a Pacific goal that could be achieved through martial means.

In his enthusiasm, Gilpin often ran roughshod over the facts.

He preached that the Mississippi Basin would be easily capable of supporting more than 1 billion people; that the semiarid plains east of the Rockies sat atop a limitless reservoir of artesian waters; that although the western plains lacked surface timber, settlers there could easily dig for firewood; that the warm western weather obviated the need for houses; that the same forces that had created homogeneity among all the Indian tribes would ultimately do the same for all Americans, "a people one and indivisible . . . imbued with the same opinions and having the same political liberties"; in short, that nothing could or should prevent the region from tenfold expansion.[15] "He saw the West through a blaze of mystical fervor," wrote historian Wallace Stegner, "as part of a grand geopolitical design, the overture to global harmony."[16]

Inevitably, Gilpin's fanatical interest in the West began to turn from lobbying to marketing, just like his contemporary Missourian, Benton. He wrote several magazine articles on the topic in the 1850s; authored lengthy newspaper treatises about the "isothermal zodiac," the favorable climatic and resource zone that was a central physiographic tenet of his expansion theory; and in his 1860 book *The Central Gold Region: The Grain, Pastoral and Gold Regions of North America* (actually a compilation of his public addresses), he laid out a bold, booming geomorphologic vision that would "disinfect ourselves of inane nepotism to Europe," enabling us to "pursue the divine mission chalked out for us by the Creator's hand." The American Republic, he said, was "*predestined* to expand and fit itself to the continent . . . brightening the world with its radiance."[17]

Soon, others picked up the spirit of Gilpin's overzealous boosting, and they naturally turned to the one promotional tool that could reach a national audience and lend credibility to their efforts: books. The very

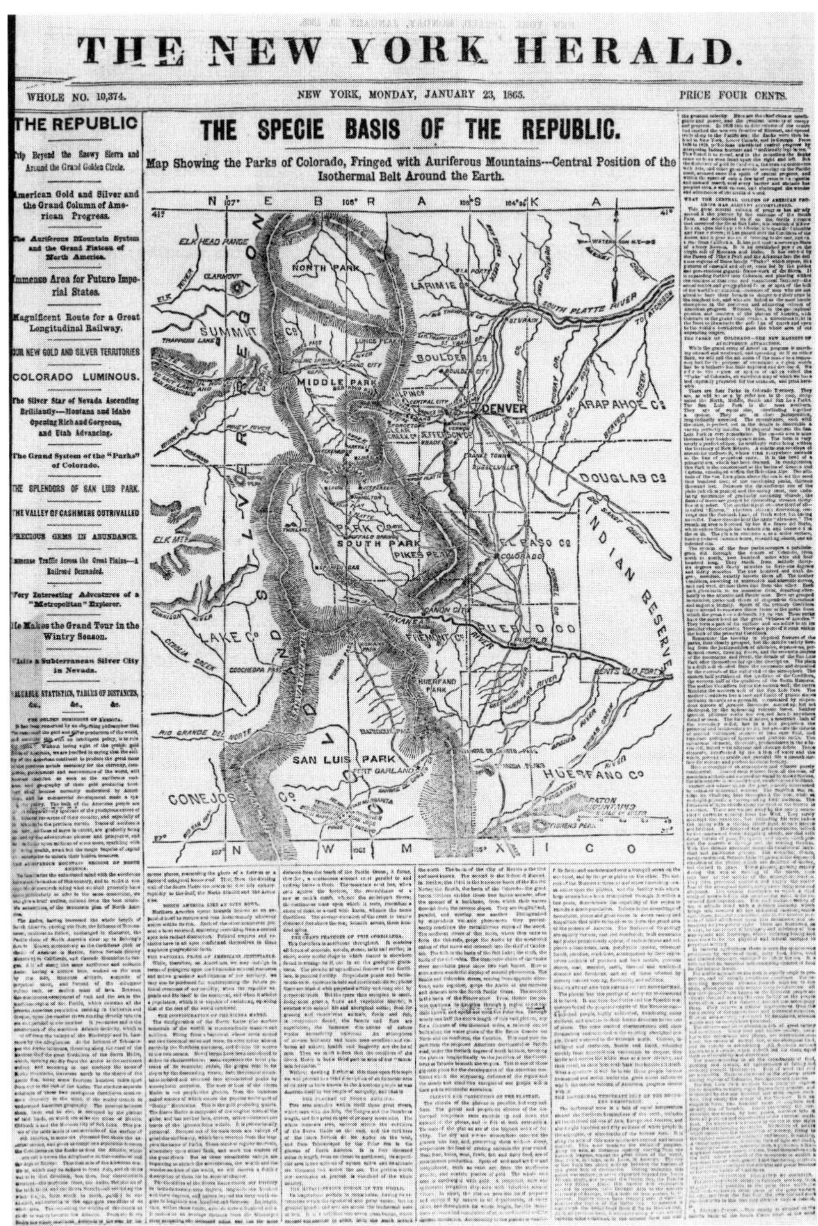

THE NEW YORK HERALD.

WHOLE NO. 10,374. NEW YORK, MONDAY, JANUARY 23, 1865. PRICE FOUR CENTS.

THE SPECIE BASIS OF THE REPUBLIC.

Map Showing the Parks of Colorado, Fringed with Auriferous Mountains---Central Position of the Isothermal Belt Around the Earth.

THE REPUBLIC

Trip Beyond the Snowy Sierra and Around the Grand Golden Circle.

American Gold and Silver and the Grand Column of American Progress.

The Auriferous Mountain System and the Grand Plateau of North America.

Immense Area for Future Imperial States.

Magnificent Route for a Great Longitudinal Railway.

OUR NEW GOLD AND SILVER TERRITORIES

COLORADO LUMINOUS.

The Silver Star of Nevada Ascending Brilliantly---Montana and Idaho Opening Rich and Gorgeous, and Utah Advancing.

The Grand System of the "Parks" of Colorado.

THE SPLENDORS OF SAN LUIS PARK.

THE VALLEY OF CASHMERE OUTRIVALLED

PRECIOUS GEMS IN ABUNDANCE.

Immense Traffic Across the Great Plains---A Railroad Demanded.

Very Interesting Adventures of a "Metropolitan" Explorer.

He Makes the Grand Tour in the Wintry Season.

Visits a Subterranean Silver City in Nevada.

VALUABLE STATISTICS, TABLES OF DISTANCES, &c., &c., &c.

WILLIAM GILPIN, a leading western booster of the mid-nineteenth century, did not put his name on this 1865 article that took up more than an entire page of the *New York Herald*, but its exploitative optimism and reference to the "isothermal zodiac" clearly bore his fingerprints. *New York Herald*, January 23, 1865, Library of Congress, Chronicling America: Historic American Newspapers; http://chroniclingamerica.loc.gov/lccn/sn83030313/1865-01-23/ed-1/seq-1/.

solemnity of leather binding seemingly lent legitimacy to some of their specious claims and hence lifted them above reproach.

One of the more impressive booster books was Frederick B. Goddard's 1869 volume *Where to Emigrate, and Why*—591 pages of territory-by-territory reviews complete with maps, illustrations, travel routes and fares, wages, advice on how to secure public lands, and more. In the opening chapter, Goddard belted out an anthem of manifest destiny so bellwether clear that readers must have been tempted to stand up and sing.

> We want yet more people to wake our sleeping wealth; strong-armed men to press to the front in our march of civilization, and conquer easy victories with the plowshare—to "tickle our prairies with a hoe that they may laugh with a harvest." We offer them the greatest boon on earth—Manhood and Independence. . . .
>
> If past experience be worth anything—if we may judge from the rapid settlement and appreciation in value of the lands of Ohio, Illinois and Indiana—surely the lands of the newer States and Territories, with their genial climate, great fertility, and vast mineral wealth—under the added stimulus of the great railroads opening up to their products the markets of the West as well as the East, and a larger national immigration than ever before—cannot idly linger in their advancement. On the contrary, all reasonable inference tells us that they will as far outstrip the older States of the West in rapidity of development, as the emigrant of to-day upon the iron horse outrides the pioneers of those States moving slowly on in the lumbering wagons of the past.[18]

California, Goddard wrote, with a rapidly growing population of 550,000, "sits enthroned in opulence and power, Queen of the Pacific and Pride of the Nation. Behind the 'Golden Gate' her metropolis sits regnant, and the oldest nations of the earth pay her peaceful tribute. Vessels from every part of the civilized world furl their sails in her beautiful harbor, mingling their masts and spars to the semblance of a leafless forest." He praised the Arizona Territory's fertility, mineral resources, and climate. "Excepting upon the Lower Gila and Colorado, the climate of the entire Territory is represented as delightful. The days are not excessively warm, and the nights are refreshingly cool." And Wyoming Territory, though currently contested by Indians, also had much to offer:

> The climate of Wyoming is almost unsurpassed for salubrity and healthfulness. The winters are mild and open, and in many parts stock feed and fatten upon the standing grasses, requiring no shelter from November to April. . . .
>
> Already the germs of a splendid State have taken root around the Black Hills, and the young tendrils are nourished by resources and natural advantages which promise to rival those of any other region of the far West. Ere long the westward tending engine, freighted with thousands of eager emigrants, will pause at Wyoming to discharge its precious burden. Before the advancing footsteps of civilization the Indian must retire. His hunting-grounds will be turned into corn-fields, and the smoke of his wigwam superseded by the rising incense of a thousand hearth-fires.[19]

Apparently, settlers' firsthand reports of the truth about Arizona summers and Wyoming winters made it back east, too, since the territories remained sparsely populated for many more decades.

A similar book was *Crofutt's Trans-Continental Tourist* (1875), by George Crofutt, progenitor of the American travel guide genre that would later produce *Baedeker's*, *Frommer's*, *Lonely Planet*, and many others, and nothing if not a booster shot of boosterism. Crofutt's title page not-so-succinctly said it all:

CONTAINING A
FULL AND AUTHENTIC DESCRIPTION OF OVER FIVE HUNDRED CITIES,
TOWNS, VILLAGES, STATIONS, GOVERNMENT FORTS AND CAMPS,
MOUNTAINS, LAKES, RIVERS; SULPHUR SODA, AND HOT SPRINGS; SCENERY,
WATERING PLACES, SUMMER RESORTS;
WHERE TO
LOOK FOR AND HUNT THE BUFFALO, ANTELOPE, DEER AND OTHER GAME;
TROUT FISHING, ETC., ETC.
IN FACT, TO TELL YOU WHAT IS WORTH SEEING—WHERE TO SEE IT—WHERE
TO GO—HOW TO GO—AND WHOM TO STOP WITH WHILE PASSING OVER THE
UNION PACIFIC RAILROAD, CENTRAL PACIFIC RAILROAD OF CALIFORNIA,
THEIR BRANCHES AND CONNECTIONS BY STAGE AND WATER
FROM THE ATLANTIC TO THE PACIFIC OCEAN.[20]

Still another earnest foot soldier in the publicity revolution that overtook the West was Robert Strahorn, author of more than a dozen guidebooks and long pamphlets, including *The Rockies and Beyond* (1879), *The Enchanted Land, Or An October Rumble in Yellowstone National Park* (1881), and *Where Rolls the Oregon* (1882).

Strahorn was one of the first of an entirely new kind of booster, or publicist, the scribe-for-hire—for most of his work was done at the behest and on the payroll of a sponsor (first, the Union Pacific Railroad; later, the Idaho-Oregon Land Improvement Company) with an ulterior marketing motive.

Strahorn had been a freelance correspondent for the *New York Times, Chicago Tribune, Rocky Mountain News,* and *Omaha Republican,* reporting on the Sioux War campaigns of General George Crook throughout the West. After witnessing the surrender of Crazy Horse and 889 Oglala Sioux at Camp Robinson, Nebraska, in May 1877, he said he "sensed the oncoming tide of settlers and capital" and decided to write a guidebook about Wyoming—which he cranked out, longhand, in about sixty days.

The Hand-Book of Wyoming and Guide to the Black Hills and Big Horn Regions for Citizen, Emigrant and Tourist was filled with utilitarian facts and statistics and a minimum of romance, but it articulated a view of the rising West that caught the eye of others who were a bit more marketing-savvy. Shortly thereafter, he was hired by Union Pacific president Jay Gould to start up a "literary bureau" for the railroad, where his job would be to travel around to the lands the railroad served or hoped to serve, gathering facts and impressions and writing guidebooks to encourage settlement (which, in turn, would create more freight tonnage and passenger business for the railroad and more opportunities for it to win the rights to expand its burgeoning real estate empire).

For the next six years, Strahorn and his intrepid young wife, Carrie—a refined, University of Michigan–educated doctor's daughter from Marengo, Illinois, and herself a journalist—did just that. Enduring many hardships, traveling by train, stagecoach, wagon, and horse, the couple traversed huge swaths of territory, gathered data and observations, and transformed it all into publications.

Carrie wrote articles for the *Omaha Republican,* and eventually (1911) produced a book about their experiences, entitled *Fifteen Thousand Miles by Stage,* which has emerged as an important work among early western female writers.

Robert's books became stealth promotional tools for the Union Pacific, extending the railroads' tradition of using promotional lectures and pamphlets to advance its causes, and helping to usher in the golden age of railroad publicity, without ever overtly identifying the Union Pacific as their backer. Strahorn continued to report plenty of dispassionate statistics (population, altitude, bank deposits, hotel registrations, telegraph rates, land prices, crop yields, etc.), but his reportorial flair painted an enticing picture, as for example of Cheyenne, Wyoming:

> A feature always refreshing and pleasing to the new comer here is the wonderful thrift, bustle, and unfaltering courage which is everywhere apparent. From the peanut vender [*sic*] on the street corner to the wholesale merchant we traced this same nerve, which in the west is said to "laugh at impossibilities." Of course we caught the infection, and were soon ready to embark in any number of prodigious enterprises. Then here we received our first really unmistakable blast of the mining atmosphere, which comes down strong and fresh from the Black Hills. Bronzed and enthusiastic miners are constantly arriving with glittering specimens from their "finds," while new seekers for treasure are bound northward on every coach, or are seen leaving by every other conceivable means of transportation. The bank windows and counters are always lined with tempting displays of yellow nuggets, huge retorts of gold from the Black Hills scamp-mills, or fine dust from the rich gulches of that famous northland.[21]

In her book, Carrie speculated about the influence of her husband (whom she referred to as "Pard," short for Pardner, a common term of endearment in the day): "How much of the vast influx of settlers has been due to Pard's facile pen and untiring energies none may ever know, but we have watched the flow of immigration until it has become a tidal wave of humanity sweeping over the broad western domains and obliterating every vestige of the pioneer trails."[22]

Historian Oliver Knight wrote in a 1968 article for *Pacific Northwest Quarterly*, "It is easy to see how Strahorn's guidebooks could have encouraged itchy feet and bright new dreams in a day when optimism infused emigrants and when, presumably, readers had not yet become wary of pitchmen in print." Indeed, the legislatures of Wyoming, Idaho, and Montana all sanctioned Strahorn's books, in some instances publishing them under their own imprints, and they purchased thousands of copies for about 7½ cents each (which, since the books had been underwritten from the start by the Union Pacific, must have brought a sly smile to Jay Gould's face).[23]

Robert Strahorn went on to a long career in business, development, railroads, and philanthropy, and became quite wealthy, but his legacy as a sort of evolved booster, one of the new generation of promoters, was best captured by Knight, who dubbed him simply "Propagandist for the West."

Of course, not all Americans were rubes who unconditionally accepted the boosters' claims. There were doubters and detractors who sniffed out the duplicity in these sometimes-putrid promotional efforts, just as they did with Barnum's early humbugs.

This spirit of growing cynicism was perfectly captured by Rep. J. Proctor Knott of Kentucky, who in January 1871 took to the floor of Congress to address the question of whether federal lands should be deeded to the St. Croix and Lake Superior Railroad to build a spur line near the town of Duluth, Minnesota, population three thousand, as the region's boosters no doubt had argued.

In a savage parody speech that was interrupted by laughter sixty-two times, Knott was pitch perfect, praising the "region of sand and pine-shrubbery . . . that would not produce vegetation enough in ten years to fatten a grasshopper," and even skewering Gilpin's "isothermal zodiac" theory:

> I became satisfied that the construction of a railroad from that raging torrent [the St. Croix River] to some point in the civilized world was essential to the happiness and prosperity of the American people, if not absolutely indispensable to the perpetuity of republican institutions on this continent. . . .
>
> Duluth [is] not only in the center of the map, but represented in the center of a series of concentric circles one hundred miles apart, and some of them as much as four thousand miles in diameter, embracing alike in their tremendous sweep the fragrant savannas of the sunlit South and the eternal solitudes of snow that mantle the ice-bound North. . . .
>
> Then, sir, there is the climate of Duluth, unquestionably the most salubrious and delightful to be found anywhere on the Lord's earth. Now, I have always been under the impression, as I presume

> other gentlemen have, that in the region around Lake Superior it was cold enough for at least nine months in the year to freeze the smoke-stack off a locomotive. But I see it represented on this map that Duluth is situated exactly half way between the latitudes of Paris and Venice so that gentlemen who have inhaled the exhilarating airs of the one or basked in the golden sunlight of the other may see at a glance that Duluth must be a place of untold delights, a terrestrial paradise, fanned by the balmy zephyrs of an eternal spring, clothed in the gorgeous sheen of ever-blooming flowers, and vocal with the silvery melody of nature's choicest songsters. . . .
>
> Here are inexhaustible mines of gold, immeasurable veins of silver, impenetrable depths of boundless forest, vast coal-measures, wide, extended plains of richest pasturage, all, all embraced in this vast territory, which must, in the very nature of things, empty the untold treasures of its commerce into the lap of Duluth.[24]

The railroad bill was defeated, but its boosters received enormous publicity when the speech was reprinted in newspapers around the country. They eventually named their car-sorting yards near Duluth "Proctor Knott."

Perhaps boosterism would *not* become the ultimate expression of the American promotional impulse after all, any more than Barnumism would. Still, an important shift had taken place with the application of promotional techniques not just to dry goods and amusements, but to aspirations—with the West as both medium and message.

There would be one more shift ahead, this one subtle rather than seismic, but indispensable to the evolution of the modern marketing industry and the development of twentieth-century marketing-centric culture. While the western boosters had been squarely focused on the future, a theoretical "place to go," a resource to be literally and figuratively mined for possibility, there was also real marketing value in the West of the *past*. This was a place, rapidly disappearing, which even in its heyday, while the Conestogas were still rolling and the bullets still flying, was already being eulogized in sentimental works like Erastus Beadle's Dime Novels (which first appeared in 1860) and Francis Parkman's *The Oregon Trail* (1872). Boosterism had invoked aspirations, but nostalgia marketing would tap into the deeper wellspring of memories.

This West of the past, the Old West, was in reality ephemeral and in reverie eternal. No stage of its development—not the fur trade, not the gold rush, not homesteading, not the Indian wars, not the mining boom, not the gunslingers, not cattle ranching, not sod busting—had lasted for long, but they would all be preserved as part of a powerful narrative. Within a critical ten-year span around the turn of the century, this frontier time would be remembered fondly by novelist Frank Norris as "the firing line where there was action and fighting, and where men held each other's lives in the crook of the forefinger."[25] It would be etched into popular culture for all time in the brave, laconic cowboy title character of Owen Wister's novel *The Virginian*. And it would be codified with a flourish by historian Frederick Jackson Turner in his 1893 address to the American Historical Association at the World's Columbian Exposition, in which he described the "successive waves across the continent" which had now come to an end: "Stand at Cumberland Gap and watch the procession of civilization, marching single file—the buffalo following the trail to the salt springs, the Indian, the fur trader and hunter, the cattle-raiser, the pioneer farmer—and the frontier has passed by."[26]

Most significantly, the frontier would also be co-opted for commercial use. For at the very same time Turner was delivering his paper, Stephen Mather of the Pacific Coast Borax Company was literally harnessing the growing nostalgia for the West into a brilliant marketing tool. Mather had commissioned books and articles to tell the story of the twenty-mule teams, which from 1883 to 1888 had heroically hauled borax ore 165 miles across the blazing salt sink of Death Valley. Now he brought them out of retirement, photographed them, and turned them into an iconic image that would henceforth evoke the rugged heroism of the West on every package of borax, while also incorporating them into a brand name (see plate 3). Certainly for Americans of the 1890s, the concept of buying borax *because of* the 20 Mule Team name was probably about as strange and unnecessary as the concept to Americans of the 1990s of buying bottled water because of the Evian or Perrier brand name. But it worked: 20 Mule Team Borax became a household name. Mather's strategy would trigger a trend of attaching the symbols and values of the American West to products, eventually manifesting in the long-lasting advertising of Wells Fargo, Marlboro cigarettes, and many other consumer companies.

But that was all in the future.

For now, on the cusp of the 1870s, the promotional industry had reached an inflection point, a figurative crossroads at the hundredth meridian of the mind.

A century that had begun with only a modest amount of basic mercantile advertising had now seen the art of promotion expand into humbuggery, indirect advertising, creative imagery, subtle deception, brash boosterism, and dewy-eyed nostalgia at the hands of the clever people manipulating the industry's reins.

Meanwhile, a marketing culture had taken root in America, and with the spread of wealth, the growth in population, and each new technological advancement making communication faster and easier, it was becoming more entrenched. Whether it was Barnum in the East or the boosters in the West, these early nineteenth-century promoters had helped to plant the seeds of a new industry, a new ethic, a new age of persuasion, all of which were growing at a steady and predictable rate.

But in the last quarter of the century, a new class of promoters would appear, no less clever yet infinitely more professional than their forebears. Armed with the new promotional tools of aspiration and emotion, courtesy of the marketing power of the West, and, perhaps, with the development of an American sense of memory and sweet sorrow over what was being lost to the breakneck pace of progress, they would significantly accelerate the industry's growth.

Chief among them were John M. Burke of Buffalo Bill's Wild West and Moses P. Handy of the Columbian Exposition, who would emerge as the standard bearers of these differing views of how to use the West as a promotional tool. Burke's plan was to turn back into the dust of time, entertaining and educating people with all that had been heroic on the adventurous edges of the frontier. Handy would focus on positioning Chicago as the consummate expression of the future, a new and decidedly western metropolis. One was a jovial master of style and images, the other a promoter of solemnity, substance, and words. And for six months in that remarkable year 1893, their efforts would be on display, side by side, for 27 million people to witness firsthand and for all the world to see.

Theirs would be the legacies that would carry the new industry of marketing forward into the modern era.

4

THE HERO CODY AND THE MYTHMAKER BURKE

"The finest specimen of God's handiwork I had ever seen"

All night long, without a thought of sleep or even a sign of fatigue, Buffalo Bill and his mate rode around, gathering men and making preparations for the expedition in search of his lost sister.

By sunrise they were all assembled, had breakfasted and were ready for a start.

Not uniformed, scarce one dressed or armed alike; some mounted on noble thorough-breds, others on hardy wild-eyed mustangs; some young and slender; others tall, weather-bronzed, all bone and muscle—they looked like *true* fighting men.

Ned Buntline, *Buffalo Bill: The King of Border Men!* (1870)

It has now been more than one hundred years since William F. Cody—in his characteristic thigh-high boots, fringe-trimmed buckskin coat, ornately embroidered shirt, and belt with the huge square buckle—last galloped into an arena aboard his white horse, doffed his pale Stetson with a sweeping gesture as the horse bent one knee as if to bow, and proclaimed, "Ladies and gentlemen, permit me to introduce you to a Congress of Rough Riders of the World!" Later, Cody and horse would back up, out of sight, and Buffalo Bill's Wild West—unquestionably one of the most original, popular, and memorable forms of entertainment ever created—would commence its two hours of rip-roaring shoot-'em-up re-creations of life on the plains. This scene played out thousands of times during his long career as America's foremost showman, from 1883 through 1916.

In his final years, even though the fringe and square buckle were still present, and there was still enough muscle memory to walk through the paces of equine showmanship and trick-shooting exhibitions, things were not quite so regal. Hounded by debt, Cody had lost control of his own show and the freedom to use the Buffalo Bill name, and he was forced to perform as an employee in other shows and circuses. The Stetson on his head was no longer just an icon but a way to hide a toupee. And Cody, weary from a lifetime of performances, overweight, and tired as any man is in his late sixties, sometimes had to be helped in and out of the saddle.

Still, after he backed out of the arena in his last performance, in November 1916, Buffalo Bill never truly exited the public stage. Today, a century later, his name and at least some vague image—a long-haired scout, a hero, a westerner, an entertainer—linger, even among young kids whose great-grandparents had not yet been born when Cody died; meanwhile, most of the other names that dominated the headlines in his era have been relegated to dusty history books and *Wikipedia*. Indeed, Buffalo Bill appears to have entered that strange pantheon of larger-than-life legends, where real people and fictional ones (George Washington, Johnny Appleseed, Davy Crockett, Paul Bunyan, Pecos Bill, John Henry, Babe Ruth) dwell side by side in a murky world of perpetual stories, myths, and singsong nursery rhymes, and in so doing get passed down to new generations despite the loss of their original context and the advent of child rearing by smartphone.

More than anyone else, we have John M. Burke to thank for that. He developed the myth and devised the ingenious methods to market it.

To understand what Buffalo Bill *became*, however, it is first necessary to understand what William F. Cody *did*.

His was one of the best-documented lives of the nineteenth century (the details of which could once be recited by millions of schoolchildren, much as later generations of celebrity followers would be able to recall the life histories of the Barrymores or tick off Mickey Mantle's statistics). Cody's life was chronicled many times and in many ways—from the ubiquitous Buffalo Bill dime novels of the 1870s, '80s, and '90s, to thousands upon thousands of contemporaneous newspaper and magazine articles that detailed his every move; from his first autobiography in 1879 and numerous later adaptations, to a spate of biographies written by two of his sisters, his wife, people who knew him and worked with him, and historians of every stripe; from a single daguerreotype of eleven-year-old Will looking hollowly right into the camera, to thousands of cabinet cards and lithographs of Buffalo Bill in staged poses before trompe l'oeil backdrops; from the first primitive Edison Kinetoscope movies of him in 1894, to Hollywood blockbusters starring Roy Rogers, Joel McCrea, Charlton Heston, and Paul Newman.

In fact, Cody's life is *still* the focus of intensive scholarship well into the twenty-first century, sometimes by revisionists who are delving into persistent disputes over whether some of the most familiar tales of his derring-do were fact, fiction, or just plain embellishment. Some of the Cody scholarship, for example, gets hung up on questions about whether he truly fought in certain battles, killed certain Indians, or hosted four kings of Europe in the Deadwood Stagecoach at the same time. Other studies have reexamined earlier historical critiques and argued that they were misguided, because Cody's contributions as a showman may have been far more significant than any real work he did on the plains.

But when measuring Cody not as a historical figure or showman, but as a marketer, such disputes are beside the point: the fictions and embellishments that helped to create the Buffalo Bill phenomenon may in fact have been his, and John M. Burke's, greatest accomplishment.

William Frederick Cody was born in a log cabin in LeClaire, Iowa Territory, in February 1846, just as the Great Plains were becoming enmeshed in the Indian wars; he died nearly seventy-one years later, three months before the United States entered World War I. In between was a yawning chasm of American history that closed with frightening alacrity, as the vast empty spaces on the North American map quickly filled with dots and lines, stagecoach ruts were replaced by iron rails and paved roads, and the American Revolution faded as the industrial one began.

Cody's role as an emblem of transition and a vanguard of change was evident even in his own times. There was a keen awareness about the pace of change, and a conflicted feeling (similar to the one we experience today) brought about by the simultaneous love for technological advances and a wistfulness about days gone by. “Only Buffalo Bill remains as a reminder of the past,” his sister Helen Cody Wetmore wrote in 1899. “He is the vanishing point between the rugged wilderness of the past in Western life and the vast achievement in the present.”[1]

But of course, no life is truly that dichotomous. Historians have tended to carve up Cody’s life into four overlapping phases, each one infused with its own version of the rugged, masculine sense of adventure that was so characteristic of the American frontier (although some phases involved real gunslingers desperately fending off hot-leaded trouble, while others were merely imitations populated by self-reverent caricatures the cowboys and Indians created of themselves, firing blanks and repeating the same holdups and battles to the death twice a day before retreating to camp for a cozy night’s sleep):

1. Youth, largely spent in “Bleeding Kansas,” where the volatile question of whether that territory should enter the Union as a free state or a slave state dominated his upbringing and ensnared his abolitionist-leaning father, Isaac
2. Frontiersman, roughly a decade long, from the time he joined the Union Army in 1864 through his many exploits as a scout and buffalo hunter
3. Stage actor, which began almost by accident in late 1872 and continued as his winter job for another decade, even while he returned to scouting and other frontier activities during most summers
4. Showman, his curious new form of re-creating the great adventures and battles of the West using many of the original participants, which began with the Old Glory Blow-Out rodeo he organized in 1882 and quickly mutated into the highly polished Buffalo Bill’s Wild West, one form or another of which he organized right up until his death

In the first three phases, Cody used his survival skills, majestic physical bearing, and flat-out gumption to accomplish much and achieve a certain degree of notoriety. But for that fourth and most spectacular phase of his life to succeed—to cash in that garden-variety popularity for the eternal stuff of the Gods, *fame*—would take something more. It would take the megaphone of the press, the reputation-transforming power of marketing, an impresario of imagery. It would take John M. Burke.

YOUTH

As a boy, Will Cody showed more aptitude for horsemanship than for scholarship, and this frequently served him in good stead. When Isaac Cody spoke out against Kansas becoming a slave state, he was threatened, stabbed, and forced into hiding; on one occasion, Will furiously rode his pony to warn his father that trouble was coming, outracing grown men on larger horses. In 1855, Will was hired as a messenger and cattle herder by Russell & Majors (later called Russell, Majors & Waddell), a huge freight company that was sending thousands of wagon trains through nearby Leavenworth, Kansas, to points west. After Isaac Cody's death in 1857, the family needed money, so Will, age eleven, was hired by Russell, Majors & Waddell as an extra hand and wagon driver to take caravans from Leavenworth to Salt Lake City.

It was a dangerous life, but one filled with nonstop adventure. Will Cody befriended the Kickapoo Indians; lived with the teamsters; went on his first buffalo hunt in 1857; met hardened men like Wild Bill Hickok, Kit Carson, and Jim Bridger; joined the Pike's Peak gold rush in 1859; and quickly began to experience for himself the wide-eyed, wandering life of a true westerner at a time when most Americans lived sedate lives, never traveling beyond one hundred miles from the place of their birth. On one caravan trip, the Danites, a group of Mormon vigilantes, intercepted him and burned his wagon train; the boy had to walk most of the one thousand miles home.

As the country's westward expansion continued at a furious pace, Russell, Majors & Waddell developed a new service to capitalize on it: the Pony Express. It began operation in 1860. Up until that time, the record for getting a letter from New York to San Francisco had been twenty-one days. But now that the railroad had reached the Missouri-Kansas line, the only missing link in rapid transcontinental communication was the stretch from the Missouri River to the Pacific. By establishing 190 relay stations between St. Joseph, Missouri, and Sacramento, California, and deploying eighty riders to gallop thirty miles at breakneck speed on a succession of three ponies, handing off mailbags on the fly, the Pony Express cut the delivery time down to just ten days.

William F. Cody, age fourteen, was one of those riders—probably. He certainly described his Pony Express experiences in his autobiography in convincing detail. And several other people, including his sisters and the freighter Alexander Majors, later provided corroboration. As with many incidents in Cody's early life, however, the dates and facts of his stories don't always hold up to scrutiny. Besides, the sisters were writing about it many years later, with a family legacy to protect; and Majors only got around to writing about it in his 1893 book, *Seventy Years on the Frontier*, after a then-world-famous Cody rescued him from poverty and paid for the book's publication (Burke purportedly even wrote the preface under Cody's name).[2]

Whether William F. Cody actually rode for the Pony Express, he certainly was close enough to it to learn its intricacies and therefore able to re-create it in the Wild West shows. Thus, as Steve Friesen, former director of the Buffalo Bill Museum and Grave, noted in his book *Buffalo Bill: Scout, Showman, Visionary*, although the Pony Express lasted only sixteen months, the Wild West version of it endured for thirty years. Without that reenactment, "it might have ended up as a minor footnote in American history."[3]

FRONTIERSMAN

The Civil War erupted in April 1861, and for the next few years the teenage Cody got swept up in the guerrilla activities of groups in Kansas that were continuing to fight the antislavery battle for which Isaac Cody had given his life.

His mother prevented him from becoming too deeply involved, however, and since there was still the need to provide for the family, Will used his growing knowledge of the land and his considerable survival skills to guide military detachments and drive wagon trains across the Great Plains. In February 1864, at the age of eighteen and now a virile young man, Cody enlisted with the Seventh Kansas Regiment and served with them for nineteen months—during which time (depending on whose histories are to be believed), he may have fought in Mississippi and Missouri; encountered old friend Wild Bill Hickok when both were posing as Confederates on a spying mission; or mostly served as a hospital orderly.

After the war, now over six feet tall and inordinately handsome and broad shouldered, he married Louisa Frederici in St. Louis (here again, history provides little clarity: at least three different stories emerged about how they met, one of which of course originated with Burke). After failed diversions as a hotel keeper and real estate speculator, Cody settled into a life of scouting and frontier work that would last for several years and would bring him not just his nickname and his first brush with fame, but the substance and style of a brand so powerful that it would demand new promotional tools and communications tactics to harness.

The stories from this frontiersman period of Cody's life are so big and heroic that it is hard to imagine they weren't dreamed up by some latter-day Aesop of the trans-Mississippi. Mounted on Brigham ("the fleetest steed I ever owned" and a horse that "on several subsequent occasions . . . saved my life"), with his trusty 1866 Springfield hunting rifle in hand (a weapon he nicknamed Lucretia Borgia), Cody the contract hunter killed 4,280 buffalo in seventeen months to supply meat to the workers of the Kansas Pacific Railroad.[4] His hunting and marksmanship became so renowned that the railroad workers started calling him Buffalo Bill, and a jingle supposedly written at that time went

> Buffalo Bill, Buffalo Bill
> Never missed and never will;
> Always aims and shoots to kill
> And the company pays his buffalo bill.[5]

In an eight-hour shooting competition against renowned marksman Bill Comstock (remarkably, the grandnephew of James Fenimore Cooper, whose fictitious character Natty Bumppo in the five Leatherstocking Tales was a model Cody and Comstock both seem to have emulated), Cody killed sixty-nine buffalo—the last thirteen of which he bagged riding bareback on Brigham, to impress the lady spectators who had made the trip out from St. Louis in wagons filled with champagne. Comstock tallied forty-six.

Buffalo hunting, whether for subsistence or for sport, was one thing. But these were also dangerous times on the Great Plains. In late 1868 the Indian wars were escalating, as more and more settlers moved west through areas that had been tribal lands, while the natives grew resentful about the restrictions placed on them by the Medicine Lodge Treaty of October 1867, which had largely confined them to reservations. Thus, the Cheyennes, Sioux, Kiowas, and Comanches, among others, were periodically on the warpath, and in response, the U.S. military was dispatched to build forts, bolster defenses, and try to pacify (or in some cases eradicate) them. Cody was frequently hired as a civilian scout on these military expeditions because he had spent years traversing the area, knew the Indians' ways, and had great skill using his breech-loading rifle.

WILLIAM F. CODY'S PROWESS at hunting buffalo earned him a nickname for eternity and was often depicted in images used by Burke and his team to remind people about the exploits of their authentic hero. Buffalo Bill Museum and Grave, Golden, Colorado.

He was also apparently brave and tireless. On one occasion, Cody carried messages sixty-five miles from Fort Larned, Kansas, to Fort Hays, Kansas; and then, when no other courier was willing to take messages through the dangerous territory ninety-five miles south to Fort Dodge, Kansas, Cody volunteered and took off after only four or five hours' rest. He slept another six hours at Fort Dodge, then returned with more dispatches back to Fort Larned—only to learn, a few hours later, that he needed to return to Fort Hays. As General Phil Sheridan summarized in his *Personal Memoirs*, "Thus, in all, Cody rode about 350 miles in less than sixty hours, and such an exhibition of endurance and courage was more than enough to convince me that his services would be extremely valuable in the campaign, so I retained him at Fort Hays till the battalion of the Fifth Cavalry arrived, and then made him chief of scouts for that regiment." The precise distance covered may have been somewhat less, but it was a remarkable feat, especially given, as biographer Don Russell noted, that "for a part of the journey he was riding parallel with the Indians he was carrying information about," and that for the last thirty-five miles, he actually had to walk because he had been thrown from his mule and the animal kept up what Cody called "a little jog trot" that he could not match.[6] "So I trudged on after the obstinate 'critter,'" Cody wrote, "and if there ever was a government mule that deserved and received a good round of cursing it was that one." Four miles from Fort Larned, Cody finally raised his gun at the mule and "continued to pour the lead into him until I had him completely laid out."[7] (Which of the two was the more stubborn is not clear, but as was so often the case, the Winchester won the West.)

Throughout this period of Cody's life, he engaged in all sorts of mad dashes, narrow escapes, breakaway stagecoach rides, and other assorted acts of prairie heroism; one of the lesser ones, a skirmish at Loupe Fork, Nebraska, in 1872, in which he scouted for the Third Cavalry Regiment and displayed "gallantry in action," won him the Congressional Medal of Honor.[8]

But the most notable of his scouting assignments was his participation in the Battle of Summit Springs in July 1869. The Cheyenne Dog Soldiers, led by Tall Bull, had gone on a murderous rampage through the white settlements of Kansas and Nebraska, and had taken two white women back to their camp as hostages. Now the Fifth Cavalry, under the command of General Eugene A. Carr, was sent to stop them. Guided brilliantly by Cody and scouts Frank and Luther North, 244 soldiers and 50 Pawnee scouts set upon the Cheyenne camp in Summit Springs, Colorado, killing 52 Indians, rescuing one of the hostages, and suffering no casualties themselves. Tall Bull himself was killed—perhaps by Cody, although Luther North disputed that in some of the many contradictory accounts he later provided (all after Cody had become famous, and thus rather suspect)—and although the official dispatches sent to the newspapers did not mention Cody, over time his would come to be the only name associated with the battle (see plate 4).

STAGE ACTOR

In the aftermath of Summit Springs, Cody and the troops returned to their base at Fort McPherson, Nebraska, on July 23, 1869. And it was there, one day later, that a chance meeting would change his life forever.

Edward Zane Carroll Judson, also known as Ned Buntline, was a roguish character. In 1849 he had been confined to the penitentiary on Blackwell's Island for a year because of his purported role in instigating the Astor Place riot, which had left more than twenty people dead. Among other

STREET AND SMITH'S

NEW YORK WEEKLY

A JOURNAL OF USEFUL KNOWLEDGE, ROMANCE, AMUSEMENT &c.

Vol. XXV | FRANCIS S. STREET, FRANCIS S. SMITH, Proprietors. | NEW YORK, DECEMBER 30, 1869. | TERMS Three Dollars Per Year. Single Copy, Six Cents. | No. 7.

THE PILOT.

Ned Buntline's Great Story!!

Buffalo Bill.

THE KING OF BORDER MEN!

"The Wildest and Truest Story I Ever Wrote."

BY NED BUNTLINE.

CHAPTER V.

WILD BILL.

NED BUNTLINE'S Buffalo Bill dramas were serialized in publications like Street and Smith's *New York Weekly*, creating a new western hero to stir the imagination of people in the East. Buffalo Bill Museum and Grave, Golden, Colorado.

dubious achievements, he had also deserted during the Civil War; survived a hanging; killed a jaguar with his bare hands; and married many women, including some simultaneously. At this point in his career, however, he was a writer cranking out a magazine and numerous dime novels—as many as six a week, he claimed.

Cody later wrote that Buntline came through Fort McPherson to deliver a temperance lecture. Some historians looking back at the event said that he was there in search of a new western hero to write about; Burke himself told a reporter in 1881 that Buntline "searched the West personally for a living hero, and traveled eight hundred miles to find Cody and [Texas] Jack on their hunting grounds."[9] Whatever the reason, the two men met and were impressed with each other—Buntline by Cody's charisma, the scout by Buntline's riding ability and bravado—and before long there was a new Buntline story appearing in serial form in the *New York Weekly* entitled *Buffalo Bill: The King of Border Men! The Wildest and Truest Story I Ever Wrote.*

Cody seems to have been amused by the popularity of the fictionalized Buffalo Bill and began to sense that, though it was merely a caricature, this altered alter ego had considerable potential. Out on the plains, riding for his life or firing his rifle or tapping into all his senses to sniff out the slightest hint of danger, he had always enjoyed a visceral life, one that included occasional machismo but contained no artifice. But as the dangers of the West began to recede, and with them the animating purpose of Cody's early life, stagecraft and spectacle started to creep into his work, and he reluctantly embraced them.

Cody led two rather theatrical buffalo hunts in late 1871 and early 1872, the latter a grand affair for Russia's twenty-one-year-old Grand Duke Alexis, fourth son of the czar, which was arranged with the explicit help of General Phil Sheridan, Colonel George Armstrong Custer, and the U.S. Army. Preparations for the hunt, said Cody, involved the shipment from Chicago of "a large supply of provisions, liquors . . . [plus] bedding and furniture for the tents."[10] The army issued seventy-five of its best horses for use by the hunting party and sent along two companies of infantry in wagons and two companies of cavalry, who helped by removing the snow from the fields so that campgrounds could be established. There were cooks, couriers, Sibley stoves to heat the tents against the bracing Nebraska winter evenings, three wagons filled with "champagne and royal spirits," and an expensive Oriental carpet for Alexis's tent. Cody had even arranged for Chief Spotted Tail and one hundred members of his Brulé Sioux tribe to perform "exhibitions of horsemanship, sham fights . . . [and a] grand war dance." It was, in the always fustian words of Cody's sister Helen Cody Wetmore, a "Terpsichorean revelry."[11]

But just as important as the choreography of the event was the publicity. Some of Cody's past escapades had made it into the newspapers, but that was largely because of dispatches sent out by military officers after the fact. In contrast, the buffalo hunt with Grand Duke Alexis was attended by numerous reporters and photographers and was enthusiastically covered while it was unfolding by newspapers across the country. A dispatch to the *New York Herald* on January 16, 1872, for example, was widely reprinted and resulted in a story of more than 2,200 words.[12] Cody was keenly aware of the journalists' efforts: later, in his autobiography, he would even note errors in their reportage of how Grand Duke Alexis had bagged his first buffalo. He had clearly begun to realize that the newspapers could wield more power in the life that lay ahead of him than the warpath Indians and desperadoes ever had in the life that stretched out behind him.

Hence, while these "dude hunts" weren't genuine, per se, they did help to legitimize the notion of showmanship and publicity in Cody's eyes. In turn, wrote biographers Henry Blackman Sell and Victor Weybright, "[Cody] seemed to grow in stature as he achieved a new conception of himself, in the mirror of [the easterners'] admiration . . . [and] comradely feeling of social equality."[13] In the eastern conception, Cody began to realize, the West was a highly marketable concept.

On the heels of the highly successful Grand Duke Alexis hunt, Cody was given one offer to visit Russia and another to become a commissioned officer in the army. He was not inclined to accept either. But having shown the journalists and other eastern elites his West, he did soon accept an invitation to visit New York and have them show him their East.

He traveled first to Chicago, where he met with leading journalists, professors, and military men, enjoyed some "'swell' dinners," and attended a formal ball where "I became so embarrassed that it was more difficult for me to face the throng of beautiful ladies than it would have been to confront a hundred hostile Indians."[14] From there it was on through Niagara Falls, Buffalo, and Rochester to Manhattan, where his publicity-primed fame preceded him—and even if it hadn't, his buckskin-and-colored-bead jacket set against the anonymous mass of dark, formal Prince Albert coats, bowler hats, and crinoline dresses hustling up and down the avenues made for quite a sight.

In New York, on February 20, 1872, Buntline invited Cody to the Bowery Theater to see a performance of the writer's stage adaptation of his Buffalo Bill novel; in between acts, the crowd learned of the scout's presence and bade him come up on stage so that they could get a good look at the genuine article (Cody wrote: "I never felt more relieved in my life than when I got out of the view of that immense crowd").[15] In the ensuing months, Buntline quickly cranked out two more dime novels—in March, *Buffalo Bill's Best Shot; or, The Heart of Spotted Tail;* and in July, *Buffalo Bill's Last Victory; or, Dove Eye, the Lodge Queen*—rapidly establishing a popular and heroic character at precisely the time when interest in the American West was beginning to surge, thus inspiring other authors, including the prolific and redoubtable Prentiss Ingraham, to work Buffalo Bill into hundreds of additional dime novels.[16] Throughout the summer, Buntline wrote a series of letters beseeching Cody to consider leaving the field for the footlights and appear on stage as himself in a Buntline-written play ("There's money in it," wrote Buntline, "and you will prove a big card").[17] And when Cody finally relented and decided to take him up on that offer, arriving in Chicago on December 11, 1872, with another acting recruit—his scout friend Texas Jack Omohundro—Buntline, in just four hours' time and using hotel bellboys as scribes, penned another adaptation of one of his dime novels, entitled *Scouts of the Prairie.* Buntline *had* to work fast: it was a mere five days before the scheduled premier of the show in a ramshackle canvas-topped venue called Nixon's Amphitheatre.

The play and its actors turned out to be perfectly wretched—what Sell and Weybright termed a "preposterous extravaganza."[18] There was no real plot, and the scouts could not remember their lines; "Indians"—actually local actors in tan frocks and cambric pantalets—were killed in some scenes and then came back to life in others. Critics hated it. The *Chicago Times* wondered what, if Buntline had truly written the show in four hours, he had been doing all that time.[19] The *Chicago Tribune* wrote that Cody "speaks his lines after the diffident manner of a schoolboy," and said the Indians delivered "bombastic speeches about the dew, the clouds, and the baseness of white men." The paper concluded: "Such a combination of incongruous dialogue, execrable acting, renowned performers, mixed audience, intolerable stench, scalping, blood and thunder, is not likely to be vouchsafed to a city for a second time—even Chicago."[20] The *Auburn (N.Y.) Daily Advertiser* called Cody's acting "crude and unnatural."[21]

Buntline, playing the role of Cale Durg, was perhaps the worst of all, droning on with a stage version of his real-life temperance lecture, often bringing the catcalls of patrons who cheered when his character died. When the play reached New York the following spring, the *New York Herald* wailed: "Ned Buntline is simply maundering imbecility. The applause savored of derision and the derision of applause. Everything was so wonderfully bad it was almost good. The whole performance was so far aside of human experience, so wonderful in its daring feebleness, that no ordinary intellect is capable of comprehending it."[22]

It mattered not. The gunplay, the sight of a hero in the flesh, the very incursion of the untamed West into the decorous and effete East—it all played to full houses and raucous applause from Chicago to St. Louis to Cincinnati, and on to Rochester, Buffalo, Boston, and New York. The *Boston Journal* said there were "more wild Indians, scalping knives and gun powder to the square inch than any drama ever before heard of."[23] The *New York Herald* acknowledged that "whatever close criticism may detect, there is a certain flavor of realism and of nationality about the play well calculated to gratify a general audience."[24]

That was William F. Cody's story, up until the age of twenty-seven. It was a rich life, an unusual life, a colorful life, though not a life that was quite the stuff of legends. He had led what his first serious biographer, Richard Walsh, called a "worthy record" but one that was unspectacular:

> No single act of Cody had been of prime importance in the pioneering of the West. Other men were already recognized as the greater pony express riders, greater scouts, greater gun-fighters, greater soldiers. Even the tremendous buffalo slaughter which gave him his nickname was done, not for the transcontinental railroad, but for a secondary line. His dispatch-riding and guiding, brilliant as they had been, did not happen to have been connected with any major military operation. As luck would have it, he had missed all of the fights which live in history.[25]

A more recent and insightful biographer, Louis Warren, called his track record “a shimmering mirage of frontier success.”[26]

Cody *had* begun to trade some of that western equity for a role in eastern society; but that role was one characterized by uncertainty and stage fright, a newborn calf on quavering legs. Once the novelty of the repertory cowboys-and-Indians had worn off, once the savage literary rapiers of the critics took their toll, there was no guarantee that the boards and greasepaint held any future for Buffalo Bill.

But for the arrival of John M. Burke, that is as far as that career might have gone.

For someone who always had facts on the tip of his tongue and who was an inveterate self-promoter, John M. Burke left behind a surprisingly scant biographical trail.

He was born in 1842, second son of an Irish immigrant father and Swiss mother, somewhere on the East Coast, either New York, or Wilmington, Delaware, or Cecil County, Maryland, or the old Seventh Ward of Philadelphia—the newspaper record offers contradictory evidence.[27] He was adopted by an uncle after being orphaned at a very young age—one article said his mother, Mary Frances, died when John was fourteen months old, and his father, Peter, died six months later; other articles pegged their deaths at somewhere between two months and two years into young John's life. He was then raised in Wilmington, near the family's home in the New Castle subdivision of Brandywine Hundred (his name appears on the U.S. census there in 1850 and 1860), but probably also in Maryland or Washington, D.C., as indicated in later newspaper articles about Burke's life.

The fact that he had neither a large close family nor a rooted upbringing would have great significance in his later life: it freed him to travel in search of adventure, to identify himself as a westerner, and to live large chunks of his life on the road. It also seemingly encouraged him to latch on to surrogate families of theater troupes and the Wild West like the proverbial boy who had run off to join the circus. As Burke himself later mused, “Being devoid of the usual domestic attachments, is it any wonder that I, at the time, fell a willing victim to the fascination of the subject of Western plains lore, the picturesque heroes, the military celebrities, Indian chiefs, famed plainsmen, and, above all, the Indian fighting trailers, the daring American scouts of that exciting era?"[28]

Indeed, throughout his life Burke always took great pleasure in his rootlessness. He was, as the great twentieth-century writer Wallace Stegner would define a westerner, "the quintessentially deculturated American, born artless and without history into a world of opportunity."[29] Newspaper articles would describe him as "Major John M. Burke, of the world at-large," or the "famous nomad," and would comment with just a little irony that "he comes from everywhere" or that the "world traveler . . . is . . . 'back home' in Washington for a few days."[30] Although he did sometimes spend a few weeks in a room at the home of Colonel and Mrs. Allison Nailor at 1315 15th Street NW in Washington, well into his sixties he took pride in telling people that for forty years he had not lived in any one place for more than a year at a time. His was mostly a life spent in transit, and when he signed registry books at hotels with John Hancock–style flourishes of penmanship, it was always as "John M. Burke, U.S.A." (Cody would eventually do him one better, filling in *his* place of residence as "world."[31])

Nothing is known about Burke's education, but he must have been exposed to more than just the usual *McGuffey's Readers*, or even the Greek, Latin, chemistry, and classics that were typical of American curricula in the middle of the nineteenth century—because he would quickly demonstrate a worldliness, a sophistication, and an expansive vocabulary that was as identifiable as a fingerprint (albeit with a syntax that was often twisted beyond recognition).

Burke apparently did not fight during the Civil War, at least not in uniform. An 1882 newspaper profile of him indicated that he started working as a theatrical manager in 1861–1862, just as the war was beginning; another article mentioned that he teamed up with Leonard Grover, an entrepreneur in drama, opera, and low vaudeville, at Washington's National Theatre in 1863.[32] That was the year in which the Draft Act was passed, which might otherwise have subjected the twenty-one-year-old to conscription. But Burke would later write that because he was an orphan, "the war had put me in the category of what would be called the 'irregulars,'" presumably granting him an exemption. He also referred vaguely to some "tumultuous experiences at the theatre of the Civil War of quite an adventurous kind."[33]

It *is* known that he spent the war years in Maryland, Virginia, and Washington, and was, according to him, one of three civilians present in the District of Columbia in July 1864 when Confederate forces under Major General John C. Breckenridge and Lieutenant General Jubal A. Early threatened the capital. Early's troops swooped past Harpers Ferry, fought their way through Frederick, Maryland, and confronted Union troops at Fort Stevens, a mere five miles from the White House. A steamer waited on the Potomac to whisk President Lincoln away to safety, but he remained in the city and actually went out to Fort Stevens to observe the fighting; in later years, Burke provided one of many firsthand accounts of how the president came under fire on the fort's parapet and watched as a surgeon standing next to him was hit—the only time a sitting president has ever come under enemy fire.[34]

Several months later, Burke, on horseback, was also witness to Lincoln's intimate discussion of reconstruction from the porch of the White House, on the night of the Grand Illumination, when streetlamps throughout the city were lit to celebrate the end of the Civil War—one day before the president was assassinated. (To the modern American, accustomed to the phalanx of barriers that keep the president away from the citizenry and out of harm's way, this sort of access seems unusual. But in those days, the White House was truly thought of as "the people's house," and it was common for presidents to receive visitors. Still, Burke's charm and connections through people like his occasional landlord, Colonel Allison Nailor, may have granted him an unusual degree of access: he met every president from James Buchanan through Theodore Roosevelt, and although he seldom talked about it later in life, he did tell one newspaper in 1882 that "I of course knew [Lincoln] well."[35])

He apparently continued his theatrical work, promoting shows and theaters and managing actors, and in the process became acquainted with many of the most famous thespians of the day, including all three Booth brothers. (Burke was particularly friendly with John Wilkes Booth and even witnessed him riding up Washington's Four and a Half Street just before the actor assassinated the president.) But in 1865 he became a military man—accounts vary as to whether he enlisted or joined as a civilian employee of the Quartermaster Corps—and may have fought in some skirmishes with the Indians.[36] Either that year or the next, Burke ventured westward as a member of the advance guard and confidential secretary of General Green Clay Smith, who had been appointed governor of Montana Territory. The detachment never reached its destination, however, because

Indian uprisings made it unsafe to travel, so they camped just west of the Missouri River, in the settlement of Nebraska City, and hung around the gold prospectors.

Over the next few years, Burke seems to have bounced back and forth between scouting and theater work. It was during this phase of his life—likely 1869—that Burke, en route home from California, stopped at a camp in North Platte, Nebraska. As someone who had scouted in this area and had begun to breathe deeply of the mythic western air, Burke already knew about Buffalo Bill: as he said, "His deeds of daring and his reckless confidence in self were the daily theme of border camps gossip. . . . [The] numerous daguerreotypes in the traveling picture men's tents . . . enhanced one's desire to see this almost mystical spirit of prairieland."[37] Lo and behold, in rode Cody. As Burke later recounted,

> I drank in from the subject of the great West and was not only delighted but surprised when the famed huntsman and scout, Bill Cody, galloped into camp. For once realization excelled anticipation. Physically superb, trained to the limit, in the zenith of manhood, features cast in nature's most perfect mold, on a prancing charger, foaming, chafing at the bit, and in his picturesque beaded buckskin garb, he was indeed a picture.
>
> When he dismounted I was introduced to the finest specimen of God's handiwork I had ever seen, and felt that for once there was that nearest approach to that ideal human—visual interpretation given to the assertion that man was intended as a replica of "His Maker."[38]

That was Burke in 1917, his writing as turgid as ever but at that moment suffused with the warm glow of memory triggered by Cody's death a few weeks earlier. Still, there can be little doubt that those words echoed his true feelings back in 1869, for in that very first glance, Burke seems to have had a moment of extraordinary insight—seeing the sun setting on the Old West, but its shadows growing into legends the farther east (and the closer to the twentieth century) one headed. Burke may not at that moment have imagined how much of a celebrity Buffalo Bill would become, but in Cody he at least recognized the potential for a heroic leather-and-fringe idol—a "central . . . figure in the most stirring times in the history of the conquering of a continent"—to be the commercial standard-bearer in the march toward the modern era.[39] If not love at first sight, it was certainly marketing at first sight and the Athena-like birth of the modern concept of celebrity, straight from John M. Zeus's forehead.

Cody, however, wasn't ready for any of that. Ned Buntline's fictionalized Buffalo Bill had not yet appeared in print. The gaudy celebrity buffalo hunts, the over-the-top stage dramas—all lay in the future. At age twenty-three, William F. Cody was still living life in the saddle, the blood coursing through his adventurous life.

Here, history again loses track of Burke. He may have continued to do some scouting work, although at some point he apparently returned to the East: the 1870 census again has him listed with a Wilmington, Delaware, address, now, suddenly, with the middle initial "M."[40] Over the next few years, he worked as a newspaper drama critic and city editor; an assistant manager for theater impresario C. D. Hess; a manager of a traveling acrobatic troupe, a series of Japanese and Arabian acts, and McDonough and Earnshaw's Wooden-Headed Marionettes; and a stock-company actor who sometimes appeared in blackface.[41] He ran theatrical companies that put on some of the more popular stage dramas of the era, including Bartley Campbell's *The Galley Slave*, George Jessop's *Samuel of Posen*, and R. G. Morris's *Old Shipmates*, and was manager or supporting actor to famous stars of the stage, including Edwin Booth, Edward Davenport, Robert McWade, Ada Cavendish, and John McCullough.

For a time he also helped bring legitimate theater to the Southwest—"introducing civilization . . . or at least educating the public to the beauties of the theatrical business," as he later told the *Arizona Republican*, by outfitting opera houses and having his company mount performances in remote outposts like Las Vegas, Tombstone, Tucson, and Santa Fe.[42] (Burke was especially fond of Tombstone, and just months after the famous gunfight at the OK Corral in November of 1881, took his troupe there; audience members, per town regulations, were required to deposit their weapons at the box office, and eighty revolvers plus numerous knives were collected.[43])

By the late 1860s and early 1870s, Burke, now in his late twenties and sometimes known by the sobriquet Arizona John, had grown into a large, heavyset man, reportedly six feet tall and pushing three hundred pounds, with the unique combination of both stage presence and a talent for stage management.[44] He clearly had a flair for the dramatic, and as with many people who suffer from that affliction, he could not quite decide whether he wanted to be center stage or in the wings—a paradox that would remain for the rest of his life.

Simply being associated with the theater provided him with a thorough schooling in what was then called press agentry, the clever art of feeding information to newspaper editors to obtain editorial coverage in lieu of paying for "reading notices" (advertisements). Stage drama was the most prevalent form of entertainment in America; and theatrical press agents such as Jerome Eddy had been among the first to create regular communications to keep editors informed about their clients: by the 1860s, his "press sheet," called *Eddy's Squib*, was well known in newspaper offices throughout the major cities.

So as John M. Burke began to take his theatrical companies and clients around the country, often playing one-night stands or short runs, he relied heavily on the local newspapers to help fill the theater seats. And little by little, he began to build relationships with editors and figure out what kinds of verbiage, stories, characters, and strategies would earn him the most ink.

Now it was 1872, and Cody had temporarily shifted from the theater of war to the theater itself. Fortunately for him, and for history, Texas Jack Omohundro, Ned Buntline, and a bunch of fake Indians were not the only other company members of the "preposterous extravaganza" called *Scouts of the Prairie*; there was also a graceful, talented, legitimate thespian by the name of Giuseppina Morlacchi, who happened to be performing in Chicago when Buntline and his rogue's gallery arrived and was soon pulled in to play the role of Dove Eye the Indian Princess.

Born in Milan in 1846, Morlacchi had trained at the famous La Scala opera and was a popular performer in Italy, Portugal, and London before coming to the United States in 1867. She was also a dancer of some renown, who formed her own ballet troupe and is credited with introducing the can-can to America. The *New York Times* said she possessed "not what might be called a beautiful face, but she is interesting," although other critics were more generous with their praise.[45] She lent class and legitimacy to Cody's act, sometimes staging an operetta before the shooting show began. One such performance, a comedy called *Thrice Married*, featured Morlacchi playing four characters, speaking five languages, and singing a cavatina from Giuseppe Verdi's *Ernani*.

THE BUFFALO BILL COMBINATION in its first year, 1872, managed by John M. Burke and featuring Ned Buntline, William F. Cody, Giuseppina Morlacchi, and Texas Jack Omohundro. Buffalo Bill Museum and Grave, Golden, Colorado.

She also lent her manager to the act—a large, affable, vagabond of a man who had developed a certain expertise in promoting the theater.

So John M. Burke was once again pulled into the orbit of William F. Cody.

Precisely where and how Burke met Morlacchi is not known—historical sleuthing would seem to peg it as 1868, for by September of that year he was being referred to in the press as the agent of "this incomparable artist of the ballet school . . . this talented lady . . . [who] created a great sensation."[46] At one point Burke claimed that his first chance meeting with Cody, in 1869, had occurred while he was returning from a tour with Morlacchi to the Rockies and San Francisco. Certainly by the time of the debut of *Scouts of the Prairie* in December 1872, he had been serving as manager of the dark-haired, dark-eyed actress for several years. At one point, they teamed up on a play he had written called *Flomelli, the Demon Page*, with Morlacchi serving as producer and star in what one paper called "the greatest success of her stage career."[47] (Coincidentally, Morlacchi was a featured performer in a December 1871 ball in Boston honoring Grand

Duke Alexis of Russia, one month before he participated in the buffalo hunt that would set in motion the sequence of events that brought Burke and Cody back together.)

Burke elicited from the press some high praise for Morlacchi: she was frequently billed as "the peerless danseuse, vocaliste and comedienne" and "pantomime actress."[48] For her role in *The French Spy* in 1872–1873, the *Pittsburgh Commercial* said she "exhibited great proficiency in the broad sword exercise, and in her dances was rapturously applauded."[49] The *Rochester Democrat and Chronicle* wrote that "Her impersonation of Hamet, the wild Arab mute, is certainly superb, and as a pantomimist Morlacchi may be unhesitatingly declared to have few, if any, equals."[50] The *Louisville Courier-Journal* raved about this "Queen of Terpsichore," noting the "purity of sentiment which pervades all of her performances" and calling her "a refined and gifted artiste, with exalted ideas relating to her profession."[51] Two years later, the *Atlanta Constitution* raved about her "versatile talents" and "dancing both graceful and splendid," concluding, "She is an *artiste* in the true sense of the term."[52]

Yet Burke's interest in Morlacchi was more than just professional, for he had worked his way into her Mediterranean heart. Burke presented her with rings at some point, and they began to plan a future together. As Dexter Fellows, one of Burke's protégés, would later explain, "Their affair had progressed to the point where he had furnished a home in Billerica, near Lowell, Massachusetts," and Burke expressed "ineffable joy" at the experience of buying furniture for the first permanent home he would occupy since his youth.[53] (This was, presumably, the forty-acre farm that she had purchased in early 1870. It was described in the *Boston Saturday Evening Gazette* as a modern wood-frame two-story building with two elegantly furnished parlors and a library filled with French, German, Italian, and English volumes, in which Morlacchi "attend[ed] to her household duties . . . [in] a neat calico dress, her hair hanging below her waist in two plain braids."[54] Is it any wonder this brought out Burke's nascent domesticity?)

Alas, it was to be a largely unrequited love. Sometime during that first season of the Cody troupe's performances, Morlacchi fell for her costar Texas Jack Omohundro instead.

Louisa Cody, in a sanitized but otherwise engagingly written posthumous (1919) biography of her husband, described Burke's heartbreak. She recalled standing in the wings of a theater with a forlorn Burke, watching what she sardonically punctuated as the "performance": "Mrs. Cody," Burke told her,

> I have met a god and a goddess in my life. The god was Bill Cody. I came on him just at sunset one night, out on the Missouri, and the reflection of the light from the river was shining up straight into his face and lighting it up like some kind of an aura. He was on horseback, and I thought then that he was the handsomest, straightest, finest man that I had ever seen in my life. I still think so.

Then he leaned closer.

> The goddess was Mlle. Morlacchi. But I can't have her, Mrs. Cody. I wouldn't be the man that I want to be if I tried. Jack's a better man—he's fought the West, and he's had far more hardships than I've ever seen and—and—he deserves his reward. I'll never love any other woman—but there's one thing I can do, I can turn all my affection from the goddess to the god, and so help me, I'll never fail from worshipping him![55]

Morlacchi returned the rings—Burke would wear them himself for the rest of his life—and on August 31, 1873, married Texas Jack in Saint Mary's Catholic Cathedral in Rochester, New York. Never a bitter man, just one week later Burke traveled together with the newlyweds to Chicago to rejoin Cody and the theater company. Burke would stick with Omohundro and Morlacchi even after their split with Cody in fall 1876 and would go on to manage Texas Jack during his subsequent theatrical career.[56]

Starting in that second season of Cody's stage career, 1873, Burke took over for Buntline as manager in booking venues, arranging travel, placing ads, and generating publicity. (Occasionally he also took a turn on stage—as, for example, on December 4, 1874, when he played Antelope Ned during a show in his hometown of Wilmington; or on the night of April 21, 1876, when Cody needed to leave in the middle of a performance in Springfield, Massachusetts, to attend to his dying son, and Burke took over as Buffalo Bill.) This would be the formative period of his mythmaking.

He filled this managerial role on and off for the next few years as the Buffalo Bill Combination staged a series of similar-sounding "border dramas," including *Scouts of the Plains; or, Red Deviltry As It Is*; *The Red Right Hand; or, Buffalo Bill's First Scalp for Custer*; *May Cody; or, Lost and Won*; and *The Knights of the Plains; or, Buffalo Bill's Best Trail.* They all featured true western scouts transplanted from the plains, Indians (eventually real ones), lots of shooting, little plot, and nary a hint of true dramaturgy. The audiences loved it all. Thus, the *Albany (N.Y.) Argus* previewed the 1874 show by promising, "Morlacchi will dance and sing, and fun, powder, blood, hair, etc. will be promiscuously mixed in one conglomerate mass." The *Rochester Daily Union and Advertiser* said, "It is not probable that even an ordinary earthquake could keep away the crowd." And while acknowledging that the 1875 Cody show *Life on the Border* was "not a drama of notable merit," the reviewer for the *Atlanta Constitution* still said, "The great original Cody himself . . . did not 'hold the mirror up to nature' but showed us nature's self" and "was greeted by thunderous applause at every stage of the play." (The *Constitution* also noted, "'Arizona John' was there, too, and proved himself a 'square man'"—perhaps the very first instance of what would become a long and appreciative relationship between this newspaper and Burke.[57])

The incongruity and inanity of it all was well captured by Louisa Cody, who called the plays "weird things" and noted that "when the lines became dull, it was always possible for someone to pull out a revolver and start shooting." She described Cody and one of his costars going about their work:

> Can't you hear them, these two great-lunged men of the plains, roaring this at each other? Can't you imagine the gestures, the strutting, the pursing of lips as these scouts of the silent places, accustomed to the long, stealthy searches, the hours of waiting, the days of trailing, bellowed this travesty, while out over the footlights, a tenderfoot audience waited, gaping on every word, and assured itself that here was the true spirit of the West, the real manner in which the paleface and the Indian fought the great fight? But one cannot transport the prairie to the boarded stage, and still keep within the mileage limits. And, besides, those audiences wanted their kind of thrills. They got them.[58]

Burke's marketing efforts were vital in countering the sneering and harsh reviews of the critics, and building the public's fascination with Buffalo Bill.

It was a big job, especially in the second season, when the troupe included Wild Bill Hickok, another genuine western legend yet also a prankster who never took the role seriously and enjoyed holding his prop gun close enough to the legs of the Indian actors to burn them. (Admittedly, as a man of true grit and obdurate character, it would have been hard to remain straight-faced while delivering lines like "Fear not, fair maid! By heavens, you are safe with Wild Bill, who is ever ready to risk his life and die, if need be, in defense of weak and defenseless womanhood!"[59])

But Burke began to find the ideal words to help people see this show in the way he wanted them to—"positioning," we would call it today. In ads for the show *Scouts of the Plains*, for example, Burke called them "Astonishing Attractions! The Originals. Living Heroes. Links between Civilization and Savagery."[60] These would be themes he would return to again and again.

Burke also drummed up interest for the show by feeding editors biographical tidbits about its actors. Before *Scouts of the Plains* played at the Nashville Opera House, for instance, the *Nashville Union and American* wrote a story that recapped some of the exploits of "the celebrated scout" Cody, including the buffalo hunt for Grand Duke Alexis, and described him as "a splendid looking man, being over six feet tall, and straight as an arrow." It also said of Hickok that he had been "brought in contact with desperate men who constantly set the laws of the land at defiance, and in the many bloody frays he has had with these characters, he has always come out conqueror."[61] Who in Nashville could have resisted the urge to see such heroes in the flesh? That was John M. Burke's strategy.

The troupe generally performed from the fall through the spring, and during the summers Cody would return to his scouting duties. In 1876, these included one of his most striking encounters—and with Burke's masterful publicity, what would also become one of his most famous. Just three weeks after his friend Custer's demise at the Battle of the Little Big Horn, Cody, as chief of scouts for the Fifth Cavalry, led a party of troopers into battle against a group of Cheyenne warriors at Warbonnet Creek in Nebraska. Cody killed a subchief named Yellow Hand with his Winchester rifle, and then used his Bowie knife to scalp the Indian. Holding the flesh and headdress high in the air, he yelled, "The first scalp for Custer!"

Details of this act of bravado were reported by eyewitnesses, printed in dispatches to the *New York Herald*, incorporated into the stage shows, embellished in many dime novels, and later written about by many historians.

Few of the accounts line up. The warrior was either named Yellow Hand or Yellow Hair. It was either a standoff on charging horses or hand-to-hand combat. Cody either did or didn't fire the fatal shot. He was either still wearing a garish black velvet Mexican vaquero outfit from his last theatrical show, had changed into that costume specifically for battle, or was in his customary buckskins. Certainly, the event did take place, since the scalp, treated with chemicals to preserve it, was shipped back to Louisa—to her utter horror—and subsequently displayed at Moses Kerngood's Pickwick Cigar Store in Rochester, the city in which the Codys were then living.[62]

Whatever the truth, the "Duel with Yellow Hand" would become a staple of the Buffalo Bill legend, a central act in the Wild West show, and a potent tool in John M. Burke's publicity arsenal. He would recycle it in Wild West printed programs, in his own book, in books he apparently ghostwrote for Cody, and in many a late-night visit to a newspaper office—which, more often than not, resulted in a recitation of the old story in the paper a day or two later. Frequently, there would be dramatic imagery showing Cody holding the scalp aloft. Late in his career, when doubts were cast by some editors about what had really happened at Warbonnet Creek, Burke even took to carrying around with him thirty-year-old articles clipped out of the newspapers during 1876, several of which would then get reprinted, verbatim, by the now-contrite editors.[63] Burke, the human Google of his day, was always well armed with research.

With each successive season of the Buffalo Bill Combination, Burke began to square up the focus of his marketing and identify layers of leitmotifs. *This was not just entertainment; it was education. It was not just dramatic; it was authentic. It was about bringing the real story of the West to the rest of the world. It was a chance for everyone to see the true legends of the frontier reenact some of the scenes of their heroics. It was the story of the fading West and a rising star.* Indeed, it quickly became Burke's mission to elevate Cody into what Henry Nash Smith, the historian who founded the American Studies discipline, called in his 1950 book *Virgin Land: The American West as Symbol and Myth*, "an epic hero laden with the enormous weight of universal history." Smith said, "He was to be placed beside Boone and Fremont and Carson in the roster of American heroes, and like them was to be interpreted as a pioneer of civilization and a standard bearer of progress"—even if there wasn't much truth to it.[64]

Advertising and bill posting were still the chief means for promotion in this era, and certainly Burke used them. A standard Buffalo Bill

Combination contract called for the theater to provide "the usual advertising in all daily, weekly, and [S]unday newspapers published in this place 5 squares 6 days in advance; programmes for street and house," as well as a certain number of three-sheet posters and the expenses of all bill posting and distributing; Burke and the company would provide "the usual amount of advance pictorial printing, lithographs and half sheets."[65]

But within and outside those media, the main mythmaking tool at his disposal was the written word, and Burke wielded it with increasing effectiveness and panache—carefully beginning to rescript Cody's story and tap into the emotional appeal of the fading West to enhance the growing legend of Buffalo Bill. Thus, after Cody himself apparently wrote three Buffalo Bill dime novels that appeared in serial form in the *New York Weekly* and *Saturday Evening Post* during summer 1875, Burke soon took over the pen himself. In early 1877, he rewrote *The Red Right Hand* to add some of his bombast and to incorporate the duel with Yellow Hand.[66] Burke is also given credit by Cody's chief biographers for being the literary force behind Cody's autobiography in 1879, and possibly also the second edition in 1888, which was cleverly interwoven with biographies of Daniel Boone, Davy Crockett, and Kit Carson in a bravura bit of frontier packaging.[67] And at times he whipped the Cody backstory into a fine frenzy of fiction (*at age nine, Will single-handedly held a group of desperadoes at bay and shot their leader through the heart! . . . Cody bore 193 scars from bullets and arrows!*).[68] It was all part of his effort to cultivate an image of Buffalo Bill that would stand the test of time.

There was considerable genius in this approach. Burke understood, as few others did, that the West was more than a place but a state of mind. To define themselves, the foundling Americans had long looked east, across the pond, measuring their material wealth and cultural worth with a European yardstick. That is precisely what Barnum had done. But decades of taming the land, pursuing (and occasionally extracting) wealth, and suppressing the natives had created a modern, western, and in many respects more appealing narrative. California, Oregon, Nevada, and Colorado had all achieved statehood, so the West was literally a part of the country; but it was only beginning to become a part of the American sense of identity.

The nuance in Burke's thinking was that he saw the real value of the conceptual West not in its exploitation but in its commemoration. The Thomas Hart Bentons and William Gilpins and Robert Strahorns had predicated their marketing on the West of the future; Burke looked to the past. The boomers had sold the land, but Burke was selling the legend.

To make this strategic tack westward work, even as the hyperbole reached new heights, Burke realized that everything he did needed the appearance of authenticity. So he positioned the Buffalo Bill Combination not as a depiction but as a re-creation. In the fall of 1877, with the launch of the new show *May Cody*, Burke insisted that real Indians be used and worked with an interpreter named Gordon Lillie (aka Pawnee Bill, who would later play a major role in Cody's life) to hire them from the Red Cloud Agency, in the northwestern corner of Nebraska.[69]

He was meticulous about sculpting the perception of Cody as a *true* western hero, frequently repeating and embellishing his scouting and Indian-fighting exploits, and contrasting him with the pseudo-westerner. He told the *Cincinnati Enquirer* in 1881, "I believe him to be the representative man of the frontiersman of the past—that is, not the bar-room traveler or bully of the settlements, but a genuine specimen of Western manhood—a child of the plains who was raised there and familiar with the country previous to railroads, and when it was known on our maps as the 'Great American Desert.'"[70]

Burke was always quick to ride to Cody's defense when critics appeared—"reputation management," we might call it in today's marketing lingo. Cody-the-actor was, Burke wrote a few years later, "a meteor [who] flashed upon the people of the East, impersonating upon the stage none other than himself, living over before the footlights his own life." Repeating in a book words he had doubtless spoken in many an editor's office, Burke said, "Men who have criticised Buffalo Bill as an actor forget wholly that he is the only man who is *playing himself*. He plays his part as he knows it, as he has acted it upon many a field, acting naturally and without bombast and forced tragic effect."[71]

Similarly, after the killing of Wild Bill Hickok in a Deadwood, South Dakota, saloon in 1876, Burke, according to historian Louis Warren, "tended to the deceased Hickok's reputation, and defended him in the press, because the two scouts were so closely linked in the popular mind that to allow bad press about Hickok would ill betide Cody."[72] (Indeed, this continued throughout his life. In a letter to the *Washington Post* in 1894, Burke took exception to the characterization of Hickok that had been written by a Brooklyn paper and reprinted in the *Post:* "Referring to him as a desperado does an injustice to a man whose career as a government scout illumined the history of the Army in the Southwest . . . and whose greater portion of life was spent as a marshal whose extraordinary career and record as an executioner was on the side of law and order."[73] As late as 1915, Burke was still at it, writing in the *El Paso Herald* that he had come across an old photo of Hickok that showed him to possess "a more mellow, thoughtful, professor-like cast of countenance that this great law and order marshal of the west showed as the fearless, dashing spy, guide, scout and ranger in more youthful days."[74])

Still, for all his obsession about Cody's image and imagery, in the mid-1870s the Buffalo Bill Combination was just one of several stage shows that John M. Burke was promoting.

Another was the Texas Jack Combination, for which Burke continued to play the dual role of promoter and occasional actor. When *Texas Jack in the Black Hills* came to St. Louis, the *Globe Democrat* wrote that "no one . . . can annihilate whole tribes of Indians with greater facility than 'Arizona' John. Armed with a revolver filled with blank cartridges, he kills six of the 'red demons' at a single fire."[75] This troupe continued to tour for a little while, though with diminishing success; as the *Brooklyn Daily Eagle* wrote in 1878, "the novelty of seeing two real backwoodsmen in sham circumstances wore off," and Omohundro, lacking Cody's charisma, was a "broken actor" who was "utterly unfitted" for theatrical life.[76] Omohundro went into debt and died of pneumonia in Leadville, Colorado, in 1880. The widow Morlacchi would die six years later in Billerica, Massachusetts; Burke quietly showed up for her funeral.

Burke had greater success with his own production of a show called *Old Shipmates*, which made a tour from San Francisco through Kansas in summer 1882, and on to an engagement at Pope's Theatre in St. Louis in January 1883. Also in 1882, Burke began managing the actor Frank Mordaunt, who had appeared in *Scouts of the Prairie;* in mentioning this new business relationship, the *New Orleans Times-Picayune* took note that Burke had also been the one to put Cody on stage, "the only theatrical act for which he need feel ashamed."[77] Around this time, too, John M. Burke's name was listed as general manager for a trap-shooting show headed by the expert marksman Captain Adam Bogardus.[78]

Clearly, Burke had a remarkable instinct for promotion at a time when the most cutting-edge work usually consisted of a few lines of single-column type in a newspaper ad. But for his genius to truly shine, and to pave the way for modern marketing, he was going to need a bigger stage.

Fortunately, Cody provided just that. Back in his hometown of North Platte, Nebraska, for the summer of 1882, the scout organized an Independence Day parade/rodeo/riding/shooting competition called the Old Glory Blow-Out, and it was a wild success, attracting more than one thousand cowboy participants and many times that number of spectators. So, possibly in consultation with Burke, he soon decided to shift his western reenactment from the small stage to the big arena.[79] It would be a new kind of entertainment, one that would require intricate logistical planning to produce thrilling extravaganzas in the great outdoors. Since the show would move on to a new town every day or two, it would also demand a massive promotional effort to build awareness, establish its reputation, create enormous anticipation, sell tickets, and keep it in the news year after year.

John M. Burke had finally found his true calling.

5

THE NEWSMAKER, MOSES P. HANDY

"Your despatch magnificent beat"

The Press! What is the Press! I cried:
When thus a wondrous voice replied:–
In me all human knowledge dwells;
The oracle of oracles,
Past, present, future, I reveal,
Or in oblivion silence seal;
What I preserve can perish never—
What I forego is lost for ever.

James Montgomery, *The Press* (1845)

On December 19, 1873, the front page of the *Harrisburg Daily Telegraph* featured a lengthy article about P. T. Barnum, who had recently lost his wife, Charity, at the age of sixty-five. The reporter noted that Barnum's career had begun with Joice Heth and had "ended" with his Great Travelling Museum, Menagerie, Caravan & Hippodrome. "Barnum has suffered in public estimation by his profession," the article read. "Had he been in some other business than that of showman his genius would have commanded more respect."[1] Barnum's great fame, of course, still lay ahead; but when the Greatest Show on Earth returned to Harrisburg, in 1876, it is doubtful that a certain reporter received a free pass.

Four columns over from the story about Barnum was an advertisement for the stage show that was to appear at the Harrisburg Grand Opera House that evening, for one night only: *Scouts of the Plains*, starring Buffalo Bill, Texas Jack, Wild Bill, and the peerless Morlacchi. "The original Living Heroes," said the ad. "Links between Civilization and Savagery."[2]

All that entertainment news came as a pleasant distraction, because for most of the week, the *Telegraph* had been filled with stories about how Spain and the United States were on the brink of war over Cuba. Indeed, the paper had provided extensive coverage of Spain's surrender of the USS *Virginius*, based on special reports from a correspondent in Cuba that had been telegraphed to New York and then to the rest of the world. That correspondent, unnamed in the newspaper reports but known well to his journalistic brethren, was a twenty-six-year-old named Moses Purnell Handy, descendant of a long line of Virginia military heroes, who had cleverly managed to embed himself right in the middle of the naval action as the only civilian on the scene. It was a singular act of journalistic bravado, a defining moment in a brilliant career that would eventually prove as important to the development of the new marketing industry as those of Tody Hamilton and John M. Burke.

The details leading up to Handy's triumphant reporting were somewhat convoluted. The United States had long had its eye on Cuba, "the Pearl of the Antilles," which was under Spanish control, and had even considered annexing it before settling on a surreptitious policy of support for Cuban insurrectionists. This support included the sale of a former Confederate blockade runner renamed the *Virginius* to help supply the rebels. The Spanish had finally caught up with and captured the vessel in late October 1873, summarily executing fifty-three members of its crew, including several Americans and British. War was in the air, and it blanketed the pages of every major newspaper. The New York dailies, especially the *Herald*, *Tribune*, and *Times*, were scrambling to report every little scrap of news and cover whatever might happen next, and reports from the enterprising reporters of those papers often found their way into smaller papers like the *Harrisburg Daily Telegraph*.

The U.S. government secretly decided to send the flagship of its North Atlantic squadron, the man-of-war *Worcester*, which was docked at Norfolk, to intercede and get the *Virginius* back. Handy, then the news editor of the *Richmond Dispatch* and a "correspondent on call" for the *New-York Tribune*, learned of these details on the night of Saturday, November 17, 1873, while sitting with several other newspapermen in the Richmond office of the New York Associated Press, and telegraphed *Tribune* editor Whitelaw Reid in New York to seek instructions. The reply came back the next day: "Go. Orders at Norfolk. Draw for expenses." But the message came too late for Handy to catch the last train from Richmond to Norfolk. So he scoured the wharves for a ship to charter before finding a city tugboat (although he had to drag the president of the city council out of a church pew to get permission to use it). The price was three hundred dollars, one hundred times what the train fare would have been, but Reid had told him to spare no expense, and there was no time to be lost because the other correspondents were also now hustling toward Norfolk.

The tugboat steamed down the James River in a blinding rain, but when it arrived in Norfolk, Handy was unable to secure permission to sail to Cuba on the *Worcester.* Instead, he turned in the other direction, taking a train to New York and then a fast mail steamer from New York to Key West, where at last he caught up with the *Worcester,* ahead of the rival reporters. "Within a week I was exchanging dinner with the admiral and had established friendly relations with the officers generally by fitting up my rooms at the St. James Hotel as a club and head-quarters for their use when ashore."[3] Handy's bonhomie enabled him to learn, "without resort to bribery or breach of faith," the details of where and when the *Virginius* would be surrendered by the Spanish to the U.S. Navy; and after stowing away aboard the ship that would receive the *Virginius,* courtesy of a friendly officer, he was present to witness the historic event—the only reporter, or civilian of any kind, to do so. He was among the first to board the *Virginius,* and he spent the night there before working his way back to Key West so that he could telegraph his story to New York.

"The Spanish Surrender," read the headline in the *New-York Tribune* the next day. And there, in a story that spanned several columns, "from the very full report of a special correspondent," was the only eyewitness account of the whole incident, written in a telltale narrative prose that was both clear and gripping:

> The Virginius proved to be in a most filthy condition, and was stripped of almost everything movable, save for a few vermin which haunted the mattresses and cushions in the cabin, and half-a-dozen casks of water. The decks were caked with dirt and nuisances recently

> committed, combined with mold and decomposition, which caused a foul stench in the forecastle and below the hatches. In the cabin the odor of carbolic acid gave evidence that a faint attempt had been made to make that part of the vessel more inhabitable.[4]

Handy was hailed as a hero in the journalistic community. Whitelaw Reid sent a telegram to prove how Handy's scoop had demoralized the competition. "Your despatch magnificent beat. The *Herald* kept printers and made second edition at seven o'clock to copy it in full." The *Petersburg (Va.) Index & Appeal* wrote, "And HANDY crept up on all of 'em, and was the only living correspondent who beheld the surrender of the Virginius! Good for the minister plenipotentiary of the *Index-Appeal* in Cuba and the thereto adjacent islands!" The *Norfolk (Va.) Landmark* called him "the newspaper hero of the Virginius." The *Charleston (N.C.) News* soon included him in its column of comings and goings of famous people: "Mr. P. Handy [*sic*], of the New York Tribune, the only correspondent who witnessed the Virginius surrender, was in the city yesterday. Mr. Handy is a Virginian and an ex-Reb."[5]

It was one of those dramatic moments when luck and skill coincide to change the course of a life. But Handy's was a life that had already experienced a great deal of drama.

Although the United States was viewed as a grand experiment in democracy, in the middle of the nineteenth century, how that experiment would turn out was not necessarily evident. For one thing, there were no equal rights under the law: it was still a country that relied on the institution of slavery and denied the vote to women, so Franklin Pierce was elected president in 1852 based on the voting of 3 million white men over twenty-one years old, or roughly 12 percent of the total population. Even more fundamentally, the country still retained echoes of the feudal systems from which its founders had fled: where you were born still largely determined who you would become.

Thus, while the Handy family had been in America since long before the founding of the republic, and had loyally served God and country for generations, by the time of Moses Purnell Handy's birth in 1847, the soil in which the family had planted its roots—at the precise border of the growing North-South schism—would come to define his early life.

This was a family well aware of its genealogy, which by then had already been traced all the way back to the year 1273 and the personages of Thomas, John, and Robert le Hendy of Norfolk County, England. There was even a Handy coat of arms.[6]

The first family immigrant to the New World was Samuel Handy, who settled in Somerset County, Maryland, on the eastern shore of the Chesapeake Bay, south of what would become Washington, D.C., possibly as early as 1635. The succeeding generations included many prim and starchy names that today radiate with the biblical solemnity of the colonial era: Asa, Isaac, Josephus, Caleb, Silas, Ebenezer, Levi, Elias, Elisha, Job, Levi, Salathiel, Samuel.

It was a pious clan, a well-educated clan, landowners who were fair minded, intellectual, and highly patriotic. More than three dozen Handys served in the Revolutionary War, including Captain George Handy (great-great-grandfather of Moses), who gave an eight-thousand-dollar loan to the Continental Congress and who supplied ships to the Committee of Safety out of his large shipbuilding yard in Salisbury, Maryland, called Handy's Landing.[7] Sometime in the late 1750s George and his wife, Nelly, built Handy Hall on the Wicomico River, three miles from Salisbury—part of a block of land that would remain in family hands for centuries and would in many ways come to define the family as northern-minded people living in a southern place. This, after all, was the northerly edge of plantation country, about the same latitude as Charlottesville, Virginia, and Lexington, Kentucky, and over many years, the family became inured to slavery and accustomed to the southern way of life. George Handy's grandson James Henry Handy, who was born at Handy Hall in 1789, continued to own house slaves up until his death in 1832, although he was supposedly a kind master who offered to free his servants and send them to Liberia; they declined.

His son Isaac William Ker Handy would also wrestle with the moral dilemma of slavery, especially after graduating from Princeton Theological Seminary in 1838 and moving to Berlin, Maryland, to become a minister of the Presbyterian Church—for the Presbyterians themselves were at first outspoken abolitionists.

Although his personal and professional selves were already at war with each other, Isaac did not shrink from the debate. He moved his wife, Mary Jane, and their three young children to an even more hotly contested border state, Missouri, to take up work as a missionary. Slavery and sectionalism had long defined life in Missouri and continued to do so: in the Missouri Compromise of 1820, it had been admitted to the Union as a slave state, counterbalanced by Maine's admission as a free state, but that had resolved little. Indeed, while Isaac and his family were living in Missouri, Senator Thomas Hart Benton (who had supported the Missouri Compromise) was making speeches against the institution of slavery, and the freed black man Dred Scott was suing for freedom, kicking off an eleven-year legal battle that would end with the Supreme Court declaring him a slave, affirming that slaves were not citizens of the United States, and thereby confirming the constitutionality of slavery.

The Handys settled in Warsaw, a tiny town halfway between Jefferson City and Kansas City that had recently been home to Osage and Kickapoo Indians, but that had been incorporated one year before the Handys' arrival in 1844.

On April 14, 1847, Mary Jane gave birth to their fourth child, Moses Purnell Handy, named for her father; but she died ten months later, and Isaac had little choice but to move the family back to the East, closer to his relatives. He accepted a call to a pastorate in Delaware, and then worked as a traveling evangelist in Delaware and Maryland before becoming pastor of the First Presbyterian Church in Portsmouth, Virginia, in 1854. There, in summer 1855, he provided help during a yellow fever epidemic that killed more than one-quarter of Portsmouth's four thousand residents.[8]

Throughout this time, Isaac Handy again became embroiled in controversy. "Opposed to slavery in principle, but a southerner by heritage, Handy supported the southern interests to the point of debating the anti-slavery advocate Albert Barnes," wrote Galen Wilson in a 1987 biographical summary that today is part of the finding guide for the Handy Family Papers.[9]

At the General Assembly of the Presbyterian Church in Cleveland in 1857, Isaac Handy was one of twenty-two southern ministers and ruling elders who filed a complaint against the church's official statement on slavery, declaring it "unrighteous, oppressive, uncalled for . . . [and] adding to the peril of the Union of these United States."[10] His rebellious flank soon seceded from the larger body to form what eventually became the Presbyterian Church of the Confederate States.

Isaac remarried, twice, and raised his ten children, including Moses, in an increasingly divided world that was being swamped by the great issues of the day. According to Wilson, Isaac "was slowly won over to the Confederate cause, but became an ardent secessionist after the election of Abraham Lincoln at which point he believed peaceful union to be an impossibility."[11]

Moses, meanwhile, was proving himself to be a pious young man, a diligent student with a facile mind, a keen sense of observation, and a budding awareness of the dangerous and conflicted world around him. From an early age, he took to writing—starting his private journal on January 29, 1857, when he was just nine, in a little notebook with a cover made (appropriately, given what would follow) out of wrapped newspaper.

"A bier come along with a black boy who fell on a hatchet and killed himself," he scrawled as part of his first entry. "There has been a great many accidents happened here this months [*sic*] one of them was the one just mentioned." Then on February 2: "To day is the second day of the month the 14th of this month is sister Trudy's birth day and valentine day and it will be a month that I have not eat any butter." And three days later: "I am going to the temperance meeting tonight at the Methodist Church."[12]

His secondary education occurred at the Virginia Collegiate Institute in Portsmouth, a school founded in 1850 by a twenty-nine-year-old man named Nathan Burnham Webster. Webster was a displaced New Englander who had a far-reaching intellect, with knowledge spanning Latin, Greek, physics, chemistry, astronomy, and biology; he had even spent two years as civil engineer of the Gosport Navy Yard (forerunner of today's Norfolk Naval Shipyard). Still, the pedagogical style of the era was disciplined and unyielding, and most of twelve-year-old Moses's notes from his 1859 chemistry notebook reflect the rote lessons. On one page entitled "Laws of Combination," Handy dutifully wrote: "There are 62 elements which are divided into metals and metalloids all elementary substances are composed of minute atoms, combination consists in the attraction and guxtaposition [*sic*] of their individual molecules."[13] The omission of punctuation almost enables the reader to hear the parched and inflectionless lesson being read at the front of the room, all these decades later.

But even while he was soaking up Webster's wisdom of the known universe, Moses's thoughts were often elsewhere. He doodled all over his notebook, writing his name and his initials in many different ways—in print, in three dimensions. And he tucked away a card for an extracurricular event he apparently wanted to attend: "Exercises in Elocution," to be held at the VC Institute's Oxford Hall on Friday evening, July 8, 1859.[14]

Soon, too soon, the world caught up with him and brought an abrupt end to his innocent school days.

When fighting began at Fort Sumter on April 12, 1861, Moses Purnell Handy was two days shy of his fourteenth birthday, an age at which he would have been begun thinking about college. But it was not to be. Portsmouth lay just across the Elizabeth River from Norfolk, home of the shipyard at which Handy's schoolmaster Webster had served as engineer. It was a facility of enormous strategic importance for control of all the port cities of the Atlantic seaboard, so federal troops were determined to keep it out of rebel hands. On April 20, fearing the approach of Confederate troops, the yard's commandant, C. S. McCauley, set fire to several of the ships.

> I then commenced scuttling the Germantown, Plymouth, Dolphin, and Merrimack, destroying engine and machinery of the latter, cutting away the large shears, spiking all the guns in the yard and on board the ships in ordinary, including the Pennsylvania, and destroying such arms of the old and obsolete pattern as could not be placed on board the Cumberland and throwing them overboard, making the destruction of other things, with the exception of the public buildings, as complete as possible.[15]

But McCauley's sabotage was actually quite incomplete. Confederate troops were still able to seize 1,195 heavy guns; and the *Merrimack*, though damaged, was not destroyed; it would be salvaged, outfitted with armor plating, and rechristened the CSS *Virginia*. Eleven months later, it would engage in the famous battle of the ironclads with the USS *Monitor* just a few miles upriver from the Handys' Portsmouth home; Isaac Handy would be an eyewitness to it and write about the encounter in his journal.

By May 1862, the Union troops had gained the upper hand in Hampton Roads, and as they prepared to invade, Confederate troops set the navy yard ablaze again and retreated. Norfolk and Portsmouth were evacuated. Fearing trouble, in January 1863 Isaac Handy sent Moses and his half-brother James off to Baltimore to stay with Moses's maternal uncle William H. Purnell, who was Baltimore postmaster and a Union Army colonel, and who had hosted Handy's children in the past.

Briefly, Moses returned to the lessons of the classroom at a school called the Rugby Institute. But in July, while visiting family in New Castle, Delaware, his father was arrested for voicing his Southern sympathies and was incarcerated at Fort Delaware Prison. Moses left his school in Baltimore for Delaware City, opposite the fort, to be near him. There he remained for fifteen months, supporting himself as a farm laborer and apothecary worker.

These were unsettling times for Moses Handy. He was a Southerner in a Northern state, a budding intellectual in a senseless and martial world. His older brother, Frederick, was in a Confederate uniform, and his father was in a Union prison. People tend to grow up fast during wartime, but he was only fifteen, sixteen years old, too young to fight yet too old to ignore the swirling tempest around him.

Some young men of his age and social standing *did* choose scholarly asceticism over patriotism, and college would have been an option for Handy: he was well read and advanced for his age, and among the two hundred or so colleges operating in the country at that time, nearly a dozen were in nearby Delaware and Maryland.

Life on such campuses, with their rigid and archaic curricula, continued into the beginning of the Civil War much as it had for decades—with instruction in ancient languages and the classics, recitations in international law or philology, debates in literary societies, and commencement orations on timeless topics like "The Youth of Milton," "Arabian Fiction," "Monumental Testimony to the Historic Truth of the Scriptures," and "The Philosophic Method of Study."[16] As President Cornelius Conway Felton of Harvard said in a speech in 1861,

> One of the misfortunes which have sometimes attended a condition of war, is, that progress in literature and science ceases; school houses are closed; the halls of universities are deserted; and liberal studies, that before occupied so large a portion of the best and most ingenuous minds, lose their interest in the midst of the clang of arms. But . . . it has been to me a matter of pride, in visiting schools and academies, high-schools and colleges, to find that, while this great subject of civil liberty and national existence fills our minds, and stirs up every heart, the great interests of literature, science, and education have not ceased to have their hold on the New England mind.[17]

Yet as the war dragged on, the drumbeat grew harder to resist.

THE HANDY FAMILY. Moses (*left*) and brother Fred flank their father, Isaac, in an image likely made around 1867, when Moses was twenty years old. Handy Family Papers, William L. Clements Library, University of Michigan, Ann Arbor.

On many campuses students formed paramilitary organizations and drilled after classes on school grounds. Decorum gave way in some classrooms as instructors ditched their lesson plans for discussions about current events. And gradually, more and more students abandoned their studies for the glories of tent and field.

In one especially telling and humorous incident in summer 1863, rumor had it that the Confederate ship *Taconey* was planning to head up Narragansett Bay in Rhode Island. Governor James Y. Smith called for fortification of the area and guaranteed exemption from examinations to all Brown University students who would join in the defense effort. Many did, in what became, in the words of Brown historian Walter Bronson, a "delightful fortnight."[18] As Francis T. Hazlewood, class of 1864, sardonically described it,

> Of the tearful embraces, of the long farewells, of the gentle waving of handkerchiefs, as the pilot boat streamed down the bay, I cannot speak. . . . But of the long exile of *two* weeks, broken by only an *occasional* furlough,—of the tedious night watches, spent in sound sleep within the fold of warm blankets,—of the blistered hands, won in preparing clambakes,—of the heavy marches, in quest of berries and milk,—of the midnight attacks, on poultry yards and sheep folds,—of the daily exposure, to the hot sun on the beach, . . . it is fitting that I should speak. For these are the records of a patriotism, which could willingly sacrifice the examinations of the University for the recreations of the Bonnet, and the mush and milk, and bread puddings, and pork stews, of the commons, for fresh fish, and sweet berries, and baked apples swimming in cream.

He continued with stories of how the heroes' "hard service" was broken up by baseball and musical concerts, then concluded:

> To the future historian, whose duty it shall be to analyze the motives which led to such self-sacrifice, nothing but the most unselfish devotion to the interest of the country will be apparent. What else could induce men absorbed in literary pursuits to forego, in the heat of summer, the subtleties of logic, the intricacies of mathematics, the familiar talks of Thucydides and Demosthenes and Socrates and Plato, for clambakes, and surfbathing, and fishing, in a locality more beautiful than the Utopia of More and of Southey.[19]

War, as William Tecumseh Sherman would later say, is hell.

But for Moses Purnell Handy, caught in between worlds, formal education was not on his mind. Instead, he bided his time awaiting his father's release and perhaps a return to the South.

Beginning in 1863, he started to record some of the moments of his daily life in a tiny Excelsior Pocket Diary—a habit he picked up from his father, and one to which he would sporadically return for more than thirty years.

He was not a fanatical daily diarist like many people in that era, nor a self-reflective one, but instead a chronicler of facts and minutiae. His 1863 journal, for example, recorded lists of letters written and received, and a ledger of expenses ($3.00 for a linen coat, $2.50 for one pair of shoes, $1.00 for a straw hat, $.25 for repair of a breast pin, and $.20 for soda water) and revenues ($1.75 paid by Capt. S. Jefferson for 1¾ days' work in Harvest @$1.00). It also included the names and in some cases formulas of various remedies that he must have discovered through his work at the apothecary (a private recipe for cough mixture from Dr. E. W. of Delaware City; Pancoast's Gargle; Number Six Rheumatic Drops; and something called Cuban Hair Invigorator, which included glycerin, alcohol, spirits of ammonia, and blood root—a delicious irony, given that an abundance of hair would later become one of Handy's trademarks).

But Handy's journal also contained occasional moments of insight into his difficult plight. On October 18, 1863, for example, he noted: "Father's parole has been taken from him and he is now confined as at first. There are several cases of Small Pox on the island."

When Isaac was released from prison in October 1864, his son, now seventeen and usually going by the name Purnell, was finally ready to act. He declined his uncle's offer to stay in the North to attend college (and avoid the war) and instead slipped through the blockade and made it to Richmond, where he joined the staff of Confederate Brigadier General Walter Hustad Stevens as a lieutenant, inaugurating a brief but eventful military career.

He remained near the Virginia capital, serving as a reserve courier, until Richmond fell in the first week of April 1865, at which point he and other troops beat a hasty and circuitous retreat. First, he headed west, through the tiny towns of Cumberland Courthouse and Farmville. Then Handy found himself in Appomattox Depot, Virginia, on April 9, 1865, the day after General George Armstrong Custer battled with Confederate troops there and delivered one of the final blows to the Lost Cause; Robert E. Lee would surrender to Ulysses S. Grant at Appomattox Court House three days later.[20]

Along with three others, Handy then volunteered to deliver some of Lee's maps to General Joseph E. Johnston in Greensboro, North Carolina, perhaps 150 miles to the southwest.[21] They crossed the Blackwater River and spent the night of April 14—his eighteenth birthday—camping near Rocky Mount, Virginia. He and his companions continued pushing south, traveling eighteen miles in the rain over rough road on April 16, knowing that the war was in its final throes and longing for home. Upon reaching Greensboro on April 17, they heard that Johnston had already surrendered, so they decided to head back north to Virginia to "go up the spout" (surrender) there; they were captured by Union troops at Halifax Court House, near Danville, where Handy was paroled on April 26 and offered safe passage.

He eventually made it back home and was reunited with his father and brother Fred, who had spent the war close to home, serving on gunboats in the James River Squadron of the signal service of Virginia.

During his six months in the Confederate Army, Moses Purnell Handy had jotted down a few notes about his war experiences in microscopic script in his Excelsior Pocket Diary, in some cases writing right over notes he had made two years earlier. But these were mere annotations, reminders that could be used to open the floodgates of information he had committed to his impressive schoolroom-honed memory; months later, he would be able to recall every name, every town, every little detail of the Confederate retreat in a series of seven articles he wrote and sold to a New York publication called the *Watchman*, for which he was paid five dollars each. "This constituted the first money I ever earned by writing for the press," he would later write in a scrapbook.[22]

The *Watchman* articles were remarkable works of reportage, not just because of their detailed eyewitness accounts of the dramatic Confederate retreat, but because of their *tone*. Though still a teenager, Handy had already developed a unique journalistic style that was a dramatic departure from the overstuffed pomposity of the antebellum newspaper correspondent, a style that would be one of his hallmarks throughout the coming decades and would enable him to become a highly effective publicity and promotion man. It was neither florid, like the magazines, nor lurid, like the penny press. It was honest, clear, accessible, and visceral. Handy narrated stories with verbal dexterity, skillfully using words to convey emotions and paint pictures of scenes that were far outside the pale of most readers' experiences.

In one article, for example, Handy described the army's hastily abandoned camp outside the city of Richmond as the end neared:

> Passing for the last time the formidable earthworks, the magazine, the quarters, the chapel, and the frowning river-batteries, I delivered my dispatch, and turned my horse's head toward home, or the place which, for six months, had been to me a dwelling-place. Sally cantered along at a moderate gait, and at eleven o'clock we reached the old camp. I saw in a moment that we were too late—it was deserted. I gave my horse a free rein, and she trod the well-known path between the tents, and halted before the door of my cabin. Hitching my horse to a swinging bough, I dismounted and entered the door. The fire was smouldering upon the hearth, the table was upset, and the bed of pine-straw was scattered over the earthen floor. I opened the door of every cabin, but the only living thing visible was the General's little dog, which came out to meet me, followed by three whining puppies, and trotted after me as she had often done before. In the office and upon the floor of the draughtsman's tent, stationery, maps, and drawings were scattered about, and piles of documents with the official red tape had been thrown into the fire.[23]

He also wrote in the *Watchman* articles about the looting that erupted throughout the city of Richmond on the night of April 2, 1865:

> When I reached the scene of the riot [of a confectioner's store], he stood upon the counter, surveying, with gloomy countenance, the ruins of his stock. Broken glassware, candy, oranges, cakes and jellies; fancy goods and children's toys had been trampled under foot in delightful confusion, and if any of the half-starved little urchins, who crowd the streets of Richmond, had been about at that unseasonable hour, they would doubtless have extracted many a palate-pleasing morsel from the heterogeneous mass. . . . I passed by a jeweler's. His shelves were empty, and the broken glass and mashed woodwork of the windows told me that the removal of the goods

> had been accomplished by violence. A neighboring bakery was in the same manner stripped of its goods. Two reserves were guarding, with loaded muskets, a large clothing-house, but it was evident that they could not long withstand a mob of soldiers and citizens, who were threatening to "gut" the establishment.[24]

The next day Handy witnessed more disturbing sights and emotions, and wrote about those, too:

> In viewing this work of plunder [of the quartermasters' supplies], one could not refrain from asking why all these immense stores of clothing, blankets, and breadstuffs had been so long hoarded . . . while so many of our brave boys in the field were drawing their single thin blankets around their bodies, shivering with cold or almost perishing with hunger. Loud were the murmurs of some of the war-worn veterans as they marched from the capital, witnessing upon every side the waste of those things of which they have been deprived for many months.
>
> Many a poor fellow, whose tattered gray barely hid his emaciated form, felt his heart glow with a sense of injustice when he beheld bolts and bales of the finest cloth and warmest blankets thrown out to those who had never lifted a hand for the cause, and who were already loud in their words of welcome to the foe.[25]

The *Watchman* was a new and obscure publication in 1866, and Handy's articles in it did not attract much attention. But having spent the months immediately following the war tackling a variety of jobs in and around his father's new home in Orange Court House, Virginia—including selling door-to-door "subscriptions" to a biography of Stonewall Jackson—he now discovered his great talent and passion for journalism, and his life resumed its forward momentum.

In fall 1866 he moved to Richmond in pursuit of newspaper work and landed a job as clerk at the *Christian Observer*, earning ten dollars a month plus board. His tasks were menial—marking papers, writing letters, making fires, and perhaps also some promotional work: once again, in his trusty diary he jotted down some kind of sales pitch, echoes of the rote schoolroom lessons of Nathan Burnham Webster, listing a series of reasons one might want to subscribe:

> It is the duty of every man to have a good religious paper for the use of his family and we offer the Christian Observer as such, not because it is the only religious journal of any denomination in the Southern states at the present time.
>
> 2nd, it is conducted by a (Telegram?) Editor. . . . Conducted by Rev. A. Converse D.O. of Philadelphia for the past half century.
>
> 3rd It is the only organ of the Presbyterian Church in Va . . .
>
> 4th It will keep church members thoroughly posted.[26]

But the world of promotion was still well off in Handy's future. For now, he wanted to write, and he soon used his dash and resourcefulness to do just that.

In April 1867 he volunteered to report on a speech being given by Rep. Henry Wilson of Massachusetts—a once-ardent abolitionist, radical Republican, and future (1873–1875) vice president of the United States—for the *Richmond Dispatch.*

> Hearing that Wilson was to speak at Orange C.H. (where father then lived) & apprehending the importance of his mission, I went to Mr. Ellyson of the Dispatch & offered to go to Orange & report the speech for $5 & a free ticket.—A number of reporters were on the ground, but to my surprise I succeeded in getting the fullest report & having a "clean beat" on the negotiations of Wilson with the old Whigs. When Dr. Brock of the Examiner was taunted with letting "that country boy" beat him, he said—Well, he ought to have done it: he had six men sharpening pencils for him.[27]

This led to other work, including an assignment to cover a speech by Horace Greeley in Richmond, and soon Moses P. Handy was offered a staff position on the *Dispatch.* He would remain with that paper for six years in various roles (reporter, local editor, news editor, political department manager during the election of 1872), which would give him complete vocational training in journalism, newspaper production, business, and politics—in effect, the college education he never had.

Handy was not just smart and resourceful, but exceptionally affable, and this won him many plaudits: "REPORTER BY INSTINCT," read a short piece in an Orange, Virginia, newspaper. "Whenever anything of importance is about to happen in this place, MOSES HANDY, led by unerring reportorial instinct, is sure to come up on a visit to his venerable father. He is a good newspaper man."[28] He was elected to join the Knights of Pythias, a fraternal organization that gave its members swords inscribed with the letters F.C.B. for Friendship, Charity, and Benevolence.

On April 15, 1869, he married Sarah Ann Matthews in a ceremony performed by Isaac Handy at a friend's home in Cumberland County, Virginia—the very place through which Moses had retreated four years earlier, almost to the day, in the wake of the fall of Richmond.[29] The wedding was celebrated in print by some of Moses's fellow journalists, including one at the rival *Richmond Journal:* "*Married.*—Our talented friend and confrere, MOSES P. HANDY of the Dispatch, became a Benedict in Cumberland county Thursday. In extending our felicitations on this auspicious event, we can but wish him a long life and a merry one with the bride of his choice. May she always find him a handy man to have in the house."[30]

Their union would prove to be one of deep and abiding love, as well as significant professional collaboration. Two years his senior, Sarah had attended school in Richmond and was herself an aspiring writer. In October 1872, for example, she wrote a lengthy feature article for the *Century* magazine entitled "On the Tobacco Plantation," describing in detail the operations of tobacco production in the part of Virginia in which she had grown up; a similar feature ran in *Harper's Monthly* one year later. She carved out a fairly complex dual life, tackling in-depth feature writing ("Witchcraft Among the Negroes," *Appleton's Magazine,* 1872) while juggling more traditional activities such as child rearing (Sarah and Moses would eventually raise seven kids together) and entering works of embroidery in the Virginia State Fair.

Moses, meanwhile, began plying his trade as a professional writer. After narrowly surviving the collapse of the Virginia state capitol in 1870—an event that injured Handy and 250 others, killing 62 people, including the very same Dr. Joseph Brock who had derided Handy as "that country boy" during the coverage of Congressman Wilson's speech three years earlier—he began writing dispatches in the *New York World* and other newspapers, signed "Purnell." He also coauthored a book entitled *Visitor's Guide to Richmond and Vicinity* (which, he stated in the prefatory note, "makes no pretensions to literary merit").[31] Then late in 1873 he demonstrated all that pluck in landing the scoop on the *Virginius,* and life for the Handys began to change quickly.

By June 1874, he had accepted an offer to join the staff of the *New-York Tribune,* the paper whose fortunes he had so gallantly advanced by his derring-do in Cuba. With Sarah and their three children, Moses moved to Manhattan—much to the delight of his old pals back in the South, who saw their small-town boy, "Brother Handy," making it big. In one snippet some weeks later, the *Farmville (Va.) Mercury* crowed, "Our old friend, Moses P., flourishes abundantly in New York. He has got a position on the Tribune, where he is so useful the boys call him 'Handy Handy.' He told me he was coming among his old friends shortly to write up Virginia for the Tribune. I have called on a great many editorial friends but have had no pleasanter time than I spent with Handy."[32] The *Wilmington (N.C.) Morning Star* commented, "He has won a good position on the staff of that great journal, which is a pleasant fact seeing he is a Southern man 'to the manner born,' a young and ambitious journalist of character and talent."[33]

Moses Handy would remain with the *Tribune* for only about a year and a half, beginning a regular pattern of switching newspapers as opportunities arose. During that time, however, he traveled extensively, covering everything from the women's temperance crusade in Ohio and Indiana to shady monetary dealings of carpetbagger politicians in Louisiana and the centennial celebrations of the Revolutionary War battles of Lexington, Concord, Ticonderoga, Bunker Hill, and Mecklenburg.

Politics was his forte, but Handy also had a sharp wit that lent itself to social commentary. At one point during his time with the *Tribune,* Handy even contributed some verse to a ditty that was making the rounds, much like the "Macarena" would in the mid-1990s. It was, according to the *Saline County (Kans.) Journal,* an "absurd little street-car jingle," based on an instructional sign that had been posted in cars of the New York and Harlem Railroads after they switched to a system of punching passenger tickets. The riff "has been running through American newspapers [and] . . . has even invaded the continent of Europe and made its appearance in French and German translations." With some embellishment by Handy, it went:

> Punch, boys, punch! Punch with care!
> Punch in the presence of the passinjare.
> A blue trip slip for an 8-cent fare;
> A buff trip slip for a 6-cent fare;
> A pink trip slip for a 3-cent fare;
> All in the presence of the passinjare.

The verse was printed in the *Tribune* and then in other papers, before it was co-opted by an umbrella manufacturer and some political promoters. Even Mark Twain got in the act, penning a short story for the *Atlantic Monthly* about the contagious but "idiotic burden" of these lines in a piece appropriately called "A Literary Nightmare."[34] Surely there must have been a twinkle in Moses Handy's gray eyes when he read that story.

In October 1875, Handy joined with two others to purchase the *Richmond Enquirer* and remake it as a conservative Democratic paper. Moses's brother Fred also joined the editorial management team. The paper was going through a great deal of strife, and Moses had to deal with the business side as much as the editorial. Nevertheless, he was a frequent contributor, producing thirty-two articles between January and March 1876 (despite spending three weeks in Washington in February), with headlines such as "Mr. Wheeler Pockets His Conscience," "Reform in the Kitchen," and "Rip Van Winkle Outdone." He carefully documented all his writing in a school composition notebook, perhaps borrowed from one of his children—a remarkable 158 articles published between January and September. The *Cincinnati Enquirer* was one of many newspapers that took notice, remarking that "A young, vigorous writer, Mr. HANDY made the paper a just competitor with its local contemporaries."[35]

During his time with the *Richmond Enquirer*, in summer 1876, Moses Handy was appointed as Virginia's commissioner to the Centennial Exhibition in Philadelphia. It was common for newspapermen and other leading citizens to be connected to expositions in this way, in official positions with semiofficial responsibilities that often amounted to a lot of observation and reporting. Typically, they served on committees for each administrative and exhibition department, such as Tariffs and Transportation, Manufactures, Commerce, and Opening Ceremonies. Handy had previously been appointed by President Ulysses S. Grant as a commissioner to the World Exposition 1873 in Vienna; however, he had been unable to serve. This time, Handy accepted the honor and hence got a glimpse of the first major world's fair to be held in the United States.

Laid out on a handsome 285-acre tract along the Schuylkill River, the Centennial Exhibition featured official buildings of eleven other nations and attracted more than 9 million visitors, many of whom saw displays of the mighty Corliss steam engine and Alexander Graham Bell's new invention, the telephone.

The Exhibition was neither a financial nor an artistic success. But it did dramatically demonstrate to visitors, including Handy, the appeal of a grand spectacle, the power of the press to attract a mass audience (twenty-seven daily and weekly newspapers from Philadelphia alone provided coverage), and the promotional potential of nationalism and patriotic pride. The latter was an especially poignant lesson, because the day after the centennial of the Declaration of Independence was celebrated at the Exhibition ("Gunpowder and Glory," read the headline of the *Philadelphia Times*; "The Two Hemispheres and the Four Quarters Revolving Around Our Big Centennial Magnet"), word reached Philadelphia about the army's devastating defeat at the Battle of the Little Big Horn ("An Indian Massacre: Custer's Command Cut to Pieces").[36]

When Handy returned to the *Richmond Enquirer* following the Centennial Exhibition, the paper was in financial trouble and the partners decided to shut it down. "Were the standard lowered, its publication might be indefinitely continued," they wrote, "but to lower this standard would be to surrender privileges and ideas which, in our view, are essential to independent journalism and true public policy."[37]

But this was only a minor setback. Impressed by what he had seen in the City of Brotherly Love, Handy agreed to become associate editor of the *Philadelphia Times* in fall 1876. Philadelphia would be home base for the Handys for the next fourteen years, at first in a four-story masonry row house with basement at 924 Clinton Street, in the Society Hill neighborhood, for which they paid $175 rent per month. It was a home large enough to accommodate their growing family (their three youngest children were born right there) and a shifting cast of others, including servants, boarders, and relatives.

Moses continued to change jobs frequently, becoming managing editor of the *Philadelphia Press* in late 1880, owner and editor of the *Philadelphia Daily News* two years later, managing editor of the *New York World* in 1887, and a special Philadelphia-based correspondent to the *Boston Herald, Chicago Daily News, Cincinnati Enquirer,* and other papers in 1888. (At a dinner, his friend Colonel Alexander McClure, founder of the *Philadelphia Times*, teased him about this: "No one knows just where to find Handy, he used to be with the *Times*, then with the *Press*, now I understand he is the Washington correspondent for the *New York World*." "True," said Handy. "I tried the flesh and the devil, now I'm trying the *World*."[38]) Along the way, Handy built a formidable reputation in the journalism community. The *Raleigh Observer* called him "one of the most brilliant young journalists in the country," and the *Boston Globe* dubbed him "one of the most candid journalists in America."[39]

In 1881, Handy traveled abroad for the first time, departing Philadelphia for Liverpool on May 19. (He would return to Europe in 1884, and again in 1886, making him a seasoned traveler and cosmopolite before age forty, and preparing him for the great tasks that lay, unbeknownst to him, ahead.) The trip would take him to London, Paris, and most of the great cities of Italy. He noted many little facts about the journey in his diary—latitudes and longitudes, the mileage between cities (3,292), arrival times at hotels, some of the attractions he visited (St. Peter's Basilica, the Colosseum, the Forum), and the costs of each sundry item ("cab in London 1s 6d, Postal Cards 1s 5d, Barber 2s 6d, coffee 4d, Stewards Fees 8s, Hotel Royal 24s, Cigars 2s").[40]

These were all ostensibly work trips, spent talking to European politicians and journalists, American expatriates and cultural icons, studying the Old World but mostly observing the United States in the continental mirror, warts and all. As Handy caustically wrote in a column entitled "Entre Nous" following his 1884 trip,

> "Been abroad this summer?" Yes, along with fifty thousand other Americans, more or less, on business or on pleasure bent. Fighting for good berths and getting the worst; packed like sardines, three in a room, that would make a Summer hotel point with pride to its attic chambers; homesick or seasick; doing sight-seeing to death and calling it enjoyment; buying foreign trash and calling it business; committing whole cities to memory in a day; climbing mountains by buying stereoscopic views for our drawing-room tables; wearing Winter clothes all summer; overdrawing letters of credit, and thanking Lord that we bought return tickets before we left New York; bored to death in English hotels and making believe we were hilarious on Parisian boulevards; praising French cookery and sighing for our modest home tables; bragging about all things American, and feeling at heart, with all our greatness that other nations can do many things better than we can; ridiculing aristocracy and tickled to death to be dined by a lord; all going shearing to come home shorn; all going with the air of taking possession of our inheritance as lords

of the universe, and returning either greater fools than ever or with more conceit knocked out of us than we ever knew we had—This going to Europe is a big thing.[41]

It was a hectic life for Moses, spent riding the trains up and down the Atlantic seaboard in a frantic effort to stay ahead of the news and build his network; meeting with government officials to research his stories; writing numerous letters and articles longhand in a large, loping, elongated script that looked like Arabic, with just four or five words per line; attending the theater and innumerable social clubs; and helping Sarah with the children. He also spent a great deal of time in Washington, D.C., and while there could often be found milling with the VIPs at Chamberlin's, a legendary restaurant and hotel on 15th and I Streets NW, where high-stakes card games took place in back rooms, waiters brought out live terrapins that special guests would select for their soup, and proprietor John Chamberlin was "as silent on other people's affairs as the Egyptian sphinx."[42] Somehow in the midst of it all Handy helped campaign for two presidential candidates: family friend James G. Blaine, the former Republican senator from Maine, in 1884; and Benjamin Harrison in 1888.

His most passionate social commitment was to the Clover Club, a gathering of journalists, Philadelphia's solid citizens, visiting dignitaries like President Grover Cleveland, entertainers like the actor Edwin Booth, and cultivated hail-fellows-well-met; one of his boarders, the newspaperman W. B. Merrill, was a frequent guest. They called themselves "A Club for Social Enjoyments, the Cultivation of Literary Tastes, and the Encouragement of Hospitable Intercourse." Handy was a founding member of the Clover Club in 1881 and its first president. They would meet on Thursday nights around a clover-shaped table at the Hotel Bellevue, act out silly but formalized customs (the youngest or last-elected member would sit in the Baby Member's Chair, with a rattle in hand and bib under his chin), engage in witty banter, break out in songs ("Mamie," "The Band Played On," "Sidewalks of New York"), and dine sumptuously on extravagances like oysters on shell, consommé printanier royal, canvasback duck with jelly, English pheasants, and charlotte russe.

Handy was the consummate host, networker, and raconteur—a man of grace, intellect, and bon mots, a planet around which the satellite literati of Philadelphia happily orbited. His southern gentility charmed one and all, and his Confederate war record always lent the festivities an air of gallantry.

He became known as Major Handy, "Major" an honorific adopted by many men in the postwar era, even though his rank in the army had never risen above lieutenant. He was described in an 1897 commemorative book about the Clover Club with humorous reverence:

> Mr. Moses Purnell Handy, "Major" Handy in the North and "Majah" below the line, seems to have been a special creation just fitted to handle the gavel at a dinner. There is hardly any term that can be used to comprehensively state his qualifications as the presiding genius at table. It is no more his whiskers (irreverently called, at times, "His Lug's," "Siders," or "Picadilly [*sic*] Weepers") than his head and no more his head than his face, and no more his face than his body; but above all is his personality, culture, brain and good sense. He is chief at a dinner; he puts the men in front through their paces, knows their values, and blends song, story and speech as to make one harmonious whole. He may be surpassed, in time to come, as a presiding officer at a dinner or feast, but so far he is incomparable.[43]

Handy even nicknamed his youngest daughter Clover.

He kept track of his multiple obligations in his pocket diaries, recording a dizzying pace of life. In one eighteen-day span in spring 1886, he traveled from Philadelphia to Washington, attended several club meetings, saw President Cleveland, took in a performance of *Othello* at the Academy of Music starring Edwin Booth, saw *Hamlet* at the Academy of Music also starring Edwin Booth, and then presided over a farewell dinner to the actor Henry E. Dixey at the famous Delmonico's Restaurant in New York. Other weeks, he had receptions at the Journalist's Club, dinners at the Catholic Club, charity balls, and obligations to the Press News Association, of which he was elected president in June 1887. During another short stretch in early 1889, his schedule was frantic—beginning on February 27, when he traveled from Philadelphia to New York to attend the annual dinner of the New York Press Club, and then a reception in Philadelphia the next day, a trip to Washington two days after that for a dinner and a night at Chamberlin's, another dinner the next night, the inauguration ceremony and ball for President Harrison on March 4, and a return trip to Philadelphia on March 6.

Little wonder that his health sometimes gave out; in both 1887 and 1888, he needed to take several months off to recuperate—in the latter year, traveling to Europe for the fourth time in eight years.

THE "PICCADILLY WEEPERS" (sideburns) of Moses P. Handy, before they really took on a life of their own, circa 1870s, printed from a glass wet collodion negative. Library of Congress, Brady-Handy Photograph Collection; LC-DIG-cwpbh-04272.

Sarah, meanwhile, began to emerge from the burdens of motherhood. Although Moses was on the road frequently, or in the newspaper office, or at social club meetings, or otherwise working at his meticulously organized rolltop desk, she resumed her writing career, albeit now with a focus on stereotypically "feminine" topics. She authored articles about advice to young wives ("The husband won must also be *kept*, and he who having wooed a dainty and attractive girl finds himself wedded to a dowdy, careless wife is *swindled!*") and new mothers ("Teeth are a mysterious dispensation, on the whole, and it might be well if they could be abolished by act of Congress and sets provided for us all by dentists at once").[44] She ran the Household Department in the *Philadelphia Weekly Times* from 1877 to 1880, and in the *Philadelphia Press* from 1880 to 1884. She also contributed occasional articles to the quarterly catalog put out by Strawbridge Clothiers, on predictably domestic topics such as "How to Shop." And she wrote very clever poetry as well—in one case, summoning the dilemma of a young woman going to an Ivy League regatta with multiple suitors asking her to wear their colors:

> There's Jack Arundel just from Princeton—
> You know I think oceans of Jack;
> And he vows that he'll never forgive me
> If I don't wear the orange and black.
>
> Black lace would be awfully stylish,
> With marigold flowers; but then,
> You see, Lou's betrothed and his brother
> Are here, and they're both Harvard men.
>
> I've half promised Mr. De Lancey,
> To please him I'll wear the Yale blue:
> They say he is worth a cool million—
> I really don't know what to do.[45]

There were not a great many female journalists at the time—the 1880 U.S. census listed 12,308 people with the profession of journalist, only 288 of whom were women—and while Sarah likely did not consider journalism her full-time job, she was a talented and passionate writer.[46]

Beneath it all, however, the workload, caregiving, and solitude took their toll on her. From time to time she traveled with her husband or took in a show; sometimes she was simply summoned by telegram to Chamberlin's in Washington to take care of him when "la grippe" (an archaic term for influenza) wore him down—on which occasions, she might take dictation from him to make sure his stories still made deadline.

Sarah, too, kept a pocket diary, and it was often filled with curt little complaints and pessimistic remarks that revealed a darker side of her gentle soul.

> Took notes for Haines article, sheer force of will.
> New cook a failure—left in a fuss.
> Dress making by my lone self.
> Mr. H telegraphs home tomorrow. Hallelujah!
> Another profitless day, lounging around & suffering.
> Backache & misery in my bones.[47]

Despite all the ailments, she would ultimately survive to age eighty-eight, outliving her husband and three of her children.

SARAH MATTHEWS HANDY, in 1893, in a feature about "World's Fair Women" that lists her numerous literary credits, while also mentioning that she "is very domestic and retiring." *A Souvenir of World's Fair Women,* 1893, courtesy of North Central College Archives and Special Collections, Oesterle Library, Naperville, Illinois.

In 1887, for the third time in his life, Moses P. Handy was tapped to participate in the organizational committee for a major celebration—this time, the Constitution Centennial, for which he served as chairman of the Committee on Press, a new function created since the time of his work on the 1876 Centennial Exhibition, necessitated by the tremendous expansion of the newspaper industry and the growing focus on publicity and promotion.

The event itself was held in Philadelphia, a three-day affair that began with a Civic and Industrial Procession down Broad Street that drew 21,029 representatives of the city's trade and commercial organizations, 2,106 musicians, and 497 floats. On the following day, with President Grover Cleveland in attendance, organizers staged what was hailed as the largest military parade in the nation's history, with thirty thousand uniformed men led by General Phil Sheridan on his sorrel steed. It was "A Grand, Good Time," declared the *Salt Lake Herald:* "Broad Street from end to end presented a sight never [to be] forgotten. The brilliant raiment of ladies and children lent a pretty effect to the picture, and with a clear sky, wide street, handsome uniforms of military and police, it was an inspiring scene."[48]

All told, the events drew about five hundred thousand visitors and 1 million local residents. Handy had clearly put his extensive network and newspaper skills to use, since news of the event—from the often-mundane advance-planning activities to detailed coverage of the parade and the president's involvement—graced all the major dailies as well as obscure newspapers like the *Concordia (Kans.) Daily Blade, Pittston (Pa.) Evening Gazette, Waterloo (Ind.) Press, and Muskogee (Okla.) Indian Journal.* Indeed, with telephone lines beginning to crisscross the nation, more than 50 million telegraph messages being transmitted each year, and the wire services disseminating news using both technologies, the Constitution Centennial was one of the first planned special events in history that could be efficiently covered by the nation's press—and Moses Handy took full advantage of it.

His work on the Constitution Centennial probably felt to Handy like a civic responsibility, a way for him to use his considerable journalistic skills to report the event and, perhaps, to continue to close the national rift that the southerner with the northern mentality had experienced so viscerally two decades earlier.

But through the application of substantive journalistic techniques to the work of promotion, he was also bringing innovation and credibility to a field that thus far had been dominated by the high-flying style of the entertainment press agents. And of course, *their* work was only getting started.

PLATE 1. **MASTODONIC MARVEL.** In 1882, Jumbo quickly became the centerpiece of Tody Hamilton's promotional efforts for Barnum & Bailey.

Circus World Museum, Baraboo, Wisconsin; CWi 15239.

PLATE 2. **IN THE ERA BEFORE PHOTOGRAPHY** took hold, idyllic artwork—such as Fanny Palmer's *Across the Continent, "Westward the Course of Empire Takes Its Way"* (1869)—was often used by the boosters to portray progress and the dominion of mankind in the West.
Courtesy of the Newberry Library, Chicago, Illinois; Poole 24.

PLATE 3. **THE TWENTY-MULE TEAMS** operated in Death Valley for only five years, but they became a long-lasting symbol of the rugged West that was built into a brand by the Pacific Coast Borax Company.

U.S. Borax; author's collection.

PLATE 4. **EARLY WILD WEST POSTERS** depicted scenes from Cody's career with equal doses of realism and idolatry. Buffalo Bill Museum and Grave, Golden, Colorado.

PLATE 5. **GEORGE CATLIN'S PAINTINGS** became part of his own early version of a Wild West show—including this dual portrait of the Assiniboine chief Wi-Jun-Jon, who traveled to Washington and came back looking rather different.
George Catlin, *Wi-Jun-Jon, The Pigeon's Egg Head*, 1837, Library of Congress; LC-USZC2-331.

PLATE 6. **THE WILD WEST POSTER STYLE** evolved to reflect the high drama that was injected into the show in 1886 by Steele MacKaye. Buffalo Bill Museum and Grave, Golden, Colorado.

PLATE 7. **THE PORTRAYAL OF AMERICAN INDIANS** in Wild West promotional materials came to reflect the progressive views of Burke and Cody. This poster from 1893 is very restrained and identifies the Indian only as "The American."
Buffalo Bill Museum and Grave, Golden, Colorado.

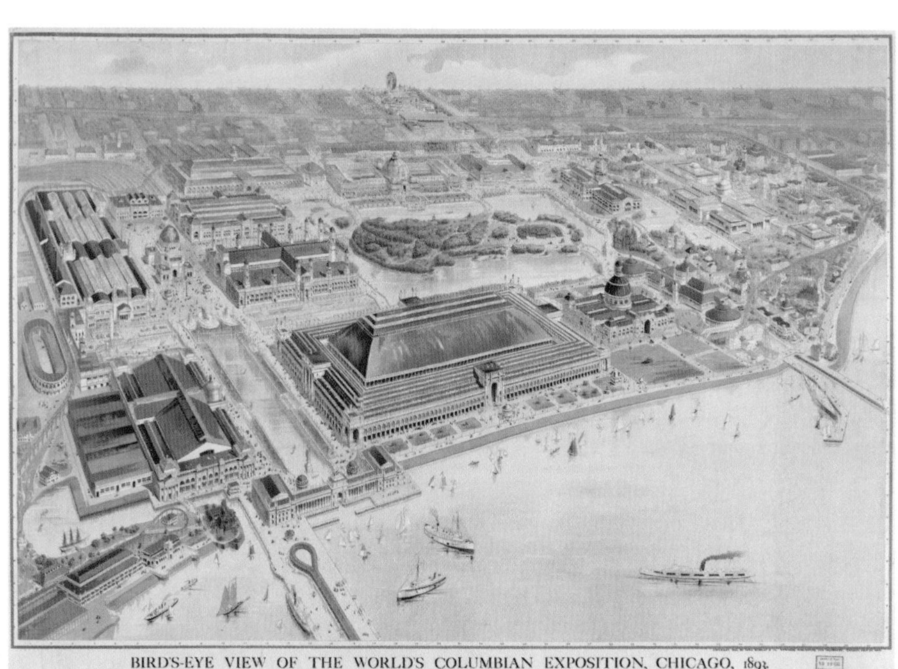

PLATE 8. **THE BIRD'S-EYE VIEW** lithograph of the World's Columbian Exposition helped fixate an image of scale and grandeur in the public's mind. Rand McNally, 1893, Library of Congress Prints and Photographs Division; LC-DIG-ppmsca-09328.

PLATE 9. **DISTRIBUTING FREE PASSES** to the Exposition was one of the Department of Publicity and Promotion's many tasks. Handy apparently even had to issue passes to himself.
Handy Family Papers, William L. Clements Library, University of Michigan, Ann Arbor.

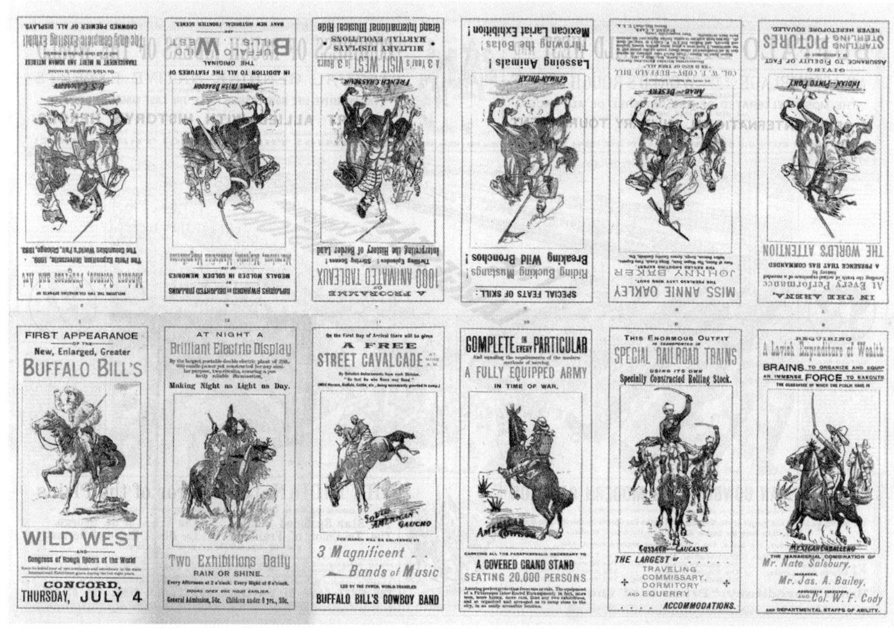

PLATE 10. **A WILD WEST COURIER** from 1895.
These intricate pieces folded up as tabloid booklets or could be posted flat.
Buffalo Bill Center of the West, Cody, Wyoming; MS327.1895.

PLATE 11. **THE OVER-THE-TOP ALLITERATIVE WORD PLAY** of Tody Hamilton is evident in this Barnum & Bailey poster from 1906.

Courtesy of Chris Berry.

FROM DESERT SANDS TO PRAIRIE WILDS

BUFFALO BILL'S WILD WEST

COMBINED WITH PAWNEE BILL'S GREAT FAR EAST

ORIGINAL PRESS COPY

"READY TO PRINT AND NOT DUPLICATED"

SERIES E

PRESS DEPARTMENT

BUFFALO BILL'S WILD WEST COMBINED WITH PAWNEE BILL'S FAR EAST

LOUIS E. COOKE, General Agent.

Press representatives who will visit the newspapers in advance and with the exhibition:

LESTER W. MURRAY, Contracting Agent.
Maj. JOHN M. BURKE, "The Story Man."
FRANK WINCH, With the Show.

Who will arrive in the order given.

OUR DATE IN THIS CITY IS

PLATE 12. **A NEW PUBLICITY INNOVATION**. The 1911 *From Desert Sands to Prairie Wilds* booklet distributed by the Wild West was the forerunner of the modern press kit.
Buffalo Bill Center of the West, Cody, Wyoming; MS327.02.11.006.

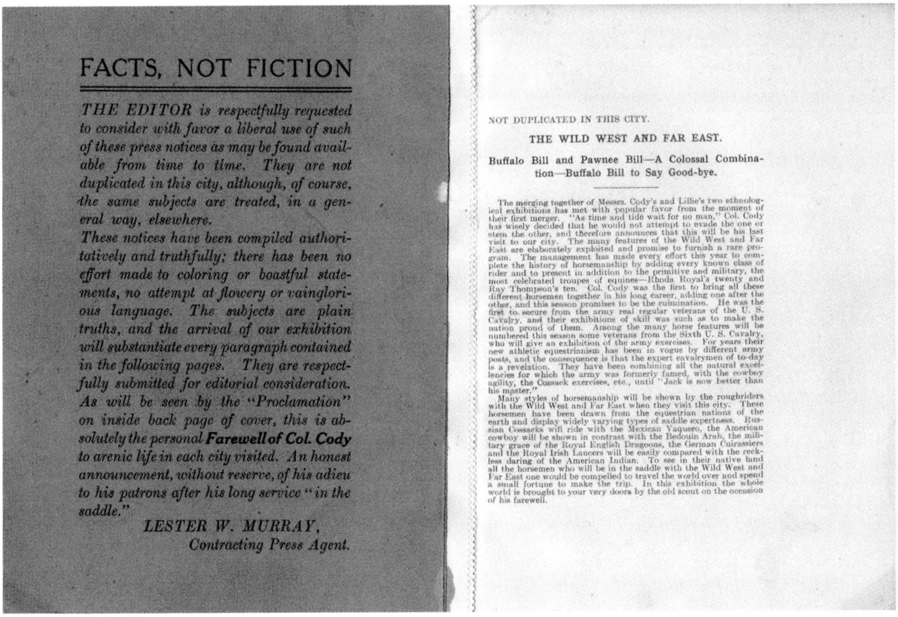

FACTS, NOT FICTION

THE EDITOR is respectfully requested to consider with favor a liberal use of such of these press notices as may be found available from time to time. They are not duplicated in this city, although, of course, the same subjects are treated, in a general way, elsewhere.

These notices have been compiled authoritatively and truthfully; there has been no effort made to coloring or boastful statements, no attempt at flowery or vainglorious language. The subjects are plain truths, and the arrival of our exhibition will substantiate every paragraph contained in the following pages. They are respectfully submitted for editorial consideration. As will be seen by the "Proclamation" on inside back page of cover, this is absolutely the personal ***Farewell of Col. Cody*** *to arenic life in each city visited. An honest announcement, without reserve, of his adieu to his patrons after his long service "in the saddle."*

LESTER W. MURRAY,
Contracting Press Agent.

NOT DUPLICATED IN THIS CITY.

THE WILD WEST AND FAR EAST.

Buffalo Bill and Pawnee Bill—A Colossal Combination—Buffalo Bill to Say Good-bye.

The merging together of Messrs. Cody's and Lillie's two ethnological exhibitions has met with popular favor from the moment of their first merger. "As time and tide wait for no man," Col. Cody has wisely decided that he would not attempt to evade the one or stem the other, and therefore announces that this will be his last visit to our city. The many features of the Wild West and Far East are elaborately exploited and promise to furnish a rare program. The management has made every effort this year to complete the history of horsemanship by adding every known class of rider and to present in addition to the primitive and military, the most celebrated troupes of equines—Rhoda Royal's twenty and Ray Thompson's ten. Col. Cody was the first to bring all these different horsemen together in his long career, adding one after the other, and this season promises to be the culmination. He was the first to secure from the army real regular veterans of the U. S. Cavalry, and their exhibitions of skill was such as to make the nation proud of them. Among the many horse features will be numbered this season some veterans from the Sixth U. S. Cavalry, who will give an exhibition of the army exercises. For years their new athletic equestrianism has been in vogue by different army posts, and the consequence is that the expert cavalrymen of to-day is a revelation. They have been combining all the natural excellencies for which the army was formerly famed, with the cowboy agility, the Cossack exercises, etc., until "Jack is now better than his master."

Many styles of horsemanship will be shown by the roughriders with the Wild West and Far East when they visit this city. These horsemen have been drawn from the equestrian nations of the earth and display widely varying types of saddle expertness. Russian Cossacks will ride with the Mexican Vaquero, the American cowboy will be shown in contrast with the Bedouin Arab, the military grace of the Royal English Dragoons, the German Cuirassiers and the Royal Irish Lancers will be easily compared with the reckless daring of the American Indian. To see in their native land all the horsemen who will be in the saddle with the Wild West and Far East one would be compelled to travel the world over and spend a small fortune to make the trip. In this exhibition the whole world is brought to your very doors by the old scout on the occasion of his farewell.

PLATE 13. **THE BOOKLET** *From Desert Sands to Prairie Wilds* contained several complete articles and images that could be torn out and used by local newspapers, with the assurance that no competing news outlet had run them in that market.
Buffalo Bill Center of the West, Cody, Wyoming; MS327.02.11.006.

PLATE 14. **LEGENDS OF THE OLD WEST**. In 1910 Burke appears to have engineered a licensing deal to get Buffalo Bill and Pawnee Bill more exposure through this American Caramel Company card set—and he also slipped himself into the group of legends. American Caramel Company; author's collection.

PLATE 15. **THE 1895 WILD WEST PROGRAM** featured seventy pages of stories, pictures, historical sketches—and plenty of ads.
Buffalo Bill Museum and Grave, Golden, Colorado.

PLATE 16. **MISTAKEN IDENTITY?** Later in the 1895 season, a second edition of the program was published, on the cover of which the image labeled "Cowboy" was replaced by one of John M. Burke. Buffalo Bill Museum and Grave, Golden, Colorado.

6

BIRTH AND GROWTH OF THE WILD WEST

"Thunder of hoofs, clank of spurs, rattle of pistols"

Prepare the triumph car for me
And purple throne to sit on,
For I've done more than Julius C.–
He could not down the Briton!
Caesar and Cicero shall bow,
And ancient warriors famous,
Before the myrtle-bandaged brow
of Buffalo Williamus.

S. W. Foss, *Buffalo Bill and the Romans* (1890)

In printed programs, newspaper articles, and undoubtedly many a hotel bar, too, John M. Burke would forever perpetuate the notion that the show known as the Wild West was the direct lineal descendant of Buffalo Bill's Old Glory Blow-Out rodeo of 1882, the ingenious creation of his friend and boss, William F. Cody. But that was just Burke's marketing handicraft. Who truly deserves credit for originating the idea is not clear.

In 1843, P. T. Barnum had staged a buffalo hunt in the unlikely outpost of Hoboken, New Jersey—a typically clever and opportunistic Barnum stunt in which he drew twenty-four thousand people to see a free event but profited handsomely because of a deal he had cut with the Hoboken ferry operators to transport spectators from New York. The concept of a western show was long on his mind, and in his 1869 autobiography he even described the theoretical spectacle, including "the Indians in all the glory of paint and feathers, beads and bright blankets, riding on their ponies, followed by tame buffaloes, elks and antelopes; then an exhibition on a lot large enough to admit of a display of all the Indian games and dances, their method of hunting, their style of cooking, living, etc." Barnum was focused on other ideas at the moment, but felt that "such an exhibition is perfectly practicable now to any one who has the capital and tact to undertake it, and a sure fortune would follow the enterprise."[1]

Others were heading down the same path.

In 1872, just before joining Cody on stage for a season, Wild Bill Hickok served as master of ceremonies for a "Grand Buffalo Hunt" at Niagara Falls with some cowboys and Indians. And Nate Salsbury, a renowned troubadour who became Cody's Wild West business partner in 1884, also seems to have thought of this same idea. Indeed, he wrote a stern defense of his own claims as the originator of the concept in an article so bitter that he apparently insisted it not be published until fifty years after his death. According to Salsbury, he had come up with the idea while traveling home from Australia in 1876, six years before Cody's Old Glory Blow-Out.

> I know that there will be a world of protest to these lines, but that the Wild West Show was an invention of my own entirely, is proven by the letters in Cody's own hand which I have preserved as indeed I have preserved every scrap of writing he has ever signed and addressed to me. It is lovely to be thus fortified against protestations and abuse that would surely follow if proof did not exist of what I have stated.[2]

Yet well before these pretenders to the throne, there was George Catlin—a Pennsylvania-born painter of some renown (portraitist of Governor DeWitt Clinton of New York and General Sam Houston, among others) who in the 1830s had gone to live among American Indians, documenting the lives, customs, and costumes of some forty-eight tribes.

Catlin came to believe in a sort of ethnological mandate to capture and preserve the ways of the Indians before they were inevitably conquered or absorbed into modern society:

> I have seen him shrinking from the soil and haunts of his boyhood, bursting the strongest ties which bound him to the earth and its

pleasures; I have seen him set fire to his wigwam and smooth over the graves of his fathers; I have seen him . . . with tears of grief sliding over his cheeks, clap his hand in silence over his mouth, and take the *last look* over his fair hunting grounds, and turn his face in sadness to the setting sun. . . . I have seen . . . the grand and irresistible march of civilization. I have seen this splendid Juggernaut rolling on and beheld its sweeping desolation.[3]

But Catlin also realized that there was money to be made by educating and entertaining white men with stories of the red men, as he would have put it. And so, beginning with a series of lyceum lectures and painting exhibitions in the cities of the East (see plate 5), gradually donning Indian costumes and imitating their dances, and eventually touring with real Ojibwa and Iowa Indians in London, Paris, and Brussels, George Catlin set out to bring the wild western world of the Great Plains to the seats of Western civilization.

Based on what he saw of the major entertainments of the day—circuses, concerts, menageries, puppet shows, orations—he understood how important promotion would be. (Indeed, he wrote to his father that London "is filled with Ex[hibitio]ns. & places of amusement in proportion to the number of its inhabitants, and all strive & struggle for their proportion of visitors, who seem divided and drawn so many ways."[4]) So he inundated towns with broadsides, handbills, and newspaper ads. In one six-week period in 1838, Catlin paid a printer $82.35 to create 5,100 advertisements, 350 circulars, 1,000 handbills, 200 prospectuses for his prints of Seminole leader Osceola, and 2,000 copies of his catalog of paintings.[5]

Catlin possessed other good marketing instincts. He gave free passes to editors to persuade them to write about his shows and created special promotional feasts featuring buffalo tongue, venison, and peace pipes. In 1840, to truly create a sensation, Catlin, his partner, and his nephew dressed up as Indians and crashed the posh Caledonian Ball at London's exclusive Almack's Assembly Rooms. He also occasionally ventured out with the Ojibwas onto horse-drawn omnibuses and into ballet halls, simply because he knew it would get people talking.

Catlin's time on the world stage did not last long. Over the course of his intermittent six-year European tour, his performances lost some of their novelty and appeal, and in response he gradually made them more active and sanguinary. The shows evolved from passive displays of Indian paintings on easels, to demonstrations of war dances and whoops, to the presentation of a "Tableaux Vivant of Red Indians," which included re-creations of bloody battles and scalping. His career as a showman and promoter ended in Brussels in January 1846, when eight Indians in his show contracted smallpox and two of them died. The survivors were sent back to England and on home to America—arriving, coincidentally, at nearly the precise moment when Isaac and Mary Cody welcomed their new son William Frederick into the world. Their contiguous places in the grand processional of the American West, by pure happenstance, would ensure the continuity of the historical narrative.

Catlin briefly contemplated exhibiting his Indian paintings at the London World's Fair in 1851, but in the final two decades of his life, he never again performed with Indians or promoted his work much at all. He died on December 23, 1872—five days after Cody made his acting debut in *Scouts of the Prairie.* Catlin was buried in the Green-Wood Cemetery in Brooklyn, in a grave that remained unmarked for nearly a century, an indignity that his spiritual successor in promotion, John M. Burke—who adopted, adapted, and perfected nearly every one of Catlin's promotional tactics—would suffer as well.

Whether the credit for conceiving the western reenactment show ultimately went to Catlin, Barnum, Hickok, Salsbury, or Cody, the *idea* would not be sufficient; it would take an iconic image to headline it, and a brilliant promoter to turn that image into fame and fortune. After all, history does not remember Fargo's Wild West, Hennessy's Wild West, or Adam Forepaugh's Wild West Combination, all of which launched about the same time.

In Buffalo Bill's first season, which began in Omaha, Nebraska, on May 17, 1883, the show was called Cody and Carver's Wild West, Prairie and Rocky Mountain Exhibition.[6] (The absurdly verbose Burke, ironically, is generally credited with succinctly renaming it Buffalo Bill's Wild West.[7]) From the very beginning, it was a form of entertainment unlike any other. Huge in scale, bold in vision, it combined a series of riding exhibitions, shooting demonstrations, races, and reenactments of high-drama moments from Cody's career on the plains—some of which required mythic embellishment and rescripting from the pen of Burke. Cody's sister Julia Cody Goodman later wrote a wonderful description of it:

With the sky as a roof and the hard earth as a huge stage, the performers brought the tumult of the West almost into the laps of the spectators. Indians, riding bareback, participated in elimination races. Cowboys competed in bronco busting, trick-riding, fancy roping, foot racing, bison riding, shooting on foot and on horseback and knife throwing. Mock battles were waged between the red men and the scouts. At the climax of the show a pony express rider dashed through the grounds, followed shortly by the Deadwood Mail Coach. A band of "hostile" Indians attacked the coach. And the scouts, led by Buffalo Bill on a magnificent white charger, galloped to the rescue, completely routing the attackers.[8]

The opening show at the Omaha fairgrounds drew 10,000 people, and the second show that day drew 20,000; the total population of Omaha in the 1880 census was 30,518.[9] From there, the show moved on to Iowa, Illinois, and Ohio before heading to the big cities of the East Coast, and eventually back to Omaha, five months later.

The crowds were large and enthusiastic everywhere. People were excited to see the tall, handsome, long-haired chief of scouts and guide for the U.S. Army Buffalo Bill (Hon. W. F. Cody)—Burke made certain that the name always appeared exactly so—about whom they had already heard so much. There were also elk races, buffalo hunts, an imitation cyclone, glass ball target shooting (Cody, riding at a gallop, hit eighty-seven out of one hundred that were tossed in the air ahead of him at that first Omaha performance, a fairly routine display of accuracy for him), and Indian dances.

In the weeks leading up to the opening, Burke had told reporters what to expect in a rather mundane fashion:

> The proposed show is intended to give to civilized communities an accurate representation of how white men and Indians live in the far West. There will be 200 Sioux and Pawnee Indians, with their entire outfit of squaws, tepees, dogs, ponies, &c. under command of Major Frank North, for a number of years the Captain of a company of Pawnee scouts in the United States service. He and his men have had many a bloody fight with the Sioux but the hatchet is now buried between the two tribes—at least between those of them engaged for this show.[10]

But that may have been the last time he showed any promotional restraint. In the printed program he came up with swashbuckling language meant to raise the pulse and stir the soul:

> BUFFALO BILL
> (Hon. W. F. Cody) the terror of the red men,—at home,
> in the camp, and in the saddle
>
> Dr. W. F. Carver
>
> The wizard rifleman of the West, known among the Sioux as "THE EVIL SPIRIT OF THE PLAINS." Champion All-Round Shot of the Universe. Conqueror of all America and Europe. The Pride of Columbia. Cynosure of the Admiration of People, Princes, Warriors, and Kings. . . .
>
> A Grand Indian Camp. Genuine Blanket Indians. Pawnees, Shoshones, Sioux, Cheyennes, Brawny Braves of Bloody Records, from the Virgin Wilderness of the Land of the Setting Sun, showing a LIVING, PICTURESQUE REPRODUCTION OF SAVAGE LIFE. Instructive, Interesting and Thrilling. The Largest Delegation of Wild Indians brought East.

The stars, he wrote in the program, were "keen of eye, sturdy in build, inured to hardship, experienced in the knowledge of Indian habits and language, familiar with the hunt, and trustworthy in the hour of extremest danger, they belong to a class that is rapidly disappearing from our country."[11]

In time, his programs would grow to a hefty sixty-four pages full of similar purple-patched varnish about the performers and the show he took to calling "America's National Entertainment." He often recycled some of the copy in his newspaper ads, along with headlines like "The Most Thrilling, Romantic and Novel Exhibition Ever Known."[12]

To help convey the epic nature of the show and its hero, Burke also used stunning lithographic posters with detailed painted vignettes depicting Cody's magnificent achievements as scout, wagon master, Pony Express rider, Indian fighter, beaver trapper, stage driver, consort to Grand Duke Alexis, and more. "The Amusement Triumph of the Age," they heralded. "The Romantic West Brought East in Reality. Everything Genuine . . . A Year's Visit West in Three Hours. Actual Scenes in the Nation's Progress

JOHN M. BURKE was a recognizable figure in nearly every newspaper office in the country, although his western affectations sometimes made people on the street mistake him for Buffalo Bill. Buffalo Bill Center of the West, Cody, Wyoming; P.69.1405.

to Delight, Please, Gratify, Chain and Interest the Visitor."[13] Posters like this were sold as souvenirs and used in bill-posting operations. They would become a primary method for advertising western shows and circuses, and thus a clear precursor to the world of billboards and "out-of-home" advertising that are now so familiar to us.

Burke instinctively knew that the key to his promotional efforts was the press. As a former newspaper man himself, and a longtime theatrical press agent, he had already experienced how the reach and implied endorsement of the newspapers could make the difference between a sustained run and abject failure.

Oversize in both girth and storytelling reputation, affable, and easily caricatured (by 1883 he was calling himself Major and wearing a western-style sombrero to cover up his long, curly Cody-style hair and decidedly Wilmington heritage), Burke made friends in every newsroom on the tour. In Cincinnati, in early June 1883, he hosted the local press corps at a special western banquet, where food was served on tin plates—the first instance of a Catlinesque tactic he would use frequently to help reporters experience the westernness for themselves.[14] One year later he upped the ante, inviting New York reporters to a similar feast at the Polo Grounds but arranging for them to get there in spectacular fashion.[15] As the *New York Herald* told it,

> The small boy who found himself in Fifth avenue between two and three P.M. yesterday, might have been observed to suddenly come to a halt, open wide his eyes and assume the expression of one who beholds a vision[:] a resplendent stage coach, drawn by six fiery, untamed steeds, which were being driven by a large man of powerful build, whose dark eyes blinked not in the glare of the sunlight, whose sweeping mustachios were black as the raven's wing and whose unshorn locks fell far over his massive shoulders. Upon the top of the coach were three other bronzed faced men, also equipped with broad-brimmed sombreros, eagle eyes, and sweeping mustachios. They were surrounded by some half dozen modest looking men, who clung tenaciously to the seats of the coach, and seemed very much alarmed at the public attention they were attracting. The resplendent coach, with the fiery steeds, was part of the property of the "Buffalo Bill Wild West, Rockey [*sic*] Mountain and Prairie exhibition." The driver was the popular scout, known in legislative halls as the Hon. William F. Cody and on the boundless plains as Buffalo Bill . . . and the six timid looking men were reporters.[16]

At the Polo Grounds, the reporters were escorted into a tent with animal skin rugs for a floor and served ox that had been roasted whole over an open fire as part of a menu reported to include "SOUP: Whisky with Water; FISH: Whisky Straight; ENTREE: Crackers with Pepper, Salt and Whisky, etc." and "Ambulances to order." It was, perhaps, the first modern press junket, and Major Burke was not only cultivating powerful allies but quickly indoctrinating them with his grand mythology.

And they, in turn, responded, echoing the same Big Western imagery that he had spewed to them. "Thunder of hoofs, clank of spurs, rattle of pistols, glint of shattered glass balls, odor of gunpowder and cattle made it authentic," the *Hartford Courant* reported after its first look at the show.[17] "A picturesque profusion of long curls, gaudy-colored blankets, sombreros, Indian women and papooses and corduroy breeches tucked in high boots presented so realistic a scene of the 'Wild West' to the spectators that the enthusiasm was boundless," wrote the *Philadelphia Times*.[18] The *New Haven Morning Journal and Courier* called the morning parade "a temptation too strong to be resisted," praised the "plucky riding" in the show, and noted the "paralysis of wonder when the Indians of three tribes burst down the race course in a bareback pony race."[19]

Burke was always exceedingly careful in how he positioned the Wild West. To be seen merely as entertainment, as sort of a western circus, would reduce the exposure it received in the newspapers and therefore limit its livelihood. He thus stringently enforced a rule among the press agents he hired that this was never to be referred to as a "show." It was simply Buffalo Bill's Wild West. (In an era when manual typesetting was the rule and the newspapers were rife with compositors' errors, it is simply amazing how consistently this principle was adhered to: if the word "show" appeared after "Buffalo Bill's Wild West," it was almost always in lower case.) As one of those agents, Dexter Fellows, told it, "Never, [Burke] admonished, was I to refer to the site where we played as 'show grounds' but only as 'exhibition grounds,' and on no account was I to use the word 'lot,' a vulgar term common to the circus, an enterprise which didn't deserve to be mentioned in the same breath with Buffalo Bill's Wild West."[20] In fact, according to a 1910 story in the *Duluth (Minn.) Evening Herald*, Burke worked to ensure that *all* Wild West participants followed his nomenclature:

> Doubtless you've heard of the major's first instruction to all new recruits of the organization.
>
> "If at any time," the major begins as he lines up before his trembling bands of Indians, cowboys and veteran cavalrymen, "I hear you call this educational exhibition 'a show,' damme. I'll throw you out of the exhibition. If any of you call it the 'Bill show' I'll tear you limb from limb as I would a diamondback rattlesnake."

The newspaper then continued quoting the Major as he went on one of his classic digressions, perhaps more akin to a different pseudomilitary man, Gilbert and Sullivan's "Very Model of a Modern Major-General," with "information vegetable, animal, and mineral," from *The Pirates of Penzance*, which had debuted five years before the Wild West:

> "This is the Buffalo Bill Educational Exhibition, remember. Personally, I should prefer to have it called the Bison William Educational Exposition. Buffalo as applied to the animal in question is a misnomer. The bison from the Latin Bos or Bison Americanus is a bovine ruminant, nearly related to the true ox but much fiercer—oh, much—having the withers higher than the hind quarters, consequently causing the hind quarters to sag much nearer the ground than any other portion of the ruminant. Bill is an over-familiar abbreviation of William, and the animal is not related to either the yak or digdig. Fall out."[21]

Burke was legendary for this sort of obliquity. As the trade newspaper *Black and White* wrote of him in 1888, "His conversation on American topics—whether it be political, social, geographical, agricultural, mineral, or climatic—is sound, entertaining, and exhaustive; indeed it would be difficult to find a man so admirably fitted to his position, having so complete a grasp of details and generalities, and being withal so genial and so thorough. Honest, sincere, and generous, he is a friend to all the world."[22]

Another remarkable example of this occurred in a Burke interview with the Portsmouth, England, *Evening News* in 1903, when, apparently extemporaneously, Burke began riffing on the name "Portsmouth" and its counterpart in New England, summoning an incredible wealth of extraneous detail:

> The American town of Portsmouth, New Hampshire . . . is a seaport city and a great Naval station. The harbour was visited in 1603 by thirty Englishmen on the ship Speedwell, and thirteen on the schooner Discoverer, and was first called Strawberry Bank, on account of the wild strawberries which grew in luxuriance. This party came back to Bristol in the following October. In 1623 an expedition on the ship Jonathan, 150 tons, commanded by David Thompson, landed with the intention of permanent settlement, and the memory of these men is cherished as that of first settlers of the State of New Hampshire.[23]

Still another publication parodied Burke's gift for gab and elephantine memory of trivia by claiming that he was "born 27 years before the creation of the world," was "chummy with Noah" and "[took] charge of the press work for the great ark excursion," and then "built the Great Pyramid . . . solved the riddle of the Sphinx with one hand tied behind him, and undid the Gordian knot with his teeth."[24] (He is—the keen observer of twenty-first-century advertising might expect to hear next—the most interesting man in the world.)

The early Wild West posters and ads were always quick to point out that this was an educational exhibition and went out of their way to steer clear of Barnum's legacy. "The Green Sward Our Carpet, Azure Canopy Our Canvas, No Tinsel, No Gilding, No Humbug! No Side Shows or Freaks!"[25] This careful parsing continued even well after the Wild West had established its credibility. In 1894 Burke was still assuring newspaper readers, "There will be no tinsel, no baggage wagon, nothing that is like a circus."[26] In 1898 the *Rocky Mountain News* matter-of-factly noted, "There will be no tinsel or familiar circus features."[27] Burke was positioning not only the Wild West, but Cody as well, to the point at which they would eventually become inseparable and indistinguishable.

At the end of the first season, Cody and Carver began feuding over ownership of the show, its copyright, and Cody's drinking; they soon split, with Cody winning a coin toss to claim the assets. Burke wanted no word of this to sully the reputation of his boss and friend and began sending out press releases praising Cody and disparaging Carver. When Carver then created his own show, Burke's posters would sometimes disparage that, too.[28]

In the second season, 1884, with Salsbury now running the business end of things, the Wild West started off strong. It opened in St. Louis and moved on to Chicago, where it played to an astounding 41,448 people during a single performance. Thanks in no small part to Burke's cultivation of the press corps through western banquets, stagecoach rides, balloon ascensions, and more, huge crowds turned out everywhere the show performed. The Wild West was, the papers said, "as fascinating as a circus, and better and more wholesome than a dime novel"; "a picturesque profusion" for which "[the spectators'] enthusiasm was boundless."[29]

During that second season, for the first time, Major pulled another potent arrow from his publicity quiver: celebrity endorsements.

While the Wild West was performing in Elmira, New York, September 6 through 10, 1884, it received two visits from one of the most famous men

St. Louis Daily Globe-Democrat, Saturday Morning, May 3, 1884.

REAL ESTATE AT AUCTION.

REAL ESTATE
FOR SALE AT
PUBLIC AUCTION!
AT THE
REAL ESTATE EXCHANGE,
NOS. 14 and 16 N. SEVENTH ST.,
On Thursday, May 15, 1884,
AT 10 O'CLOCK A. M.

NO. 1. Lot No. 1, in city block No. 1638, fronting 34 feet 9 in. on the north line of Keokuk st., by a depth along the western line of California avenue of 125 feet to an alley 20 feet wide.

NO. 2. Lot No. 14, in city block No. 810, fronting 25 feet on the west line of Carondelet avenue by a depth of 120 feet to an alley 17 1-2 feet wide.

NO. 3. Lot No. 21 and the north half of lot No. 20 in city block No. 795, having a front in the aggregate of 37 feet and 6 inches on the west line of Carondelet ave. by a depth of 120 feet to an alley.

NO. 4. Lots Nos. 11 and 12 and the south half of Lot No. 10, in city block 796, fronting in the aggregate 62 feet and 6 inches on the east line of Eighth, or Decatur st., by a depth of 100 feet along the north line of Ohio street.

NO. 5. Lot No. 5, in city block No. 809, fronting 25 feet on the east line of Eighth or Decatur st., by a depth of 100 feet to an alley 15 feet wide.

NO. 6. Lot No. 2, in city block No. 4172, fronting 50 feet on the north line of Dunnica avenue, by a depth of 163 feet.

REAL ESTATE AT AUCTION.

REAL ESTATE
FOR SALE AT
PUBLIC AUCTION
AT THE
Real Estate Exchange,
Nos. 14 and 16 N. Seventh St.,
On Saturday, May 17, 1884,
COMMENCING
AT TEN O'CLOCK A. M.

No. 1. Lot in block 930 of St. Louis, fronting 125 feet on the southern line of Christy avenue, by a depth southwardly of 140 feet to an alley, and being composed of lots Nos. 22, 23, 24, 25 and 26 of block No. 1 of Beaumont's addition. Said lots being 155 feet 8 inches west from Jefferson ave.

No. 2. Lot 25x150 on the southern line of Washington avenue, 116 feet 6 1-2 inches west from Twenty-second street. Block 2009.

No. 3. Lot on the southern line of Washington avenue, consisting of all of block No. 2008 in the City of St. Louis, between Twenty-first and Twenty-second streets, fronting 388 feet on Washington avenue by a depth of 150 feet to St. Charles street, on which it fronts 338 feet 2 inches.

No. 4. Lot on southern line of

AMUSEMENTS.

BUFFALO BILL'S WILD WEST
The Great Realistic National Entertainment of America
MAY 3 TO 11,
JOCKEY CLUB PARK.
Admission, 50c; Children, 25c.

Gate open at 1 p. m. Performance begins at 2:30 p.m. The Franklin Avenue Line runs cars to the Grounds. The Narrow-Gauge Railroad will run excursion trains. A grand street parade will be given on the morning of May 3.

CARVER'S WILD WEST AT THE FAIR GROUNDS,
To-day and Sunday, Continuing for Five Days.
PROGRAMME.

1. GRAND INTRODUCTORY MARCH OF THE WILD WEST—Champion shot of the World—the Pawnee, Winnebago and Sioux Indians. Mexicans, Buffalo, Elk, Deer, Texas Steers, Spanish and Wild Broncho Ponies, Cow Boys, etc. 2. Exciting War between Omahas. Sioux and Pawnee Indians. 3. Showing the method of carrying dispatches before the telegraph. 4. A Startling and Soul-Stirring Attack upon the Mail Coach by Indians. Rescued by Cow Boys, "Evil Spirit of the Plains." 5. Indian on Foot vs. Indian on Pony, turning stake at 50 yards. 6. Champion Shot of the World—Shooting on Foot and on Horseback. 7. A Spirited and Lively Fight by Mounted Cow Boys. 8. Cow Boys' Fun. Bucking and Kicking Ponies. 9. Roping, Tying and Riding Wild Texas Steers. 10. Indian War and Scalp Dancing. 11. Capture, Torture and Death of a hunter by Savages of the Plain, and the Rescue by the Cow Boys, led by "Evil Spirit of the Plains."
To-day and Sunday, continuing for five days, from 3:30 to 5:30 p. m. Adults, 25c; Children, 15c.

AMUSEMENTS.

GRAND OPERA HOUSE.
MATINEE TO-DAY AND TO-NIGHT.
LEON & CUSHMAN'S
MINSTREL
COMEDY COMPANY,
Comprising a coterie of Selected Artists, whose well-directed efforts have met with extraordinary favor in a new comedy satire entitled

AUCTIONEERS.

HAGGERTY & DEWES,
General Auctioneers and Commission Merchants, 411 and 413 N. Broadway.
Special Trade Sale of 1,000 Cases

EVEN IN ITS SECOND SEASON, the Wild West was being touted by Burke as "realistic," and Cody's well-known visage was being turned into an icon. Buffalo Bill Museum and Grave, Golden, Colorado.

of the day, the acclaimed writer and raconteur Samuel L. Clemens (Mark Twain). He wrote a letter to Cody in which he said he had "enjoyed it thoroughly" and that it "stirred me like a war-song. Down to its smallest details, the show is genuine—cowboys, vaqueros, Indians, stage coach, costumes and all: it is wholly free from sham and insincerity; and the effects produced upon me by its spectacles were identical with those wrought upon me long ago by the same spectacles on the frontier."[30] Burke instinctively realized what a goldmine Twain's testimonial represented, and in an inspired pivot, turned that simple encomium into a commercial endorsement by forwarding the letter to many of his newspaper friends, who printed it verbatim. Later, he would incorporate it into the show program. It's the sort of celebrity-fueled pitch that is commonplace in our era, but in 1884, there had rarely been anything like it.[31]

How, exactly, did Burke manage to duplicate Twain's letter, or any of the other documents he was constantly sending off to editors? Here in the twenty-first century, perhaps seven generations of copying and transmission technology down the road from Burke (mimeograph, ditto machine, Xerox copy, fax, e-mail, text message, Twitter), marketers don't think twice about such things; but in the 1880s, it was a considerable challenge.

He could have used one of the "press exchanges" (today's wire services), such as the New York Associated Press, the Western Associated Press, or United Press, which would have transmitted the letter to the smaller papers by telegraph.[32] Throughout his decades with Buffalo Bill, Burke always gravitated to new technologies like this. For example, he embraced—perhaps even abused—the telegraph for personal correspondence. In winter 1886–1887, he enraged Nate Salsbury by sending all his scouting reports from London via telegraph instead of the far less expensive mail.

But the Twain letter ran 192 words, which would have made for an expensive telegram—the average (much shorter) telegram sent from San Francisco to New York in this era cost about $2.50—and with the Wild West still in the red in 1884, that expense would have been hard to justify.[33] Besides, there was no guarantee that the smaller papers along the route of the Wild West were going to pick up the story, or were even subscribing to the press exchanges, for that matter.

A slower and cheaper method would have been to rely on the newspapers to circulate the Twain letter themselves. From colonial days up through the middle of the nineteenth century, U.S. postal policy permitted newspapers to be sent through the mail for free. So most of the smaller papers subscribed to the larger papers and then freely copied material from them. The fact that the Twain letter appeared in newspapers over a relatively long period (more than six months) may indicate that this methodology was in use.

On the other hand, Burke had a huge personal network of editor friends and may have been inclined to reach out to at least some of them directly; with first class postage costing just two cents, that would have been an inexpensive, if still cumbersome and slow, solution. Of course, he would have needed multiple physical copies of the Twain letter. To get them, he might have relied on copy clerks to rewrite letters by hand, an age-old method still widely used in the late nineteenth century. Or he could have used the typewriter, a fairly new invention (1868) that could be paired up with carbon paper (commercialized earlier in the nineteenth century) to make at least a few copies. Alternatively, he might have paid to have Twain's letter set in type and run through a letter press or printing press. Or he could have used other new copying technologies, including a process invented in 1869 called "hectography," which used special aniline dyes in ink to create a master document that was then placed in a reusable pan of gelatin. The gelatin absorbed the dye and essentially created a mirror image of the document, so that a sheet of paper could then be pressed onto the gelatin pan, and the image would transfer with precision. One company that manufactured these "transfer tablets," J. R. Holcombe & Co. of Mallet Creek, Ohio, advertised them as "A Perfect Copying Process . . . Simplicity, Rapidity and Cheapness Combined. . . . Every Man His Own Printer." Their letter-size tablets sold for $4.50 and were said to be good for making fifty to one hundred copies of any document in fifteen minutes. "It is the greatest time, labor, and money saving article ever introduced" read the Holcombe ad.[34]

How Burke operated is not known, but the expanding array of options available to him and other press agents of the day was starting to make their job easier. The Twain letter was widely reproduced in papers like the *Wheeling Daily Intelligencer* (October 1, 1884), the *Daily Cairo (Ill.) Bulletin* (November 19), the *Memphis Daily Appeal* (November 23), and the *Montgomery (Ala.) Advertiser* (April 11, 1885). Thus, Twain became the first celebrity to provide unwitting fuel for Burke's marketing fire.

There would be others. Two years later, in 1886, Major Burke wrote to many of the military leaders with whom Cody had served, requesting what amounted to letters of commendation prior to the show's scheduled trip to Great Britain the following spring—where, it was assumed, praise from high commanders would elevate Cody's stature in the British mind and enable him to be presented to members of high society and even to the royal family.

In they came—from General William Tecumseh Sherman, Lieutenant General Phil Sheridan, Brigadier General Nelson Miles, Brigadier General George Crook, and many of the heroes of the Civil War and Indian wars. Typical of the messages was the one written by Brevet Major General Eugene A. Carr: "I take pleasure in saying that in an experience of about thirty years on the plains and in the mountains I have seen a great many guides, scouts, trailers, and hunters, and Buffalo Bill (W. F. Cody) is 'king of them all.' He has been with me in seven Indian fights, and his services have been invaluable."

Carr addressed his letter directly to Burke, but his use of Burke's very specific nomenclature—"Buffalo Bill (W. F. Cody)"—makes it clear that

CELEBRITY ENDORSEMENTS, including those of many military heroes actively solicited by Burke, were a new way to promote Cody and the Wild West. Buffalo Bill Center of the West, Cody, Wyoming; MS327.01.40.01.04.

the letter was solicited and carefully guided by the press agent. Indeed, most of the letters used very similar language: "I take pleasure in commending him," "I take pleasure in observing your success," "I take great pleasure in testifying to the very efficient service rendered by you," "I full, and with pleasure, indorse [*sic*] you as the veritable Buffalo Bill," and "I take great pleasure in recommending you to the public."[35] Clearly, the hand of a skilled publicist was at work here, one who could foresee the value of endorsements and manipulate some of the most powerful men in the land to say exactly what he wanted them to say. Burke and Cody even designed a poster to be used on the European tour showing Cody's image surrounded by those of all the gallant and admiring generals. The Major would also include their letters and photographs in Wild West programs and press materials for many years to come.[36]

As if the military commendations were not sufficiently impressive, Burke also capitalized on other celebrity appearances, converting them into implicit endorsements. Among other visitors to the show in 1886–1887—most of whom Burke likely greeted with exaggerated kindness and courtesy, before gossiping to the press about their attendance—were Elizabeth Custer, the great English stage actor Henry Irving, and Prince Dom Augusta of Brazil.[37]

Burke also had bigger game in his promotional gunsights: P. T. Barnum, with whom he had built an "intimate acquaintance" over dinners of pinfish at Bridgeport's Sterling House Hotel. To considerable fanfare, the seventy-six-year-old Barnum came into New York from Connecticut to see the Wild West, and Burke made a great fuss over the "fact" (specious at best) that the Wild West was the first competing entertainment Barnum had gone to see in forty years.[38] Barnum found the show highly entertaining and praised it to reporters.

Cody, for his part, clearly liked the comparison to Barnum. In 1883 he wrote to his sister that "the papers say I am the coming Barnum."[39] And in a later-life photo of Cody, taken in the hotel he built in Wyoming and named for his daughter Irma, a portrait of Barnum is clearly visible on the back wall.

It was apparently also Burke's brilliant endorsement handiwork that, on March 8, 1887, just three weeks before the Wild West was to set sail for England, resulted in Nebraska governor John M. Thayer commissioning Cody as aide-de-camp of his staff with the rank of colonel (one notch higher than Burke's own assumed title!). The civilian scout could use an honorary military title on his tour through Europe, and would do so for the rest of his life.[40]

The Wild West was an expensive show to produce. The payroll expanded rapidly from 200 to more than 450 people. Expenses included rental fees for the venues, railcars for transportation, and the daily food necessary to feed people and beasts (including, according to various reports, more than 250 dozen eggs, 400 chickens for a single meal, and 900 meals a day).[41] The production also included what Burke described as "an immense amount of paraphernalia such as tents, wagons, stage-coach, arms, ammunition, costumes, and all equipage necessary."[42]

And then there was the campaign to promote and market the show, including the huge bills for lithography and the bill-posting teams. With each passing season, the Wild West bill-posting operation grew more sophisticated. Much as with Barnum & Bailey, dedicated teams of bill posters traveled ahead of the show in elaborate, specially designed railroad cars, buying lumber, constructing billboards, leapfrogging each other to make

BILL-POSTING TEAMS—working here in Washington, Iowa, in 1909—often tried to cover everything in sight, including each other's posters. Buffalo Bill Museum and Grave, Golden, Colorado.

sure that every barn and shop window in every nearby town and hamlet was covered—and that no one had torn down a poster or pasted over it with a competing one after the first team left town. As many as eight thousand posters might go up in a two hundred-mile radius around each show, real estate for which the Wild West either traded free tickets (a custom known as "dead-heading") or paid between three and twelve cents apiece.[43]

The posters were made using state-of-the-art lithographic printing techniques by companies like A. Hoen of Baltimore (which was so successful that it remained in business until 1981). The standard one-sheet poster was large, at twenty-eight by forty-two inches, but was cleverly designed so that it could stand alone or be combined with up to twenty-seven other posters to form huge mosaics.

Burke and his team added another dimension to many of the posters by using richly saturated color artwork, heavy in western symbolism, some of which was likely created by the famous artists Frederic Remington and Charles Russell.[44] The Wild West posters were intended not just to draw a crowd, but to moralize, to tell a story, to pontificate. They used light, color, and design to show Cody in calm, heroic poses. They depicted Indians as noble and almost sad figures. They juxtaposed Buffalo Bill with historical figures such as Napoleon and Columbus. They used captions like "A Factor of International Amity." And they certainly attracted a lot of attention. "Far more of the public was introduced to the West through the proliferation of posters than was able to view Buffalo Bill's Wild West performances," noted authors R. L. Wilson and Greg Martin.[45]

All these expenses left the show on delicate financial footing for its first few years, and unfortunately this was compounded by the occasional tragedy. For example, several months into the second season, on December 9, 1884, the Wild West's riverboat sank near Rodney, Mississippi, killing most of the animals. Salsbury provided the funds to replace them, but the subsequent three-month stay at the World's Industrial and Cotton Centennial in New Orleans was hampered by forty-four straight days of rain. Cody became despondent, writing to Salsbury:

> My Dear Pard
>
> The cammels [*sic*] back is broken. This day I looked forward to as one to help us out, worked every possible means to make it a success—but, but God, Christ and the devil is against me. The

> morning opened bright. I started with a full parade. Thousands of people in the darned city. And we would surely have played to $2,000 had it not been so ordained that we should not. At 10-30 it clouded up all of a sudden and poured rain until 4pm. Then it cleared up again just as pleasant as before. It's plain to me. I can read it clearly. Fate if there is such a thing is against me. There is not one bit of use trying more. The longer we stick at this the worse off we are. The sooner we give this outfit away the better. I am thoroughly discouraged, I am a damned condemned Joner and the sooner you get clear from me the better for you. . . . [I am] disgusted with myself & the world. There is no heaven—if so it can stay there and be damned.
>
> Your Pard & take my advice & quit him
> Cody[46]

The Wild West closed out its run in New Orleans in spring 1885, uncertain about the future. It had generally filled the arenas in which it played, yet it still lost money. To survive they would have to produce more shows, in larger venues, with bigger crowds.

There was, however, hope on the horizon.

Beginning in 1885, the use of calcium flares would enable the Wild West to perform at night, when it would be easier to fill every seat. And with some help from John M. Burke, there would also be new attractions worth lighting up, for in the coming weeks, he signed both Annie Oakley and Sitting Bull to appear in the show.

Oakley, born Phoebe Ann Moses to a Quaker family in Ohio, was a petite woman possessed of preternatural marksmanship skills. As a small girl, using a sixteen-bore single-barrel muzzle-loader, she had bagged birds and rabbits in the fields near her home and soon turned to competitions and exhibitions in variety theaters and skating rinks. "The Peerless Wing Shot," she was called. But once she signed on with Buffalo Bill's Wild West, Burke dialed up the melodrama and added just enough intrigue and, perhaps, embellishment, to make her into a celebrity in her own right. According to his press materials, she shot enough game at the age of fourteen to pay off the mortgage on her father's house. Moreover, "At Tiffin, Ohio, she once shot a ten-cent piece held between the thumb and forefinger of an attendant, at a distance of 30 feet. In April 1884, she attempted to beat the best record made at balls thrown in the air, using a 22 cal. rifle. The best record was 979, made by Dr. [A. H.] Ruth. Miss Oakley used a Stevens 22 cal. rifle and broke 943." In February 1885, the press biography continued, she broke 4,772 tossed balls out of 5,000, and "besides her wonderful marksmanship, Miss Oakley is an accomplished housewife, as the neat and cheery appearance of her tent [attests]."[47] Apparently, glass balls could be broken, but gender barriers could not.

Sitting Bull, the famed Lakota chief and holy man who had led his warriors against Custer at the Little Big Horn, was by this time in his mid-fifties, living on the Standing Rock Reservation straddling the Dakotas; he knew that his fighting days were past. By 1884 he had seemingly come to terms with the changing world and went on a tour of twenty-five eastern cities. Cody had tried to recruit him for the Wild West that year but could not gain approval of the military agent overseeing Standing Rock, Major James McLaughlin. In 1885, Cody tried again. He sent his old scout friend and Wild West performer Major Frank North as an emissary to McLaughlin, trying to negotiate for Sitting Bull's participation. But after North died on March 15, Burke was sent in his place. During a five-week trip, the Major visited with many tribes, enlisted dozens of Indians for the show, and met with Sitting Bull at Standing Rock. The chief did not at first seem inclined to accept the offer, but Burke noticed a photograph of Annie Oakley in Sitting Bull's tent (they had met the previous year in St. Paul, Minnesota), and since she had also just joined the show, Burke used that as leverage to sign the chief to a contract on June 6. McLaughlin acceeded.

Burke always had a way with the Indians. He himself was perfectly at home living in tents and seeing the world through their eyes. He picked up a little of the Siouan languages, and found other ways to bridge the linguistic barrier.[48] And he bore a long scar on his cheek from some unspecified encounter, which may have helped establish his credibility with the Indians: Sitting Bull, for one, called him Big Chief Scar Face.[49] (Cody sometimes also referred to Burke as Old Scarface, although for him it was not a matter of respect but playful mockery: he teased the press agent that the only Indian he had ever killed was one on his grandfather's Delaware farm, whom he had worked to death. In 1908, when both Burke and Cody were in their sixties, Cody told a reporter that the scar had actually been the result of a disciplinary action when Burke was just a boy, but over the years the Major had grown so proud of his "duelmark" that "he would not have it eradicated for a million dollars."[50])

Yet, while Burke's treatment of the Indians may have been far more respectful than most people of his times, he also had an ulterior motive: he saw tremendous publicity value in their story.

Thus, en route from the reservations to Buffalo, New York, to meet up with the Wild West in summer 1885, braving violent storms and swollen streams with fifty-two Sioux and Pawnees and Sitting Bull in tow, Burke made a pointed effort to talk about his mission with every newspaper reporter he could find, generating extensive coverage. This culminated in a dramatic account in the *Buffalo Courier* by a reporter to whom Burke had apparently given an exclusive: the opportunity to ride in the coach with Sitting Bull as it rolled up to the driving park where Cody awaited. The reporter wrote,

> Major Burke went toward Buffalo Bill and shook him heartily by the hand. Said Burke: "I am here, governor. I've got him. Come and shake hands. He's a fine fellow. See, he is coming." Cody hesitated for a moment. At this time Sitting Bull, who had advanced several paces, also halted. There was a strange pause and then the famous redskin and the equally noted white hunter, pressed by the interpreter and Major Burke, advanced, and Buffalo Bill, drawing himself up and assuming a very striking and really handsome pose, held out his hand to the redskin warrior. They grasped hands. For several seconds they eyed each other. It was a truly dramatic spectacle and entirely unrehearsed in its striking effects. Drawn up at the inner fence opposite the grand stand were all the Indians, Mexicans, and cowboys of the "Wild West" show; outside of the track was lined with carriages, and the grand stand as well as the space for a long distance along the stretch was crowded with spectators, all watching with breathless interest the novel and interesting interview.

Cody then addressed the gathered throng in statesman-like fashion, saying in part,

> "I have never been insensible to the abstract rights that civilization, as our progress is called, has perhaps unconsciously trodden upon, and in time of peace I am strongly the red man's friend. The man who stands before you to-day has been a great warrior; his deeds, divested of our personal feelings to the victims of his success, occupy

> the blood-red pages of the nation's history. He, from his standpoint, fought for what he believed was right, and made a name for himself to be known forever. The man I now introduce you to is Sitting Bull, the Napoleon of the red race, who has journeyed thousands of miles to be present with us here to-day."[51]

Burke knew a good thing when he had one: he reprinted the article in the Wild West program.

Sitting Bull would remain with the show for just four months, spending most of his time sitting impassively—sneering, some people thought—and signing his name on photographs. (Already wise to the new ways of the world, he had shrewdly negotiated with Burke that he would receive all proceeds from the sale of his photographs and autographs, in addition to his fifty-dollar weekly salary.) Sitting Bull was surprised that there were so many beggars in this wealthy white man's world, and he gave away most of his earnings to indigent children who swirled about the camp, though he did spend some money on food, having developed a fondness for oyster stew and hard candy.[52]

But even in that short time, he became a huge attraction, and Burke opportunistically squeezed every drop of marketing value he could out of him.

He courted the press to write about Sitting Bull in every single town, and they did—though the Sioux chief was in many ways a prouder man than Cody and would not be "handled" in the same manner. When journalists pressed him about Custer and the Battle of the Little Big Horn, he steadfastly refused to answer. One reporter wrote that the chief "raised his hand and shook it warningly," saying through an interpreter, "That is another day. I fought for my people."[53]

Burke also arranged a "very impressive and solemn" ceremony in which Sitting Bull "adopted' Nate Salsbury as "Little White Chief."[54] He staged a photograph of Sitting Bull in full headdress and Cody in ornate show costume, standing side by side with their hands both braced against Cody's rifle; thousands of souvenir copies were sold, with the ingenious caption "Enemies in '76, Friends in '85." And even at the very end of the tour, Burke was undoubtedly the force behind an awkward meeting between Sitting Bull and his old battlefield nemesis Brevet Major General Eugene A. Carr, in the Southern Hotel in St. Louis; lo and behold, Cody walked in on the encounter with a group of reporters.[55]

It was all exceptionally clever and innovative communications work. There had never been a publicity campaign as sophisticated, as multidimensional, as the one John M. Burke unleashed in the early years of the Wild West, and neither the newspaper reporters nor the public fully knew what had hit them. Fueled by his efforts, the exhibition played to more than 1 million visitors in its 1885 tour and raked in more than one hundred thousand dollars in profits.[56]

By 1886, its fourth season, the Wild West was a raging success at the gate, often attracting fifteen thousand people twice each day to its shows at Madison Square Garden; "The Greatest Triumph Ever Known in the History of the City," its ads immodestly proclaimed.[57]

Part of the success was because the show had been enhanced and professionalized, outclassing every competitive form of entertainment. For example, an entirely new script was written and designed by noted dramatist Steele MacKaye for the run at Madison Square Garden, entitled the "Drama of Civilization." MacKaye outlined his meticulous and melodramatic stagecraft design in a letter to Salsbury on November 8, 1886, that described the opening of the show:

> 1st Each group of Indians—and separately each chief will be introduced
> 2nd The vacheros [*sic*]
> 3rd The soldiers
> 4th The cowboys
> 5th Cody by himself
>
> The introductions will be managed in this manner.
>
> The grand curtains in the Proscenium will part—just wide enough to admit each group as it is introduced to emerge and dash up to the grand stand—where each of them give a salute—and parting in the centre suddenly disappear directly under the seats—as they go under seats they ride back underneath there and form in platoon—behind the curtain—When Cody is introduced he dashes madly down toward the grand stand—salutes—and says "Ladies and Gentlemen, permit me to introduce the equestrian portion of the Wild West exhibition." Then he turns and gives the word—instantly the luminous curtains

> are drawn fully up on each side—and the whole force of the Wild West is in platoon four deep—They ride like an avalanche toward Cody as though this would trample him down—Stop short salute Cody and dividing into two divisions then fall into single file ride quickly through the arena making beautiful spiral lines in opposition to each other—and disappear. As the whole force dashes forward the curtains fall behind them—and as they divide on each side Cody dashes to the central point of the curtains—turns and surveys the spiral movements of the forces and as they disappear—Cody salutes the public—and backing his horse exits between the curtains. This finished Richmond [Frank Richmond, the announcer] tells the story of the First Act—and the performance begins.
>
> In this first act I shall show even the glow worms in the forest at night—and as the dawn creeps in the malarial mists of the winds will appear hanging over the pools of water—and evaporating before the eyes of the public in the most mysterious manner. I desire to illustrate fully all the obstacles to the white man's advance that exist in the wilderness—even the toads and frogs and katy-dids—and crickets—will be heard.[58]

MacKaye's sets for the Wild West included elaborate painted backdrops by noted artist and cartoonist Matt Morgan; a wind machine strong enough to blow the Deadwood Stagecoach across the arena; and lighting effects to simulate a western cyclone. The preparations cost sixty thousand dollars.[59]

But at the heart of the Wild West's ascent into profitability were Major Burke's visionary promotional efforts.

He established the brand of Buffalo Bill's Wild West (Cody had been granted a copyright for the name and script the previous June) and constructed a halo around it with celebrity endorsements. He took an already-famous man, built up his image, and elevated him to mythic status. By combining information and imagery in a media relations charm offensive, he left the old criticism of Cody the stage actor in the dust. Burke used the latest technology to distribute information quickly through the media to the masses, and he helped engineer a broad and sophisticated poster campaign that burned Wild West show imagery and subliminal heroic messages into the national consciousness (see plate 6).

Most remarkably, Burke transformed the old forward-looking view of the West into a new backward-looking one, addled with misty-eyed nostalgia, and he strategically positioned the Wild West as an educational exhibition, a show with a message, an instructive narrative of a time and place that were no more. After all, by 1886 Custer and Crazy Horse were long dead, as were Billy the Kid and Jesse James; before the year was out, Doc Holliday and even Ned Buntline would be gone, too. The gunfight at the OK Corral was a fading memory. The Great Western Cattle Trail was shut down, and Dodge City was becoming a sleepy little town. Sitting Bull was retired, a darling of the media, and Geronimo was about to be subdued. The West was all but gone. But the Wild West was very much alive.

Larger than any circus, more popular than any stage performance, more innovative than any spectator sport, Buffalo Bill's show had no precedent—and therefore no blueprint for how to market it. No one had ever done this before. Burke invented and improvised as he went.

In July 1886, for example, he placed ads in New York newspapers offering free show tickets for all newsboys and shoeshine boys who would meet the ferry from Manhattan to Staten Island, where the Wild West was performing. Buffalo Bill's sister Julia Cody Goodman estimated that 1,500 boys responded; they received a free round-trip ferry ticket, a toy boat, a brown bag lunch, a Wild West ticket, and the opportunity to meet Buffalo Bill after the show—in the process, adding layers of heroic patina to his already golden image, and creating a small army of Wild West promoters around the city.[60]

Another of his innovations was the press kit.

That fall and winter, as the show prepared for its first trip abroad, Burke sailed ahead to England to make arrangements. The Wild West arena was being built on grounds adjacent to the American Exhibition in Earl's Court, West Brompton, where Queen Victoria's Golden Jubilee would be celebrated. The arena would be capable of seating twenty thousand and accommodating twenty thousand more in standing-room or "open air" slots, along with corrals, stables, barns, a huge field kitchen, and a massive landscaping background built with seventeen thousand train-car loads of rock and earth meant to evoke the American West.[61] Finding construction way behind schedule, Burke took over daily management of the project, making twice-daily visits and bribing workers with show tickets to encourage them to move faster. But in between, he began to lay the marketing groundwork in London by visiting with newspaper editors and leaving behind a kit complete with background material, biographies, stories, photographs, or "cuts" (engraved blocks or plates for making images, as in "woodcuts" or "electrotype cuts"), and this list of the "15 Good Reasons to Visit Buffalo Bill's Wild West," which had first appeared in a Wild West program the previous year:

1. Over 1 million people have set you the example.
2. Because it is a living picture of life on the frontier.
3. It is an opportunity afforded your family but once in a lifetime.
4. See how cowboys, Indians and Mexicans live.
5. You will see buffalo, elk, wild horses and a multitude of curiosities.
6. You will see an Indian village transplanted from the plains.
7. You will see the most wonderful riders the world can produce.
8. You will see the greatest marksmen in America.
9. You will see Indian warfare depicted in true colours.
10. You will see the attack on the Deadwood stagecoach.
11. You will see a method of capturing wild horses and cattle.
12. You will see a buffalo hunt in all its realistic detail.
13. You will see your neighbours there in full force.
14. You will see Buffalo Bill (Hon. W.F. Cody)!
15. You will see an exhibition which has been witnessed and endorsed by President Arthur and his cabinet, General Sheridan and staff, Generals Cook, Miles, Sherman, Carr, etc. and tens of thousands of well informed people in every walk of life.[62]

The spellings, of course, were Anglicized; Burke was always extremely conscious of playing to the local audience.

Burke also helped to create a massive bill-posting effort, the likes of which the old town had never seen. Indeed, so ubiquitous and brazenly *American* was the posting effort that it elicited commentary from the humor magazine *Punch* ("At present we don't know much about 'Buffalo Bill,' but one thing is certain, that the Buffalo Bill-poster is doing its work uncommonly well") and inspired the *London Globe* to write verse that included these lines:

> I may walk it, or 'bus it, or hansom it; still
> I am faced by the features of Buffalo Bill.
> Every hoarding is plastered, from East-end to West,
> With his hat, coat, and countenance, lovelocks and vest.
> Plunge in City or fly suburbwards—go where I will,
> Bill and Bill's 'Billy-ruffians' appear on the bill.[63]

BEFORE THE OPENING IN ENGLAND in 1887, Burke (*center*) took charge of the preparations for the arena at Earl's Court. Buffalo Bill Museum and Grave, Golden, Colorado.

When Cody and his troupe set sail for London from New York aboard the ship *State of Nebraska* on March 31, 1887, thousands of well-wishers lined the piers to see them off—the same sort of media-whipped hysteria that seventy-seven years later would welcome The Beatles coming in the other direction. Burke had learned how to do this with the shoeshine boy promotion the previous year (although, of course, Barnum had done it years earlier with Jenny Lind).

Meanwhile, British papers were abuzz with Burke-stoked anticipation. "It will be curious to learn how an Indian will be affected by *mal de mer*," wrote the *London Observer*, "and whether the stoicism which enables him to die by torture unmoved will suffice to enable him to resist the horrible qualms of seasickness."[64]

Similarly, with the *State of Nebraska* still four days from port, the *London Daily News* wrote:

> There is considerable speculation about the Red Indians composing Buffalo Bill's troupe. On the presumption that Nature never

> intended that interesting race for the functions of the mariner, it is thought possible that strange things may result from the voyage. Will the brave warriors exchanging the wigwam for the forecastle perish miserably from sickness? Will they rise with a whoop of vengeance, flourishing the tomahawk as they hold onto the weather shrouds, and scalp Jack Tar for putting the indignity upon them?[65]

(In reality, other than some queasiness, the first-time mariners—of whom Cody was one—managed just fine.)

Upon arrival, Burke unveiled a deft bit of stagecraft: arranging for an American-flag-flying tugboat to meet the ship in the Gravesend harbor with some special guests on board, including a band playing the "Star Spangled Banner"—and, of course, a handful of reporters. From there, a train he had commissioned, called the Buffalo Bill Special, would transport the VIPs into London and the show cast and apparatus to the Midland Railway Depot adjoining the fairgrounds. "Trivial as these details may appear at first sight," Burke would write, "the rapidity with which the Wild West had transported its materials from dock to depot, and depot to ground, had an immense effect upon the people of London. A number of notable visitors present, especially the representatives of the press, expressed great astonishment at the enterprise of the Americans, and communicated that feeling throughout London."[66]

Burke's smart and sophisticated marketing campaign was under way. It was still more than five weeks before the exhibition would open, but clearly the press agent had already succeeded in heating things up to a rolling boil.

Upon Cody's first visit to see the arena construction site, the workers stopped what they were doing to take a look at the larger-than-life figure ("The interest evinced by the British workmen in my presence detracting somewhat from their attention to business, caused us to retire after a brief inspection," he noted).[67] Then with each passing day, as Cody made the rounds from St. James to Belgravia, in parlors, salons, and social clubs—even dining with Lord and Lady Randolph Churchill and their thirteen-year-old son, Winston—Burke was there to fan the glowing embers of celebrity.[68] The *Times of London* wrote that "Buffalo Bill has found himself the hero of the London season. Notwithstanding his daily engagements and his punctual fulfillment of them, he finds time to go everywhere, to see everything and be seen by the whole world."[69] (On one such occasion, leaving the Columbia Club in a coach, Burke, with his sombrero, long hair, and western waistcoat, was mistaken for Cody and gleefully tossed half-pence to the "street arabs."[70])

This was, said British historian Alan Gallop in his 2001 book *Buffalo Bill's British Wild West*, probably Victorian London's first encounter with someone like Burke: "Public relations consultants, press agents, promoters and spin-doctors were unheard of in England in 1887. . . . They admired his brash American business methods and ability to come up with fresh and exciting stories about Buffalo Bill and the Wild West every day, everything from a small tit-bit [*sic*] of information which would make a paragraph or two to a front page lead story, already prepared for a newspaper 'incognito' by the pen of Major John M. Burke."[71]

During setup and rehearsal, dignitaries occasionally visited the Wild West, which played right into Burke's strategy of celebrity endorsement. Henry Irving, the actor, stopped by, having been so impressed by the show in New York that he even promoted its arrival in the British press. The Wild West would "take the town by storm," he predicted in the *Pall Mall Gazette*, and he praised its "graphic vividness and scrupulosity of details," including the buffalo, which he called "snorting monsters with bloodshot eyes." Burke's assistance was evident in Irving's article, which closely mimicked the biography Burke had penned for Cody in the Wild West program.[72]

Other actors visited, and so did some members of Parliament. On April 28, then-three-time former British prime minister William Gladstone came to Earl's Court for a visit and chatted with Lakota chief Red Shirt; magically, their conversation ended up being reprinted in the *London Daily Telegraph*.[73] And when the Prince and Princess of Wales accepted an invitation to a special preview performance on May 5, along with a coterie of royals, Burke not only alerted the newspapers but also transformed news of their interest in the show into endorsements that were later incorporated into posters and broadsides.[74]

Indeed, much as twenty-first-century marketers sometimes use the attendance of the president and his family or certain prominent lawmakers as publicity tools (the Chicago 2016 Olympic Committee famously persuaded President and Mrs. Obama to accompany them to the International Olympic Committee presentation in Copenhagen), Burke instinctively knew that distinguished visitors were a golden ticket for the Wild West. The requests for free passes arrived daily on calling cards and embossed letterhead ("Dear Colonel Cody: The Grand Duke & Duchess . . . of Russia, the

THE DEADWOOD STAGECOACH was a centerpiece of Buffalo Bill's show, a rickety symbol of the fast-fading West. Burke is third from left, just behind Cody's right shoulder. Buffalo Bill Center of the West, Cody, Wyoming; P.69.2041.1.

Duke & Duchess of Edinburgh and their suite will attend the 'Wild West' Exhibition this afternoon. Will you have the kindness to retain boxes for them."[75]). Burke kept detailed records of their visits, published a brochure of "Distinguished Personages" who had come to the Wild West, and had lithographs designed, too.

Queen Victoria came to see the show at Earl's Court on May 11, just two days after it had officially opened, and forty days later she was treated to a command performance on the grounds of Windsor Castle, with an audience that included the kings of Denmark, Greece, Belgium, and Saxony; the crown princes of Germany, Austria, Sweden, and Norway; and many other members of the European royalty in town to celebrate her Jubilee. Their names, alone, would provide Burke with sufficient fodder for weeks of newspaper articles, many of which he cabled back to the United States, where they were immediately reprinted in U.S. papers. But during this performance, two other magical marketing moments occurred, and Burke didn't miss them.

First, the queen rose and bowed at the presentation of the American flag—a relatively simple gesture that Burke would elevate into a grandiose act of statesmanship. "Then there arose such a genuine heart-stirring American yell as seemed to shake the sky," said Burke. "For the first time in history since the Declaration of Independence a sovereign of Great Britain saluted the Star-Spangled Banner."[76] Unsurprisingly, a Wild West poster would soon commemorate this event with an added quotation from the *Times of London:* "Buffalo Bill has done his part in bringing America and England together."[77]

Then, after the kings of Denmark, Greece, Belgium, and Saxony all joined the Prince of Wales for a ride in the Deadwood Stagecoach, with Buffalo Bill driving, Cody quipped that although he had "held four kings" before, "four kings and the Prince of Wales makes a royal flush, such as no man ever held before."[78] This story, too, took on a life of its own and was retold many times and in many versions—all because John M. Burke had the insight to understand the marketing power of celebrity.[79]

The Wild West was a spectacular success in Great Britain. The crowds were vast. During that first run, it played more than three hundred London shows in front of a total of 1 million people—helping to rescue the second-rate American Exhibition at Earl's Court.[80] As Nate Salsbury told the *New York Sun* in January 1888, "There has not been a day since we opened in England that has not been prosperous."[81]

The press coverage was everything that Burke had engineered it to be. "The magnificent appearance of Buffalo Bill, and the almost legendary stories of his valour, have made him one of the most popular personages in contemporary American history," wrote the *London Magnet* in a fairly representative article.[82] The *Sporting Life* said it was "one of the most signal successes of recent years. . . . It is new, it is brilliant, it is startling, it will 'go!'"[83] Back in the United States, the magazine *Puck* tub-thumped:

> The success of "our own" Buffalo Bill—W. F. Cody—in England is very gratifying to his thousands of admirers on this side. There was more truth than many imagined in his reply to the inquiry:
>
> "What are you doing in England?"
>
> "Chiefly playing poker with Duchesses."

> The English nobility quickly "cottoned to" Buffalo Bill because they recognized that he belonged to a higher order than their own—Nature's nobility.[84]

After London, the Wild West headed for Manchester and the Midlands. There, Burke staged another rib roast for reporters, in which they were served grub steak, Boston baked pork and beans, "Arizona John Relishes"—and were fed a steady diet of his frontier mythology and balderdash, which they dutifully reported as their own. "Not less instructive than interesting is the big show," wrote the *Manchester Courier and Lancashire General Advertiser*, "for it gives one an insight into the habits and customs of the aboriginal inhabitants of the Far West, and furnishes the visitor with information as to the usages of frontier life, and almost from the very realism of the scenes presented makes one feel that he is thousands of miles away on the trackless prairie, in the mining camp, or in the depths of the primeval forest."[85] Best of all, news of the show's popularity was eagerly reported back home and made American chests swell with pride.

For example, the stacked headlines in column one of the *St. Paul Daily Globe* on April 29, 1887, went from "Awful Loss of Life" (describing Australian boating accidents that had killed more than seven hundred people) right to "Gladstone Visits the Wild West Show and Has a Chat with a Sioux Indian" and "Buffalo Bill to Be Entertained at a Swell Dinner in London To-Day."

The *Peninsula Enterprise* in tiny Accomac, Virginia, among others, reprinted a note from a *New York World* columnist observing that Cody was already as well known to the masses in London as the queen. "You could not pick up in the most obscure quarter of London any one so ignorant as not to know who and what he is. His name is on every wall. His picture is in nearly every window."[86]

The *New York Times*, under the headline "Buffalo Bill Happy," reprinted a letter that Cody had written to an old "chum," Colonel William Ray, in which he described the London run. "I have captured this country from the Queen down—am doing to the tune of $10,000 a day. Talk about show business! There never was anything like it ever known, and never will be again, and with my European reputation you can easily guess the business I will do when I get back to my own country."[87]

Another good friend, General William T. Sherman, wrote to Cody, "Our papers have kept us well 'posted,'" and declared in another letter,

"You have caught one epoch of the world's history, have illustrated it in the very heart of the modern world—London—and I want you to feel that on this side of the water we appreciate it."[88]

Then, like waves bouncing back and forth across the Big Pond, the British press began to pick up on the American reporting of the British reception for the Wild West—proving just how small the transatlantic cable had made the world. The *Pall Mall Gazette* wrote, "Nothing (says the New York *Evening Post*) can well be odder than the attention paid in England to 'Buffalo Bill. . . . ' In fact, he has had a far more flattering reception than any foreigner without official rank or antecedents."[89]

This was all part of Burke's grand plan. He was always looking for new adornments to hang onto Buffalo Bill's Wild West to make it more popular, more authentic, more interesting. He now had, effectively, a royal imprimatur and the affectionate embrace of the world's most staid bastion of high culture—all validating the emotional, promotional appeal of a moribund time and place.

The Wild West departed England on May 4 amid send-off crowds so large that a police escort was required. They returned to the United States triumphant, arriving aboard the *Persian Monarch* with flags of all nations rippling in the wind, Cody on the captain's bridge with his long hair fluttering, and the Indians decked in their colorful outfits along the railing. Burke, who had traveled home early, was there on a guide boat to call out a traditional Indian greeting of "How koolah! How! How!" The *New York World* reported, "The harbor probably has never witnessed a more picturesque scene than that of yesterday."[90]

7

EVOLUTION OF A MARKETING VIRTUOSO

"The vandal hands of John Burke"

It is not fulsome adulation to say that the newspapers only honor themselves in honoring Major Burke, and they, knowing it, inevitably place their columns at his command. Reminiscence, history, anecdote, story fall from his lips in as graceful stream as ever water flowed from a fountain, and they are eagerly caught up by the editors and repeated in print in the genuine and generous effort to let their readers share in the "feast of reason and flow of soul."

Whiting Allen, *Wild West Route Book* (1896)

Although Erastina had briefly housed the Wild West in summer 1886 and would later become a resort and eventually a posh neighborhood called Mariners Harbor, in 1888 it was still just a large patch of vacant land on New York's Staten Island. But for six weeks that summer, it was transformed into another crucible for experiments in promotional alchemy by John M. Burke, which were growing ever more sophisticated, nuanced, and effective.

Now flush with cash, the Wild West built four miles of railroad track to reach Erastina, brought in portable grandstands and electric generators that would soon become part of its retinue, and operated sixteen steamboats in New York Harbor to get fans there. It was a Muhammad-to-the-Mountains strategy, but it worked: thirty thousand people turned out on Memorial Day for the opening.[1]

Having hit on a successful marketing formula, Burke now had plenty of momentum and a friendly American press corps hungry for copy. "BUFFALO BILL'S DAZZLER," blared the *New York Herald*, and (no doubt to the delight of the man it called "the big hearted, enthusiastic manager of the Wild West") it described the show in vivid detail:

> On came the Indians, dashing wildly from the corral a third of a mile off to the grand stand in splendid fashion. Here were the Ogallallas [*sic*], the Brule Sioux, the Arapahoes, the Cheyennes, the Detached Sioux and their chiefs, Yellow Hand, Black Face, Blue Hand, Spotted Eagle and the singularly noble featured Red Shirt. Many of the braves wore nothing but paint, feathered head dresses and breech cloths. They were all scored, seamed and bedizened [decorated gaudily] in the most savagely picturesque manner. On they came fiercely, grandly, amid the cheers and yells of the white and colored spectators. It was the finest display of Indians by long odds ever seen by the inhabitants of New York.[2]

Cody had achieved a level of fame that accompanied him everywhere. The *New York World* reported, "Buffalo Bill is probably the best known man in New York City. Wherever he goes he is recognized and pointed out by the crowds." Riding in an omnibus from East 24th Street across the city,

> all along the route on the east side children recognized the gallant scout and cheered him lustily. Some of them ran after the vehicle for entire blocks and shouted as they ran. Heads were popped out of windows—pretty girls paused to exchange glances, and workingmen with their tin buckets in hand nudged each other and said "That's him!" as the omnibus rolled by. It was an ovation all along the line. And Col. Cody bore it all with that quiet, gentle modest [*sic*] which is so becoming to him.[3]

Still, even if there was less need for Burke to build awareness of Cody's name, the press agent continued to cultivate the image that he had worked so hard to create. He meticulously tended to Cody's reputation, working on a new version of his autobiography and constantly scanning the newspapers from around the country for bad reviews or words of disparagement, which Burke always countered with a pointed letter to the editor. When Annie Oakley defected to appear in several others shows (such as the similar-sounding Comanche Bill Wild West and Pawnee Bill's Historical Wild West Exhibition and Indian Encampment) in 1888 and 1889—a potentially large blow to the Wild West—Burke merely responded by creating posters that urged people to "Wait for the big show. Buffalo Bill is coming."[4] And, always mindful of the powerful imagery of the changing West, at the end of the show season in October 1888, Burke joined Cody and Salsbury in taking a group of seventy-five show Indians to Washington, D.C., to meet President Grover Cleveland and smoke a peace pipe at the Bureau of Indian Affairs.[5]

Back in his beloved homeland, John M. Burke, U.S.A., also began to undergo a transformation. Now in his forties, and nearly as closely associated with the West as was Cody, Burke started to look the part. He had grown his hair long, like Cody's, though he usually kept it pinned up under his sombrero. (At Windsor Castle, apparently, he showed no such modesty; Salsbury facetiously reported, "Major Burke let his hair down, and we knew the afternoon was bound to be a success, for whenever the Major let his hair down the world stood in awe."[6]) Around the show, Burke dressed in buckskins and high boots, like Cody's, and began to supplement his droopy mustache with flying-buttress whiskers that would later become the subject of an entire newspaper article in the *Richmond Times Dispatch* ("The queerest bunch of whiskers that ever sprouted from the human face," they were called. "They grow out from the side of his face, shoot upward, then downward, and then start over again, cutting the pigeon wing on the bias before they turn backward to seek their couch for the night."[7])

When he wasn't traveling out ahead of the show, Burke took up residence in a tent in the encampment, just like Cody and Oakley and the Indians. It was thus not unusual, and not unwelcomed, for this oversize man with the oversize personality to be thought of as a real westerner (as, for example, the *New York Times* did in 1901, referring to him as both a "native of Indian Territory" and "fond of his prairie descent"[8]) or even to be mistaken for Cody himself—which, according to the press agent Dexter Fellows, "was an episode of infinite enjoyment for the Major." It was, perhaps, all part of what Louisa Cody called Burke's "blind adoration" for her husband, and Fellows agreed. "His emulation of Cody did not spring from vanity. Actually he adored the Colonel with all the intensity of a high-school boy at the shrine of an athletic hero. Anyone making the slightest disparaging remark about his idol immediately felt Burke's displeasure."[9]

And yet, despite his western affectations, Burke easily shifted back into the cultivated comforts of the East. Outside of the show, he "always appeared to be the picture of sartorial perfection," said Fellows. He wore a Prince Albert coat, striped pants, and, as Fellows described it, not a shirt but "a false white bosom of starched linen, and attached to the sleeves of his undershirt were white cuffs." (The *St. Paul Daily Globe* concurred, saying, "Excepting his broad brimmed white felt hat, he dresses in the height of fashion"—to which Burke replied, "I suppose that hat looks odd and attracts attention [but] I am independent enough to wear what I please.")[10] He usually sported a large diamond horseshoe pin on his cravat. He checked into fine hotels, smoked his "seegars" in the lobby while palling around with an ever-present circle of friends, ordered terrapin soup, and engaged bartenders in arguments about the best way to prepare a mint julep. He liked to pop into newspaper offices, often late at night, and hold court with the editors and cub reporters, regaling them with stories of the road and flattering them with compliments about how much their town had grown since his last visit.[11] And even if the office were just around the corner, he would always hail a carriage to get there. "He hated to walk," said Fellows. "It wasn't that he was in a hurry, for should the driver urge his nag into anything but the most gentle jog, the Major would stick his head out the window and shout: 'Slow down! We're not going to a fire!'"[12]

During the offseason, he would frequently return to the Washington home of Colonel and Mrs. Allison Nailor, or to a room in Joe Schmitt's Hotel on the southeast corner of Union Square in New York, where in shirtsleeves he would drink beers in the lobby while sitting at the head of a table full of old-crony reporters, actors, sculptors, press agents, and diamond merchants. Here, he was no longer Arizona John, or the Major, but simply Jack.[13]

For now, though, there was little time for Burke to enjoy himself. Salsbury, ever analytical and meticulous, had concluded that the best strategy for the Wild West was to go where the people were. Hence, just as he had booked their time in Britain to coincide with Queen Victoria's Golden Jubilee, he had arranged their debut on the Continent to align with the Exposition Universelle, a world's fair marking the centennial of the start of the French Revolution, which would feature many bold innovations. Already, Gustave

Eiffel's miraculous feat of ironwork engineering was rising nearly one thousand feet above the Champ de Mars—"the tallest edifice ever erected by man," he boasted.[14] And with more than sixty thousand exhibits, including electrical displays and Edison's multilingual phonographs, the fair promised to be perhaps the best-attended event in world history. Salsbury committed the Wild West to a five-month run in Paris, followed by an extended tour into Southern France, Spain, Italy, Germany, Austria, and Britain.

Burke understood the inherent appeal that the famous Buffalo Bill and the Indians would have for the French, but he was not going to rely on reputation alone to do his bidding. So in preparation for the trip, he decided that he would learn French.

In the months leading up to the troupe's departure in April 1889, Burke toted around a French primer, studying it every day while he sat at French restaurant tables in Union Square; aboard the horse cars, elevated railroads, and steamboats he took to get around New York; and for an hour every night in his hotel room. "I'm determined to speak pretty good French when we open in Paris," he told a reporter who happened to see him with his French book at a restaurant. "I dream in French, I think in French, and inside of three months I'll wager that I'll parley vous as well as any ordinary Frenchman."[15] He succeeded, at least to a degree, and was soon conversant enough to be able to listen in on debates in the Chamber of Deputies in Paris and write sonnets in French.

As they had done in Britain, the Wild West's advance advertising crew arrived early in Paris and began plastering posters all over town. Some of them featured Cody's image, and simply proclaimed—with the confidence of a brand that had been well-marketed—"Je Viens" (I am coming). At first, this seemed like quite a novelty. Emma Bullet, a correspondent for the *Brooklyn Daily Eagle*, observed that "the immense painted posters all over the city to advertise Buffalo Bill—his portraits pasted all in a row, many times larger than natural; the cowboys on their wild horses; the Indians looking very savage—amuse the Parisians immensely. It is something new."[16] Some of the journalists-cum-cultural-arbiters sniffed. "Have we had enough of this Buffalo Bill for the past fifteen days?" asked one. But *Le Temps* pooh-poohed the dissent: "Eh bien! All that ingenious and bold American advertising enterprise has proved to be as honest as our tame [publicity] ever was. Nothing has been pictured or said too much."[17] Burke was beginning to unleash his modern marketing methods on the world.

BY 1905, when the Wild West returned to Paris, the publicity team was large enough to warrant its own office. Burke is fourth from right. Buffalo Bill Center of the West, Cody, Wyoming; FYIEWBB.037.2.

Beyond that, Burke's team seems to have had an influence on fashion and merchandising. Many observers noted the fact that western American gear started showing up in Parisian stores as interest in the Wild West began to mount. Burke himself would later reflect, "It became a fad to introduce curios and bijouterie from the American plains and mountains. Buffalo robes of Indian tanning, bear-skins embroidered with porcupine quills, and mats woven in redskin camps became fashionable; while lassos, bows and arrows, Mexican bridles and saddles, and other things from the American borderland became most popular as souvenirs."[18]

The stage was set. Burke joined 218 cast members of the Wild West when they set sail on April 27, 1889—and once again, he orchestrated a glittering send-off spectacle that was attended by many friends (including the lawyer John Dos Passos, father of the future novelist of the same name; Canadian journalist and land developer Erastus Wiman, who had lent his name to the Staten Island grounds—Erastina—on which the Wild West had enjoyed such a successful 1888 season; but not General William T. Sherman, who was supposed to be there until his daughter would not let him go out in the rain) and was well covered by the media.[19] "The cowboy band thumped away vigorously at 'A Life on the Ocean Wave,'" wrote the *Chicago Tribune,* "while the steamship *Persian Monarch* backed out into the stream this afternoon with the whole 'Wild West' on board. Col. Cody himself stood on the bridge, his big hat in his hand and his long hair glistening with the rain. The band played, the cowboys yelled, the Indians ki-yied, and the dripping crowds cheered. Buffalo Bill waved his hat in a comprehensive farewell to everybody, and the steamer started for Havre."[20]

Twelve days later, Burke's team coordinated an almost equally grand reception on the other side, with a chartered ship full of French reporters and Moet et Chandon to greet the *Monarch* in the harbor, as well as a press banquet that night.

On opening day in Paris, President Marie François Sadi Carnot of France was among the ten thousand spectators at the Wild West, and just as Burke had scripted it, the newspapers launched in with almost daily coverage.

Of course, the Major was often hard at work behind the scenes. In the second week, Burke donned a tricolored handkerchief, reminiscent of the French flag, while addressing a group of reporters. On June 10, he was with a group of celebrities (including Cody, Oakley, and the Prince and Princess of Wales) who were among the first to ascend the Eiffel Tower; one of the cowboys pinned a lithograph of Cody on the tower's lightning rod. One month later, on Bastille Day, July 14, Burke led a group of Wild West Indians back up the tower. Newspapers quoted one of the Indians, Red Shirt, as saying, "If people look so little to us up here, how very much smaller they must seem to One [Wakantanka] who is up higher."[21]

This tactic—the ironic incongruity of taking Native Americans to the temples of high culture—was one of Burke's favorites. He had used it frequently in America (Indians go through tunnels, Indians shop in department stores) because he knew these peculiar meetings of Old World and New would generate a lot of ink. Burke would later write that these dramatic encounters reinforced the educational component of the Wild West; the show was a "civilizing" influence on the "savages," and they in turn were a powerful symbol of the honor, nobility, and tradition that were being sacrificed in society's headlong dash toward the future.

Europe presented many new opportunities for the Major's didacticism. So Burke had the Indians photographed on the gondolas of Venice. He staged a wide shot of them in Naples with Mount Vesuvius in the

MOUNT VESUVIUS looms in the background of the Wild West arena in Naples in 1890. Buffalo Bill Museum and Grave, Golden, Colorado.

background. Always the Indians were dressed in their full native regalia, instead of the dull pants, vests, and shirts that had become their everyday clothes—all the more to emphasize the contrasts, attract attention from the public, and generate press coverage.

The more majestic the setting, the more Burke hyperventilated. He brought them to the Colosseum in Rome and later wrote what he undoubtedly said aloud at the time to anyone who would listen: "The stately ruin seemed silently and solemnly to regret that its famed ancient arena was too small for this modern exhibition of the mimic struggle between that civilization born and emanating from 'neath its very walls, and a primitive people who were ne'er dreamed of in Rome's world-conquering creators' wildest flights of vivid imaginings."[22] Standing in the amphitheater in Verona, built by Diocletian in A.D. 290, he cried out, "Hoary antiquity and bounding youth kiss each other under the sunny Italian skies!"[23] And posing for a photograph with a group of show Indians at the statue of Columbus in Barcelona, he pompously pronounced, "On this very spot Christopher Columbus landed from his caravels upon his return after discovering America." Pointing toward Columbus he added, "There stands our advance agent, four hundred years ahead of us."[24]

The Barcelona photo was not picked up by the press, but the opportunity to play out this stunt had clearly been taking shape in Burke's mind for some time. In publicity materials he created for the Spanish tour, Burke highlighted the irony of the Indians discovering Columbus's roots nearly four hundred years after he had discovered theirs.[25] And in Nate Salsbury's unpublished memoirs, he recalled traveling to Barcelona in advance of the show to make arrangements and being met by Burke on a small boat in Barcelona harbor:

> As the boat neared the shore at a snails [*sic*] pace, Burke suddenly jumped to his feet, and taking off his hat he fixed his enraptured gaze on the monument of Columbus. . . . In spite of the uncomfortable surroundings I could not help laughing at the droll figure he cut, with his long hair trailing down his back and a miniature ocean streaming over his upturned face. . . . After a few minutes of this pantomime, I yelled at him a question as to why he was making such a blankety blank ass of himself. With the fine scorn inherited from a race of Irish kings curling his upper lip he said:—"Is it possible that you see nothing to pay homage to in that beautiful counterpart of your best friend in this country? . . . Damn this utilitarian age of money grubbers. Oh, man without a soul, you should go down on your knees in adoration of the man that statue typifies. . . . Because he has been your ADVANCE AGENT FOR THE LAST FOUR HUNDRED YEARS."[26]

Burke also carefully prepped the Indians for a visit to the Vatican in March 1890, on the twelfth anniversary of Pope Leo XIII's coronation. "For a week before this day," recalled Salsbury, "John Burke, who is a devout Catholic, had worked on the Indians to impress them with the solemnity of the occasion we were about to assist in celebrating. He impressed them with the idea that they were going to see the Representative of God on Earth, and to those of them who had been under Catholic instruction at the Reservation, the coming event was of great interest."[27]

The event elicited extraordinary coverage in the newspapers back home. "[A] tremendous rush for tickets to the Vatican to-day," observed the *Salt Lake Herald*. "A curious juxtaposition," acknowledged the *Richmond Dispatch*, but still "a magnificent and impressive pageant." "One of the strangest spectacles ever seen within the venerable walls of the Vatican," wrote the *Sacramento Daily Record-Union*.[28] Burke would add historical polish (and a dash of his usual patronizing tone) in his 1893 book: "The grandeur of the spectacle, the heavenly music, the entrancing singing and impressive adjuncts produced a most profound impression on the astonished children of the prairie." And he would refer back to this seminal event in interviews for years to come.[29]

It would be easy to view John M. Burke through the comforting filter of twenty-first-century enlightenment and see his efforts to use the Wild West Indians as marketing tools as paternalistic, racist, and just another chapter in the well-worn book of exploitation of the less fortunate. After all, the 1800s had already seen big crowds turn out for blackface minstrel performances and for Barnum's freaks, sideshows, and humbugs. Was this really any different?

Yet Burke had a complicated relationship with the Indians.

On the one hand, he opportunistically retold and embellished the stories about Cody's battles with Tall Bull and Yellow Hand, and never protested when newspapers described Burke himself as an Indian fighter. (In 1892, the *Arizona Weekly Journal-Miner* went so far as to say that he had been with Custer at the Battle of the Little Big Horn "and is one of the few survivors of that sanguinary engagement"; one wonders whether, upon reading the article, Burke laughed at their preposterous error, or smiled at their gullibility. With John Burke, the real truth was always somewhat elusive.[30])

He commonly used pejoratives like "savage," "red man," "bronzed warrior," and "primitive" to describe the Indians and frequently echoed the condescending tone of the Great White Father. For example, he told the *Boston Globe* that he had been able to sign Sitting Bull to a Wild West contract in 1885 because "the authorities believe it better for him that some one has been found who will care and provide for him, educate and civilize him, and let him see that the white man is not his enemy."[31]

Burke's view of the Indians was paternalistic but also pragmatic. By the mid-1880s he had spent a great deal of time working with and living among them, and in his view at least, this gave him the qualifications to advocate for them intelligently. He earnestly (if somewhat naively) believed that all Indians would benefit from the involvement of some of them in the Wild West because "they will tell to their children and their companions, and it will be repeated all over the reservations, what grand times they had abroad, and what wonderful things they saw concerning the great numbers, power and science of the white race. It will do them all good. It is like the kindergarten system of training children."[32]

In an interview with the *Philadelphia Times* in 1888, Burke railed against proposed reforms that would effectively wall off the reservations from further settlement:

> The talk of impractical theorists, rank hypocrites and interested, designing schemers that 'it is for the good of the Indians' that they want civilization kept out of the Territory is the most arrant, impudent nonsense. It is precisely for his good that I want to see the example of thrifty agriculture set him upon all sides; towns, school houses and churches established about him; railroads extended through his land to enhance their value; commerce and manufacturers flourishing in his vicinity. Then his land will become of great value to him; he will have learned the white man's lessons of industry, economy and self-help, and he will be in time a contented, happy, law-abiding citizen and—with the start he will have from the sale of his surplus land—a very well-to-do one, much better off than the average white agriculturalist. But keep him in his present isolated condition and you compel him to become a savage, or rather to remain one.[33]

Over time, he chiseled out an even more plausible rationalization for the benefits to the show Indians and used his two thousand-grit vocabulary to sand it smooth. "This little band of Sioux have been in seventeen different countries," he would tell a reporter in 1906, after the final Wild West European tour: "They have visited almost every commercial, artistic, architectural and natural point of interest in Europe. And they have been keen and intelligent observers. They have seen the burning mountain, Vesuvius; the glories of the art of the old world, splendid palaces and castles, the wonderful cathedrals. And so they will go back to the reservation to teach. They will tell the story of the different peoples, their languages and customs more effectively than ever books could."[34]

Conveniently, he could see that what was good for the Indian was also good for the Wild West. He knew that the Indians' participation in the show helped to underscore the point he had tried to make time and time again: that the Wild West was not a show or a circus, but an educational exhibition that was completely authentic. "The Wild West, although bringing the genuine blanket Indians to the East, has always found a doubting Thomas as to the genuine article being with us," he told that same *Boston Globe* reporter, "so we thought the surest way was to bring a man and some of his most noted chiefs whose careers are associated with the dark pages of Western history."[35]

He also clearly understood how much publicity they could generate for him. Burke knew there would be great interest among newspaper audiences in learning how the natives reacted to the civilized world—the bustling train stations full of white men, the cacophony of the cities with their street cars and cobblestones, the spectacle of all the cultural and commercial wonders of the built-up world east of the Mississippi. In a manner that sounded utterly amusing to his contemporary audience, and rather horrifying to a modern one, Burke described how the Indians

> are constantly astonished at what they see, and ask any number of questions. As an instance, Frisking Elk, on seeing the large six and seven-story houses in Chicago, wanted to know how it was that the white man could build one "tepee" and then another and another on top of that until it reached the sky. The great depots with "stam engins" [*sic*] and hurley gurley surroundings made him say that he was going crazy and ask the people to watch him, as his head was all going round. He wanted the interpreter to bandage his eyes so that he would not see too much until he recovered. Crow Eagle, in going through a tunnel, was met by the interpreter in the aisle of the car. The latter asked, "Who's that?" Crow Eagle answered that he did not know. He was then asked his name and said: "I have traveled so fast that I have left my name far behind. . . ." They stood in wonderment at what appeared to them the marvelous skill of the white man. None spoke but Crow's Ghost, the most stoical one of the lot. He said, with a shrug of the shoulders: "That settles it; Injun no good."[36]

On the other hand, John M. Burke had great empathy for Native Americans and held few illusions about the problems of the reservation Indian, "emasculated by the vices of the whites, by whom he was environed and defrauded."[37] He told that same Boston reporter that Sitting Bull's "expressions of astonishment and delight while on the trip would cause the bitterest enemy of the Indian to feel a sympathy for their simplicity and ignorance in

ONE OF BURKE'S FAVORITE TRICKS was to take the Indians, in full regalia, and photograph them in strange and iconic landmarks (here with Cody, in Venice, 1890). Buffalo Bill Center of the West, Cody, Wyoming; P.69.1147.

regard to the East."[38] And he would later relate a story about the trip with Sitting Bull to his friend Macon McCormick, a well-known sportswriter then working for the *New York Advertiser*, which captured the paradox of his attitude toward the Indians, at once patronizing and enlightened:

> But what [Sitting Bull] could least understand was the way the wonderful man-away-back-in-the-dark treated his own people, who were white like himself. The Indian by his treaty had the right to ride free on the steps and platforms of the cars, which were pulled so fast by the strange iron horse, but if a white man tried to ride with him and didn't have money to pay for the little pieces of white paper which were sold at the stations, the chief of the train, who was dressed in a blue coat and wore brass buttons like a soldier, would put him off and he would have to walk the rest of the way. The Indian thought that was a very cruel thing to do. He couldn't understand, either, why it was that this great man-away-back-in-the-dark, who was so very rich and so powerful, would let so many of his people be so poor that they had to beg for the means to buy food.[39]

This balanced view also came through in his evolving characterization of Cody as a reformer, a man who had come around, someone who had "educated the people to seeing the hated and ever-dreaded red men in another light." Although Cody had killed Indians in the performance of his duties, argued Burke, "Buffalo Bill may properly wear the laurels and deserve the plaudits of civilization . . . for the friendship he has displayed for the red man in times of peace."[40] The Wild West advertising posters, which Burke influenced and sometimes helped create, also frequently depicted the Indians in a positive light—at worst, as worthy adversaries, but often as proud warriors, near equals of the white man. One such poster, from 1890, was dominated by a beautiful and realistic scene of Indians in a canoe gazing across a lake, with one inset circle featuring a picture of Cody, and another ever-so-slightly-smaller circle featuring a picture of an Indian described simply as "The American" (see plate 7). In 1909, Burke would even advocate a plan for "erecting a colossal bronze statue of an Indian with arm outstretched, in New York harbor, as a tribute to the aborigines, whom the present population supplanted." This notion was laid out in a Baltimore newspaper article whose headline strikes the modern reader with a refulgent bolt of irony: "Favors Shaft to Red Men."[41]

Thus, although caught up in the currents of the social prejudices characteristic of his era, Burke nevertheless was able to eddy out into a more progressive way of thinking. He saw honesty and decency in the American Indians' character and sadness in their inevitable plight as "helpless, idle, dispirited wards of the government" being forced to "accept in spirit as well as deed the altered conditions of life."[42]

But amid the European tour of 1889–1890, the marketing of Wild West Indians started to become much more challenging for Burke. Two of the Indians, Swift Hawk and Featherman, became ill; Burke paid to put them in private hospital rooms in Marseilles, but they eventually died. Other Lakotas became ill in Barcelona, and Burke sent them home to the United States. Then Goes Flying died in Naples (of smallpox) and Little Ring died in Rome (of a heart attack). Suddenly, there were reports in the papers—possibly stirred up by the ambitious James O'Beirne, U.S. assistant superintendent of immigration of the Port of New York, and by others from the Reformist Progressive movement—that the Wild West was mistreating its Indians, providing inadequate food, and sending them home on ships in steerage.

Burke immediately went on the offensive, not only because he was trying to manage Cody's reputation, but also because the issue was deeply personal to him. He cabled the papers in New York, referring to those leveling the charges as "notoriety-seeking busybodies," "the forked-tongue of human serpents" attempting "without reason or rhyme, truth or reason to stain a fair record."[43] He also sent a dispatch from Berlin to the *New York Herald* bureau in Paris, calmly refuting the charges one by one (and sounding very much like a modern political spin doctor):

> The statements and general inference about starvation and cruelty in the Wild West camp are ridiculously untruthful, and unjust to Cody and Salsbury. I appeal to your sense of justice to fully deny the same. The Wild West is under the public eyes daily, and in all the countries and cities visited, under rigid police and health inspection. Our cuisine is the same as in New York, Paris and London, and has challenged the admiration and astonishment of the citizens of every place visited for its quality and quantity. Our contracts and beef bills will bear witness as well as the United States consuls and local officials, and thousands of others who have daily visited our camp. Our pride as well as our interest lies in the good food and good health of our people. As regards the steerage passage, the steamships don't want to give cabin passages to Indians. Many a good white man has gone across the ocean in the steerage. Would that every white man in the world was as well fed, clothed and looked after as our red tourists on Buffalo Bill's Wild West.[44]

(Burke did fess up to the *Herald* that he had had to punish one Indian for translating Tolstoy's *The Kreutzer Sonata*—a controversial work, highly censored, that led Theodore Roosevelt to call Tolstoy a "sexual moral pervert"—by cutting back his meat to three pounds a day and suspending his ice cream and pudding. "This will probably be cabled to America as an instance of the hardships the noble red men are subjected to in Europe," reported the paper.[45]) Burke also invited three European-based American diplomats to inspect the Wild West camp, which they did—and found nothing wrong.

Nevertheless, when the Wild West season ended in October 1890, Cody, Salsbury, and Burke decided it would be prudent to return to the United States with the thirty-nine Oglala Sioux in their troupe to defend themselves in person against the charges of mistreatment. Burke cabled the New York newspapers with a typically florid explanation:

> The Indians are being repatriated to give the lie to current slanders and to show the refining and enobling [*sic*] influence which European travel had on them. . . . The Indian folds his tents and follows on the brine's deep blue the trail of Columbus, Vespucci, De Soto and Hendrik Hudson. Thence wandering westward he braves the bleak blizzards of the Bad Lands of Dakota and will imbibe in his wild native solitude those graces and virtues that contact with modern civilization in the intellectual centers of Europe may have blunted.[46]

A few years earlier, the Major had assured the Bureau of Indian Affairs that it was Cody's "honorable ambition to instruct and educate the Eastern public to respect the denizens of the West by giving them a true, untinselled representation of a page of frontier history that is fast passing away."[47] Now he was determined to prove that despite the show's commercial success since, nothing had changed.

In the nation's capital, Burke and the Indians met with senators, congressmen, Secretary of the Interior John W. Noble, and the Bureau of Indian Affairs, none of whom heard anything to be alarmed about. The episode passed without further incident, and Burke escorted his charges back home to the plains.

Now, however, there was trouble brewing on the reservations, where a quasi-religious movement called the Ghost Dance had stirred unrest among some natives and in turn among the troops who were watching them. Cody was summoned by his old boss and friend General Nelson Miles to try to meet with Sitting Bull at the Standing Rock Agency to help defuse the situation. (The orders were rescinded, however, and Cody was detained at nearby Fort Yates without ever reaching Sitting Bull.)

Precisely what Burke did next is unclear. Some reports indicate that he first went to Chicago to meet with newspaper editors to promote Cody's possible role as peacemaker—although by his own account, provided to an Oklahoma reporter years later, Burke simply said that when in Washington he had received instructions (from whom, he did not say) to go to the Pine Ridge Agency in southern South Dakota to encourage the Indians there to remain peaceful.[48] In late November, he sent a telegram from Pine Ridge to Allison Nailor in Washington, D.C., stating, "Situation greatly improved.

About 500 lodges have come in and more coming over the hills. More troops coming. My Indian friends are level headed."[49] Other reports say he made it to Standing Rock, three hundred miles to the north of Pine Ridge, and since, as one army officer reportedly said, "he was the only man in the United States that at least stood a chance of riding up to Sitting Bull and his tribes and getting away with it," he did just that—going alone, in zero-degree weather, on a forty-mile journey.[50] Still other reports say he was there when, in the early morning hours of December 15, Sitting Bull was killed in a chaotic scene while Indian policemen tried to arrest him.[51] (Burke did later send a telegram to Standing Rock agent James McLaughlin, asking him to "save me some memento of Sitting Bull, for with all his faults I love him still." McLaughlin sent a lock of the Indian chief's hair, which Burke kept in a strong box alongside the jeweled pin given to him by Queen Victoria.[52])

Burke may have even been present December 29, 1890, at Wounded Knee Creek back on the Pine Ridge Agency, when in a confusing and tragic episode, the Seventh Cavalry opened fire with revolving-barrel Hotchkiss guns on an encampment of Lakotas, killing more than two hundred men, women, and children.

But as with everything Burke, it was then—and is now even more so—nearly impossible to tell the truth from the tall tale. In his retelling of the story to the Oklahoma reporter, Burke provided extremely detailed descriptions of the battle, never once mentioning himself. Yet Dexter Fellows, Burke's protégé, recalled that Burke sometimes maintained that he had killed an Indian in hand-to-hand combat at the Battle of Wounded Knee. Cody, knowing his press agent's penchant for exaggeration, offered a different version: "The Major had constructed a shelter of wood into which he could crawl, and if the fighting got too hot, he would kick out one of the supports and be safely hidden under a pile of debris." (Years later, at a Press Representatives' Association dinner in New York, Burke told the same story. Afterward, the Sioux chief Black Horn got up to speak, and his interpreter then reported, "The Chief says that after the battle he found the woodpile. . . . [H]e still has the Major's clothes in his possession. Would the Major like them back?"[53]) Fellows said he was never able to figure out the truth about Burke's role at Wounded Knee, but that "evidently it was a great moment in his life and, if I reminded him that I had already heard him tell of the exploit many times, he would take on the look of a wounded dog that has been called down for being naughty and say: 'I suppose you don't believe it.'"[54]

Who would? Burke was forty-eight years old in 1890 and weighed in at three hundred pounds—hardly battle ready. Moreover, he idolized Cody, even to the point of looking and dressing like him, and could thus be forgiven for imagining himself to be back on the western stage rather than in the wings. But he was also bighearted; and whether he had actually taken up arms or cowered under his copse during the fighting, or was even present, afterward he engaged in an act of great kindness when he helped to rescue and adopt a young Indian boy who had been left orphaned by the battle, naming him Johnny Burke No-Neck. The boy would become a part of the Wild West show, although there were few mentions of him in later articles about Burke, and with his travel schedule, it is unlikely that the Major played an active role in the boy's life.[55]

Still, the events at Wounded Knee had a profound impact on John M. Burke. He told Macon McCormick that after the battle, he had encountered a young Indian who had been educated at the Carlisle Indian Industrial School but had returned to his tribe to fight. "You ought to have had sense and you ought to have taught your people that the proper thing for them to do was to keep peace with the whites and engage in farming," Burke chided the young man.

The Indian looked quizzically down from his pony and said, "Major, you and I have seen a good deal of the white man's country. Will you tell me where he erects monuments to farmers? I have seen plenty that he has put up for soldiers, but never one for a farmer."

"That was a knockout argument," said Burke, "and I hadn't a word to say in reply."[56]

He eventually wove these incidents from Wounded Knee into a narrative that demonstrated his progressive thinking while continuing to inflate the heroic image of Buffalo Bill's Wild West. As he would tell the *St. Albans (Vt.) Messenger*, Sitting Bull "played a tragic part in the last chapter, possibly the final contest between the original inhabitants of this grand American empire and that civilization that excuses the Saxon for conquests in the name of a higher law than what an impartial jury might consider poetic justice or equity." In that struggle, Burke concluded, "the influence of Buffalo Bill and his Wild West travelled and educated Indian allies played an honorable and influential part in bringing about peace."[57]

That may reek of historical revisionism, but Cody *did* negotiate to allow fifteen leaders of the Ghost Dance movement and dozens of their friends and relatives to join his Wild West cast instead of going to jail. And Burke *did* try to play an "influential part." Two weeks after the horrific events at Wounded Knee, hundreds of Oglala and Brulé Indians gathered near Pine Ridge in a peace conference of sorts and requested that Burke (along with Captain Jesse Lee, former military agent for the Brulés at the Rosebud Agency) play the role of "peace commissioner." Burke and Lee rode eight miles from the agency to meet them ("no spring morning ramble, as you may imagine," Burke would later say; "the dangers from cold and the Indians were considerable") and spent five or six hours talking peace.[58] Burke delivered what the *Washington Post* referred to as an "eloquent and effective plea for a peaceful solution":

> I do not come here in behalf of the Government or any society, but because I travel and live with the Indians, and they are my friends for many years. When I first heard of this trouble, Gen. Cody (Buffalo Bill) sent me to do what I could for you. I have been here eight or nine weeks—have listened, heard, and seen a great deal. From the first I saw no necessity for this trouble. A great deal of it came from a misunderstanding and the lack of confidence among the Indians as regards the intention of the Government. . . . I, too, show you what confidence I have in Gen. Miles that he will not fire upon you and your women and children when you are disarmed. I will promise to live in your camp until you have confidence that the white chief will see no harm come to you. I am glad to hear that some chiefs are going to Washington, and hope instead of ten, twenty or twenty-five will go. I will be there to see you and may go with you. I will do all I can in my humble way for you. Let us all work for peace between the white men and the red—not for a moment, a day, a year, but forever, for eternity.[59]

Throughout all these incidents, and indeed throughout his career, Burke clearly regarded the Indians with great respect, affection, and sympathy, even while he capitalized on their marketing value. He had the vision to see beyond his own era and anticipate a world in which Indians would achieve near equality with the rest of society, and in which a member of the racial minority, like them, might rise to great heights. Thus, while

IN THE AFTERMATH OF WOUNDED KNEE, Burke (*far right*) stayed with the Indians for several weeks, and then served as a "peace commissioner" at Pine Ridge in 1891, where he delivered a moving speech. John C. H. Gabrill, photographer, Library of Congress Prints and Photographs Division; (LC-DIG-ppmsc-02619).

visiting the grave of Charlemagne in Germany in 1891 with a group of descendants of the "dusky African prototypes," the irony and possibility struck him: "Here by the grave of the founder of Christianity stood the latest novitiates to its efforts, who may yet, in following its teaching, it is hoped, make such progress through its aid and education as to furnish one of their race capable of holding the exalted chieftainship, the presidency in their native land—the Empire of the West. Who can say? Why not?"[60]

With the Indian unrest in America now over, and the show back on tour in Germany, Burke put down his peace pipe, picked up his cigars, and resumed his role as general manager, press agent, promoter, and icon builder. He had plenty of new material with which to work his magic, because Nate Salsbury, fearing that the events of the preceding winter might prevent the Indians from returning to the show, had reconstituted the act as Buffalo

Bill's Wild West and Congress of Rough Riders of the World. It now incorporated Russian cossacks, South American gauchos, English lancers, and other skilled horsemen from around the world.

Some of John M. Burke's marketing work in Germany was groundbreaking and, in the most literal sense of the word, anachronistic, for it was well ahead of its time. For example, special brochures entitled *Buffalo Bill's Wild West Journal* were handed out to reporters. These were ingenious marketing pieces that looked like magazines. They included the usual fanfare about the fading American West, Cody's scouting career, his military endorsements, and more. They also boasted (in typical Burkean when-in-Rome fashion) that the Wild West would be of particular interest to Germans because of how many of their countrymen had already emigrated to the United States. And they were peppered with new versions of some of Burke's standard positioning statements: the show featured "real personalities, only true, no false equipment," and was not just a "theater production" but an educational exhibition in which "one sees here actual life, as it was in the west . . . a genuine, unvarnished picture of the past." Sure enough, these "copy points" regularly made their way into the German press.[61]

Burke also created the equivalent of a modern-day rock tour backstage pass—for example, inviting German journalists to one of his "Indian Breakfasts" on June 20, 1890, followed by a tour led by Cody. One reporter from Berlin noted with obvious surprise and delight that after he identified himself as a journalist, "all doors flung open wide," and he was allowed to walk around the grounds before they were open to the public.[62]

Furthermore, Burke and his team introduced a marketing innovation that still captivates and annoys motorists a century and a quarter later: the mobile billboard. In Hamburg, as Julia Stetler pointed out in her 2006 doctoral dissertation "Buffalo Bill's Wild West in Germany," there was a "colossal carriage, drawn by four horses, that was decorated with a life-size picture of Buffalo Bill and multiple other colorful pictures." And in Bremen one newspaper noted that "advertisement cars have been driving through the city daily, drawing massive attention from passers-by." Another paper in Dresden seemed as awestruck by the "press work" as by the show itself: "Already weeks in advance, the audience is prepared for the show through billboards etc. The American, in this matter as in many others, is very practically minded."[63] Other local commentators lauded the "truly American advertisements" and "adventuresome representations in pictures and words."[64]

The poet and humor writer Eugene Field, who was vacationing with his family in Germany at the time, decried Cody's "barbarous pageant" and how "Buffalo Bill posters (flaming with red and green inks) desecrated statues and turrets and walls here, there and everywhere," and that "the vandal hands of John Burk [*sic*]" had even managed to slap a three-sheet poster on the world-famous Loreley Rock in the Rhine River. Field bemoaned the fact that what his boys recalled most from their epic European trip was Buffalo Bill's Wild West.[65]

Not surprisingly, the Wild West was extremely popular in Germany. Burke would later tell the story of how, when Kaiser Wilhelm II went to visit Heligoland, a small archipelago in the North Sea, which Germany had just purchased from England in 1890, he discovered lithographs of Buffalo Bill in every home. "Who owns this island?" Wilhelm asked. "Is it I or Buffalo Bill?"[66] Burke, who was renowned to have a laugh that was "contagious" and "rollicking," probably exploded in cachinnations, and one can almost feel the reverberations still.[67]

The rest of the European tour rolled smoothly through Belgium, England, Scotland, and Wales. Mostly, Burke had great fun with it, trotting out most of his customary tricks. For example, after performing for a week each in Portsmouth and Brighton in early October, the Wild West had a week off before an engagement in Glasgow, which would last from mid-November through the end of February. Eager to keep the show in the news even during the breaks, Burke brought a group of eight Indians in full native costume on the train to London, and then to Westminster Abbey and St. Paul's Cathedral—echoing the actions of George Catlin, the Indian painter and Wild West show progenitor, fifty years earlier. At least three newspapers wrote about the visit, all commenting in remarkably similar terms about Kicking Bear. One said he showed "the bitter resentment and potential cruelty of another Sitting Bull." Another wrote that he had "a cruel-looking face, such a man as one would expect to look on unconcernedly while a prisoner was being tortured to death." A third paper remarked that Kicking Bear featured "a wide, thin-lipped mouth [that] wore a sneer oftener than not. . . . [F]or raw ferocity of expressions I never saw his equal." Burke was stirring things up. "Far from being the spontaneous reactions of independent witnesses," surmised historian Tom Cunningham, "they were prompted and even carefully choreographed by means of Major Burke's press releases."[68]

Later that spring, as the Wild West prepared for its return engagement in London, a five-month run back at Earl's Court as part of yet another exhibition, Burke unveiled a new marketing tool: his own newspaper. *Buffalo Bill's Wild West Courier and International Horticultural Exhibition Gazette* featured articles written by Burke and biographies of the famous Wild West personalities. He printed one hundred thousand copies and distributed them for free to passersby on the streets of London. P. T. Barnum had done something similar, but whereas Barnum's paper, like all his early promotions, had a halo of humbug around it—one never knew whether to believe it or not—Burke tried to add an air of legitimacy to his effort through one of his favorite tactics, glowing press reviews clipped from papers around the world. In so doing, he was anticipating the world of custom publishing that would eventually lead to in-flight magazines and the boom of slick-looking, journalistic-sounding corporate publications of the 1990s.[69] (The *Courier* may have also been part of Major Burke's response to erroneous reports that reached American newspapers in early April that Buffalo Bill's Wild West Show had "collapsed." Burke quickly straightened things out, assuring reporters that the show was as strong as ever, and it opened once again to large crowds in early May.)

During his time in Europe, Burke also helped to stage—or at least milk—a series of what we would now call publicity stunts, which were often taken at face value by the audience and covered as news by the press.

- In London, in 1887, there was a week-long indoor endurance race between Wild West horsemen and bicyclists; both groups raced about 674 miles.
- Two years later in France, there was a similar match race between a Wild West cowboy on horseback and a local man on a bicycle.
- In March 1890, Burke arranged an event in Italy to see if the Wild West cowboys could handle the Duke of Sermoneta's supposedly untamable wild horses. To make a true spectacle of it, they ostentatiously had the horses brought to the arena in chains and had barriers erected to protect the audience should things get out of hand. A crowd of twenty thousand people showed up to see the horses, and, as Commercial Cable reported to the *Herald* (and as Burke would later excerpt in his programs), "The brutes made springs into the air, darted hither and thither in all directions, and bent themselves into all sorts of shapes, but all in vain."[70] The Wild

West cowboys broke the nobleman's horses "in less than a quarter of an hour," resulting in spectacular press coverage and a certain degree of national shame in papers like *La Capitale* and *Il Diritto*.[71]

- In London in 1892, Burke and his team created a hurdle race to test national pride—pitting German, English, Mexican, and Indian jockeys on horses from around the world. The English rider won almost all the time. The crowds were exultant about the outcome, until they learned that the "local" jockey was actually an American cowboy named Harry Stanton in disguise. "His feat made a great hit all over England," Burke later chortled in an interview with the *New York Times*.[72]

Busy as he was, press agentry and advance work were only part of Burke's job. As general manager of the Wild West, he was also responsible for a lot of the show's logistics, the extent of which was revealed by the artist Frederic Remington in an article he wrote for *Harper's Weekly* in 1892. Among other tasks, Remington said that Burke had to deal with Indians who asked the camp cook for extra meat in between meals, and that he had to fine some of the cowboys who became unruly and imitated Russian cossacks by standing on their heads in the arena. "The Major will conclude that the management of a light-opera company on the road is a mere beginner's work beside the people with the Wild West show," wrote Remington, "because they are all schooled in the theory that it is the proper thing to run a ten-inch knife into the anatomy of any one who does not agree with 'their peculiar whim.'"[73]

By the end of its tour in fall 1892, the Wild West had been in existence for nine years and had spent somewhat more than half of that time in Europe. Burke had played the newspapers like a Stradivarius in the Vienna Opera House, generating enough clips to fill dozens of scrapbooks, and as a result, Buffalo Bill had become an international celebrity. After the first trip to England, Cody had said, "The press were generous to us to an extent possibly never before known. Its columns were teeming daily with information about us, so eulogistic that I almost feared we would not cup to expectations."[74] And the coverage had gained momentum with each successful stop in the cities of the Old World.

Thus, while the Wild West had become a commercial success and international sensation—establishing the "mimic arena" as a new form of educational entertainment, mythologizing the West, proudly shouldering the task of bearing the American standard, and "everywhere winning the plaudits of royalty, the press, and the public"—Major John M. Burke had perhaps done something even more impressive.[75] Through his press agentry, he had invented a whole new set of promotional tools, the sturdiest and most effective "tent poles" yet for supporting the expanding canvas of the new industry of marketing. Burke had proved that by harnessing the flow of information, manipulating imagery, and tapping into the emotional appeal of the West, one could define and refine perceptions, persuade people, change behavior, stimulate demand, and attract enormous audiences. Moreover, he had elevated William F. Cody into Buffalo Bill, whose exploits, Burke wrote, "have been so numerous, involving a display of such extraordinary daring and magnificent nerve, that language can not exaggerate them"—although Burke certainly tried.[76]

Of course, like any great showmen, Burke and Cody were already thinking ahead as they staged their final European show on October 12, 1892. What could they possibly do for an encore?

On that day, Buffalo Bill rode into the arena, doffed his cap, introduced the show, and backed his horse out of the arena, just as he had on so many other occasions. The Congress of Rough Riders of the World performed their stunts. Glass balls and clay pigeons were shot out of the air. The Indians mounted their attack on the Deadwood Stagecoach. And then it was all over. Three days later, the Wild West would board the Cunard Line steamer *Servia* and head for home.

As fate would have it—and in truth, fate had little to do with it since Burke was a master of such things—that final October show marked the exact four hundredth anniversary of the date on which Christopher Columbus, aboard a westbound ship of his own, the *Santa Maria,* first sighted the Americas. It was a deft bit of marketing, for it would signal the start of the next major conquest for the Wild West.

Upon arrival in New Jersey, Burke immediately headed west to take the Indians home to the Red Cloud Agency and then went on to Denver and Flagstaff to meet up with Cody. From there, they embarked on a hiking tour of the Grand Canyon along with a group of British noblemen, plus Burke's friend-and-sometimes-landlord Allison Nailor; the prolific Buffalo Bill dime novelist and one-time member of Burke's team Prentiss

Ingraham; Brigham Young, grandson of the Mormon leader; and others.

But for the showman and the publicist, the Grand Canyon was merely a diversion. Their ultimate destination was the same as that of millions of other people around the world that fall who were busily checking railroad and steamship schedules and planning ahead for the trip of their lives—to that 633-acre former swampland called Jackson Park, seven miles south of Chicago, where the shimmering ethereal wonder of the World's Columbian Exposition would soon open, presenting yet another opportunity to redefine the boundaries of promotion.

John M. Burke had his encore all mapped out.

8

THE BATTLE FOR THE WORLD'S FAIR

"An extraordinary exhibition of indecorum"

Chicago, when it put forth its impertinent claim for the World's Fair, had never seen itself as others see it. Having always flattered itself that it was the greatest place on earth, it took no thought of how other people sized it up. It is now suffering a painfully rude awakening from its dream.

"As in a Looking Glass," *New York World* (August 3, 1889)

For truly grand twenty-first-century marketing theater, nothing quite compares to the spectacle of major sporting events.

The Super Bowl, for example, regularly attracts more than 100 million viewers. The 2015 game pulled in the largest audience for a televised event in U.S. history, with an average of 114.4 million viewers; the halftime show, featuring Katy Perry, did even better, with 118.5 million viewers—more than one-third of the country's population. That game was also telecast on national networks in Australia, Canada, New Zealand, the United Kingdom, and Ireland, and by rights holders in dozens of other countries, including questionable football strongholds such as Bulgaria, Poland, and Finland. A Spanish-language version ran on NBC Universo in the United States. A webcast on NBCSports.com and the radio broadcast on Westwood One reached millions more. On Facebook, 65 million people joined in the Super Bowl conversation, generating 265 million interactions. There were also 70,288 people in attendance at the game at University of Phoenix Stadium in Glendale, Arizona, and the week-long Verizon Super Bowl Central fan festival that preceded it drew more than 1 million additional visitors. The National Football League projected an overall economic impact on the local market of about $719 million.[1]

And of course, Super Bowl TV advertising has become a spectacle in its own right, with an unfathomable amount of news coverage, feature programs, websites, polls, critical reviews, tweets, and digital navel gazing. In one study, 17.7 percent of adults said the advertisements were the most important part of the event.[2] Anheuser-Busch, Coca-Cola, Google, Intel, GoDaddy, and dozens of other advertisers paid Fox more than $5 million for each thirty-second commercial in 2017. Audi, Buick, Fiat Chrysler, Ford, Honda, Kia, Lexus, and Mercedes-Benz all ran spots. Turkish Airlines and Avocados From Mexico advertised, and so did Fiji Water and King's Hawaiian. There was a little bit of something for everyone, although nothing about the Super Bowl is little anymore. It has become a multidimensional marketing melee that is the ultimate expression of American enterprise, verve, and commercialization.

And it actually pales in comparison to other global events. The 2016 Summer Olympics in Rio were viewed by an estimated 3.5 billion people, half the world's population. The month-long 2014 FIFA World Cup in Brazil had an audience of more than 1 billion viewers, in addition to 3 billion Facebook interactions and 672 million tweets; in Germany, Belgium, the Netherlands, and Italy, certain World Cup matches earned an astonishing television audience share of greater than 80 percent.

Once upon a time, promoting a special event was much simpler. There was no radio or satellite TV, no targeted Facebook posts or weighted media buys, no video trailers, or spin control, or "cookies" that silently capture the identities of even casually interested consumers for promoters to then "retarget." There was only printed advertising.

By 1860 the United States had about three thousand newspapers and two thousand magazines, and they often featured dense little text ads for temperance lectures, concerts, operas, or the latest theatrical production at halls like the three thousand-seat Niblo's Garden in New York, one of the larger performance venues in the country. If you wanted to tell the public what you were promoting, you just ran some ads.

So imagine for a moment what would have happened if a modern day mega-event—a Super Bowl, say, or the Summer Olympics—could have been plucked out of some fantastical future dreamed up by Edward Bellamy and transplanted into the middle of the nineteenth century. With all the hype, the press coverage, the personalities and their agents and publicists, the news feeds in different languages, the vivid images, the competing needs of sponsors—a few newspaper ads in agate type wouldn't have cut it.

The whole scenario sounds ridiculous, of course; but it is very much akin to the challenge faced by the promoters of the World's Columbian Exposition of 1893—the biggest special event of its era, and the closest thing that nineteenth-century America had to a Super Bowl or a modern Olympiad.

In a time when world's fairs were massive, intricate, immensely popular spectacles steeped with nationalistic pride and intertwined with culture and technology (London's Great Exhibition and the Crystal Palace of 1851, which attracted 6 million visitors; Vienna's International Exposition of 1873, which covered an enormous 576 acres; Paris's magnificent Exposition Universelle in 1878, which cost a whopping $11 million to produce, or the next one in 1889, when the Eiffel Tower was introduced), the Columbian Exposition was designed to outshine them all. It was to be an architectural, technological, and cultural expression of the audacious American experiment itself, a manifestation of all the progress that had been made since Columbus had first set out for the New World four hundred years earlier—all ingeniously embedded in the buildings, grounds, and exhibits of a magical White City in America's heartland, one thousand miles from the eastern coastal cities that were the country's graven monuments to Old World civilization.

The promoters would need to go well beyond mere newspaper ads to beckon the whole world to the young city on the shores of Lake Michigan—a task made all the more difficult by the fact that Chicago had many detractors and disgruntled rivals. To make the World's Columbian Exposition a success, they would need a whole new arsenal of promotional weapons, and a visionary leader to deploy them.

Between 1801 and 1849, international expositions and trade fairs had been held almost every year—and sometimes even more frequently—in places such as Vienna, Berlin, Dresden, Lausanne, Berne, St. Gall, Zurich, Brussels, Ghent, Moscow, St. Petersburg, Warsaw, Lisbon, Sardinia, Barcelona, Sydney, Melbourne, and of course London and Paris; but after

London's Great Exhibition of 1851 and its magnificent Crystal Palace, which encompassed nineteen acres under one roof, the whole magnitude of the enterprise had changed. There was no sense in holding a world's fair if it couldn't be big; and there was no sense in making it big unless it could be bigger and better than all others. Thus, after midcentury, the smaller countries resigned themselves to sending impressive representations to the fairs of larger ones, while London and Paris engaged in yet another bout of cross-channel one-upmanship. London attracted 13,939 exhibitors in 1851; Paris drew 20,839 in 1855. Paris covered 24½ acres and tallied slightly more than 5 million visitors in 1855; London expanded to 25 acres in 1862, and boasted of more than 28,000 exhibitors and over 6.2 million visitors. Paris came back in 1867 with a 41-acre exposition, 43,217 exhibits, and 6.8 million in attendance.[3] On the surface it was a game, a "tournament of industry" for measuring technological and cultural supremacy; but it only thinly veiled the wellspring of patriotism and nationalism that was characteristic of the age. "The prime object of the modern World's Fair," San Francisco journalist M. H. de Young would write in the *Cosmopolitan* in 1892, "is national glory. No matter how urgently the utilitarian spirit of the age argues that it pays to hold such exhibitions, that is not their animating purpose. The overshadowing aim is to win glory by showing the progress made in the arts and industries, and not to sell the goods exhibited."[4]

Thus, in Paris, in 1889, the French organized the Exposition Universelle to commemorate the centennial of the French Revolution. Although many European monarchies boycotted the Exposition—feeling that a celebration commemorating the guillotining of royals was perhaps inappropriate—the event was still a rousing success, a showcase for glittering belle époque Paris that featured six hundred paintings, including some by Manet, Monet, and Meissonier; the massive 375-foot-long Galleries des Machines, with its two rolling platforms high overhead to afford a bird's-eye view of all the fulminating equipment below; the cultural curiosities of French colonies like Senegal, Cambodia, Tonkin, and Tahiti; and of course the towering architectural achievement of M. Eiffel. Twenty-eight million people visited—by far the largest exposition to date, thus serving as the ultimate affirmation that the nineteen-year-old La Troisième République had arrived on the modern world stage.

There was, however, considerable disappointment among the Americans about their representation at the Exposition Universelle. Thomas

Edison, whose electric bulbs lit up the fairgrounds at night and whose phonograph was probably the single most popular attraction, arrived for a visit as a conquering hero; but Edison's inventions were not part of the official American exhibit (nor was Buffalo Bill's Wild West, which decamped in Neuilly, a few miles away). Indeed, he expressed grave dissatisfaction at the American showing. "Very poor. Even the little South American republics beat us hollow," he told the *New York World*.[5] Historian Hubert Howe Bancroft classified the U.S. displays in the Mechanic and Liberal Arts as "feeble," while Senator Chauncey Depew of New York commented that he "entered the grounds with the Stars and Stripes flying and came out with the flag in [my] pocket."[6]

Fortunately, there would soon be a chance for redemption. For even while tens of thousands of American visitors were ambling about the Champ de Mars in summer 1889, idly twirling parasols in their hands and gazing admiringly up at the Eiffel Tower, various entities in the United States were hard at work planning—and battling over—something better: a World's Columbian Exposition, to mark the four hundredth anniversary of the discovery of America, in 1892.

The idea had been kicking around for many years.

Bancroft declared in his *The Book of the Fair*, published in 1893 as one of several full-length histories of the subject, that Carlos W. Zaremba was the first to conceive of a Columbian Exposition, and that he made his ideas public "about the time of the Centennial."[7] In its 1893 *History of the World's Fair*, the *Chicago Record* stated that "claimants to the honor of having first suggested an Exposition to commemorate the discovery of America are almost innumerable," but still mentioned that "Dr. Charles W. Zaremba of Chicago issued circulars to the foreign ministers at Washington in 1884 asking them to confer with him on the subject of the Columbian fair."[8] The *Dedicatory and Opening Ceremonies of the World's Columbian Exposition* claimed that the idea was originated by "T. Zaremba, M.D., of Mexico," who had been "deeply impressed" by the 1876 Centennial Exhibition.[9] Meanwhile, Ben Truman, author of yet another 1893 *History of the World's Fair*, gave the credit to "Dr. T. W. Zaremba, a well-known German-American." Obviously he was not too well known, since no one could get his name or nationality straight.[10]

Zaremba was granted a license in November 1885 by the Illinois secretary of state to organize the Chicago Columbian Centenary World's Fair and Exposition Company, and the following year presented the idea to the American Historical Society in Washington, D.C., which appointed a committee to call on President Grover Cleveland. Philadelphia kept a close watch on these proceedings, and then sent a committee of its own to Washington. Meanwhile, a Board of Promotion was organized in New England to secure congressional action on Boston's behalf. And on July 31, 1886, Senator George Frisbie Hoar of Massachusetts introduced a resolution to appoint a joint congressional committee of fourteen to pursue the idea of erecting permanent and temporary exposition buildings in Washington—a notion that was summarily dismissed by the *New York Times*: "The project of founding a 'permanent exposition,' or shop show, in Washington to commemorate the landing is about the most unsuitable that could be devised. Nothing would more surely belittle and vulgarize the occasion and give foreigners warrant for doubting the extent of the benefit conferred upon mankind by COLUMBUS's discovery."[11] Yet despite the aspirations and wishful thinking of all these other cities, most people assumed that the Columbian Exposition would be held in New York.

On July 17, 1889, Mayor Hugh J. Grant of New York, issued an invitation to one hundred distinguished New Yorkers for a meeting, at which he and the city council resolved what all good New Yorkers already knew: that New York was the only suitable venue for a world's fair. This, indeed, was the opinion of many Americans, particularly easterners. P. T. Barnum, for one, wrote in the *North American Review*,

> There is only one place in the United States to hold the world's fair, and that is New York city. No one appreciates or admires the enterprise of our great Western cities more than I do, but I am sure their populations will consent to put aside selfish considerations in order to make the exhibition of '92 a credit to our republic in the highest degree. . . . New York is our metropolis, and the foremost city of America in the best American sense.[12]

Mostly, the newspaper and magazine editors just debated which New York park would make the best site or who were the best people for directing the various committees, because they considered it inevitable that New York would outdistance any and all rivals.

There were sound reasons for believing this. For one, New York was the most populous city in the country—the fourth largest in the world—so it was logical to assume that she could drum up greater industrial, labor, and managerial support than Chicago or Washington. Then there was New York's great concentration of wealth: the newspapers took pride in stressing the number of millionaires who lived in New York, who, it was assumed, would give generously to help finance the exposition. New York was also the primary American seaport and was near the great population centers of the Atlantic seaboard. *Harper's Weekly* summed up the feelings of many when it wrote, in August 1889,

> There can hardly be a question that New York is the suitable place for the great fair which will commemorate the event, not because there are not other great cities in the country, but because New York is the chief city, the great mart of commerce and seat of manufactures, with unequalled facilities of transport and accommodation. . . . The chief scene of the event of 1892, which is designed to commemorate the material growth and prosperity of America, should be the great city, which is itself one of the most imposing movements of that progress, and already the fourth city in the world.[13]

Edison, fresh from the Exposition Universelle in October 1889, reinforced this line of thinking. He told the *Times*, "New-York is by long odds the Paris of the United States," and even suggested that the north end of Central Park would make the perfect site for the fair and for the erection of a tower that would dwarf Eiffel's, perhaps 1,500 or 2,000 feet tall.[14]

But the battle had not yet truly been joined, for one thousand miles to the west lay Chicago—America's second city, population over 1 million, so recently arisen Phoenix-like from the disastrous fire of 1871—and while the New York papers and most of the rest of the eastern establishment were firmly decided on Gotham's suitability, Chicagoans began a campaign of their own, a campaign that would ultimately set the entire promotional tenor of the world's fair to follow.

First, Mayor DeWitt C. Cregier of Chicago responded to the urgings of newspapers and prominent citizens by calling upon the city council "to push Chicago's claims to consideration as the city to hold the Exposition" and noted that he was in receipt of (supposedly) unsolicited letters of support from Wisconsin, Iowa, Indiana, Ohio, and Missouri. Next, a committee of one hundred citizens met on July 25, 1889—just one week after the similar meeting in New York—and passed resolutions favoring Chicago as the host, concluding with determination, "Men who helped build Chicago want the Fair and having a just and well-sustained claim they intend to have it."[15]

The resolutions were telegraphed all over the world within an hour, and Chicago's massive publicity campaign was under way. Almost immediately, agents scurried about trying to secure "subscriptions" to the fair stock to match New York's pledge of $5 million. Subcommittees were appointed to attend to such urgent matters as "National Co-operation," "Press," "Addresses and Local Agitation," and "Addresses, Information and National Agitation."[16] The finance committee sent circulars to newspaper editors, to counter pamphlets that had been developed by New York. And "in furtherance of the task," President Harlow Higinbotham of the Columbian Exposition would later write, "missionary work was carried out in the several States. At many places addresses were delivered in favor of Chicago, and persistent efforts were made to win public sentiment in sections which had been indifferent or hostile."[17] It was, in other words, an all-out national campaign aimed at convincing citizens and the congressmen who would vote on the issue that Chicago was the best site.

The city had several claims to press. The organizing committee, for example, published the following list in August 1889:

1. Chicago's refrigerator, the Lake, renders her summer climate more comfortable than that of any other great city for an exhibition of that season.
2. Her exceptional railroad and hotel accommodations insure the comfort and convenience of visitors, however numerous.
3. A limitless supply of water and the immense area of the city are adequate to all the demands of an Exposition.
4. Chicago citizens have the money, and the public spirit to advance it freely in a good cause.
5. Whilst New York is nearer England than to our Pacific Coast, Chicago is so centrally located, with her thirty-eight railroads pointing out in all directions, as to be accessible to all exhibitors and visitors from every quarter of the globe, and especially to millions in the west who would be debarred visiting the Fair if held at the seaboard.[18]

These arguments were, of course, about practicality, and they were made over and over by Chicago's promoters. *Chicago's public transportation systems carry over 200 million people each year. Chicago has spacious park facilities along the lake where the fairgrounds could be built, while New Yorkers are loath to give up Central Park. A 500-mile radius circle around Chicago encompasses millions more people than a comparable circle around New York.* They were the same kinds of pragmatic claims New York was making; for each strength of one city, there was a corresponding strength for the other.

But just like the New Yorkers, the Chicagoans had begun to learn that effective marketing taps pride and emotions. They, of course, could not boast of the rich traditions of their city, for it had none; Chicago's roots dated back no further than the 1840s. What the Chicagoans could and did promote was the world of new American values that their metropolis represented: exponential growth, vastness, persistence, the subjugation of nature, industrial-scale agriculture, boundless enterprise, and boisterous energy: the boosters' West. Thus, the committee's list of reasons supporting Chicago also included the following:

6. Foreigners, and indeed many of our countrymen at the East, should have the opportunity presented them of seeing for themselves the growing cities of the West, that they may better realize that the discoveries of Columbus embraced not merely a narrow strip of territory along one seaboard, but a mighty empire of almost limitless expanse and destiny.
7. What more eligible location can be desired than Chicago from the fact alone that her marvelous growth within the memory of the natives, from the frontier camp to the active city of over a million souls, with a corresponding advance in commercial, industrial and intellectual activities, can best typify the giant young nation whose discovery the projected Fair is to commemorate?[19]

The *real* reason the World's Fair should go to Chicago, its promoters went on to say, was because it is "our turn now." That is, it is our *time* now; you have had your glories, but now the star of the West must rise!

Suddenly, after this declaration was issued on August 1, the whole nature of the battle for the fair changed.

The Chicago promoters knew that their strength was the city's appeal to the future, the America-to-be, the *West*: dynamos and electric lightbulbs, vast industry and energy, and perhaps above all else, bustle and growth. Mayor Cregier, born a New Yorker, acknowledged that the eastern capital was "the brilliant star of this continent, the flower of our civilization," but insisted that "now there exists a new country on the other side of the Alleghanies [*sic*], where powerful commonwealths have arisen, where population has multiplied, where the ground gives forth its increase a hundredfold; and of that beautiful domain, CHICAGO IS THE QUEEN."[20]

Chicago's promoters printed up little star-shaped "Chicago World's Fair 1892" stickers, sent former congressman (and future vice president) Adlai Stevenson to the South to drum up support among legislators, dispatched former railroad executive Edward T. Jeffery to Paris to study that exposition and to influence the foreign press, formed "state associations" comprising former residents of other states who now supported Chicago, and repeatedly stressed Chicago's material and climatic advantages over its rivals. The appeal to the western spirit was both the underlying message and the method—the logical, evolved, somewhat saner metropolitan version of William Gilpin's West—and the *Chicago Tribune* neatly summarized the Chicago philosophy when it said, "It is not Chicago versus the rest of the country. It is the West versus the thin fringe of people on the Atlantic seaboard."[21]

In New York, the promoters began to recognize the legitimate challenge for the fair posed by Chicago—and the implicit threat of western equality—and responded accordingly. As P. T. Barnum said, "To expect every visitor to travel half way across the continent, after making the ocean journey, would have the same effect upon prospective visitors as the thought to an American of a journey to St. Petersburg instead of London."[22]

In a revealing editorial remark, the *New York Times* reminded Chicago "that the exhibition is not to be a show of the great West, but a grand exposition of all nations," and reprimanded its western rival as "really too big and important a town to persist in making a silly exhibition of itself because it cannot have the great international exhibition of 1892 within its liberal limits. . . . She would appear ridiculous when the time comes if she should persist in flocking all by herself on the shores of Lake Michigan.[23]

As the cloak of civility wore thin, antiwestern prejudices could not be contained. For example, state politician William Waldorf Astor wrote a letter to the *Cosmopolitan*, widely republished or referenced in newspapers, in which he derided Chicago homes as "built with borrowed money, and . . . mortgaged from corner-stone to skylight," homes in which the doors are opened by housemaids instead of liveried footmen, and "whose occupants are 'all out on their doorsteps,' as they used to sit in New York seventy years ago."[24]

Similarly, in describing the activities of the "wild boomers" who were promoting the City by the Lake, the *New York Times* observed, "In this as in many of its public endeavors, the methods of Chicago are noisy and more or less offensive to dignity and good taste; . . . they are of the kind that tell in the buoyant West. . . . [I]n the creation of sentiment in favor of Chicago as against all other cities as a site for the Exposition . . . the genius of the Chicago 'hustler' has fairly blazed."[25] One correspondent actually reported, "Chicago is one of the worst governed cities in the world. The saloons are wide open seven days and nights in the week, and gambling halls flourish on every side with the knowledge and connivance of the municipal authorities. Crime is committed with impunity or is dealt with in such a manner as to render the law contemptible in the eyes of thieves, thugs and murderers."[26]

Chicago—noisy, greedy, uncouth, unrefined *Chicago*—while perhaps a credit to American industry and primitive enterprise, would doubtless be an embarrassment to the nation in any undertaking as important as the Columbian Exposition. The city selected as host would be a showcase to the world, the paramount achievement of American civilization. Therefore, reasoned the *New York Times*, "It would be well if the red-hot Chicagoans should quietly commune with themselves a little and ask themselves why in reality any strangers should wish to visit their town or what there is intrinsically attractive in the city to lead anybody to yearn after a sight of it who is not a drummer [traveling salesman] nor yet interested in a wheat corner or pork deal."[27] New Yorkers even came up with nicknames to deride Chicago. Richard Henry Dana of the *New York Sun* dubbed Chicago "the windy city" in reference to the "hot air" emanating from her boosters.[28] The *New York Times* crowned it "the city of dressed beef."[29]

Compounding the problem for Chicago was the fact that much of the Old World felt as New York did. Chicago was thought to be on the very edge of civilization itself, just a step removed from barbarism. The noise, the confusion, the filth, the stockyards, the overeager capitalism, and the coarse, vulgar character of the people were all favorite topics. The *Times of London*, in 1887, described the prominent characteristics of Chicago as "an overhanging pall of smoke; streets filled with busy, quick-moving people; a vast aggregation of railways, vessels, and traffic of all kinds; and a paramount devotion to the Almighty Dollar."[30] Playwright Giuseppe Giacosa visited Chicago and probably dissuaded a whole generation of Italians from doing likewise:

> To the eye, the city appears abominable. . . . I would not want to live there for anything in the world. . . .
>
> During my stay of one week, I did not see in Chicago anything but darkness, smoke, clouds, dirt, and an extraordinary number of sad and grieved persons. . . .
>
> The dominant characteristic of the exterior life of Chicago is violence. Everything leads you to extreme impressions: dimensions, movements, noises, rumors, window displays, spectacles, ostentation, misery, activity and alcoholic degradation.[31]

Giacosa also could not help noticing the tendency of bars in Chicago to provide a "common service" for wiping one's mustache and mouth [i.e., towels], rather than individual table napkins. "I believe, however, that they [the towels] did not receive more than they gave."[32]

Some foreign visitors, of course, were impressed by Chicago's gumption, if not by its urban charm. London's *Saturday Review* referred to Chicago as the "concentrated essence of Americanism," and Frenchman Paul de Roussiers said that Chicago was "the most active, the boldest, the most American, of the cities in the Union."[33] Even Giacosa commented on how Chicago exemplified the "intellectual and physical energies, of which man is capable; the ideas of a social order, simple and progressive." It was, he conceded, the "ultimate expression" of the nineteenth century.[34]

But to the refined sensibilities of most Continental visitors, the line between perfervid American enterprise and outright crudity was threadbare. Chicago's profusion of billboards and advertisements alone were enough to raise Europeans' dander, like the one that read, "Gentlemen chew Fraxy because it sweetens the breath after drinking. Ladies who play tennis chew it because it lubricates the throat"; or the one that promised "Business lunch—quick and cheap."[35]

Most damning of all, though, were the words of writer Rudyard Kipling, who passed through Chicago on a holiday to the United States in 1889 and then penned *From Sea to Sea: Letters of Travel.* "This place is the first American city I have encountered," he wrote. "It holds rather more than a million people with bodies, and stands on the same sort of soil as Calcutta. Having seen it, I urgently desire never to see it again." Kipling then related a series of frightening incidents:

> [At the Palmer House hotel] . . . I found a huge hall of tessellated marble, crammed with people talking about money and spitting about everywhere. Other barbarians charged in and out of this inferno with letters and telegrams in their hands, and yet others shouted at each other. . . .
>
> There was no colour in the street and no beauty—only a maze of wire-ropes overhead and dirty stone flagging underfoot. . . . [A cab driver] took me to canals, black as ink, and filled with untold abominations, and bade me watch the stream of traffic across the bridges. . . . The papers tell the readers in language fitted to their comprehension that the snarling together of telegraph wires, the heaving up of houses, and the making of money is progress.
>
> I spent ten hours in that huge wilderness, wandering through scores of miles of those terrible streets, and jostling some few hundred thousand of these terrible people who talked money through their noses. . . .
>
> Sunday brought me the queerest experience of all—a revelation of barbarism complete. I found a place that was officially described as a church. It was a circus really, but that the worshippers did not know.[36]

Chicago, of course, did not take the name calling lightly; on the contrary, the promoters and newspapermen fought back with might and main—both by defending their own character, and by attacking that of New York.

Throughout July and August 1889, for instance, the *Chicago Tribune* solicited from congressmen (chiefly western congressmen) responses to the question of where the fair should be held. "The replies show that Chicago . . . is preeminently the place for the fair." P. S. Post of the Tenth Illinois District, for one, wrote that the world's fair should be held at Chicago, "the most progressive city in the world, the centre of the continent, the centre of the universe."[37] The *Inter Ocean* ran a story describing how by 1892, New York would be running a deficit of 75 million gallons of water a day. "New York could not supply the Exposition visitors with water enough to clean their teeth with. Nice place for a world's fair, indeed!"[38] The *Tribune* editors urged Chicago's committees to "get that fair in spite of Washington bluff and New York bluster and braggadocio. . . . The natural advantages of this city are pretty well known. He who cannot see them is obstinate or blind."[39] Brash headlines heralded their confidence:

CHICAGO MUST HAVE IT (August 1)

BEGINNING OF THE END.
CHICAGO TAKES THE FIRST STEPS TO SECURE THE WORLD'S FAIR (August 2)

CHICAGO THE FAVORITE.
IT IS TWO-THIRDS OF THE NATION AGAINST MANHATTAN ISLAND (August 7)

MUST HAVE THAT FAIR (August 17)

SINEWS OF WAR (August 19)

IT MAKES GOTHAM SICK.
CHICAGO'S HAND STILL NEARER THAT WORLD'S FAIR PLUM. (August 20)

IT WON'T WORK, GOTHAM (August 23)

One Chicago pundit remarked that the real event to be celebrated was the discovery of Christopher Columbus by Chicago, which had been dated to September 1889.[40] A news bureau published "Three Hundred Reasons" (why Chicago should have the fair), ranging from the "popular fallacies about the large feet of Chicago ladies" to the devotion to pork of Chicago men.[41]

As the competition mounted, the Chicago editors turned to character attacks and leveled fantastic charges of corruption and ulterior motivation against the New York promoters. Manhattan was "the meanest city in America," "too much on the make," "a dead cock in the pit," and liable to produce the "national scandal of the century."[42] According to the *Tribune*, New York was playing a "grab game"—scheming to make the federal government foot the whole bill and to sponge visitors for everything they were worth. Moreover, New York had a proven record of incompetence—failing, for example, to build Grant's tomb, or to erect monuments to George Washington and Horace Greeley.[43] The paper added:

> New York has made and broken so many promises, has talked too much and done so little, that no one believes it any longer. It has been weighed in the balance and found wanting. Instead of reaching out for the World's Fair and claiming that it alone is entitled to it, it should clothe itself in sack cloth, put ashes on its head, beat its breast, recite the penitential Psalms, and make a full confession of its manifold iniquities.[44]

Others seemed to enjoy this war of the words. *Harper's New Monthly* magazine called it "an active, and even violent, certainly an amusing, controversy."[45] The *Milwaukee Sentinel* said that "Chicago proposes to 'use her lungs' to their utmost to secure the World's Fair. What she needs to do is to use her brains and her purse. This isn't a yacht race where wind counts." The *Atlanta Constitution* "observe[d] with some regret that Chicago continues to talk about holding a World's Fair somewhere in her confines in 1892. This means, of course, a sort of sideshow in a pig-killing establishment, where a fresh hog is turned into several links of smoked sausage in seven minutes by the watch." The *St. Paul Daily Globe*, while stating that "Chicago is unquestionably the fittest place for the great fair," nevertheless chastised the city as being "apparently content to rely on bluff and bluster to win the prize." The *Omaha Republican* chimed in: "New York is simply a place to come into and go out of. The West is the place to learn."[46] Many of these remarks were reprinted in the Chicago papers under recurring columns with names like "Our Envious Surroundings" or "Tips on the World's Fair."

The battle ran tit for tat, especially between the *Times* and the *Tribune*. For every insult one side hurled, the other countered. New York lambasted Chicago for its pollution and its rowdiness, and printed articles such as "One Week's Record of Murder and Butchery in Chicago"; Chicago advised New York that only when it would "check the lawlessness which of late has taken possession of the city" could it resume the discussion of the world's fair question.[47] The Chicago papers criticized New York's infighting over location, stinginess in raising subscriptions to stock, and lack of civic pride or spirit; the New York papers belittled Chicago's youthful exuberance, comparative lack of wealth, and unseemly stockyards.

Then amid this sectional slugfest, St. Louis joined the fray. The group promoting St. Louis's bid—led by Governor David R. Francis of Missouri and Colonel C. H. Jones, editor of the *St. Louis Republic*—made claims that were very similar to the practical ones put forth by Chicago:

- The city was centrally located, encompassing 2 million people more than Chicago within a five hundred-mile radius.
- The railroad and hotel facilities were more than adequate for the task.
- Foreign visitors would naturally want to see some of the country, and St. Louis would afford them that opportunity.
- St. Louis "is the best-watered and best-sewered city in the United States"[48]

The St. Louis organizers sent tens of thousands of circulars to every prominent city and every congressman in the country. Francis and Jones both went to New York to lobby, and the newspapers took to printing inflammatory (and erroneous) headlines, such as

BOTH ARE IN THE SOUP.

NEW YORK AND CHICAGO ADMIT THEIR DEFEAT AND STATE ITS CAUSE.

Neither the City by the Big Bay nor the City by the Big Sewer Can Hope for the World's Fair.[49]

Clearly, the St. Louisans had stolen a page from the publicity books of New York and Chicago; the promotional tone had affected the whole country.

Scribner's magazine called the entire battle an "extraordinary exhibition of indecorum," which "reflected unpleasantly upon American civilization."[50]

Kipling was witness to the contest during his stay in Chicago, and he felt the same way about the newspaper war as about most things American:

> Imprimis, there was some sort of dispute between New York and Chicago as to which town should give an exhibition of products to be hereafter holden, and through the medium of their more dignified journals the two cities were ya-hooing and hi-yi-ing at each other like opposition newsboys. They called it humour but it sounded like something quite different. . . . all that made me weep was that, in these papers, were faithfully reproduced all the war-cries and "back-talk" of the Palmer House bar, the slang of the barbers' shops, the mental elevation and integrity of the Pullman-car porter, the dignity of the Dime Museum, and the accuracy of the excited fishwife.[51]

And so the stage was set. In December 1889, each contender sent a committee to Washington, D.C., to lobby for its interests, as Congress began, at last, to take up the issue of who would host the World's Columbian Exposition.

Throughout much of January 1890 and into February, the House Committee on Foreign Affairs, and then a special Select Committee on the World's Fair, met to hear the formal arguments of the cities, which had been trumpeted by their respective newspapers for the past six months. Long speeches were delivered by the members of the New York and Chicago delegations on January 11, 1890.

New York's Chauncey Depew stated that a national exposition must be located in the metropolis of the country holding it, and New York was the metropolis of this country; that New York's transit system could handle two hundred thousand people per hour, compared to twenty-five thousand in Chicago; that New York was "pleading for the immense number of mechanics, of wageworkers, who would be within reach of it"; and all the familiar arguments.

Mayor Cregier of Chicago and others insisted that their city, unlike New York, had "a park which seems to have been made and left there unoccupied for this express purpose"; that the country "must depend for her future progress and her greatness—not altogether but largely—on those fertile miles and acres in the West"; even that Chicago was in the process of building a canal to connect the Great Lakes and the Mississippi River.[52]

Finally, on February 24, 1890, a day so dreary in Washington that the gas lamps had to be kept blazing at high noon, the great issue came to a vote before the full House.[53] The atmosphere was reminiscent of the party nominating conventions, which had taken place in summer 1888. The galleries were packed with spectators, the corridors filled to capacity, and cloak room lobbying continued up to the last moment. It took nearly six hours and eight ballots to secure a majority, but when at last this had been achieved, Chicago was the winner, with 157 votes to New York's 107, St. Louis's 25, and Washington's 18.

Within two minutes, the news was telegraphed back to the "city of dressed beef," and celebrations began. Later, "with thankful hearts the delegation . . . set their faces toward home, where like a conquering host they were met by a vast procession of citizens."[54] The *Inter Ocean* said,

> To-day the voice of Congress rings across the continent voting the location of the world's fair of 1892. The high verdict was not to be doubted—Chicago! Chicago!! Chicago!!! Continental convenience, the voice of the majority compelled the choice. Not for herself, but representing the preponderant empire of the interior, she has been raised to the purple, and the star-eyed goddess of Liberty herself will congenially assist in dispensing to the world a true American hospitality.[55]

The *Chicago Tribune* ran a front-page cartoon depicting Uncle Sam handing the world's fair bouquet to Lady Chicago, while Lady Washington cried, Lady St. Louis fainted, and Lady New York dropped a handful of dollar signs in astonishment. The *Tribune* could not resist taking a few parting shots at

Gotham, commenting that New York's "inglorious and blundering World's Fair campaign has ended in the overwhelming defeat of that city," that "New York was never really in the fight," and that her present status, along with St. Louis, was "in the big tureen." S. E. Gross of the Chicago delegation was quoted as saying that Chicago's victory was "the first historical culmination of the vast potentialities of the future seat of empire in America."[56]

In New York there was a mixture of bad feelings and reluctant congratulations. Several papers pointed the finger of blame at longtime New York politician Thomas Platt, who had "conspired" with Matthew Quay of Pennsylvania to block New York's efforts; the *Herald* promised it would "get even."[57] The *Evening World* said that "Partisan politics has had a good inning in the House."[58]

Still, there was a general consensus that West had beaten East fairly—as the *Herald* said, the victory belonged to "the magnificent West, with its large daring, its unmeasured generosity, its boundless faith in its own future and in that of the country."[59] The *Brooklyn Daily Eagle* wrote, "Now that it has failed[,] the sensible, manly course is to acquiesce in the result and do what can be done to make the Fair a credit to the country."[60] Even Chauncey Depew acknowledged that the grand national momentum had shifted, sarcastically pledging that "the effete East is behind you with such feeble efforts as she can render to help you in this great enterprise."[61]

The World's Columbian Exposition, the great Chicago World's Fair, was finally going to be a reality. The battle to host the fair had been a war of the words—a massive, modern promotional campaign fought largely through the press, the marketing manifestation of a century's worth of evolution in advertising, humbuggery, journalism, and press agentry. If little else was certain, it was clear that this was going to be the biggest, grandest, damnedest, most heavily promoted spectacle that anyone had ever seen.

And thus, over the course of the next few months, as the World's Columbian Commission organizational team came together and began its planning, one of the first and easiest decisions they made was to establish something no other exposition had ever had, a Department of Publicity and Promotion, and to appoint as its chief one of the leading journalists in the country, a man renowned for his affability, his raconteur's skills, his colossal network of contacts, his thorough knowledge of the newspaper business, and his considerable organizational ability—a man, that is, who lived in clover: Major Moses Purnell Handy.

9

THE DEPARTMENT OF PUBLICITY AND PROMOTION

"Riding on the crest of the gilded wave"

> I have just returned from a trip to Southern Europe, Asia Minor and Egypt. I was astonished everywhere, even in Palestine, at the keen interest manifested in the coming exposition. Everybody seems to know that a World's Fair is to be held in Chicago, and it is conceded that it will be the greatest in history. Palestine is in a deep slumber of centuries, and Jerusalem is dead. But their inhabitants had heard about the fair in Chicago, and our Bedouin dragoman, learning that we were Americans, triumphantly assured us that he was coming over next year to the fair. Never was anything so well advertised.

A "well-known government official and newspaper correspondent,"
Inter Ocean (August 14, 1892)

Even before the big news came in the final weeks of the year, 1890 had already been an eventful one in the Handy home at 4318 Osage Avenue in West Philadelphia.

Having taken on about one new job a year since the mid-1880s (Blaine's presidential campaign of 1884; owner and editor of the *Philadelphia Daily News* from 1884 to 1887; managing editor of the *New York World* in 1887;

organizational committee for the Constitutional Convention in 1887; Harrison's presidential campaign of 1888; manager of a news bureau in Washington, D.C., and special correspondent to several newspapers in 1888–1889), Moses P. Handy had maintained a hectic travel schedule and had continued to suffer significant health problems. In 1889, he again traveled to Europe to spend time recuperating. When the new year began, Handy had just recovered from another bout with la grippe, but he fell ill again on February 1 in Washington, and Sarah had to take the train down from Philadelphia to nurse him back to health at Chamberlin's, at 15th and I Streets NW.

Two miles away, under the elegant ellipsoidal dome on East Capitol Street, the House Committee on Foreign Affairs and the Select Committee on the World's Fair were in the middle of their highly contentious hearings to decide whether New York or Chicago would host the Columbian Exposition—a decision which, unbeknownst to the Handys, would soon change the course of their lives.

Sarah adored her husband and shouldered most of the parenting responsibilities for their seven children, now aged four to twenty, yet she also diligently maintained her own career. She had built a strong journalistic resume with her many contributions to publications like *Scribner's* and *Harper's Bazaar*, and her Home and Society column in the *Philadelphia Weekly Times*. Now, in early 1890, she produced one article after another for a variety of publications—"The Englishwoman at Home" for the *Philadelphia Press*, "Upholstering at Home" for the *Philadelphia Times*, and with unwitting prescience, a piece entitled "How to Move Easily and Well" for the *Ladies Home Journal*. In this, she noted that moving is "among the minor miseries of life" and that "not unfrequently the best advice which can be given to persons contemplating such a step is . . . *Don't!*" She then offered a great number of practical suggestions, such as "The first thing sent to the new house should be a stock of coal," and "In engaging your dray men, stipulate that the furniture is to be taken in and set up properly just where you want it, not dumped down anywhere for you to arrange afterward as best you can."[1]

On the first of March 1890, both servants employed by the Handys quit, throwing the planning for the family picnic the next day into chaos. "Everybody at the wheel," Sarah wrote in her pocket diary. Less than three months later, one of the replacement servants also bolted. "New cook a failure," Sarah huffed, "left in a fuss."[2] She got by as best she could, mending clothes and making favorites like cucumber catsup, but there would be a revolving cast of household staff throughout the year.

And of course, it didn't help that Moses was on the road again for much of the spring and summer—the usual trips to Washington, D.C., and New York several times a month, followed by a swing through Tacoma, Portland, San Francisco, and Denver. In August he made three trips to Washington, D.C., missing her forty-fifth birthday on the 22nd.

But change was in the air, and it was blowing from some far-off ports of call.

First, some of Moses's political allies floated his name as a possible replacement for the U.S. consul-general (a nineteenth-century term for ambassador) to Egypt, Eugene Schuyler, who had died of malaria in July. Handy was well known by the power brokers in Washington and by President Benjamin Harrison himself and had traveled abroad numerous times—credentials enough to land a top diplomatic post. Both he and Harrison were in Cape May, New Jersey, in July and likely discussed it during their meeting there on July 19.[3]

Yet there was another opportunity in the offing. It had now been about six months since Congress had awarded the World's Columbian Exposition to Chicago—sufficient time for the critics and skeptics in major cities of Europe to begin publicly questioning Chicago's suitability and whether they should mount exhibits or even plan to attend what some had derisively started calling the "Cook County Fair." This did not go unnoticed by the World's Columbian Commission, so on September 23, 1890, they issued a resolution for the creation of the fair's first department, overseeing publicity and promotion, which would be classified in the unsentimental patois of bureaucracy as Department O. The preamble read in part:

> **WHEREAS** reports have reached this country through the medium of correspondents and returning American tourists that the World's Columbian Exposition is practically discredited by American newspapers, and is unworthy of the serious consideration of Europeans, and
>
> **WHEREAS** such reports have received apparent confirmation from the tone of certain foreign newspapers which have mistaken the expressions of such tourists as those of the American people, and
>
> **WHEREAS** the basis of such reports is evidently an erroneous idea as to the reasons which led to the selection of Chicago as the location of

> the Exposition, and such reports being entirely based on false assumptions cannot but be harmful to the purposes of the Exposition,
>
> **RESOLVED** that the officers of the Commission be and are hereby authorized to take such steps as they deem advisable to counteract the false impressions herein referred to, and that a copy of these resolutions be forwarded to the principal newspapers of London, Paris, Berlin, Vienna, Madrid, and the other European capitals, and the other European countries.[4]

It seems quite likely that Moses P. Handy was brought in to help draft the resolution (a copy appears with handwritten corrections among his archival papers; additionally, Sarah Handy's diary noted that her husband was in Chicago from September 17 through 25). Certainly, he had already been identified as a potential leader for this department, for there was not another human being alive who combined so much direct experience on expositions with a mastery of the inner workings of the press.

Both opportunities started to become very real for the Handys in fall 1890. On December 5, a document was laid before President Harrison, signed by thirty members of the U.S. Senate and the entire Pennsylvania delegation of the House of Representatives, recommending Handy for the consul-general job in Egypt.[5] One week later, the president obliged—but on the same day, so did the World's Columbian Commission.

The choice was not a hard one. Handy was a superb journalist who had grown up with the newspaper industry, and he understood its promotional potential in a way few people of his era did. As chief of the Department of Publicity and Promotion for what was already being billed as the greatest exposition the world had ever undertaken, he would be able to capitalize on that knowledge and experience, as well as his vast network of acquaintances from the newspapers and social clubs with which he had long been associated. And at $7,500 per annum (roughly $193,000 in 2017 dollars), the compensation would be very good.

And so the decision was made, albeit without much fanfare. "Mr. H. appointed Promoter &c to World's Fair," Sarah matter-of-factly jotted in her diary entry for December 12. She probably knew at that very moment that she was about to endure another one of those "minor miseries of life," because their fourteen-year stay in Philadelphia would soon come to an end. It was time to move, again.[6]

Moses intuitively knew that his powers of persuasion and promotion could probably help rescue this already-maligned event, and perhaps even help bolster Chicago's reputation. Looking back on this period just a few years later, in a manuscript documenting the history of the Columbian Exposition, Handy recalled the skepticism among antagonists that the fair would ever come to be, and the innuendo that if it did, it would be a negligible affair.

> Outside of the local press of Chicago the attention paid to the Exposition even by American newspapers was discouragingly inadequate. Ignorance prevailed abroad and scepticism [*sic*] at home, and [were] annoying and discouraging to the public spirited men who . . . had undertaken under conditions of unsurpassed difficulty, the herculean work of building an International Exposition. It was imperative that an Exposition which was intended to represent every nation of the world should be universally exploited, if it was to be a complete success. As late as December 1890 the majority of the European press was absolutely silent as to what was proposed at Chicago. Americans traveling abroad wrote home that the fact of an Exposition being under consideration was almost unheard of in the Old World. The establishment of the Department of Publicity & Promotion therefore by the appointment and confirmation of a Chief was hailed with a satisfaction which was in itself most encouraging and stimulating to the person to whom the honor of the appointment had come unsought.[7]

On December 29, 1890, Moses P. Handy arrived in Chicago after the long train trip from Philadelphia and took a room at the Richelieu—an opulent five-year-old hotel on Michigan Avenue, "The Delmonico of Chicago," "The Most Complete, Refined, and Home-like Hotel in America"—and immediately began to piece together a plan for how to organize his department and launch a massive promotional campaign for the Exposition.[8]

That very same day, about nine hundred miles to the west at Wounded Knee Creek on the Pine Ridge Agency, the Seventh Cavalry trained its Hotchkiss guns on the Lakotas (with John M. Burke either there killing an Indian in hand-to-hand combat, or nearby cowering under a pile of debris, all the while recording every detail in his expansive memory to be unleashed later as part of his own elaborate promotional campaign). The confusing events were reported in the December 30 edition of the *Kansas City Gazette* in a series of stilted dispatches:

> The Indian men, women and children then ran to the south, the battery firing rapidly as they ran. . . . Just now it is impossible to state the exact number of dead Indians. There are many more than fifty, however, killed outright. The soldiers are shooting the Indians down wherever found, no quarter being given by any one. . . .
>
> To say that it was a most daring feat for 120 Indians to attack 500 cavalry expresses the situation but faintly. It could only have been insanity that prompted such a deed.
>
> It is doubted that either a buck or a squaw out of all of Big Foot's band will be left to tell the tale of the day's treachery.[9]

And in that same newspaper was an ad soliciting sales agents for P. T. Barnum's new book *Dollars and Sense*: "Inquire of all the American born people if they ever heard of P. T. Barnum, and you will find that at least 99 out of every 100 will answer YES; then send the publishers 50 cents for the agent's complete outfit, and go to work at once."[10]

It was quite a day for synchronicity in the development of the marketing industry.

The fact is, however, that while historians often develop timelines and talk about periods of transition, history playing out in real time usually has a lot of untidy overlap. So it was in late 1890, on the precipice of a new century and the birth of a new industry.

Chicago and Wounded Knee were both parts of the changing West, and they were playing out at the very same moment. So too with Handy and Burke.

The two men had in common an upbringing in Delaware, a background in writing, deep familiarity with the inner workings of newspapers, extensive networks of acquaintances, and experience in promoting big events. They probably already knew each other, since Burke had certainly called on the many Philadelphia newspaper offices that Handy had run. But their respective situations on December 29, 1890, were starkly different, and in a sense were emblematic of their differing approaches to promotion, which would collide two years down the road. The World's Columbian Exposition promotional effort would be about substance—lots of facts, statistics, words, and languages touting the promise of the future—while that of the Wild West would be more about style—filled with emotion, mythology, stunts, icons, and images harkening back to a time gone by. One was Chicago; the other was Wounded Knee.

Of course, embedded in their respective efforts were not just the tensions and future directions of the nascent marketing industry but the heritage—and influence—of P. T. Barnum as well. The showman was eighty years old in that winter of 1890–1891, when the curtain had begun to fall on his long-running act. Stricken in November with what at first was thought to be "influenza in its most malignant form"—later deemed a stroke—he spent the next several months at home recuperating. The newspapers described him as "gradually breaking down from old age."[11]

During the illness he periodically rallied, and in one of those instances he wrote to a friend: "The only thing lacking to make me happy on my return to good health is the chance to see what sort of lines would have been written about me." Hearing this, the *New York Evening Sun* (with Tody Hamilton's assistance) then ran a four-column obituary of him under the headline "Great and Only Barnum. He Wanted to Read His Obituary; Here It Is."[12] He died two weeks later, April 7, 1891, presumably happy with his legacy as the Prince of Humbugs, the world's greatest showman, and the very personification of the new art of marketing and promotion. Alas, the Exposition was still two years from opening, so although his legacy was secure, he would miss out on the greatest year of promotion the country had ever known.

Barnum had lived long enough, however, to see both the Wild West and the Columbian Exposition campaigns in action and, true to his character, had weighed in. When he had visited the Wild West in 1887, he declared it to be "the coming show," perhaps a worthy implementation of the buffalo-and-Indians concept he himself had entertained years earlier. "The virtue of the show was that it did not need spangles, being of itself all life and movement, the effect of which was easily grasped by everybody," he reportedly said.[13]

Barnum had also been keeping an eye on the World's Columbian Exposition. He had repeatedly endorsed the idea of holding the event in New York, but after that effort failed, he turned his attention to its substance and promotion. In March 1890, Barnum's article "What the Fair Should

Be" appeared in *North American Review* (alongside a story by the futurist author Edward Bellamy, entitled "'Looking Backward' Again") with an optimistic view of the Columbian Exposition. He challenged fair organizers to "make it bigger and better than any that have preceded it. Make it the Greatest Show on Earth—greater than my own Great Moral Show—if you can. It should differ from its predecessors in having twice as many visitors, with a hundred times better accommodations for them."[14]

Barnum went so far as to suggest one of the exhibits: the mummified corpse of Ramses II, which could be transported from Egypt. "Think of the stupendousness of the incongruity!" he wrote. "To exhibit to the people of the nineteenth century, in a country not discovered until 2,000 or 3,000 years after his death, the corpse of the king of whom we have the earliest record."[15]

Whether Handy or Burke paid serious heed to the showman's commentaries is doubtful, for by this time, the state of the art of promotion had advanced considerably beyond Barnum. Spurred by demographic and technological developments, promotion had undergone a rapid metamorphosis. The total U.S. population had more than trebled since 1840, when Barnum was in his prime as a showman, from 17 million to 63 million. The literacy rate, which had been just 36 percent in 1840, had reached 66 percent by 1890.[16] This helped fuel the first stirrings of a mass market, a surge in demand for information and consumer goods, and a consequent explosion in publishing—a jump from 4,400 newspapers in the 1880s to 13,000 in the 1890s—which then led to innovations in advertising both direct and indirect, and a surfeit of strategies for influencing the public.[17] Although newspapers of this era still frequently spoke of publicity in the context of making news public ("The report has been made, but will not be given publicity at once"), the whole notion of using information and imagery to shape public opinion or drive consumer behavior was now a key business strategy and, increasingly, an accepted part of American culture.[18] The reign of the agate-type print advertisement—inert and passive—was over. Now all advertising was being actively sculpted by the hands of clever men. This was acknowledged as early as 1884, when the trade magazine the *Journalist* declared that "any enterprise which depends to any extent upon advertising in the public press must have especial men hired solely for the purpose of 'working the press' for notices, free advertising, and the like."[19]

Indeed, by the 1890s, hundreds of press agents and press bureaus were at work cleverly trying to generate ink for their entertainment and corporate enterprises, as well as scores of advertising agencies launching multifaceted campaigns on behalf of their clients. The railroad and steamboat lines all had press agents, and so did some of the large hotels and even universities. Before long, so would the U.S. government itself.

The great industrial tycoons also increasingly relied on press agents and their creative new strategies for shaping public opinion. In their "battle of the currents" to determine which technology—Edison Electric's direct current or Westinghouse Electric's alternating current—would be adopted as the standard, both Thomas Edison and George Westinghouse turned to publicity experts for help. In fall 1889, Westinghouse hired *Pittsburgh Chronicle Telegraph* newspaper reporter Ernest H. Heinrichs to promote his company, instructing him, "All I want is to see that the papers print [matters] accurately. The truth hurts nobody."[20] But what this new class of professional press agents came to realize is that, when viewed through the lens of the media, the truth could be presented in a very different light. Thus, when New York State selected Westinghouse's alternating current system to power its electric chair in 1890, the Edison team suggested that "as Westinghouse's dynamo is going to be used for the purpose of executing criminals, why not give him the benefit of this fact in the minds of the public, and speak hereafter of a criminal as being 'westinghoused,' or (to use it as a noun) as having been *condemned to the westinghouse* in the same way that Dr. Guillotine's name was forever immortalized in France?"[21]

Westinghouse's technology would prevail (and his zeal for promotion would lead him to place an aggressive bid that won him the rights to light the World's Columbian Exposition), but Edison's name and fame—as well as a bit of nasty "spin" from time to time—would elevate him to immortality.

Handy and Burke could not help but notice that with all these new tent poles holding up the ever-expanding canvas of their industry, it was starting to get a lot more crowded inside. Still, no one had attempted to launch a promotional campaign quite on the scale of the World's Columbian Exposition.

How do you change the reputation of an entire city? How do you counteract widespread ignorance or misinformation? How do you persuade foreign governments and journalists to buy into the ludicrous and fantastical notion

THE DEPARTMENT OF PUBLICITY AND PROMOTION for the World's Columbian Exposition was organized like a newspaper office, and Moses P. Handy was essentially its publisher and editor-in-chief. Undated, unattributed photograph, Handy Family Papers, William L. Clements Library, University of Michigan, Ann Arbor.

that a glimmering White City—the paramount cultural achievement of the last four centuries—will, within two years, arise from the swampland south of a city that few of them had ever heard of? How do you convince skeptical state governments that they should set aside appropriations for exhibits to a fair that some still believed would never come to pass? And once you have accomplished all that, how do you possibly inform the polyglot people of the world about all the attractions and advancements and splendor that this fair would supposedly offer, especially when the architects and exhibitors were all working independently and were not terribly forthcoming about their plans?

Moses P. Handy spent his first hours in Chicago contemplating the daunting tasks that lay ahead of him. Although there was no obvious strategy for how to proceed, this much was clear: the traditional style of advertising, which he knew well from his many years in the newspaper industry, would be insufficient. This would be less about selling goods (a mere mercantile transaction) and more about imbuing concepts and influencing opinion (a feat of persuasion). It would be Barnum's game, played by Handy's rules.

Within days he put together a "skeleton plan of organization and a rough estimate of the probable expenses of the Department for the first year," and submitted this to Director General George R. Davis to seek approval from the board of directors. According to Handy's plan, there would be two "grand divisions"—one for publicity, the other for promotion.

By his definition, "publicity" meant any enterprise that involved a printing press, primarily newspapers and magazines. "Machinery was to be provided," Handy explained, "to furnish information through the press to the world, of the importance of the Exposition, its advantages to every department of industry, art and science, its educational features, and its unprecedented magnitude as the crowning display of civilization of the Nineteenth Century." There would be efforts to describe Chicago's location and accessibility, to explain the breadth and depth of the Exposition plan and the "high aims of its projectors," and to study the "journalistic methods . . . and tastes of each country" so that material could be provided in local languages to "tempt the editor to print it."

Yet this would-be consul-general was also keenly aware that the enterprise would rely in part on federal funding, and hence on politics, so he laid out a truly novel publicity goal: "To obtain copies of all newspapers in which articles emanating from the Department and all other articles referring to the World's Fair, appeared, and to preserve such articles not only for record but for reference, so that at any time it might be possible from such files to ascertain to the trend of public opinion about the Fair in any country, to dispel misinformation, and combat and dissipate misrepresentation and prejudice."[22]

This last task would ultimately consume the energies of several employees, who assembled scrapbooks each day (about seventy-five at any given time), counted words that were deemed to have originated from the department's editorial team, and calculated what today we would call "ad equivalencies"—the theoretical cost of obtaining the same amount of coverage in the press via advertising instead of publicity. The process was, in effect, an extensive effort to document and justify the role of publicity.

One measure of how much the art of publicity had already advanced was that now several services provided newspaper clippings, or "cuttings," from around the world, such as the Newspaper Extract and Information Bureau in London, and Agence de La Presse in Paris. Several such companies were in the United States, including Henry Romeike, Inc. (established in 1884), and Frank Burrelle's Bureau of Press Clippings (1888). They secured subscriptions to every major newspaper in the country and, once the papers arrived through the mail, scoured every article looking for their clients' key words. The cost was two cents per clip provided. (The Burrelle name is familiar to generations of public relations executives, who relied on Burrelle's press clipping services to monitor their work until the advent of the Internet. The company survives to this day as BurrelleLuce.[23])

"Promotion," to Handy, was something different. It was about "arousing public interest otherwise than through the medium of the press," especially corresponding with "State officials, Boards of Trade, National and State organizations for industrial purposes, members of Congress & of State legislatures"—more akin to a modern public affairs or lobbying function. The immediate goal of the promotional campaign was to ensure that the federal and state governments appropriated money for adequate representation at the Exposition.[24]

The plan was bold and expansive, one that probably could only have been hatched from the meticulous mind of a man whose entire life had been grounded in organization and discipline (rote schoolroom lessons, Army of Northern Virginia, numerous bustling newsrooms, house with seven children plus boarders, work on two previous expositions). And he created it within his first ten days on the job.

On January 3, 1891, Handy and Director General Davis boarded an eastbound train and began a series of meetings in New York and Washington, D.C. (including one with President Harrison, who was still without a consul-general to Egypt) to put the plan in motion. In the coming days and weeks, Handy would resume—and if anything, accelerate—the frenzied pace of work and travel to which he had become accustomed. He went on many trips to New York and Washington, with the occasional overnight stay at his home in Philadelphia or breakfast with Sarah at the Hotel Bellevue on his way back out of town. It was not unusual for him to take the overnight train back to Chicago, arrive on a Sunday, proceed directly to his office in room 422 of the Rand McNally Building, and then on to a dinner meeting, and from there to a social event, such as a gathering at the Press Club or an evening at the theater. He made several appearances and speeches each week and met over an endless string of meals with politicians, bureaucrats, financiers, journalists, and industrialists at the Palmer House, the Coaching Club, and Kinsley's—a garish five-story restaurant built in the late 1870s to resemble a Moorish castle, with a German beer hall, French café, and men's-only restaurant inside.[25]

There was even an effort to publicize the publicity effort. Just a week into his new job, Handy communicated his plan to some of his friends in the newspaper business, and they were impressed. Henry M. Hunt of Hunt's News Bureau said that Handy "has already outlined some decidedly original ideas. For one thing, he proposes to placard the leading cities of England, France, Germany, Italy, Russia and other European countries with pictures and printed matter telling of Chicago's greatness and glory, and of what she proposes to do in 1893, to an extent that will put to shame the recent onslaughts of Barnum and of the Wild West show on the billboards of the Old World."[26]

Handy asked one of his former editors and trusted lieutenants at the *Philadelphia Press*, Robert E. A. Dorr, to come to Chicago and discuss the department's job as second-in-command. Dorr had a background as a journalist but was also politically savvy and resourceful; he would be an outstanding surrogate for Handy when he was away from the office. Dorr arrived on January 23, was hired the next day at an annual salary of three thousand dollars, and went to work on February 1. Together, they quickly built out the staff, structuring it to resemble a newspaper office, with a local press division, a foreign press division, a mailing division, a press and printing division, an editorial team, and so forth.

Among the first hires were James P. Holland, a thirty-five-year-old English-born journalist whose credits included the *Chicago Tribune* and *Chicago Herald*, as well as earlier trade press work with a publication called *Shoe and Leather Review*; Thomas Weston, "a newspaperman of large experience," to supervise the foreign bureau; Henry Heinemann, twenty-six, an Englishman raised in Germany; Louis Ayme, a Columbia graduate who had traveled the world and was fluent in several languages; and Nancy

"THE VERY NERVE CENTER OF ALL ACTIVITY ON THE GROUNDS." Handy (*far left*), in his Exposition office, with (*left to right*), staffers Robert E. A. Dorr and Nancy Huston Banks, as well as visitor Richard Murphy. *World's Columbian Exposition Illustrated*, April 1891; author's collection.

Huston Banks, a talented Kentucky-born writer who in later years would report from the Boer War and pen several novels, including one called *Oldfield*—which, curiously, was a pseudonym occasionally used by Sarah Handy later in her life.[27]

Handy got right to work. During his first week on the job, he negotiated a deal with publisher James B. Campbell to produce the *World's Columbian Exposition Illustrated*—a sort of promotional magazine—in multiple languages. He also sent members of the world press an article Handy presumably wrote describing Chicago "from the point of view of a foreign traveler who had stumbled upon [it] without premonition of its greatness." This article did not say much about the Exposition—a subtle strategy to help shore up the foundations of Chicago's damaged reputation.[28] Handy later wrote in his draft report on the history of his department that this letter was reproduced verbatim in some newspapers, was incorporated into editorial copy in others, and "very frequently the editors consigned it wholesale to the waste basket." (In the draft, he then crossed out the words "very frequently" and replaced them with "occasionally" for the final report—discretion being the better part of valor.[29])

Then the Department of Publicity and Promotion began to spring to life.

By February 1, Holland reported that they had already amassed a mailing list of 5,670 names, including editors (for the publicity effort) and state officials and legislators, officers of boards of trade and chambers of commerce, and members of trade associations (for the promotion effort). Also on the department's mailing list were public library reading rooms, bankers' offices, and other public gathering places. "The mailing list thus compiled grew to such proportions [ultimately, more than fifty thousand] that every publication of the Department had a circulation equal to that of the most influential newspapers," wrote Handy.[30] Although the mail was not commonly used for marketing purposes in this era, Handy and his team would make a science of it and ultimately convert their small office into the largest second-class post office in the United States.

On February 10, department members sent out a note over Handy's signature to 2,544 trade papers and 3,305 daily and weekly newspapers, requesting that the Department of Publicity and Promotion be listed in press exchanges, so his team could start receiving and sending to these papers. At the same time, Handy mailed out a request to all the newspapers asking them for a list of the most relevant editors so that he could trim down his distribution and be more efficient.

The team also began issuing press releases and sending out literature that previewed some of the plans for the Exposition. The topics included everything from "Advantages of the Fair to Americans" and "Descriptions of the Grounds" to "Forestry Exhibit" and "Rules for State Buildings." A talented group of linguists on the editorial team translated the articles into German, French, Portuguese, Spanish, Italian, Swedish, and "Welch," and outside translators helped with another six languages.[31]

Unfortunately, these linguistic skills also brought on unwanted work, as officials from nearly every Exposition department dealing with foreign countries came to Handy's team for help in translation. Handy was repeatedly forced to complain to Davis about this unbudgeted work:

> I have to say that a very large portion of the work charged to this department under present methods, is really for other offices and departments of the Exposition; for example, we are called upon to translate all letters and documents written in foreign languages to the Director-General, President and Secretary, World's Columbian Exposition, the department Chiefs and the several officers and Committees of the Exposition. This work requires the services of

> men who are proficient in not less than four foreign languages; and translation of other languages than these four have to be paid for by the piece. The salary paid Mr. Altschul, our principle translator is inadequate, and I am threatened with the loss of his services, unless his salary is increased.[32]

The department also sent weekly newsletters that compiled information about appropriations and plans in twenty-six different states ("nearly every state was put on its metal by knowledge of what other states were doing," wrote Handy) as well as a pamphlet entitled *After Four Centuries*, a concise summary of the plans for the Exposition, which had a print run of 200,000 in nine languages.[33] During the third week of February 1891 alone, the department sent out 8,876 pamphlets and 6,562 circulars; on April 24 Holland would report that they had sent out 47,851 pieces of printed matter during the first ten days of April. Handy made sure that they tracked and counted everything that went out from or came into his office—down to the number of words.[34] While unusually meticulous, this methodology was also very much in keeping with the overall spirit of the World's Columbian Exposition organizers, who would go on to document in multivolume sets everything from building costs, daily attendance, and number of crimes committed to the amount of food served and garbage disposed.

Nevertheless, the flood of outbound materials did not necessarily guarantee the sort of coverage that the Department of Publicity and Promotion wanted. Especially in certain European countries, press releases and promotional materials were still sometimes treated as requests for paid advertising, referred to by some as "advertisement-letters."[35] Handy derisively called this the "subsidy system," which had been in wide use at previous international expositions and entertainment events. Department staffer Louis Ayme wrote to Handy, "It is a notorious fact that the Paris press, which practically controls the press of France, is utterly venal and corrupt. It was certain that a concentrated attempt would be made to force the Exposition officials to pay heavily for the insertion of articles about the World's Columbian Exposition. The 'bluff' would be made 'no pay—no publicity.'" Ayme's strategy was to call their bluff—"masterly inactivity," he called it—and assume that once the press in England and Germany started covering the World's Columbian Exposition, so, too, would the French. But it soon became clear that this was not working. "I am compelled to believe that our acknowledgement of the necessity of paying for the insertion of favorable articles on the Exposition has practically closed to us the columns of the newspapers of France. Since April 1, nearly 25,000 newsletters have been sent to between 900 and 1000 French papers. It is very questionable if 100 reprints have been made."[36]

At the same time, the French publishers smelled blood in the water and tried to strike. One in Bordeaux printed a press release for free but wrote back to Handy, "We are at your disposition to continue the insertion of such letters in our three papers, at an exceptionally low price, that is: *six francs per letter per paper*. . . . When the Exposition opens[,] the publicity of our papers might be of immense value to you as we can assure you of their circulation."[37] Another one in Lyons asked, "Would you like us to make a campaign of publicity in our journal 'La Bourse Lyonnaise' for the coming Exposition at Chicago. . . ? I place myself and my bureaux at your disposition for this special purpose if you care for it. I leave to yourself the care of fixing the remuneration or advantages which you will grant me."[38]

But Handy demurred: "The subsidy system is contrary to the spirit of American institutions, and objectionable, not to say insulting."[39] Moreover, on a practical note, there was not enough money in the budget to even begin entertaining such a notion. He fully intended to pay for advertising that was, in fact, advertising as the opening of the fair drew closer. But that would be a modest effort, geared mostly at stimulating short-term attendance. As he would later tell the congressional subcommittee that was charged with examining the preparations for the fair (and did so meticulously—even requesting at one point to know how and why there had been money spent on ice), "I can not do as Wanamaker and spend $200,000 a year . . . and Pear[s'] Soap $400,000, and Barnum $250,000 before he opens his doors. This is not a show enterprise in one sense, it is a business enterprise, but I can not do it on that scale."[40]

He acknowledged that the success of the Exposition was dependent on the press, and in such situations there was the "unquestioned sanction of unwritten law" that management would "at the proper time make return in the extension of the courtesies to editors and their families." What he had in mind were free press passes, although this would run afoul of the rule established by the World's Columbian Commission that there should be only one pass issued to each newspaper. He would have to find a way to strike the right balance.

Thus, even as this most sophisticated of promotional campaigns began to unfold, questions still lingered. Would it be driven by direct advertising or indirect—now generally referred to as "publicity"? Pay-for-play or legitimate news coverage? In effect, since there were no guidelines or precedents for how to launch such a complex international publicity campaign, Handy and his colleagues had to make it up on the fly. And as a lifelong journalist who had adhered to industry tenets of fairness and balance, the transition to the "other side of the interview table" would be rife with tension for Moses P. Handy.

Despite the advent of new "express" train service and the increasing luxuriousness of some lines with gaudy gilt-and-silver stenciling, dining cars, sleeper cars, library cars, ladies' maids, and barber shops, it was still a grueling trip for the Handys to see each other.[41] The Pennsylvania Railroad's Chicago Special, inaugurated in June 1891, left Philadelphia at 6:25 P.M., made stops at Harrisburg, Altoona, Pittsburgh, and "principal points on the Fort Wayne route," and finally arrived in Chicago nearly twenty-three hours later, at 5:15 P.M. the following day.[42]

Sarah paid her first visit to Moses in Chicago on Valentine's Day and spent the next few days getting swept up in his new world, with long hours at the office, dinners at Kinsley's with dignitaries and socialites, and a night out at the Auditorium Theater to see a London melodrama. On February 20, the snow was so heavy that she abandoned her efforts to get to the office and just stayed at the hotel; "nasty day," she wrote. But then it was back on the train, back to her writer-widow's existence in Philadelphia and a growing dreariness that peppered her diary: "another profitless day," "nothing worth chronicling," "busy all day doing the things that have no names," and her favorite, "lounging 'round & suffering."[43]

She made the trip to Chicago again in late May. And on the 27th, she and Moses went for a drive in Jackson Park, visiting the busy worksite where the World's Columbian Exposition was just beginning to rise from the sand-dune and scrub-oak swampland. It must have been a moment of great reckoning for them.

The basic layout, which would cover 633 acres, had been designed by the architects Daniel Burnham and John Root, and the landscapers Frederick Law Olmstead and Henry Codman, although neither Root nor Codman

SAND DUNES AND SCRUB OAKS dominated the Jackson Park landscape in July 1891, when this lantern slide picture was taken. Within months, the magical White City would materialize, transforming 633 acres. World's Columbian Exposition, Jackson Park, Chicago, Illinois, 1891–1893, World's Columbian Exposition Photographs by C. D. Arnold, 1891–1894, Ryerson and Burnham Archives, The Art Institute of Chicago, Illinois; Digital File #19238.

would live to see the designs realized. At its heart would be a Court of Honor, with a 1,100-foot-long basin, anchored on either end by magnificent sculptures (Frederick MacMonnies's allegorical *Columbian Fountain*, with Fame at the bow and Time at the stern of a barge guided by Columbia; and Daniel Chester French's gold-leaf-covered *Statue of the Republic*, towering sixty-five feet high on top of a forty-foot base), surrounded by seven major buildings: Manufactures and Liberal Arts, Agriculture, Electricity, Machinery, Mines and Mining, Transportation, and Administration. Waterways and an elevated electric intramural railway would connect the Court of Honor to natural landscape features, lagoons, the Wooded Island, the Midway Plaisance, and two hundred buildings on other parts of the fairgrounds; and a "moveable sidewalk" would run along the 2,400-foot pier that extended out into Lake Michigan, where many visitors would arrive by boat.

The major buildings themselves, although designed by various architects chosen by Burnham and Root, would all be of the classical Roman and Greek styles taught by the École des Beaux-Arts in Paris. They would be united by the uniform heights of their cornices and width of their bays, and by similar use of archways, domes, porticos, balustrades, and columns. All the buildings were to be constructed in like fashion: iron-and-wood frameworks, covered by "staff"—an inexpensive, lightweight but firm mixture of plaster, cement, and jute—which when painted white using

CONSTRUCTION OF THE FAIR, including the Mines and Mining Building, was well covered by the press and typically attracted thousands of paying customers each day. *Exposition Graphic,* 1893; author's collection.

compressed-air squirt guns would look to the naked eye like marble. Staff had been developed only within the past twenty years or so but had already been used at some of the great European expositions. One of its most interesting qualities was perhaps also its greatest defect: it wasn't built to last. By design, these monumental expositions and their splendid edifices were meant to be temporary—their evanescent nature serving only to enhance the illusory and magical quality of the fairy-tale fair, rising from nothing and then gone after six months of glory.

Soon there would be a maze of construction sites, with railcars and horses and wagons busily crossing paths; piles of timber and iron beams strewn about; dredging derricks and hoisting engines groaning day and night; electric-powered sawmills and tool sharpeners producing a droning industrial symphony; an army of ten thousand workers laboring away; and the half-finished iron-and-wood skeletons of what looked like gigantic train sheds rising into the air and then arching just enough to hint at the majestic shapes of the buildings that were to materialize.

On their visit to the park that day in May 1891, the Handys could only begin to imagine what grand edifices were to come. Work would not begin on the first of the major buildings, Mines and Mining and Transportation, until July. The gargantuan construction effort would then quickly become a popular tourist attraction in its own right, and fair organizers, who started out issuing free passes, began charging twenty-five cents and then fifty cents admission; on many days some five thousand spectators would pay their way in just to watch the crews at work and stimulate their own imaginations. Handy would even create a guidebook, entitled *Official World's Fair Guide, Map and Directory, During Construction,* which was published by Rand McNally and sold for ten cents.

For now, though, the grand spectacle of the White City existed only in Burnham's blueprints and the Department of Publicity and Promotion's lithographs and electrotypes. What the Handys saw on that day was the tabula rasa that would magically evolve into a magnificent painting. The site had essentially been scraped to a level plain. The grading for the temporary construction railroad was complete, though rails had not yet been laid beyond the entrance to the park. A workforce of six hundred men, 225 teams of horses, and four dredging boats was laboring around the clock. The sites for most of the primary buildings had been blocked off and readied for construction crews, and the excavation of the Grand Basin and canal were about to begin. There were tents where the workers lived, but only one building: the two-story white clapboard construction office.[44]

This bustling scene reflected, perhaps, the industriousness that had won the West, built the railroads, and led to the creation of the new metropolitan colossus that was Chicago. But how to articulate that vision? How to capture in verbs and adjectives and statistics all that the World's Columbian Exposition would represent, all the symbolism, all the object lessons that the exhibits and cultural artifacts and industrial displays would teach? This was Handy's challenge, and it was every bit as difficult as the one that still lay ahead for Burnham, Root, Olmstead, and Codman, in converting this morass into their ethereal dream.

Three days after their tour of Jackson Park, the Handys watched the Decoration Day Parade from the windows of the Hotel Richelieu. Then it was time to part again, and Sarah headed back to Philadelphia, with visions of the White City in her heart, and thoughts about the so-called Gray City (Chicago) in her mind, for she planned to join her husband there later in the year.

In contrast to John M. Burke's promotional efforts on behalf of the Wild West, Handy's campaign for the Columbian Exposition was serious, fact laden, and as yet somewhat devoid of emotion.

But in June, the Exposition marketing literally began to take on more color with the issuance of a vivid lithograph of the massive 490-by-1,391-foot Machinery Hall, which would be one of the most impressive buildings at the world's fair (the *Chicago Herald* later rhapsodized about how "its lofty dome, its stately colonnades and splendid vistas, its spacious galleries and the apparently endless perspective of its vast corridors, was something calculated to excite awe and astonishment").[45] Also nearly complete was a beautiful bird's-eye view of the fair, which would become one of the most requested and popular prints (see plate 8). Together, these two vivid images would give Handy a promotional tool he had never had during the ink-black years of his newspaper work.

Meanwhile, just six months into his campaign, Handy estimated that newspapers were now printing about one hundred thousand words about the Exposition, or the equivalent of a three hundred-page book, *every single day*. But there remained some gnawing doubt, especially overseas. Would Chicago really be able to pull it off? Would the World's Columbian Exposition open on time?

On June 27, 1891, a London paper called the *Oracle* ran a typically skeptical article, saying, "[Chicago] is a great city, energetic and full of life, but in this case it really looks questionable whether it will rise to the occasion or not," and suggesting that the fair might end up being "a gigantic fizzle." The article was entitled, "Will the World's Fair Be a Failure?"[46] A newspaper in Birmingham, England, expressed its concerns, too, citing the raw feelings still lingering from the battle over which city would get to host the fair. "If any Birmingham citizens chance to remember the satire poured upon Chicago when New York was a competitor for the fair, and its then idea that land speculators were at the bottom of Chicago's desire, they will smile at this sudden enthusiasm for the city of pork."[47] The newspaper the *Colonies and India* went even further, repeatedly referring to the host city as "Porkopolis."[48] And the *Times of London* provided regular coverage of each failure by a state legislature (Alabama, California) to appropriate enough money for a building at the fair—and indeed went on to speculate about how much Britain would or should appropriate.

In response, Handy and other commissioners of the World's Columbian Exposition prepared for a summertime trip to Europe to stir up interest. His Clover Club–honed charm, his persuasive promotional skills, his newspaperman's instinct for fairness—surely these would open doors and minds. And in case they couldn't, he also sought out letters of introduction, such as the one to a prominent British lord that said, "The indubitable indications now are that the Fair will be the greatest and grandest exposition that the world has ever seen."[49]

On July 7, Sarah saw Moses off in the pouring rain in New York on the steamer *August Victoria*. Over the next six weeks, his itinerary would take him and members of the Exposition retinue to England, France, Germany, Belgium, Switzerland, Holland, Sweden, Norway, Denmark, Austria, Hungary, and Russia.

"The plan of operations of the Commissioners was the same in all the countries that they visited," wrote the *New York Times*. "They approached the highest men in authority, and, as their mission was some what of a diplomatic character, they were first presented to the Prime Minister or Minister of Foreign Affairs, as the case might be."[50] They sought to secure appropriations for and participation in the fair—no easy task, since there was considerable displeasure with America because of the recently passed McKinley Tariff, a protectionist measure that had raised the duty on all imports by an average of 49.5 percent.

Handy also had another important agenda item: to "work" the members of the foreign press to achieve favorable coverage for Chicago and the world's fair. Even though the opening of the Exposition, which had now been set as May 1, 1893, was still twenty-two months off, there were already many opportunities to promote it in Europe.

For one, some editors had been writing poisonous copy: Handy needed to meet with them to set the record straight. For another, recalcitrant publishers needed to be disabused of the old-fashioned notion that promotional news coverage must be paid for. For example, he had received a letter from a man named Dompierre, at the Eastern Agency in Constantinople, who wanted to help spread the word—for the right price, of course: "We write to place ourselves at your disposition for all communication which you have to make to the public in Turkey, whether by means of newspapers in various languages, by hanging bills in railroad stations, in tram cars, steamboats, &c. bill-posting in the principal cities of the East: Greece, Turkey, Egypt, Bulgaria, Servia, and Roumania [*sic*]: the sale of lottery tickets, should one be created for the Exposition, and all the advertisements pertaining there to."[51] Handy also had the new lithographs of Machinery Hall to distribute, one thousand of which Dorr sent to him, mounted on wooden rollers and packed in heavy tin-fused and rubber-jointed cases to make them watertight.[52]

Major Handy carried out this promotional work with determination and solemnity, saving his candor and complaints for his letters to Sarah, which arrived back at Osage Avenue in Philadelphia several times a week, sometimes more than one per day. For example, after he met with Lord Balfour, the Prince of Wales, Lord Mayor of London David Evans, and other dignitaries, he wrote to Sarah, "Our round of official engagements continues leaving us almost no time for anything else." Similarly, although he patiently spent long stretches in transit—at one point enduring more than sixty straight hours riding a train from Novgorod to Moscow, Brest, Warsaw, and Berlin—he complained in a letter to Sarah, "We have slept on the cars every night this week . . . [and] long for a good old bed and a square meal, neither of which we are apt to get until the day after tomorrow."[53] His letters were always filled with interesting details of the trip—for example, explaining that the Russian calendar was twelve days behind the Western one. Charmingly, perhaps even journalistically, the letters also always seemed to employ different terms of endearment. "My Darling," "Dearest," "My Dear Wife," he began three letters during the third week of July. "With lots of love & kisses to match," he closed one letter. "With a heart full of love," he signed off another. "Good night, Love," in a third.

While the chief rolled across Europe, Dorr took over management of the Department of Publicity and Promotion in Chicago, and although he kept the machine humming along ("Everything is running smoothly, both personally and officially," he wrote to Handy on July 15), he also began to realize how much flak his boss had been dealing with behind the scenes. Because the World's Columbian Exposition was being overseen by both a national and a local commission, budgets were carefully scrutinized, and political considerations were often paramount. Thus, in alerting Handy that the lithographs were en route to him in Europe, Dorr added a little extracurricular commentary:

> It is a beautiful piece of work. Everyone who has seen it so far likes it. I expect, of course, that Mr. Pretyman [the Exposition's director of decoration, sometimes referred to as the director of color] will tear it to pieces some, but he would do that if the drawing was by the finest artist in the land and the work acknowledged to be superior to anything before produced. I like him very much personally, but he's a terror to do business with."[54]

A few weeks later, with Handy still away, Dorr had to deal with an urgent request from Director General Davis "for a report of the work of this Dept. from its organization & of its plans for the immediate future."[55] Perhaps because the publicity and promotion function was still so novel that it was neither understood nor valued, Department O would repeatedly need to scramble to defend and justify its methods, expenditures, and very existence. Dorr pulled together the necessary documentation, and the crisis was averted.

On September 12, 1891, Moses P. Handy arrived back in New York, and Sarah met him on the wharf. Their separation would not last much longer. On October 11, she and the children spent their last night at the home on Osage Avenue. The next day, she packed up the last of her household goods—the carpets—and then the woman who had written about "How to Move Easily and Well" scrawled her true feelings in her Excelsior Pocket Diary ("discomfort & chaos") as she embarked for Chicago and her new life.[56]

In the coming months, she would try to restore normalcy and regain some balance in her life. Notable among the seven Handy children, Will, the eldest, was already off on his own, following a well-worn family path into journalism as a correspondent for the *Philadelphia Inquirer*, for which he had written since the age of seventeen; Moses Jr. was in boarding school in Virginia; Cora Macon, the youngest girl, known as "Clover," enrolled at the Sacred Heart School in Chicago; and Henry Jamison, known as "Jam," just five years old at the time of their relocation, was frequently allowed to accompany his father to the office in lieu of school, for it was believed he would learn more watching the inner workings of the Department of Publicity and Promotion than he would in the classroom. Sarah soon resumed writing and even produced a published volume called *Bits of Verse* in 1892, as well as a poem that would be printed in a souvenir booklet for the Exposition:

CHICAGO

No city set upon a hill is she,
Proudly she stands beside her inland sea,
Upon whose breast her merchant navies ride,
Bringing her wealth with each incoming tide.
Her iron horses tramp across the plain,
Laden with cattle, oil and grain;
Her mighty engines never cease their play,
Building her bulwarks stronger night and day.
With outstretched hands and smiling face she waits,
Watching the nations thronging to her gates;
Type of the new world, young and strong, and free,
Proudly she stands beside her inland sea.[57]

A snippet of her writing that likely dates from this period, entitled "The Folly of Fretting," similarly reflected her brighter outlook as the Exposition's opening neared:

> Worry wears out more people than work does, and fretting causes more unhappiness in families than either sickness or poverty. Indeed, the secret of happiness may almost be said to be making the best of everything, and good-humor under all circumstances the most useful virtue which man, and more especially woman, can possess. There are good women to-day who would peril life and limb for husband and children, yet who daily render their dear ones uncomfortable by going forth to meet trouble half way, and by grieving over that which is past and irremediable. If a thing can be helped by any effort of yours, go to work promptly and help it; if not, waste not time in vain repining.[58]

But as always with Sarah Handy, life was never easy.

Health was one issue, and this would force her to spend some time resting with her father, who had relocated to San Jose, California. "I never thought I could miss anybody so much or that time could pass so slowly," Moses dolefully wrote to her. Around this time, too, Will Handy became embroiled in some unpleasant business, including a bad investment in which he lost all his money and a relationship with a woman ten years his senior that led to accusations of stolen jewelry and blackmail. Also, Moses's brother Fred ran into financial difficulties and wrote asking for a loan of fifty or one hundred dollars: "What is to become of my family this summer The Lord only knows."[59]

Moses no longer had the Clover Club, but he rebuilt his extensive social circles and maintained close contact with a wide range of acquaintances. His congeniality was clearly reflected in the tone people used in their correspondence to him. "Mose," many of them called him, or "Major," or "My Dear M." At one point the theatrical producer Steele MacKaye (who had designed the ingenious sets for the Wild West show at Madison Square Garden a few years earlier) wrote to praise Handy for a stance he took at a social outing: "The more I consider the splendid loyalty of your action Saturday night, in refusing to become the passive receptacle of ignoble confidences, the more I love and admire you."[60] Similarly, his friend Nathan Haskell Dole, a publisher in Boston, wrote a letter to "My dear brother Handy" in which he asked, "How are you these days? I occasionally read of you hobnobbing with Kings and Emperors. O fortunate soul to be ever riding on the crest of the gilded wave!"[61]

Handy was, indeed, starting to ingratiate himself among the upper echelons of society, which Chicago itself was desperately trying to join. The Exposition was the calling card for both. And though his name had been well known for many years, now he was becoming widely recognized throughout the country. He was of slight build (five feet ten and a half inches, 154 pounds—up 10 pounds since two years earlier, when he had been denied a life insurance policy by Equitable because "at the time I was under weight"), with gray eyes and short wavy hair he described as blond, although it appears darker in photographs and in a lock that has survived to this day, lovingly pasted into a "hair album" by daughter Rozelle in 1888. Handy was instantly recognizable wherever he went, however, because of his whiskers, which shot out in two triangular briar patches at acute angles from his left and right jowls, framing his otherwise narrow face in a most unusual way, even for a hirsute age. They seemingly had their own following. Several cartoon caricatures of Handy and his facial hair graced the newspapers. The *New York Times* described them as "flaming red" and made multiple mentions of them; the *Hamilton (Ohio) Daily Democrat* called them "whiskers of national reputation."[62] Some years after the Exposition, Robert Dorr would tease his former boss about the possibility of landing a diplomatic post in Turkey: "Just think of the effect of those wonderful whiskers on the Turkish maidens!"[63] At one point, the humorist Eugene Field—a literary compadre of Handy, and the same man who had complained about the Wild West's excessive bill posting in Germany—drew a sketch of Handy's head from behind, whiskers jutting out in silhouette, and then put it in the mail addressed only to "Philadelphia, Pennsylvania"; it arrived in Handy's mailbox without delay.

The social outings, infrequent as they now were, had a salving effect on Handy—because almost as soon as he had returned from Europe, it was "once more unto the breach." Within two weeks, pressure again mounted on him to justify his payroll and other expenditures to prevent a cut to his budget, or possibly even elimination of the department. Given all the extra work they were taking on for other departments, he wrote to Director General Davis, it simply wasn't fair. Everybody (including Davis) needed letters translated. Many departments were utilizing the scrapbooks of press clippings—work that now engaged six of Handy's staff. Moreover, a budget cut wouldn't be prudent.

> There is a great and increasing demand for the literature of the Exposition, for maps of the grounds and lithographs of the several buildings, I submit whether this demand should be ignored. . . . [B]efore the organization of this department, there was widespread ignorance and scepticism [*sic*] concerning our plans and prospects, the entire world is now kept fully advised of what we are proposing to do, and any relaxation of these efforts is almost certain to be misconstrued to our disadvantage. It is a question whether we should destroy or cripple the bridge which has so thoroughly spanned the chasm of ignorance and misrepresentation. I cannot see that there is any danger of too much publicity being given to what we desire to be made public; on the contrary, there is danger of too little publicity, and the financial failure of at least two previous International Expositions, and of one now in progress, is attributable to the failure to advertise intelligently and extensively.[64]

Throughout the fall, however, there were more complaints about the value of the department's efforts. The *Chicago Post* reported, "There are some men who think the world's fair ought to be kept a matter of close confidence among those who are getting it up. They do not see the value of publicity and think the world's fair would be a greater success if the newspapers were kept out of the building and had no opportunity to say anything about the enterprise."

Handy was nonplussed.

"If that's the idea, I'm clearly out of place," he told the *Post.* "I did not come here to keep this enterprise confidential or to suppress news about it. There is a value in publishing progress of this fair which some people do not seem to realize."

Davis defended his promotions chief to the reporter: "All this talk about dropping that department is the purest nonsense. The work under Major Handy's direction is farther advanced than the similar work of any other exposition ever held."[65]

The battle would continue throughout the fair, but in the meantime, the promotional work went on.

Handy, of course, was an old-time journalist, a man of words—and he had his staff count them as if they were precious twenty-dollar gold coins from the San Francisco Mint.[66] The June 1891 report of the department recorded that staffer William M. Knox, who produced the weekly newsletter, had written 67,075 words in the past month; that the mailing list had grown to 24,515; and that the department had mailed out 476,370 documents.[67] In August, the department's staff wrote a total of 137,650 words and counted 4,616,620 words about the Exposition in press clippings.[68] In September, Louis Ayme reported that he had received 713 clippings from foreign papers that month, totaling 554,150 words.[69]

Handy also knew that new technologies were making reproduction of pictures—in newspapers and as photographic prints—much easier and more affordable, and he clearly understood the power of imagery: "Preliminary advertising by means of lithographs and other pictures should excel anything of the kind ever before attempted by an Exposition, national or international, thereby giving additional assurance to the world of the high artistic aspirations of the projectors and managers of the World's Columbian Exposition."[70]

That first color lithograph of Machinery Hall, which Dorr had sent to Handy in Europe, was also widely distributed in the United States, in nearly every town of more than two thousand inhabitants. "In New York City, in Boston and in Philadelphia," Handy proudly wrote, "it was displayed in every first class hotel, in stock exchanges, and at the principal railroad and steamboat stations."[71]

In November 1891 the much-awaited bird's-eye lithograph, painted in watercolors by Charles Graham for the Winters Art Lithograph Company, became available for distribution after weeks of delays caused by revisions to the renderings of key buildings. The department spent twenty thousand dollars to print one hundred thousand copies. The lithograph depicted a view of the entire world's fair as it might eventually look from high over Lake Michigan, with the majestic Court of Honor, the lagoons, Wooded Island, and Midway Plaisance stretching almost to the horizon. This, for the first time, conveyed the scale and grandeur of the enterprise and began to set aside the doubts of those who had belittled it as the Cook County Fair. "Extraordinary enthusiasm occasioned by this splendid lithograph/clamor for it from every direction at home and abroad," Handy wrote. "Wherever it went it was considered, as we had expected, the best piece of advertising ever done by an international exhibition."[72] Demand for the lithograph forced Handy to temporarily reallocate every member of his staff to the mail room. It was soon hanging in the White House, congressional cloakrooms, and the officers' headquarters for the army.

During the first part of 1892, the volume of work expanded further, and the department's ranks swelled to more than fifty people, including one in Paris and two in New York. This was probably the largest promotional team that had ever been assembled, although it was still being run in a tightfisted manner. On March 15, Handy submitted his budget for the nineteen-month duration of the effort: $228,990, including $25,000 for "lithographs, portfolios and photographs"; $10,000 for "zinc etchings and electrotypes"; $65,000 for newspaper advertising; and $7,000 for postage. The budget was dutifully entered into the *Congressional Record*.[73]

Each day, there was the usual cascade of outbound stories and images; in May 1892, they distributed a daily average of 9,030 pieces of printed matter.[74] At one point, the tiny *Atchison (Kans.) Daily Patriot* wrote, "We get a great many world's fair notes from Chicago, sent by the bureau of information for the Exposition, but we never see anything about Kansas. What's the matter with our representatives in Chicago? Are they so busy putting on styles that they have no time to attend to business? Or, doesn't Kansas count?"[75] As Handy knew too well, there was no pleasing everyone.

The department's local press division, consisting of two reporters and one stenographer, formed their own miniature wire service, gathering information from the Exposition offices and the construction site and filing about 2,500 words per day for use by the Chicago newspapers, United Press, Associated Press, Reuter's Telegram Company, and special correspondents.[76] There was also the exhaustive inbound work of cataloging and scrapbooking all the press clippings; in May alone, there were enough clips to fill 878 scrapbook pages, and they encompassed more than 5 million words of coverage (2.2 million of which, the department calculated, were their own).[77] On April 1, Handy testified to a congressional subcommittee: "I do not suppose that more than twenty-five newspapers in the United States out of the whole number of many thousands have failed to print our matter, and a great part of it some print regularly."[78]

Additionally, Handy's team tackled many ad hoc projects. They generated weekly world's fair notes, distributed President Lyman Gage's World's Columbian Exposition annual report, produced pamphlets for several other departments, reproduced pictures of many of the state buildings, and compiled guidebooks to the fair in multiple languages. They worked with select journalists and publications to reprint and distribute favorable feature articles—for example, the letters of Joel Cook of the *Times of London* were made into a standalone promotional pamphlet. The department also worked to counteract misinformation in the London papers about the supposed epidemic of typhoid in Chicago in April.

Handy tapped his extensive network of contacts to negotiate syndication deals and bylined articles. In one instance, he arranged for publication of two page-long articles about the prospects for the Columbian Exposition by one of the newspaper syndicates; these ran in more than 1,200 American papers. On another occasion, he forged an agreement with his old employer, the *New York World*, to create a special world's fair edition. Moses consented to write an article for the new *McClure's* magazine, and for the *Youth's Companion* ("In a certain sense, it will be the most practical article of all," wrote editor Edward Staunch in soliciting the Major; "In short, give to the man from Texas or from Oregon, who has never been in Chicago, explicit directions as to how he shall see the World's Fair").[79] Sarah Handy agreed to write an article for *Harper's*, and the byline of "Mrs. M. P. Handy" graced several women's publications with articles about the coming Exposition. She was not on the payroll, but she was hard at work behind the scenes.

In spring 1892, the department also began an extensive new undertaking: production of a comprehensive six hundred-page catalog of all the exhibits, which visitors to the fair could use to guide them through the buildings. This would entail a painful months-long process of obtaining and then organizing detailed information about tens of thousands of individual objects that would be part of each and every exhibit at the fair, a task made all the more difficult by the lack of responsiveness from many of the foreign and state delegations. Some were unaware of the details of their exhibits at this early date. Some submitted information and then changed it, or even pulled out of the Exposition altogether, which created a domino effect of shifting exhibit sites. Handy wrote, "It seemed impossible to get anybody, even those most concerned, aroused to the importance of the work until the time for its publication. . . . It was in fact like cataloguing 100,000 books which were not on the shelves." Right up until the first edition of the catalog went to press in April 1893, the department was still waiting on information from several countries—indeed, the fair actually opened with many halls filled with unpacked crates, and as Handy noted in the case of Denmark and Russia, "their exhibits were [still] on the high seas."[80]

The difficulties encountered in producing the catalog also raised another issue, one that would become commonplace as the worlds of marketing and journalism increasingly overlapped in the coming decades. To save space, the Publicity and Promotion team decided to limit each entry in the catalog to three lines, but also made accommodations for exhibitors to pay five dollars a line to expand their listings to as many as ten lines. This created a conflict, Handy noted later, one that rages even today: "It was very difficult to draw the line at exactly the right place in saying where the free matter should end and the paid matter begin. Issues continually arose between the publisher and the exhibitor as [to] the adjacency of the gratuitous entry, and the Editor was on the one hand open to the suspicion of favoring the publisher at the expense of the exhibitor, and on the other of the exhibitor at the expense of the publisher."[81]

The catalog became one of the great crosses that Handy would have to bear, as there was much finger pointing and no appreciation of the reasons for the incomplete information or the eventual sales, which were far below expectations despite the deployment of a sales force of one hundred boys in red uniforms across the grounds. Throughout the early months of the fair, he would need to expend considerable time and energy defending his team, at the expense of actively promoting the Exposition to prospective visitors.

The whole catalog, he ultimately decided, was "thankless work."

By summertime, Handy had other problems to worry about. Congress, dissatisfied by the findings of its April scrutiny of Exposition budget management, opted to halve its next appropriation from $5 million to $2.5 million. This had repercussions throughout the fair departments, and in the newspapers. The *Chicago Tribune* in particular went after Handy and the Department of Publicity and Promotion, apparently spurred by the Exposition's firing of *Tribune* editor Joseph Medill's son-in-law.[82] The newspaper went into a vitriolic tirade on August 7:

CUT OFF MAJOR HANDY

THE MAJOR DRAWS A LARGE SALARY THAT HE DOESN'T BEGIN TO EARN AND HIS ASSISTANTS FOR THE MOST PART ARE OVERPAID—HIS BUREAU OF PUBLICITY AND PROMOTION HAS OUTGROWN ITS USEFULNESS—EXPOSITION MANAGERS LIKELY TO CUT ITS EXPENSES OR ABOLISH IT ENTIRELY

The article attacked Handy and Dorr; inferred that Handy had blackmailed his way into a large salary by threatening to use the "power of the press" if he didn't get what he wanted; and leveled charges of "waste and extravagance." It then went on:

> The bureau has been a loud-sounding, ear-filling name, but, in fact, it is nothing but the advertising department of the Fair. Its functions are the same as that branch of a patent-medicine house where the testimonials are written and the "before and after" pictures made. Its original purpose was to inform the world at large and incidentally the people of the United States that the Columbian Exposition was to be held in Chicago and ask them to come and bring their wives and children. That result has been pretty fairly accomplished, and it is safe to say that the great majority of the people of the world, outside of Africa, certain districts of China, and the Persian Empire are reasonably well informed as to the holding of the Fair and what kind of a show it will be. Those who remain in ignorance will probably continue so in spite of the best efforts of the Bureau of Publicity and Promotion.[83]

All of the carping bothered Handy, but he could not be deflected from the important goal in sight: the official dedication of the World's Columbian Exposition, which was scheduled for Columbus Day, October 12—in theory, four hundred years to the day since Columbus's discovery (and the day on which the Wild West symbolically wrapped up its European tour). This would be the first official event of the world's fair and an opportunity to generate a tremendous amount of press—"the crowning advertisement," Handy called it.[84]

His team began to prepare for it with some preliminary advertising in July, and with a letter they mailed out to more than 1,400 newspapers in August, soliciting calls for tickets. More than five thousand such requests came back, far more than could be honored.

The dedication itself was ultimately delayed until October 26, but it was a grand affair, presided over by U.S. vice president Levi Morton.

AT THE DEDICATION of the World's Columbian Exposition on October 26, 1892, tens of thousands of people packed into the Manufactures and Liberal Arts Building—including some three thousand reporters. "The amount of publicity . . . exceeded that ever given any public event on record," said Moses P. Handy. *Shepp's World's Fair Photographed*, Globe Bible Publishing, 1893; author's collection.

Most of the big buildings were still in various stages of construction, since there were still six months to go before the opening, but the gargantuan 787-by-1,687-foot Manufactures Building, spanning thirty acres and built at a cost of $1.6 million, was ready enough; thousands of people crowded in for the ceremony.

The Department of Publicity and Promotion made accommodations for press coverage, with 800 seats at reporters' tables, 1,700 more in the reserved press section, and another 1,000 general admission tickets. "The result," Handy later wrote, "was the comfortable accommodation of a larger number of newspaper men than were ever before gathered together for any purpose whatever." To help them file their stories, Western Union and Postal Telegraph were on hand with their telegraphy equipment, and in the press working room were fifty Remington typewriters, "with expert operators for gratuitous service of correspondence." Copies of every speech and prayer were distributed before the program began. It was essentially the first global press event in history, and Handy concluded that "the amount of publicity secured for the Dedicatory exercises . . . exceeded that ever given any public event on record."[85]

That was October 26, 1892.

On October 27, John M. Burke arrived back in New York on the steamship *Mohawk* with fifty-five of the Wild West Indians, the great cities of Europe behind him and the World's Columbian Exposition ahead. Opening day was still six months away, but there was much planning to do.

Nate Salsbury had tried to secure space inside the Columbian Exposition fairgrounds for the Wild West but was unable to do so. The show was apparently deemed too lowbrow, too unseemly for an exhibition of high culture, the world's consummate celebration of progress and symbolic nod to the future. As the publication *Kate Field's Washington* later told the story, "A reasonable proposition was made to the powers in control, through Mr. Nate Salisbury [*sic*]; he was told that the nature of the Wild West did not comport with the dignity of the Fair! Fancy how such an answer was received by a man who had entertained more royal personages than any American that ever lived."[86] Instead, Salsbury did something even better: he rented space between 62nd and 63rd Streets, between Madison and Stoney Island Avenues, right next to the Illinois Central Railroad's station and a primary entrance to the fair.[87] There, Buffalo Bill's Wild West would proceed to construct an eighteen thousand-seat arena.

So there would be complementary shows, two dynamic attractions side by side that would both seek to celebrate, to educate, to commemorate, to proselytize—and to extract a half-dollar from the millions of people who would descend on Jackson Park in 1893. The Exposition and the Wild West would compete for patrons, press coverage, and the supremacy of their promotional styles. They would present different visions of the significance of the West, one looking forward, the other back. How the two great pioneers of promotion, Handy and Burke, would chart those courses would not only influence the events of 1893 but would change the history of their brand new industry.

10

1893

"What could fill the eye with beauty, what could stir the soul with immensity"

Chicago is Chicago. . . . It is the belief of all of us.
It is inevitable; nothing can stop us now.

Henry Blake Fuller, *The Cliff-Dwellers* (1893)

Truss by truss, pinnacle by pinnacle, the gleaming utopian aerie of the White City rose from the ashen marshes of Jackson Park—and along with it, lithograph by lithograph, article by article, the construction of a boldly envisioned and superbly architected publicity and promotion plan took shape.

The scaffolding came down; the staff cladding went up; the press notifications went out. Daniel Burnham's glittering accomplishment was magnified by Moses Handy's towering achievement. There was no more acrimony or backbiting; Chicago had been redeemed, and all the world knew about it. Enthusiasm was bubbling over. An astonishing 9,492 people paid fifty cents to tour the site—still under construction—on April 23, 1893, eight days before the grand opening. Soon, 13 million Americans and 14 million foreign visitors would descend on the Exposition to see for themselves what they had heard about and so eagerly anticipated for the past two years.

After the dedication in October 1892, the Department of Publicity and Promotion relocated its operations from downtown Chicago to the northeast pavilion of the world's fair Administration Building in February, and then, when their need for space to accommodate the huge influx of staff and press proved too great, to the much larger pavilion C of the Administration Building later the same month. There, Handy set up what he called "the very nerve center of all activity on the grounds," with three floors of offices that accommodated his own team plus representatives of the local daily newspapers and the foreign press, many of whom were equipped with telegraphs and telephones. On the second floor, next to his office, he established a reception room and adorned the walls with five thousand headlines and front pages of newspapers and periodicals from around the world, including the *Ceylon Times*, the *Amoy Gazette*, the *Shipping Report* of Africa, the Persian journal *Il Habbar Matti*, the *South African Farmers' Representative*, the *Hiogo News* of Japan—even a copy of the *Boston Gazette* dating to 1770. The designer of the exhibit, H. P. Hubbard, slyly pasted up a picture of Major Handy, with the masthead of the *Popular Educator* below it.[1]

Throughout the first part of 1893, the department plugged away at the publicity effort despite four weeks of subzero temperatures, which left "sidewalks and wooden pavements crackling and exploding, the windows covered with hoar frost, and the snow sparkling on the many domes," occasionally forcing the team out of their offices; Handy was sometimes spotted wearing a sable fur and conducting meetings while sitting atop the steam pipes in the Administration Building.[2] Nevertheless, in January, the department mailed out more than seventy thousand articles and images, and logged 3,643,200 words written about the Exposition in newspapers it received for the scrapbooks. The world was starting to take note of the fair—and of its marketing effort. One newspaper article in early February 1893 praised Handy as "the most brilliant person that has allied himself with the fair," going on to explain,

> He has advertised it under every press cylinder, in nearly every printer's chase, on pictures at the rude ends of the earth, where language has grown dumb while the grandeur of the fair set savages dancing with delight. . . . Handy has been ubiquitous. He has made better speeches and more of them than all the Chicagoans together. He has compelled admiration wherever his talents have been subjected to honest comment, and he will end with the reputation of being the best advertiser the world has ever produced.[3]

Meanwhile, part of the team worked furiously to compile the *Official Guide* of exhibits. As of February, only a handful of nations had actually sent in any material; most of the more than thirty-five thousand items that would ultimately make it into the catalog would not be received until twenty days from its publication, and almost thirty thousand more were received after its publication.[4] Little wonder that in the midst of that winter, the catalog publisher, W. B. Conkey, tried to lure Handy to come work for him at a salary of ten thousand dollars, one-third higher than his Exposition compensation.

Another part of the team prepared to begin publishing the *Daily Columbian*, an eight-page newspaper that would debut with the fair's opening and would include original material as well as what was essentially an early version of the press pool, with content provided by five of Chicago's major daily newspapers. By publishing his own paper, Handy deftly solved the thorny issue of which outside newspapers would be allowed to hawk their issues on the fairgrounds—none.

As the opening drew near, the department also systematically canvassed English-speaking newspapers to determine how many press passes would be needed; seven thousand replied, with requests for thirty-five thousand passes. Yet the World's Columbian Commission—still operating with a mid-century mindset—had not changed the limit of only one complimentary admission for the editor or proprietor of each newspaper. Handy, however, understood that the world of publicity had changed dramatically. "Who should decide between an editor and a publisher?" he mused. "And where there are several editors and publishers who should decide between them? Where was the line to be drawn as to what were the leading papers? What editor would admit that his own was not a leading newspaper?"[5] Moreover, he believed that his rejection of the pay-for-print subsidy system obliged him to be generous in doling out passes, and his fraternal feelings toward the press inclined him similarly. And he had also invited the large press associations, such as the National Editorial Association, to visit the fair en masse during the first month. So in the end, he exercised his discretion and developed a series of photographic passes, ten-day tickets, and two kinds of single-admission tickets in order to be as generous to the press as possible—a decision that brought significant additional publicity to the World's Columbian Exposition, but also created a political imbroglio for Handy (see plate 9).

As the performers of Buffalo Bill's Wild West and Congress of Rough Riders of the World practiced for the opening of their six-month season in Chicago at the new $250,000 arena that had been constructed for them adjacent to the World's Columbian Exposition, Major John M. Burke got to work.

The Wild West would open five days before the Exposition itself, and knowing that all eyes would be focused on the fair throughout the summer, he needed to divert some of the attention. He and his team started by launching their usual sweeping bill-posting effort, carried out by 160 men, covering Chicago with messages like "AN ABSOLUTELY ORIGINAL AND HEROIC ENTERPRISE OF INIMITABLE LUSTRE . . . ITS GREAT ORIGINATOR NOW RIDES ALONG FAME'S WARPATH . . . THE NEW WORLD AND THE OLD APPEAR IN BRAVEST AND MOST BRILLIANT RIVALRIES."[6] Always a competitive process, the battle to find billboard space in Chicago was more hotly contested than ever. The city had many theaters and museums already vying for the entertainment dollar, and although Barnum & Bailey was not coming to town, Adam Forepaugh's big circus was. "The World's Fair has multiplied Chicago's places of amusements by ten, to put it mildly," wrote the *Chicago Evening Journal*. "It is an open secret . . . that it is to be war to the knife from the start between Buffalo Bill and Forepaugh." The competition sent bill-posting costs soaring, from the usual $60–$70 per week to $300–$350 per week, enriching "Chicago's knights of the paste brush."[7]

Burke and his team also developed newspaper ads linking the Wild West to the Columbian Exposition. "Voted a World-Beater," read one. "The Open Sesame to the World's Fair Subject. . . . Scenic Splenders [*sic*]. The Climax in combined interest of all Exhibitions."[8] Bolder language still was used in their "couriers"—special tabloid-style booklets that were distributed to the businesses displaying posters and selling advance tickets, or sometimes placed directly in mailboxes (see plate 10). The Wild West courier used in 1893 was 21 inches by 28 inches—ample space to accommodate even Burke's verbosity.

THE ONLY EXHIBITION IN ALL THE WORLD THAT HAS NO COUNTERPART.
EXCLUSIVELY ITS OWN CREATION. . . .
OF ITS KIND THE FIRST, THE ONLY, AND THE LAST,
IT IS A REVELATION.
THE MOST COLOSSAL AND THE STRANGEST ENTERTAINMENT
EVER ORGANIZED OR DREAMED OF.

> The Only Object Teacher history has Ever had, or Recreation Furnished. Whatever Others May Say or Claim, the Whole World Pronounces it Supremely and Originally Great. The Mirror of American Manhood. The Camp of the Makers of a Nation's History. Promoted by Kings, Honored by Nations. A Paragon at Home, a Triumph Abroad. Rough Riders Schooled to Hardship, and to Whom the Saddle is an Heirloom. An Equine and Equestrian Study, with Horse and Man a Sculptor's Beau Ideal.
>
> Realism Throned in Nature's Temple
>
> THE CENTURY'S ENTERPRISE
>
> DEFINED ALONE BY THE WORD
>
> IMMENSITY
>
> ALL TIME'S GREATEST AND MOST FAMOUS EXHIBITION
>
> IT TOWERS ALONE, IN SOLITARY AND MAGNETIC GRANDEUR[9]

And then there was the press.

By 1893, the Fourth Estate had emerged as a powerful force in society, one that was just beginning to assert its independence and sense of journalistic integrity, but that was still easily manipulated by clever press agents like Burke, Handy, and Hamilton. The size of the journalism industry was reflected by the extent of Handy's mailing list, which now included fifteen thousand newspapers, ten thousand journals and other periodicals, and five thousand class or trade papers.[10]

Chicago, like most major cities, had many daily newspapers—one contemporary source pegged the number at 34—and representatives from more than a thousand others would be in town for the Exposition, so Burke would have unprecedented opportunities to keep Cody and the Wild West in the spotlight, even though they were not an official part of the fair.[11] Since there was no advance work to be done, Burke would be staying in Chicago until the fair was over and could therefore share many a mint julep with the reporters.

Throughout April, as the two opening dates approached, Burke landed one story after another in the papers, including an interview in which Nate Salsbury magnanimously forecast an unprecedented success for the world's fair itself. "The Columbian Exposition will exceed in grandeur the wildest flights of the Frenchmen's fancy and judgment," he told the *Chicago*

Dispatch. "Nothing so extensive and constructed on such liberal lines was ever attempted in the history of the world."[12]

Burke also invited reporters out to the train station to observe the arrival of seventy-six Sioux Indians who would become part of the Wild West performance. The *Chicago Record* said that Burke "received them with amazing cordiality and they evinced the greatest pleasure to shake his hand, which they did with much grunting and waving of plumes."[13] The *Inter Ocean* similarly reported, "Before the train had come to a full stop the Indians began jumping off, and, headed by Jack Red Cloud, they made a rush toward where they saw the generously proportioned form of their old friend, Major Burke, the manager of the show. Advancing with a Brule war whoop, toned to denote pleasure rather than defiance, they surrounded the Major and gravely shook hands with him, exclaiming, 'How! How!'"[14]

Burke also continued to work the press through letters to the editor. Although he may have lacked an operation as large as the Exposition's Department of Publicity and Promotion, he too seems to have subscribed to clipping services and pasted the cuttings into scrapbooks. This vigilance gave him the opportunity, as always, to defend Cody's reputation at the slightest affront. On March 25, for example, he wrote a letter to the *Inter Ocean*, chastising it for running a *San Francisco Call* article suggesting that the Wild West had been unsuccessful in Germany:

> Buffalo Bill's Wild West never failed in Germany or elsewhere. He spent two seasons in Europe after the Hamburg engagement, leaving there with a reputation for personal conduct and financial probity equaling the Rothschilds, Morenheim's, Bank of England, or Credit Lyonnaise, inasmuch as every bond was fulfilled, and no blush of shame will mantle the cheek of any American who crosses our continental trail. Impress on the *Call* that "Bill" is not perfection, but he is honorable in all things.[15]

Furthermore, Burke had a new tool for Chicago: the book he had written over the course of the past few months, entitled *"Buffalo Bill" from Prairie to Palace: An Authentic History of the Wild West, with Sketches, Stories of Adventure, and Anecdotes of "Buffalo Bill," the Hero of the Plains.*

Even in small doses, Burke's bloated writing could be hard to follow, but this full-length (275-page) work meandered more than usual. It contained, among other things, an entire chapter of "Letters of Commendation from Prominent Military Men" of Buffalo Bill; a profile of Nate Salsbury; citations of many of Burke's favorite journalists; references to Byron and Shakespeare; a detailed recap of the Wild West's European tour; a lengthy description of Cody's physiognomy from Professor A. J. Oppenheim, which included the observation, "The downward projection of the outer corner of the eyebrows means contest—he never gives in"; and the remarkable prediction that the Alsace-Lorraine region might become "the theater of that future human tragedy for which the ear of mankind strains day and night, listening for detonations from the muzzles of the acme of invented mechanisms of destruction."[16] And of course, the book also contained some of Burke's famously florid writing—in this instance, wrapped around his insightful observations about the rapidly disappearing West: "Two thousand miles of desert waste have largely been developed in a rich and valuable agricultural and pastoral region. The iron horse has supplanted the fiery bronco, and thought flashes with lightning rapidity from ocean to ocean. Civilization has crowned that terra incognita with seven States and built large and beautiful cities. Peace has spread her halo of beauty over the savage haunts and churches have supplanted the horrible orgies of Indian massacres."[17]

The book went on sale at the Wild West show and all around town, and it was generally favorably reviewed, even if seen for the promotional tool it was. The *Chicago Globe*, for example, commented, "Inasmuch as Chicago is at present in the throes of hero worship induced by the appearance here of Buffalo Bill and his energetic followers, this book will doubtless enjoy a vogue commensurate with its merits." The reporter also noted that Arizona John's "word painting . . . merits high praise."[18]

And so they came, by the thousands, the men in their dark sack coats and bowlers, the ladies in their shirtwaists, corseted skirts, and parasols. They arrived via the Alley L, horse cars and brougham drays, the "grip" cable car and the electric train, and the packed cars of the Illinois Central Railroad. But when they reached the 63rd Street Station, they did not turn left into the World's Columbian Exposition entrance, but right, underneath the giant banner that depicted Columbus as "Pilot of the Ocean, the First Pioneer" and Cody as "Pilot of the Prairie, the Last Pioneer"—into the past, into the future, into the mythmaking machine that was Buffalo Bill's

SIDE BY SIDE, the Wild West arena and the World's Columbian Exposition, with the Ferris Wheel and some Exposition buildings in the background. Visible on the right is the rooftop hotel sign that was inescapable from inside the arena. Unattributed photograph, 1893, Buffalo Bill Museum and Grave, Golden, Colorado.

Wild West. (That the Wild West was a marketing phenomenon and not a real one was inescapable, however: an enterprising hotelier had mounted a billboard on top of his building in just such a way that it appeared to people inside the Wild West arena to be perched atop the trompe l'oeil Rocky Mountain backdrop. The Wild West management team tried to persuade him to take it down, but he knew a good promotional opportunity when he saw one.[19])

The first performance took place on April 26, five days before the opening of the Exposition, amid torrents of rain. One newspaper described how the crowd was "restless and impatient to get into the Wild West show" but then cheered wildly when the "the soldiers of all nations in bright uniforms made a brilliant scene."[20] Another reported that Cody was still "a splendid example of manhood as he galloped about the large arena mounted upon a superb chestnut steady with his long iron gray hair streaming out from beneath the broad brim of his sombrero."[21]

With its magnificent pageantry, the Wild West would fill the arena twice a day, every day, for the next six months, attracting 3 million visitors and clearing $1 million in profit. Many visitors who attended the Wild West believed that they had actually been to the Exposition. The *Chicago Post* summed up the relationship between the two attractions perfectly:

> Yes, as Major Burke would put it, the Wild West Show is a 'world-beater.' Only a true child of Barnum—a Barnumite minus the element of humbug—would ever have conceived that combination of cowboys and Indians and fearless rough riders of the earth. . . .
>
> In this annus mirabilis of the world's fair, erect, long-haired and graceful, his splendid outdoor life stamped on every limb and lineament, young in spite of the fifty-seven years [he was actually forty seven] which ought to handicap him but do not, Colonel Cody serves not only as amusement caterer on a colossal scale, combining education and recreation in his novel and ingenious programme, but also serves to illustrate in his own person vividly a species of simon-pure western manhood to which Chicago owes more than to eastern culture or eastern capital. The visitor to the Columbian Exposition who fails to see Colonel Cody on the bloodless sands of his own peculiar arena will neglect a very important adjunct of the fair.[22]

On the day before the Exposition opened, the excitement in the city reached a frenzy. Chicago had fought so hard to win the rights to host the fair, and then had fended off three years of critical commentaries and congressional budget scrutiny. It had expended nearly $20 million to transform Jackson Park into a neoclassical fairyland.

As usual, the city's many daily newspapers were the mouthpiece for its civic pride, which had been heating up like the water in a tea kettle and was now beginning to whistle loud and shrill. The Sunday *Tribune*—a forty-eight-page special edition with art supplement—was snapped up from newsboys who had opportunistically raised the price from a nickel to fifty cents; the dealer at the Palmer House hotel sold them for as much as three dollars and fifty cents apiece and reported that he could have sold five hundred copies an hour all day long, if only they had lasted.[23]

Monday, May 1, dawned like so many dreary Chicago spring days, with the wind swooping in off the lake and a stubborn blanket of cumulus clouds hovering low in the sky, leaving the daylight and the water and the city itself looking steely gray. The rain came down in the morning, driving and pelting at times, creating a sea of mud, "the softest, the dirtiest and the muddiest kind of mud," according to the *Chicago Herald*. "Every man who put his foot down splashed his neighbor."[24] The weather can sometimes make Chicago seem like a very depressing place, but on this much-anticipated day, nothing could suppress the gleeful spirit of the multitudes who converged on Jackson Park to witness this most special of special events.

At noon, as if scripted in collaboration with the heavens, the clouds broke, the sunlight slanted in, and the long-awaited opening ceremony of the World's Columbian Exposition began. Fifty thousand people crowded around the grandstand in the Court of Honor to witness the historic event, packed so tightly that not a patch of empty ground could be seen; some grew faint and had to be fanned or taken off by medical personnel. It was largely a sea of black and white, except for the red, blue, and yellow blankets and headdresses worn by the Sioux Indians of the Wild West, escorted in by John M. Burke.

On the stage were President Grover Cleveland and the Duke of Veragua, a descendant of Columbus. They were surrounded by fifty-three other dignitaries, including the key leaders of the Exposition, Director General George R. Davis and President Thomas W. Palmer of the Exposition Commission. Then came a group of two thousand special guests, including the foreign commissioners, judges, and one private citizen—William F. Cody.

When the American and Spanish flags were unfurled, the crowd roared and waved canes, handkerchiefs, and umbrellas. They watched Cleveland give a brief speech (heard by only a few people in the first rows of seats, since the loudspeaker, or "automatic enunciator," was still two decades off in the future). Following that, President Cleveland pushed an ivory button that, according to the *Chicago Tribune*, was designed to "set the colossal machinery in motion, shake out thousands of flags from their staffs, send the spray of great fountains into the air, start the activities of the World's Columbian Exposition into life, and . . . declare the Fair open to the world."[25]

And then it began.

In Machinery Hall, the 110-foot-long Reynolds-Corliss engine with the thirty-foot flywheel came to life, massive but silent, and electricity both literal and figurative surged throughout the fairgrounds. Thousands of lights illuminated. Fountains spouted. The intramural railway began circumnavigating the 633 acres. (The fair's signature icon, however, the

"THE AWESOME SOLEMNITY OF IMAGINED CREATION," reporter Amy Leslie called the World's Columbian Exposition in her coverage of the opening ceremonies of May 1, 1893. C. D. Arnold, photographer, *Administration Building*, 1893, Avery Architectural and Fine Arts Library, Columbia University, New York; plate 23.

264-foot-high Ferris Wheel, was not ready yet and would not open to the public for another six weeks; similarly, many of the exhibits were still sitting in boxes, and some doorways were barred.) The flags whipped and snapped in the breeze. The Venetian gondolas plied the lagoons. A human ebb tide five hundred thousand strong began to advance forward and gradually recede, this way and that, taking in all the splendor, catching a glimpse of the shimmering statuary or the fifty thousand rose bushes planted on Wooded Island. They went to the Government Building, the Women's Building, the Transportation Building, the battleship *Illinois*. In the Manufactures Building, visitors inspected the porcelain kitchen range and the train of cars made of spooled silk (although, according to the *Chicago Herald*, "they had no mood for the trivial or the useless" and instead opted for "what could fill the eye with beauty, what could stir the soul with

THE MAJESTIC COURT OF HONOR on opening day of the Exposition, with the sixty-five-foot-high Statue of the Republic looking across the basin to the Administration Building, home of the Department of Publicity and Promotion. C. D. Arnold, photographer, *Court of Honor: The Statue of the Republic by D.C. French*, 1893, Avery Architectural and Fine Arts Library, Columbia University, New York; plate 20.

immensity, what could quicken the blood with wonder").[26] On the Midway Plaisance, Cairo Street and Dahomey Village welcomed their first visitors.

It was a magnificent scene, the greatest day Chicago had ever known and perhaps one of the most memorable in American history, too—a carnival of grandiloquence, as the western world took stock of its achievements, momentum, and arc since the Niña, Pinta, and Santa Maria had first arrived in the Americas four hundred years earlier.

And just as Moses P. Handy had planned it, everything was neatly captured by the journalists and telegraphed around the world.

Some of them, it is true, used the opportunity to cavil. The *Boston Record* said, "Ragged and disappointing in various ways as the world's fair is to-day, it is a proud day for America." The *Boston Journal* complained that "it will lack the cosmopolitan character which it would have had if held in New

York, and in this respect will fail still further." The *New York Times* called the opening ceremony "deeply interesting to Chicago, but less so to the outside world," and the next day complained that "there was not much to see" and lambasted the Illinois Central's "cheap, coarsely-constructed . . . cattle cars" which exposed fair-bound riders to "Chicago's piercing winds and laryngitis-producing changes . . . and lay the foundation for pulmonary complaints that will last them all Summer."

But mostly there was generous praise, including that of the *Boston Transcript*, which said, "The whole nation looks on with pride and expectancy, confident in the judgment of those who ought to know that no world's fair has ever equaled the Columbian, especially in the majestic 'White City' which has been summoned into being as by Aladdin's lamp." The *New York World* instantly declared it "the greatest of world's fairs," and the *Philadelphia Record* expressed "admiration and wonder" of "the indomitable American

ST. PAUL
Daily Globe.

FAIR NOW OPEN.

VEILED BY MIST

BIRD'S-EYE VIEW OF THE WORLD'S COLUMBIAN EXPOSITION.

GUARDS OVERCOME.

GERMANY IN LINE.

GETTING TO THE PARK.

PROPHECY.

THE INDIAN CHIEFTAIN.

FRONT-PAGE NEWS. Publications large and small devoted much of their coverage on May 2, 1893, to the grand festivities of the World's Columbian Exposition opening. *St. Paul Daily Globe, Vinita Indian Chieftain,* May 2, 1893, newspapers.com.

energy and enterprise, of which Chicago itself is one of the brightest examples," and concluded that "its grounds and the magnificence of its edifices far surpasses anything of the kind that the world has accomplished."[27]

One week later, an even more magnificent scene ensued. Monday, May 8, was the night of the Grand Illumination, when the spectacular array of outdoor lighting that had been installed all along the Court of Honor was turned on in a dramatic sequence before thousands of spectators. In a portentous moment rife with symbolism, a gorgeous sunset of crimson, purple, and yellow gave way to Westinghouse's elaborate light show. This was, for many spectators, the first time they had ever seen electric lighting used at night, and the grandeur of it was beautifully captured by the newspapers. The *Chicago Tribune*, for one, ran a huge front-page story (along with an illustration—because no one had yet perfected the art of photographing electric lights at night) that read, in part,

> One by one, white globes of light glittered about the graceful sweep of the basin. They cast deep black shadows on the walls behind them and threw burnished, rippling ribbons over the dark water below. . . . Suddenly a single beam of yellow light, like a falling star, flickered and grew bright on the high dome of the Administration Building. Then lines of fire ran down its splendid sweep, and outlined in flame it stood out in splendor against the night. About its base circled a wheel of light, while above a hundred torches flared into the darkness. Within the great buildings about the basin electric coronas were ablaze and the giant pillars of the colonnades loomed white against the shadows. . . . For two hours the White City blossomed in new beauty.[28]

Arc lights brought the lines of the walkways back from their dark slumber. Search lights swept the sky in a rainbow of changing colors. "The 'White City' was transformed to-night into a city of rainbow tints," reported the *Galveston (Tex.) Daily News*.[29] "Symmetry in every outline—beautiful, soft, entrancing is the effect upon the sense," wrote a reporter for New Zealand's *Otago Daily Times* (who had been escorted to a unique vantage point on the balcony of the Administration Building and acknowledged that "Members of the Fourth Estate are well looked after out here. . . . Major Handy and his right-hand man, Mr. Holland, most certainly keep a keen and seemingly untiring eye upon the well-being of pressmen").[30] "A scene as beautiful as a dream of fairyland," said the *Louisville Courier-Journal.* "All the skill of science, the crowning triumph of the electrical age, united in portraying in the most glowing phantasy the dainty beauty of the White City."[31]

Even the European press had come around. After Handy's trip there in summer 1891, for example, there was "a nearly unanimous expression of the French press in favor of a liberal appropriation to insure a creditable representation of France at Chicago," and hundreds of stories about the fair followed, as did thousands of Frenchmen.[32] A railroad agent from Boston told his colleagues during a meeting at the start of the fair that he had been unable to avoid the Exposition throughout his travels around the world: "I saw pictures of these buildings until my dreams were highly-colored lithographs; I fled from Paris to Berlin, from Berlin to Rome, and from Rome to Athens, and I'll pay my fare home if I could find a hotel on the continent that didn't have some sort of World's Fair picture hung up where everybody had to see it."[33] One writer remarked that Handy had done such a good job that "the press notices of the Fair and its gaudy lithographs penetrated into darkest Africa and were not wholly unknown even in the impenetrable fastnesses of upper Fifth Avenue."[34]

The press coverage was so beguiling that Handy's work should have been all but done. Who could resist the fair's siren call anymore?

And yet, as so often happens in life, unforeseen circumstances intervened, for in that same opening week when there was so much revelry in Chicago, the nation's economy started crumbling. Spurred in part by the failures of the Pennsylvania and Reading Railroad and the National Cordage Company, and by a major dip in the nation's gold reserve, a panic had hit Wall Street. "Prices were cut in two and cut in two again," reported the *Chicago Tribune.*[35] On the very day of the Grand Illumination at Jackson Park, massive layoffs began elsewhere—the Tucker and Carter ropewalk in Brooklyn, for example, told 475 of its 500 workers not to come back the next day—and in the weeks and months that followed, more than 4 million others around the United States would also lose their jobs. For many people, a trip to Chicago to see the fair would come to seem like an extravagance, no matter how grand the publicity might make it sound.

One of the more fascinating reports about the opening of the World's Columbian Exposition came from the pen of an elegant thirty-seven-year-old woman with a tall column of dark curly hair and an incisive writing style that ran straight and narrow.

Lillie West had trained as an operatic singer and had starred on the stage alongside famous actors like Edwin Booth and Sarah Bernhardt. Starting in 1890, she began writing for the *Chicago Daily News* under the name Amy Leslie and soon became the drama critic. She would continue writing under that pen name for four decades, in part to protect her rather prurient personal life, which included two divorces (one from Frank Buck, whom she had married when she was forty-six and he was seventeen, long before he became a famous jungle adventurer and actor) and an affair with the writer Stephen Crane.

Leslie visited the fair on opening day, and in one graceful, lyrical swoop of the fountain pen captured the paradoxes to which the other newspapers had devoted so much angst and ink. "The beauty of the spectacle and the picturesque incompleteness of the surroundings gave the day something of the awesome solemnity of imagined creation," she wrote.

> Minor inconveniences seemed forgotten; there was only the mighty stretch toward heaven of glistening domes, marble arms and gigantic eagles' wings, brave statues and histories in emblazoned tablets. Out upon the battling whitecaps of Lake Michigan hung a thousand greetings from exultant ships. The presence of strange friends and unaccustomed tongues, costumes known to us only through the spangled veils of art and verse and with it all the tumult of life and pride and youthful hopes. To me there was nothing lacking except a more accommodating weather bureau.

She went on to describe the events as they transpired—Cleveland's speech, the pushing of the button to start the machinery—but then her focus shifted to something she found far more intriguing.

> A very pretty accident gave an unexpected American tinge to the climax of the interesting ceremonies. Cody's Indians were permitted to go upon the highest balcony of the administration building where they might see the flags run up. By an unintentional gauge of time that seemed strategic just as the machinery began to roar, the whistles blow and the magnificent chorus intone "My Country, 'Tis of Thee," these Indians in their resplendent war-paint, gorgeous necklets and representative American savagery appeared on the

> north abutment of the building, a blazing line of character moving along with high, flaunting crests of feathers and flaming blankets which stood out against the gleaming white of the staff dome like a rainbow cleft into remembrances of a lost, primitive glory. Nothing in the day's occurrences appealed in sympathetic patriotism so much as this fallen majesty slowly filing out of sight as the flags of all nations swept satin kisses through the air, waving congratulations to cultured achievement and submissive admiration to a new world.[36]

Not surprisingly (and perhaps at John M. Burke's invitation, for they almost certainly knew each other from their days in the theater), within the week Amy Leslie was a guest at Buffalo Bill's Wild West.

Leslie apparently made several visits there after that—befriending Annie Oakley; spinning yarns in the private kitchen with Cody, Salsbury, and Burke; and watching the show. All the while, she gathered personal insights, which she freely shared with her readers. Oakley was "a plain, kindly little woman," who spoke with "broad, clear gentleness" about her upbringing in Ohio, and whose tent was "a bower of comfort and taste" even though its Axminster carpet was accessorized by "guns, guns, guns everywhere." Salsbury was "a cynic, full of the bitterness of caustic humor and the spice of sarcasm." Burke was "worthy [of] his Hibernian descent" and "has a perfect volume of episodes in a repertory which changes with the weather." One of the Indians she met, Rain-in-the-Face, was "a mild, inoffensive old warrior, who looked as if he had never done anything more reprehensible than eat oatmeal all his active life."[37]

As for the show itself, it was "simply tremendous" and "intensely exciting to me." She said she understood why people raved over it because "the dramatic force of reality is always the most thrilling achievement in stupendous spectacles."[38]

But it was the warm, human, almost intimate descriptions of Cody that graced her column most poignantly and in so doing added breadth and depth to the persona of Buffalo Bill that Burke had so meticulously crafted over the past twenty years. She saw him as an "engaging story-teller," who was "quiet, rich in humor and mellow in his style as a bottle of old port." She deemed him "One of the most imposing men in appearance that America ever grew," who once had "a glint of the border desperado [lurking] in his blazing eyes and the poetic fierceness of his mien and coloring." But now, at age forty-seven,

> it is all subdued into pleasantness and he is the kindliest most benign gentleman, as simple as a village priest and learned as a savant of Chartreuse. I have just left him in his beaded regalia (which is not dress, but rest for him) and I do not think I ever spent a more delightful hour. His history, teeming with romance, is familiar to everybody in two continents, but his social personality is known to a favored few, in which treasured category I herewith enroll myself. All the gray that has been thrust into his whirlwind life has centered itself in the edges of his beautiful hair. For the rest he is ruddy, straight as the sturdiest buck in his troupe and graceful as an eagle. He talks in the quaint mountaineer language which robs English of all its proper erudities [*sic*]. It is a lazy, melodious sort of drawl tremendously fascinating and unapproachable except by a thoroughbred trapper, a cool soldier and American westerner. . . . Mr. Cody is perfectly natural. He has acquired no alien airs or manner in his marvelous travels and successes, has never lost the atmosphere of the boundless plains, the inspiration of discovery and attempt, nor the honest bravery of a lonely scout who dares break through savagery and peril for nothing much more than hardy sustenance and exciting adventure.[39]

The Barnum & Bailey Circus had spent one week in Chicago in 1891, two weeks in 1892, and had performed a total of 156 times in the Midwest during those two years; but with the presence of the World's Columbian Exposition and Buffalo Bill's Wild West in Chicago, they steered clear of the region entirely in 1893.

Instead, they presented a historical drama of their own: Imre Kiralfy's mammoth musical stage spectacle, "Columbus and the Discovery of America," which featured an almost incomprehensible 1,200 cast members. Tody Hamilton's bombast was evident in the promotions for the new act, which described it as "THE GRANDEST AND MOST COLOSSAL SPECTACLE OF ALL TIME," and "The Unparalleled Terpsichorean Spectacle . . . The Most Amazing Production Ever Devised."[40] By June 1893 Hamilton and his team had ratcheted up their rhetoric further in a courier, using the late Barnum's favorite tactic of impressing people with large sums of money: "$250,000 worth of the Grandest Costumes. $150,000 worth of Magnificent Horses.

$75,000 worth of Elegant Scenery. $50,000 worth of Rare Armor, Emblems and Trappings. TREMENDOUS PAGEANTS COVERING ACRES OF GROUND. . . . YOU HAVE OUR WORD FOR IT That you never saw a Circus before containing a tenth of what we this season bring you in THE GRANDEST CIRCUS ON EARTH. . . . PRESENTING A SERIES OF MOST AMAZING FEATS Unparalleled in the history of the world, almost surpassing human belief and utterly and for a verity far beyond and superior to ANY CIRCUS EVER HITHERTO ORGANIZED, EVEN BY OURSELVES."[41]

Still, no moment in 1893 may have been more satisfying for Tody Hamilton than the one in July when—likely traveling with the circus in New England or upstate New York, and watching the promotional success of the Exposition and the Wild West from afar—he got hold of an article by reporter Kate Field. "There's just one man who could have made the fair a gigantic financial success," the article said, "and he is dead. Of course, I mean the lamented P. T. Barnum." It went on to speculate in detail about how Barnum might have run the Exposition and used his promotional savvy to attract a crowd of three hundred thousand every day. Addressing the world's fair administration, Field wrote, "You are fine citizens, but you don't know how to run a show." In her view, the fair was ultimately nothing more than a 633-acre circus, sans the showmanship. "Resent the expression as much as you please, the World's Columbian Exposition is nothing more or less than the greatest show on earth."[42]

Barnum was dead, and Hamilton was a long way from Chicago, but their influence was certainly being felt.

Throughout the World's Columbian Exposition, there was an incredible diversity of exhibits and activities, more than enough to fill the one thousand pages of Handy's incomplete *Official Catalogue.* There were locomotives, Bach's clavichord, a California redwood, silk cocoons from Brazil, Lincoln's inaugural address manuscript, a map of the United States made out of pickles, twenty-seven dynamos, the seventy-ton Yerkes telescope, a Cuban sugar mill, a California ostrich farm, a fountain of red wine, the Liberty Bell, a prototype fax machine called the telautograph, paintings by Renoir and Picasso, a twenty-foot-long model of the U.S. Treasury Building constructed out of souvenir half-dollars, 5,978 live lectures, Norwegian snow shoes, a bottle-cleaning apparatus, Hagenbeck's Zoological Arena for trained animals (in which a lion rode a horse and a dog rode the lion), the chocolate pavilion, an Etruscan chariot, an eighty-two-foot high Tower of Light, the Ice Railway. . . . Even in the first week, visitors came back multiple times but always left unsated.

Then on May 7, the first Sunday after the Exposition had opened, fifty thousand people came down to Jackson Park only to find the gates shut tight; Sunday closure had been a requirement of the World's Columbian Commission. "The people came in spite of every public assurance that the gates would not be opened," reported the *Chicago Journal.* "It seemed to them incomprehensible and incredible that on the best and brightest day of the whole week, the day on which alone they have surcease from toil and a chance for recreation, the World's Fair should be shut out from them."[43]

The debate over whether to open the Exposition on Sundays had begun long ago. Some said it was only fair to the working people of Chicago; others said it was sacrilegious. There was also a strong financial argument to be made. In summer 1892, a man named Washington Hesing of the German-language newspaper *Illinois Staats-Zeitung* (Chicago) had estimated that if the Exposition remained open on its twenty-six Sundays it would attract 6 million additional visitors and bring in more than $5 million.[44] But in a rare example of Chicago hewing to eastern standards, such commercial interests had been set aside.

So the same scene played out on Sunday, May 14, and again on May 21. "Another big crowd beat up against the closed gates of the world's fair yesterday and vainly clamored for admission," wrote the *Chicago Mail.*[45] The impasse could not continue. The following week, a compromise was worked out, whereby the fairgrounds were opened but the exhibits remained closed. Eventually, all puritanical restraint gave way.

But on the days when the Exposition was closed, the side shows remained open. These included a whole itinerant village of merchants, "strong-voiced criers," and shysters who had taken up residence along Stoney Island Avenue just outside the fair's entrance. This motley group included, according to the *Chicago Tribune,* candy butchers, peanut and popcorn vendors, trinket dealers, picture-guide peddlers, tattooed women, snake charmers, dancers in tights, illusionists, freaks, and "black faced boys dressed in flashy costumes pounding drums and batting cymbals."[46]

And just across Stoney Island Avenue was another side show of sorts,

Buffalo Bill's Wild West, which did an enormous business on Sundays for its 3:00 and 8:00 shows.

John M. Burke's promotional instincts were finely tuned by this point in his pioneering career; he knew exactly which levers to pull. So while he and Cody told the press that they were indifferent about the issue of Sunday closure for the Exposition—remaining above the fray—the Wild West newspaper ads pointedly stated that they performed "every day, rain or shine (Sunday included)."[47]

This was a fine line that Burke walked all summer: trying not to be disrespectful of the World's Columbian Exposition next door, but capitalizing on their every shortcoming or misstep.

For example, when the heat set in during June and July, causing great discomfort to fair visitors, Burke began incorporating a new "catch line" in Wild West advertising to emphasize that a canvas covered his grandstand: "the coolest place of resort in Chicago."[48] (Burke was also frequently using lines such as "America's National Entertainment" and "A World-Beater." He was a trailblazer in the use of what we would now call taglines, which were not common in this era; and during the Chicago season he also began experimenting with icons, incorporating the image of a skeleton key into ads and printed materials as a rebus in the statement "The key to all").

Burke and his team also turned another gaffe by the Exposition management into a major promotional coup. Mayor Carter Harrison of Chicago and a group of civic-minded citizens had proposed a "poor children's day," and several newspapers called for the fair to accommodate the "newsboys, bootblacks and waifs" for free; Mrs. Potter Palmer, of the Lady Board of Managers, said she would donate her entire salary of more than six thousand dollars to the cause, and the Illinois Central Railroad offered free transportation to the fairgrounds. It was scheduled for June 29, then postponed to July 27, but the Exposition management never could agree to free admissions, and the event never happened. Instead, the Wild West stepped in, providing a picnic, parade, and entry to *their* show. Burke—an orphan himself, as he frequently reminded the press, and someone who was renowned for giving out free passes to children who hung around the camp—was likely the driving force behind this move, which resulted in considerable publicity for Cody and the Wild West, and a fortuitous ripple effect, as the *Inter Ocean* reported: "Ever since admission to the World's Fair was refused to the Waifs' Mission and the thousands of other children who celebrated Poor Children's day at Buffalo Bill's Wild West show, Superintendent Daniels has been in receipt from letters of children, and grown-up people as well, proposing to pay the admission fee for a certain number of his little charges, so that poor boys as well as the rest might have at least one day at the Fair."[49] Thereafter, for many years to come, the Wild West made regular accommodation for poor children and orphans.

And then in August, Burke again turned the power of the Wild West's popularity against the rigid fair managers after they rescinded an offer for Cody and his troupe to participate in the parade celebrating Illinois Day. President Harlow Higinbotham of the Exposition staff at first offered the rationale that the Wild West "was not an Illinois affair" and that the crowds would be too large; but then he told reporters, "Mr. Cody's show is not dignified enough for such an occasion"—the very same explanation that had been used to keep the Wild West out of the Exposition proper in the first place.[50] So Illinois Day proceeded without the Wild West.

Some newspapers got the story wrong and even reported that the Wild West Indians had caused a ruckus that disrupted the Illinois Day parade. Burke gently fired back with a letter to the editor complaining about the "misrepresentation of facts that does great injustice to the Wild West" and setting the record straight: "The members of the Wild West did not leave their own grounds during the day, but owing to the crowds being so great their parade, by understanding with the Exposition authorities, was postponed. . . . If we had been on the streets at all there might have been some excuse for your reporter making the statements he did, but under the circumstances as they were you can readily see the injustice done to us."[51]

The Wild West was then invited to stage its own parade, on Exposition grounds, the very next day.

Meanwhile, the Major kept up a steady stream of promotions throughout the summer. For example, he arranged and/or publicized visits to the show by many prominent people—among them Statue of Liberty sculptor Frederic Bartholdi, Maharaja Jagitjit Singh Bahadur of Kapurthala (British Empire of India), the Duke and Duchess of Veragua, Susan B. Anthony, James Cardinal Gibbons, and Prince Antoine of Spain.

In June, when a newspaper in Chadron, Nebraska, announced that it was organizing a cowboy horse race across one thousand miles to the World's Columbian Exposition with a two hundred-dollar prize, Burke all but co-opted it by announcing that Buffalo Bill would meet the winner at the entrance to the Wild West arena and present him with five hundred dollars as well as a Colt revolver and a saddle. Burke heavily promoted the event, and the press responded. The coverage of the race turned sour, however, when the Society for the Prevention of Cruelty to Animals (SPCA), along with the Illinois Humane Society, raised concerns about the welfare of the horses. Burke immediately shifted into reputation management mode, backpedaling about Cody's support for the race and reminding anyone who would listen about Cody's love for animals: the Colonel, said Burke, had even lobbied for the use of clay pigeons instead of live ones in shooting exhibitions. Indeed, Burke left Chicago to provide support as the race proceeded, inviting SPCA and Humane Society members in various states along the racecourse to examine the horses for themselves.[52]

When the mad dash ended, after thirteen days, Burke ran a newspaper ad that read in part, "An Equine Race Humanely Run! Humanely Won! UNDER SUPERVISION OF the Society for the Prevention of Cruelty to Animals." But he probably didn't need it. The papers were filled with breathless headlines about the "cowboy race" and reports that "Major John M. Burke was full of enthusiasm. He was more than satisfied with the race, but declared the riders to be a 'lemonade brigade.' 'They don't drink anything but lemonade. Why I've bought a string of lemonade from Iowa to Chicago and the boys just broke me.'"[53] So much for the image of two-fisted whiskey-swilling cowboy renegades.

During the season in Chicago, Burke also provided assistance to his endless network of newspaper compadres in generating novel angles and fresh copy about the Wild West. *Tag along with Rain-in-the-Face, purported slayer of Custer, as he sees the world's fair. Inspect the camp's two dynamos and 250 horsepower for its electric lighting. Marvel at the new photographic process that will be used to take a panoramic picture of the grandstand before the start of the 3:00 performance "and be of sufficient size to make the picture of each visitor clear and distinct."*[54] They rewarded him with many column inches, day after day after day, as well as occasional triumphal declarations, such as when the *Inter Ocean* said, "The success of Buffalo Bill's Wild West show is assured. Its appropriateness to the world's fair in conception and execution and the arrangement of its details have won public approval and the attendance continues to grow larger day by day."[55] Or when the *Chicago Herald* wrote, "Without question, Buffalo Bill and his exhibition have hit the public fancy harder than any entertainment that has visited this city in years."[56]

The press coverage throughout the run in Chicago was constant and unprecedented in volume, save for the even larger volume being accorded to the Exposition. There were stories about how the Indians built their tepees, how a cowboy roped a kangaroo that had escaped from Hagenbeck's Zoological Arena, how the food was prepared in the camp, how Burke and Cody dissuaded their cowboys from throwing a statue near the fair's Transportation Building into the lagoon—human interest stories, feature stories, real news, manufactured news: a torrent of daily publicity. The tone was typically excited, awestruck, and very colloquial, as befitted the subject matter. And most of it emanated in one way or another from John M. Burke. At one point, Cody declined an interview with reporter Kate Field and pushed her off to the Major. "There's Burke," Cody told her. "He's the only one at leisure. Just set him going and you'll discover the next thing to perpetual motion. He knows everything and would talk a hen off her nest."[57] (It is not hard to imagine Burke sitting on a chair outside his campground tent, taking a couple of puffs on his "seegar," reflecting on the most successful season the Wild West ever had, reading that comment, and letting out a satisfied little guffaw.)

Perhaps this publicity assault was Burke's answer to the insult of the Wild West having been deemed too undignified to be an official part of the Exposition, or maybe it was his own stylized response to the competition posed by Handy. Burke would later tell the newspapers, "Yes. We were there during the great World's Fair, and the Wild West hardly paled in human interest beside the wonders of that marvelous triumph of man's art and ingenuity."[58] Either way, it was a highly effective counterpunch.

Burke continued to spout his unique, somewhat revisionist historiography, the main tenets of which were (1) that the conquering of the western frontier was *the* key pivot point between ancient and modern society, (2) that the Wild West authentically captured and preserved that transformation (which now extended all the way back to Columbus), and therefore (3) that the Wild West was entertaining and elucidating as well as educational. The newspapers were all too happy to incorporate these themes in their reporting.

Just a few weeks after the show had opened in Chicago, he told the *Inter Ocean*,

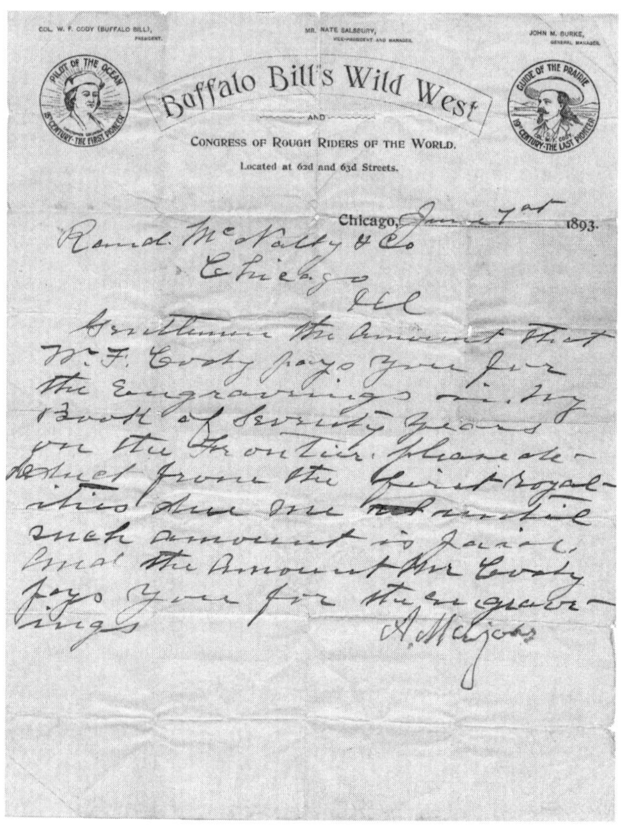

COL. W. F. CODY (BUFFALO BILL), PRESIDENT. MR. NATE SALSBURY, VICE-PRESIDENT AND MANAGER. JOHN M. BURKE, GENERAL MANAGER.

PILOT OF THE OCEAN — 15th CENTURY-THE FIRST PIONEER

Buffalo Bill's Wild West

AND

CONGRESS OF ROUGH RIDERS OF THE WORLD.

Located at 62d and 63d Streets.

GUIDE OF THE PRAIRIE — 19th CENTURY-THE LAST PIONEER

Chicago, June 7th 1893.

Rand McNally & Co
Chicago
Ill
Gentlemen the amount that W. F. Cody pays you for the Engravings in my Book of Seventy Years on the Frontier. please deduct from the first royalties due me until such amount is paid. I mean the amount Mr Cody pays you for the engravings
A. Majors

PILOT OF THE OCEAN, GUIDE OF THE PRAIRIE. In 1893, Burke's mythmaking even extended to the Wild West letterhead—equating the accomplishments of Columbus and Cody atop this letter written by Cody's one-time boss Alexander Majors. Buffalo Bill Museum and Grave, Golden, Colorado.

The Indian was the character Columbus discovered and his mode of life was all that was known in this country 400 years ago, and from that civilization in the meantime has produced the marvelous results shown in Jackson park. At Buffalo's Bill's one sees the first arch of the bridge that spans the stream of time, and in Jackson park is placed the other. To thoroughly appreciate the structure man has built, bridging these 400 years, it is necessary to study the foundations and at no other place in Chicago can this be done save at Buffalo Bill's. Not only is the Indian in his primitive state found here, engaged in the pursuits of his daily life and customs, but a strong contrast is drawn and presented to the visitor by the presence

> of the Russian Cossack, the Bedouin Arab, the Mexican vaquero, the American cowboy, and representative of the highest perfection of the military art in picked representatives of the cavalry of the armies of the four greatest nations of the world.[59]

Columbus had become another pawn in Burke's chess game of irony-and-symbolism.

But the unwitting checkmate occurred on the afternoon of July 12, 1893, when participants in the American Historical Association conference came to see Buffalo Bill's Wild West—and that very night, heard one of their own, Professor Frederick Jackson Turner of the University of Wisconsin, deliver an address from his seminal paper "The Significance of the Frontier in American History."

Turner spoke to his colleagues about the frontier, "the meeting point between savagery and civilization," a form of geographic determinism that contained echoes of Thomas Hart Benton and William Gilpin. The frontier had shifted across the country like "successive terminal moraines," Turner said. "The buffalo trail became the Indian trail, and this became the trader's 'trace'; the trails widened into roads, and the roads into turnpikes, and these in turn were transformed into railroads."[60]

It was old news by the time Turner spoke, because the 1890 census had already confirmed it; but the frontier was gone. By implication, so was the "wild" part of the "Wild West." And yet, at the hands of a masterful marketer like John M. Burke, as the historians had seen for themselves just hours earlier, the Wild West was just getting started.

During the last three days of May 1893, the American Publishers' Association gathered in Chicago for its World's Press Congress. The association comprised 150 newspapers, representing 50 percent of the total daily newspaper circulation in the country, and 85 percent of the advertising. It was an opportunity for the newspaper industry to take stock of its growth and progress, assess its newfound power as a tool not just for dissemination of news but for advertising and publicity, and resolve important operational questions such as whether to reduce the size of the Sunday paper. Many of the most powerful publishers in the country were on hand, from the trade press and the religious press as well as from leading newspapers like the *New York World*, *Chicago Herald*, *Inter Ocean*, and *Cincinnati Post*.

On Friday, May 26, the attendees wrapped up their business affairs in the morning, took a drive through the West Side parks, and then visited the plant of the Webster Manufacturing Company, where they examined the development of the Paige compositor—an eleven-foot long, five thousand-pound mechanical typesetting machine, which had been funded in part by Mark Twain with the royalties he received from *Huckleberry Finn.* The combination of technology and advertising dollars had fueled the rise of the newspaper in their very lifetimes, and this new behemoth held the promise of even faster production and greater riches. But unbeknownst to the association tour group, the machine they inspected that day, which would be completed the following year, was one of only two working Paige compositors that would ever be made. It went down in history as one of the most complex patent applications ever filed, and one of the biggest technological failures.[61]

But that evening, at the association's banquet at Kinsley's, amidst elaborate food, abundant ferns and flowers, and music from the Weber Quartet, members were able to inspect the other half of the formula that had made them so rich and powerful: human genius. Among the attendees were the two pioneers whose work over the past two decades, though so different stylistically, had combined to confer a new purpose and power to the press as a promotional vehicle, and who had already helped to make 1893 into a watershed moment for the new industry of marketing: John M. Burke and Moses P. Handy. The latter addressed the crowd of seventy-five dignitaries, recapping the accomplishments and difficulties he and his department had experienced over the past two years. According to the *Chicago Times,* "Maj. Handy was called on to tell how he had 'worked' the newspapers of the world for advertising, which if paid for would have cost the world's fair more than its buildings."[62]

There was no record of how the publishers received Handy's remarks, but by this time it was certainly clear that the idea of promotion through the newspapers was here to stay. Indeed, just four weeks earlier, on the day before the Exposition had opened, the *New York Times* had written:

> The greatest triumph of modern times might be constructed, and if its wonders were not published and advertised the greatest purpose of the exposition would fail. Doubtless, possessing the intrinsic worth it does, the fair could have advertised itself in a way, but to carry word of its grandeur and magnificence to the uttermost parts

> of the earth, to arouse the interest of mankind, required intelligent direction.
>
> [Major Moses P. Handy's] department called out all his experience and accomplishments acquired in a successful journalistic career, and it is safe to assume that so invaluable has been the aid Major Handy has given to the greatest exposition the world has ever seen that hereafter a bureau of publicity and promotion will be as indispensable a department of great exhibitions as the bureau of works.[63]

Throughout the rest of the Exposition, Handy continued to enact his promotional plan even while he kept the bureaucracy at bay and defended himself and his department against the arrows of detractors. For example, Handy was chastised for his liberality in issuing free passes, even though a statement from the auditor showed that of the forty thousand free passes thus far issued, only three thousand had truly come from the Department of Publicity and Promotion; henceforth, Handy would record and report with great precision the numbers issued—9,024 single-admission tickets given out in June, 9,870 in July, and so forth. He also issued a pointed defense of his practices, stating in his official monthly report that the Exposition had received "a plenitude of gratuitous advertising" and that it had come at a cost he calculated to be just eleven dollars in free passes to each newspaper.[64]

The accusations and innuendo continued. On June 6, Handy received a letter from Daniel Burnham blaming him (incorrectly) for misspelling the chief architect's name at a dinner, causing him "public humiliation"; Burnham wrote back the following day, admitting it had been a mistake: "I tender you a hearty apology."[65] Handy also had to deal with criticism of the cost overruns for printing the *Official Guide* and for the incompleteness of the first edition of the *Official Catalogue*. Even some of the newspapers were petty and unkind. "Major Handy's Department Doomed," read a headline in the *New York Times* on June 18, in an article incorrectly reporting that the decision had been made to eliminate his department as of July 1.

On June 30, Director General Davis informed Handy that his salary would be cut by a third, to five thousand dollars per year. By mid-July, the budget crunch got tighter, and Handy was forced to ask for the resignation of fifteen members of his staff; shortly thereafter, he encouraged his second lieutenant, J. P. Holland, to resign so that Handy could recommend him for a new job working on the upcoming Exposition in Antwerp. Later still, when Handy hired a man named Joseph Woodward as messenger, he received a stern note from Davis complaining that Woodward "was found bringing in other material than that required by your Office or any other administrative office. I wish you would inquire of Mr. Woodward what he has to say in this regard, and if his answers are not satisfactory, you would better secure some one who will respect the rules and regulations of the Exposition."[66]

All the carping and micromanagement got to Moses P. Handy. He again gave serious consideration to stepping down, and this was reflected in his correspondence with his son Will, who was posted as a newspaper correspondent in Texas, "working like a dog, night & day covering 3 towns 200 miles each from the other." Will wrote on June 5 from the Pacific Hotel in Helena, Arkansas, "I see they are talking of economy at the fair but they no longer talk of economising in your direction, which shows their wisdom." Soon Moses wrote back, "There is no news about my resignation or the future of my department. I . . . am not caring what the outcome will be. Meanwhile I am milling [?] down steadily."[67]

He would stick it out to the end, however, secure in the knowledge that he had worked diligently and honorably, and that in launching the largest promotional effort in history, he had accomplished something nearly miraculous—whether the rest of the world realized it or not.

Fortunately, at least some did.

In one of the official histories of the Exposition, published in 1893, ex–Virginia governor William E. Cameron (who, twenty years earlier, had recommended to President Grant that he appoint Handy as a commissioner to the World Exposition in Vienna) wrote that Handy's task was difficult because the field of marketing was "entirely unexplored; methods, as well as forces, had to be originated, and the territory to be covered was the globe." Cameron summarized the results: "How thoroughly the work has been accomplished is best shown by the universal interest which has been created in the enterprise. A recent traveler through the remote East said on returning home that he had encountered in the most obscure hamlet no person who had not heard of Chicago and the great Exposition."[68]

Many newspapers also came to his defense. The *New York Times* said that "Maj. Moses P. Handy will go out in a blaze of bewhiskered glory."[69] The

Albany Journal declared, "The fair has been magnificently advertised by Major Handy's bureau, and it has proved the value of advertising. . . . The fair is a great commercial enterprise, and the experience of business men is that no commercial enterprise depending for success upon the constant patronage of the public can succeed without the assistance of the press, whether such assistance takes one form of advertisement or another."[70] It was a prescient observation, because henceforth, nearly every major undertaking in American society—commercial, entertainment, government, military, or sporting—would include a marketing component, featuring many of the strategies Handy had advanced in Chicago.

A huge crowd of 716,881 people turned out for Chicago Day at the World's Columbian Exposition, October 9—the twenty-second anniversary of the Great Chicago Fire. It seemed as if the long process of planning, the war of the words, the two frenetic years of construction, and the nearly six months of euphoric entertainment were building toward a dramatic conclusion, a crescendo that would explode in an epic final harmonic chord that might reverberate in the bestilled air for a very, very long time.

But then on October 28, Mayor Carter Harrison was assassinated in his home by a disgruntled office seeker, and the city plunged into mourning.[71] The planned pomp and spectacle for the Exposition's closing day on October 30—triumphal marches, the firing of cannon, plenty of grandiloquent speechmaking—was muted. The gates then quietly closed forever.

Nevertheless, the World's Columbian Exposition had exceeded even the expectations of Chicago's "wild boomers." It had drawn 27.5 million visitors, about half of whom were from other countries. It had overcome all the budgetary concerns and actually turned a profit of about a half-million dollars. It was also the spark that ignited or popularized many cultural trends that would last for decades, including the City Beautiful movement, landscape architecture, women's suffrage, popular photography, and outdoor electric lighting.

Perhaps more significantly, it helped America's "second city" overcome its poor reputation and earn a place in the pantheon of global metropolises, which both effectuated and legitimized the rise of the West. The Chicago-born writer Hobart Chatfield-Taylor called it "Chicago's debut in the society of the world" and marveled at how far the previously "vigorous—though somewhat uncouth—exponent of Western energy" had come:

> Heretofore Chicago has formed a civilization somewhat apart from the world. Its reputation certainly has not been aesthetic. Its society, naturally sensitive to criticism it considered in a great measure undeserved, and geographically removed from the social centers of the East, has lived apart from the rest of the world. [But] it has grown and thrived and imbibed the spirit of Americanism. During recent years it has begun to acquire the subtle polish the world requires from those who aspire to social distinction.[72]

Similarly, former Kansas senator John J. Ingalls, noting that the Windy City's bid was originally considered a "frontier joke," remarked,

> The wonder that these noble, artistic conceptions were realized at all is increased by the fact that they were realized in Chicago . . . the assemblage of the highest achievements of civilization, the fraternal rivalry of nations; the uplifting of the human race. The conception was Napoleonic, and the result is an epoch in history. . . . The demonstration was a signal and unprecedented triumph, not alone of Chicago, but for the new empire of the West.[73]

The World's Columbian Exposition's astonishing splendor and punctilious display had captured the imaginations of millions, providing a fitting send-off to the nineteenth century and presenting a tantalizing glimpse of an alluring future. "Your fair," wrote the author and social critic Charles Eliot Norton, "in spite of its astounding incongruities and its broad border of vulgarities, is a great promise, a great pledge even. It at least forbids despair. I have never seen Americans from whom one could draw happier auguries for the future of America than some of the men I saw in Chicago."[74]

11

DENOUEMENT

"The last gasp in arenic marvels"

There, is an Indian mound, and here
The cabin of the pioneer;
Where once the signal torch was lit,
'Neath incandescent lights are writ
The poesy and prose, that changes tell,
From tom-tom's beat to silver bell,
Here, in modern heat, find mirth
Or jest, before the log-warmed hearth;
Go ride a broncho 'cross the plain
On auto car or trolley train.

John M. Burke, *Blue Hawk Peak* (1910)

On November 22, three weeks after the Columbian Exposition had closed, Moses P. Handy received a letter proposing a dinner in his honor:

> A number of your newspaper friends in New York City, appreciating the splendid work done by you as Chief of the Department of Publicity and Promotion of the Worlds [*sic*] Columbian Exposition for the entire publishing press of the country, desire to tender you a testimonial of such appreciation in the shape of a dinner at the Hotel Waldorf in this city. While we propose to limit the number of participants, we shall place no bounds on the enthusiasm and

> feeling of goodfellowship which prompts the entertainment of one good fellow by others who feel that they have a place under the same heading.[1]

At the dinner, held on December 7, Handy began by saying that this would be his "four hundred and seventy-second World's Fair speech," if that was what was required, but that he would prefer to talk about something else. He later told the *Reading (Pa.) Times* that this had been his 570th banquet since the fair had begun—and given his penchant for counting everything, he was probably right.[2]

Meanwhile, although the fair was over, a lively debate had broken out in Chicago about what to do with the buildings and grounds of the moribund White City. It had been an evanescent achievement, a lucid dream, a tour de force in staff—none of it built to last. Everyone knew that. Yet it had inspired such profound optimism ("There has come to pass . . . a new sense of unlimited human kinship and fellowship; a large grace of hospitality; a new measure, if not a new degree, of human sociability beyond all the bounds of any race or speech," wrote one reporter) that many civic leaders were loath to let its forward momentum come to end. All sorts of ideas were put forward. *Move the Liberal Arts Building to the lakefront. Demolish everything, pile up the materials, and landscape over it to make artificial mountains five hundred feet high. Shore up the Court of Honor with white marble or Roman brick. Burn one building each night and charge admission. Keep the buildings in place for one year. Hold another fair in 1894 or 1895.*[3]

But the question didn't linger for long. Just a few weeks after the fair closed, on the night of January 8, a massive fire broke out and destroyed a swath of the majestic Court of Honor. It was, said the *Chicago Tribune*, "the greatest pyrotechnic display of the Fair." The reporter went on to paint a vivid and grotesque picture:

> A strong breeze from the lake fanned the flames, and they shot up into the air to a height of 100 feet or more. All the grounds as far north as the north lagoon were lighted up like a midsummer's day at noon. The crowd that lined the shore could be distinctly seen in the bright light, and they could be heard, too, every time a statue or a pinnacle toppled on a crumbling cornice before taking a plunge into the fiery depths below. The crowd cheered as one after another the statues toppled and pitched head foremost, some

ON THE DAY AFTER THE FIRE ON EXPOSITION GROUNDS, January 9, 1894, the smoldering ruins of the Court of Honor signaled a sad end to the reign of the White City. *Beautiful Scenes of the White City*, part 15, May 21, 1894; author's collection.

> back into the burning building, others out toward the lake. . . .
>
> The French statue of the Republic seemed to stand in the midst of it all like a gigantic silhouette, with uplifted arms as if appealing for help. The wind blew furiously, and now and then made great rifts in the smoky wall, revealing the blood-red skeleton of arch and column.[4]

There was hardly even time for one last look, one final moment to sear the image into the nation's collective memory. Two more fires in the next six months would level the rest of the fairgrounds, leaving little more than the photographs and the Department of Publicity and Promotion's bird's-eye-view lithograph to remind 27 million people of what had stood ever so briefly, what had shone ever so brilliantly, in Jackson Park. What remained was nothing more than a lingering impression created by the ghostly images of architectural grandeur that had lined the Court of Honor, an ephemeral tribute to durability, a testament of commemorations and relics—a place that was nothing, and then was magnificent, and then was gone.

For the man whose promotion of the Exposition had contributed so much to its success—whom the *New York Times* had predicted would go out "in a blaze of bewhiskered glory"—this different sort of blaze was not momentous news. In Moses Handy's tiny Excelsior Pocket Diary, he scrawled one simple notation for Monday, January 8, 1894: "Fire at World's Fair destroying casino, Peristyle & music stall." That was it. No emotion. No elegies. He had moved on.

He soon returned to his enduring passion, newspaper work—first as a special correspondent for the *Inter Ocean* and the *New York Mail and Express* (now edited by his erstwhile protégé Dorr), and then as political writer and editor-in-chief of the *Chicago Times-Herald.* After years of nearly nonstop travel, this enabled him to spend more time with Sarah and their seven children—although Moses Purnell Handy Jr. would suddenly die of a brain embolism at the age of eighteen in 1897. He also made two tantalizing references in his diary to a novel he may have been writing, but if any such work was ever produced, it was not published and nothing survives.

Still, as much as he loved writing, politics was always an important avocation for Moses P. Handy: he had covered several presidential campaigns as a reporter, had campaigned for both Blaine and Harrison, and had almost taken the job as consul-general to Egypt in 1890. Thus, a few days after the Exposition closed, Handy wrote to Governor William McKinley of Ohio, ostensibly congratulating him on his reelection and jokingly suggesting that he must be "bored to death" by all the congratulatory letters he had received, but likely with the ulterior motive of fishing around for possible employment. McKinley wrote back on November 14 with thanks, praising Handy's "feeling of consideration."[5]

Handy would go on to organize two business-centric political groups, the American Honest Money League and the National Business League. He also worked hard to help put McKinley in the White House in 1896 ("He [Handy] was indomitable, fluent, vociferous, and picturesque," wrote the *Washington Post,* and "lent to the campaign more melody, more Italian sunset effects; more humor and more stimulus than any one of our acquaintance"), and then openly lobbied to secure a plum patronage job—perhaps running the consulate in London or Paris, or the American mission in Japan or Turkey.[6] A consular job, he learned, would pay $20,000 to $35,000 a year, compared to the $3,500 a year offer he had gotten from the *New York Mail and Express.* Among those who contacted McKinley in support of Handy were three members of the U.S. Senate and Secretary of the Treasury Lyman Gage (former head of the World's Columbian Exposition), but it was all for naught: other candidates secured the positions, and Handy never got his consular post.

He did, however, get one consolation prize from McKinley: on July 27, 1897, the president named Handy, now fifty years old, as special commissioner to the Paris International Exposition of 1900—the fourth time in his life he had been similarly honored. This one was, perhaps, something of a booby prize, because Congress cut back the number of commissioners, the size of its appropriation, and allotted Handy only a five thousand-dollar salary.[7]

The stated task would be to travel to Paris to secure space and make arrangements for the American exhibit there, as well as learn what other nations intended to do; the implied task would be to figure out how, in the wake of the success of Chicago, America could best position and promote itself at the next big international exposition. "His work will be that of the advance agent," wrote the *Inter Ocean,* and thus his achievement in Chicago "was regarded as especially fitting him for this work."[8]

On August 28, 1897, Moses and Sarah along with two of his deputies sailed aboard the steamship *Gascogne* for France, where over the course of the next two months he studied the plans for the Paris Exposition and used his well-honed diplomatic skills to negotiate with French authorities for exhibit space—securing two hundred thousand square feet, 60 percent more than was offered at the start of the negotiations.

But toward the end of his visit, he fell ill with what was called "nervous prostration" as well as "impaired circulation" and "faulty heart action." The *New York Times* would later report, "Never a very strong man, the strain of his labors had told heavily on his constitution, and he was advised by his physicians to give up the more trying work of the mission. But he persisted until two days before the date set for sailing, when he was overcome by what appeared to be temporary weakness."[9] The trip home was delayed for two weeks until Sarah could nurse him back to health. She wrote to reassure the children that all would be fine: "This morning, the Doctor says the immediate danger is past, & the corner is turned. But our Major is to be kept perfectly quiet, & have absolute rest. It is a case of complete nervous prostration, the brain kept going at the expense of the other organs of the body. Like a bloodied horse he has made his race refusing to give up until he reached the goal."[10]

They finally returned on November 1 to New York, and then back home to Chicago, where Handy prepared his report to Congress. After a relapse of his illness on December 17, Sarah took him to the Hotel Bon Air in Augusta, Georgia, to get away from the stresses of the city. But he never recuperated. Moses P. Handy died on January 8, 1898—four years to the day after the fire that had brought down the World's Columbian Exposition.

Sarah tried to find solace in writing—including two poems, never published, that survive in the Handy Family Papers. One of them, which she left untitled, still echoes her heartbreak more than a century later:

> When the light of our life goes out,
> leaving us blind and alone;
> When all the foundations are rent,
> and the house of our heart overthrown:
> Dazed mid the ruin and wreck,
> Conscious only of loss;
> How shall we rise neath the load?
> How shall we carry our cross?
> Help us, oh Christ to be still,
> Laying our mouths in the dust,
> Help us to bow to Thy will,
> Lord, and endure, since we must.[11]

The special commissioner's report to Congress on the Paris Exposition was filed, but it would be left to Sarah to carry the promotional torch to the public. This she did, in a lengthy article that was published in Dorr's *New York Mail and Express* on March 12, 1898. It began:

> All France, and more especially the city of Paris, is deeply in earnest with regard to the exposition of 1900. Thoroughly resolved that this great World's Fair, the crowning event of the century, shall eclipse anything of the sort which has ever been, national pride is fully aroused, and the work of preparation is being vigorously pushed forward in every possible manner. Frankly acknowledging the

> impossibility of equaling the Columbian Exposition of Chicago in either beauty of location or in extent, they openly avow the intention to excel it in every other respect.[12]

But perhaps the most fitting tribute to the pioneering work of Moses P. Handy appeared four days later, in the trade journal *Printers' Ink* (tagline: A Journal for Advertisers), which observed that

> whenever a great public or political enterprise is inaugurated, the formation of a literary bureau is one of the first and most important acts of its beneficiaries or promoters. . . . Take expositions, for instance. No undertaking of this kind is without a well organized department of publicity, whose business it is to secure the greatest possible circulation for all sorts of bulletins and descriptions. . . . The late Major Moses P. Handy, who was chief of the department of publicity and promotion of the World's Columbian Exposition at Chicago, probably secured more of this free advertising . . . than any man that ever lived. Moreover, he created a system of "working the press" which has, since his time, been used with excellent success.

Among those now using Handy's publicity and promotion techniques, said the author, were charitable enterprises, railroads, patriotic societies, state and national political organizations, and backers of causes.

> All want publicity, and they want it without expense. . . . [S]cores of literary men and statisticians are employed to prepare newspaper articles for every section of the country. Editorials are supplied to all publishers calling for them, and facts and figures can be obtained by mail or telegraph. . . . The chief aim and object of all is mainly to keep their ideas before the people, to convince voters that prosperity will result from the adoption of their theories and principles; just as the theatrical press agent attempts to convince newspaper readers that the particular star he represents is the greatest actor or actress in the world.[13]

It was a wholly different world than the one in which Moses Purnell Handy had been born, with an entirely new industry that he had helped create.

By 1903, a record ninety-eight circuses and menageries were operating across the United States, and the competition for arena time, ticket sales, and press coverage was fierce.[14]

Tody Hamilton's ornate linguistic stylings, clever stunts, and incessant efforts to keep Barnum & Bailey in the news during this period combined to produce a competitive promotional strategy that is largely still in use by today's publicists—for new movie releases, sports teams, and even Coke and Pepsi.

At least as early as 1886, Hamilton's title was advertising director and press agent, and this meant he had several different roles to play. Barnum & Bailey eventually built up a large team to handle the promotional responsibilities, including what was often described by the overwhelmed local newspaper editors as an "army of advance agents," as well as an extremely sophisticated bill-posting operation that comprised four entire railroad cars, each with eight to eleven men to do the posting and several lithographers, at the cost of more than one thousand dollars a week.[15] The average location might get five thousand such lithographs, but on occasion, especially when there were competing shows on tour, the bill posters might use five times that number.[16] (On the day after the advertising cars rolled into Phoenix in 1905, the *Arizona Republican* reported, "The consequence is that Phoenix before night was a different looking town. It was a vast picture book with all the pages open at once and plenty of readers to enjoy them."[17])

Hamilton's hand was in all of it. At times he was on the road ahead of the show, dropping in on newspaper offices in Keokuk, Rock Island, Wabash, Owosso, or Richmond to negotiate advertising contracts or pitch stories; on other occasions, he was writing ads, pamphlets, and press materials from the Barnum & Bailey office in New York (which, after Bailey bought an interest in the Wild West in 1895, he shared with John M. Burke).[18] Hamilton's role in developing the copy for what he called "the flaring circus posters" for which Barnum & Bailey became so famous was readily apparent in their linguistic style:

THE PEERLESS PRODIGIES OF PHYSICAL PHENOMENA

STARTLING AND SUBLIME EXHIBITION OF SAVAGE WILD BEASTS AND DOMESTIC ANIMALS EXEMPLIFYING THE DIVINE DECREE THAT "THE LION AND THE LAMB SHALL LIE DOWN TOGETHER"

Hamilton's style became synonymous with the circus style, which in turn came to be thought of as its own genre of marketing—brash, pulse racing, and over the top (see plate 11). Indeed, he even wrote copy for some of his circus competitors—an antiquated custom, but one that he successfully defended to Bailey because it would prevent the competitors from saying anything bad about Barnum & Bailey.

Late in his career with the circus, however, Hamilton would acknowledge that as a promotional tool, the venerable poster had lost its edge: "Its real value as an advertising medium is doubtful. Hereafter the newspapers will get more and dead walls less."[19] Still, it was in his capacity not as poster writer but as press agent that he did his best work. Others on his team might prepare generic and predictably positive "after-blast reviews" of the show, which would be printed in many newspapers, but Hamilton was a genius at creating fresh angles and lively content to keep Barnum & Bailey in the news, before, during, and after their stands in a town. "He was . . . a good newspaperman and knew how to provide good stories for the reporters who were sent to cover the show," wrote Frank Leroy Blanchard, the one-time managing editor of *Printers' Ink* and author of a 1921 book called *The Essentials of Advertising*. "If there was a natural dearth of news that had a punch to it, he could, seemingly, without the slightest effort, create news stories that the papers were glad to play up on the front page with scare heads."[20]

He loved to tell reporters about the oddities of some circus creatures, such as the supposed fact that kangaroos respond to different types of violin music, or the story of how Sepia the elephant, normally number twenty-seven in a parade of twenty-eight, got lost and had to count to find her proper place in line.[21] The press marveled when Hamilton took them behind the scenes to see Joanna, "the educated ape," who dined with fork and knife, poured and savored her own wine, and tipped the waiter at the end of the feast.[22] (Years earlier, he had employed the same strategy at the aquarium, where he supposedly trained oysters to recognize him, to propel themselves along in their tank and follow him, and to "whistle tunes" for reporters.[23]) It was said that Tody Hamilton could persuade even the most conservative of newspapers to write about Barnum & Bailey simply "by a screed on how elephants are captured or how monkeys educate their babies."[24] He once told a reporter, "The circus is a great field for the press agent. If anything, it is too full of material."[25]

One of his favorite tactics was to invite reporters to special press demonstrations at the show's winter quarters in Bridgeport, Connecticut, just before or after the circus season. At these outings, the reporters might be treated to an experiment in which pans of beer and whiskey were put into the cages of a polar bear and other beasts, or another in which the old story about lions being terrified of mice was put to the test. On one occasion, in 1894, Hamilton invited his guests to see the feeding of two live lambs to the leopards and Bengal tigers, and the newspapers wrote about it in excruciating detail ("Like a flash, the leopards had sprung at its throat, and, burying their fangs deeply in the neck of the lamb, they sucked its blood, their eyes gleaming with ferocious satisfaction"—this was the sort of coverage that put fannies in seats!).[26] In 1906, Hamilton even held the preopening press luncheon inside the wild animal cage. "It was a very unique affair as the table was set in the center of a large cage in which were a number of animals, including lions, tigers and several other man-eating beasts," reported the trade journal the *Fourth Estate*. "Not all of the invited guests had the courage to enter the cage, but there were a number who did, and they greatly enjoyed the meal."[27]

Certainly, the crowning glory of Tody Hamilton's questionably true publicity stunts was in 1899 when, during the show's stay in London, he orchestrated "the revolt of the freaks." Barnum had always known there was a huge popular appetite for sideshow attractions, or "freaks," as they were commonly known, and he had included many of them in his early humbugs and displays at Barnum's American Museum. The "freak show" then became a standard part of the carnival and the circus, and the Greatest Show on Earth had more than its fair share, including Fedor Jeftichew, aka Jo-Jo the Dog-Faced Boy; Annie Jones, the Bearded Lady; Harry Coffey, the Skeleton Dude; and a rogue's gallery of others known by names such as the Armless Wonder, the Wild Man of Borneo, the Tattooed Man, the Rubber-Skinned Man, the Albino Lady, and the Lightning Calculator. Hamilton referred to them as "manifestations of the merriment of nature in her morbid mood," or the "grotesque group of forty madcap merrymakers and freaky fools whose waggish ways have made millions hold their sides with laughter."[28] Fellow press agent Harvey Watkins called them "Dame Nature's Oddities."[29] It all sounds terribly cruel and exploitative today, but these were accepted norms for a society that still occasionally resonated with the memories and justifications of far worse affronts, like slavery; and this was, after all, the circus, a place apart from the starched linens of proper society, where the unusual was glorified.

Hamilton was sensitive to the exploitation, but even this he embraced and converted into an especially clever promotional angle once the circus went overseas. He sent an anonymous typewritten note to the London newspapers, stating, "Despite their protests, these unfortunate people are compelled to submit to the indignity of being billed and described as 'Human Freaks . . . ' and they feel keenly the opprobrium and outrage that is contained in the appellation." Because their concerns had not been addressed by circus management, the note said, they were going to hold a meeting "to enlist public sympathy and compel the substitution of some more dignified term for the word 'Freak.'"[30]

Reporters flocked to the meeting, where grievances were voiced and suggestions made: Hamilton himself offered the term "whams" as an alternative to "freaks," mainly because it did not exist in any language. At the end of the meeting one of the participants suggested a vote of thanks to Hamilton, and that may have been a tip-off that, as one newspaper reported, the whole thing had been a "put-up"; but as one of the better early Barnum biographers, Harvey W. Root, wrote in 1921, "so skillfully was the matter handled that no one on the outside ever even mistrusted that there had been a purpose behind any of the events."[31] Of course, the newspapers didn't care; it made for great copy.[32]

The dignified dailies on both sides of the pond debated the issue, conspiratorially including quotations from "the human snake" and "the elastic-skin man" as various ideas were tossed about. The *Times of London* gave it a column and a half on the front page. The *Chicago Journal* reported, "For some weeks Mr. Hamilton has been in a mental condition bordering on collapse owing to the violent molecular gyrations in his thought fount caused by efforts to substitute something for the word 'freak' which could fill the bill and at the same time not offend the distinguished personages whose accomplishments with their toes or whose lack of avoirdupois or whose hirsute extravagance have distinguished them from their fellow men."[33]

Mailbags full of suggestions arrived before it was finally decided to go with "prodigies."

"Wasn't that great?" Hamilton reflected three years later, again tapping into the exploitative side of promotion that was still common in this era.

> Lord, how the London papers fell to that—columns and columns! Why, for a week we had a lot of scientific specialists poling around the freak show, sent specially by the papers to write learned psychological articles about the final awakening of personal pride in abnormal specimens of the human race. Why, that went so far that I almost dreamed that I was ashamed of myself. . . .
>
> We had another revolt of the freaks just the other day. I find that a story as good as that ought to be revived once in a three or four years.[34]

Despite having been taken for a ride by Barnum & Bailey's famous press agent, or perhaps because of it, the London press grew quite enamored of Tody Hamilton. His endless stockpile of stories, manufactured news, and descriptive dexterity proved to be a sensation, the very embodiment of the American spirit of pluck. They raved about his writing in the circus program. The *Yorkshire Evening Post* reprinted a story he told about Joanna the ape, calling it "pathetic" but then acknowledging, "Mr. 'Tody' Hamilton and his colleagues, of Barnum's press department, are exceedingly clever advertisers."[35] London's *Daily Mail* called him "one of the greatest marvels of Barnum & Bailey's collection of marvels."[36] He won over so many of the legendarily skeptical British journalists that one publication referred to him as "the world-renowned Editor-Tamer."[37] As Harvey Watkins wrote in his contemporary book *Four Years in Europe: The Barnum & Bailey Greatest Show on Earth in the Old World*, "The clever manner in which they handled their department and the host of friends which they made for the show and themselves among the London journalists" resulted in "wonderful profits" by the end of the engagement.[38]

Over the course of the next four years of the circus's European tour, Hamilton and his team made similar inroads from Berlin to Vienna to Budapest to Ghent. In Paris, Hamilton overcame some initial resistance from the newspapers by bringing thirty-two French reporters to Brussels to see the circus and how well it was being covered there—a competitive challenge that generated a raft of publicity. As one trade magazine in New York described it, "Mr. Hamilton's countless friends in the journalistic world at home will be pleased to hear that his success in wooing Paris editors has been as great as in the United States, and that, as he might put it, 'an avalanche of laudatory eulogiums have thundered down the columns of the Paris press in praise of the multitudinous marvels of the mastodon of modern entertainment enterprises.'"[39]

As the circus traveled deeper into the Continent, the biggest challenge was finding a way to translate Hamilton's adjectival innovations. "What I can do with English took seven translators to turn into French," he said. German was a bit easier because of the length of its words, although he claimed to have constructed one German word to describe the circus action that was forty-six syllables and 168 letters.[40] "We had to make the posters there a size larger to accommodate all of them," said Hamilton.[41] As the *New York Clipper* described the problem, "After it had been translated from English into German, and then into Hungarian, Bohemian, Polish, Slavonish, Kroatian, Hollandish, French, and then back into English . . . it would show little traces of its first clever construction."[42] In Austria, it was said that people read his materials in the cafes with a dictionary in hand, "and the merits of the great word painter [were] discussed in flattering terms."[43] Indeed, the catchphrase he used in Austria, "10,000 Entzuckte Besucher" (10,000 delighted visitors), became a popular greeting on the street.[44] But translating what was sometimes called "Hamiltonian American" into other languages often resulted in bizarre constructions, a fact that was parodied by Hamilton himself when, upon his return to America in 1904, he greeted reporters on the dock and pulled a large banner from his valise made up of lots of X's, Y's, and Z's—supposedly a translation of one of his headlines into Hungarian. "Them's my sentiments," he quipped.[45]

Nevertheless, the combination of bombast, billboards, and publicity stunts worked well. "During the tour of the Barnum show in Europe," recapped the *Minneapolis Journal*, "Mr. Hamilton's florid style of writing created a positive sensation, and his newspaper 'dope' was eagerly sought for by all classes of publications."[46] Hamilton would call this work the "biggest achievement" of his career, for "I carried American [promotional] methods into Europe and made the newspapers over there not only sit up and take notice, but sit up and take us at our own valuation."[47]

Before he was through, Hamilton became almost as famous as the circus he was promoting.

"His name," wrote the *New York Sun* in 1906, "is known from one end of this country to the other—and then some." Or, as a wire service story written about him just before his retirement from Barnum & Bailey in 1907 said, "'Tody' Hamilton is the great original press agent, the father of the flock, the Nestor of publicity promoters. . . . He was as great in his own line as Barnum was in his. He made a new profession, one which is now a recognized necessity in the circus and theatrical businesses."[48] The *Washington Times* declared him to be the "originator of the system that hypnotizes the newspaper management into printing good publicity by simply making it so good that it 'has the pull.'" Despite the outrageous nature of what he plugged, "'Tody' got past the editors and the desks by dint of producing stories that they just naturally couldn't resist. The public liked 'em, the papers were willing to 'fall for 'em,' and the circus management could afford to pay well the genius that could squeak 'em into the news columns."[49]

That comment was written in the rose-colored afterglow following Hamilton's death in 1916, but it is fascinating to note how throughout his life the newspapers seemed to suspend their instinctive cynicism and almost delight in being persuaded into following Hamilton's lead. In a sense, it was no different than the people who, decades before, had willingly paid their nickels to visit Barnum's American Museum and be taken on a wild ride of credulity by his humbugs—or those who, decades later, would fall for the act of legendary boxing promoter Don King, laughing every step of the way. Then as now, the members of the press were not rubes. While they might have been dazzled at first by the luminous personalities of the famous press agents like Hamilton and Burke, in fairly short order they came to understand the fine line between being played and playing along. As the *Hawaiian Star* put it in 1911, "Buffalo Bill Cody, in the course of many years, had many press agents and nearly every reader of the daily newspapers from coast to coast has had occasion to wonder how much these hired historians of one of the most picturesque characters in American life drew the long bow in writing about William F. Cody."[50] Ultimately, it did not matter, because the appetite for promotion had grown as large as the appetite for reality.

Coming off the scintillating season in Chicago, William Cody, Nate Salsbury, and John Burke were at the pinnacle of their success. Eleven years in, the formula was working. Cody's celebrity had taken on a life of its own, and did not need to be developed so much as *tended.* The Wild West had become the most popular entertainment show in the country, and the regular addition of new acts stimulated curiosity even among those who had seen Cody, Oakley, and the Deadwood Stagecoach many times before.

SPECIALLY EQUIPPED RAILROAD CARS like this one from 1896 enabled the Wild West bill-posting team to hang thousands of lithographs within a two hundred-mile radius of each show. Buffalo Bill Center of the West, Cody, Wyoming; MS6.1995.268.

Burke leveraged the reach and influence of the newspapers to deploy his many clever promotional tactics. The efficient, carefully choreographed bill-posting operation—with its leapfrogging teams, precision timing, barter system of trading show passes for billboard space, and railcar boilers to heat up the poster paste—had become the promotional equivalent of "Taylorism," the system of scientific management that had lately begun to influence factory work and industrial manufacturing. On top of all that, with the Indian wars now over and the plains rapidly urbanizing, a widespread feeling of nostalgia for the spirit of the frontier and the long-lost West had begun to set in.

In fact, it had turned out more or less as Burke had designed it when he had first met Cody and sensed the "halo of glory, in the actual." The genuine and stage personas had now fused into one nearly indistinguishable entity: Col. William F. Cody (Buffalo Bill), conqueror of the plains and hero of the stage and arena; author and featured subject of biographies and fiction; progressive supporter of the Indians and employer of women.[51] He was the closest thing the nineteenth century had to a multimedia star. Burke even floated Cody's name as a potential candidate for president in 1896.

So the Wild West team doubled down, taking a big financial risk by investing $1 million to launch its 1894 season at a newly built twenty-two-thousand-seat, twenty-two-acre facility at Ambrose Park, in South Brooklyn. The show there would employ eight hundred people and operate at the almost unthinkable cost of $1,100 per day, in addition to $5,000 per week spent on bill posting.[52]

Filling all those seats and paying off all those bills would require Burke to use his charm, verve, and full arsenal of promotional tactics.

To "brand" the Ambrose Park season, as he had done in Chicago, he ordered custom stationery and an eight-page courier complete with plenty of "cuts" of Indians, generals, crowned heads of state, and images from Cody's career. In February he wrote to the German American lithographer Alfred Hoen in Baltimore: "My dear Hoen: Whar is ze letter head? Would you kindly send copies of your photograph proofs such as you took from Miner's bills for Cody's Life scenes. I am getting up an 8 page Courier there and want to make some one and two column cuts for the same." Always one to mix business and pleasure, Burke signed off with a gustatory afterthought, anticipating his next visit to Maryland: "Oh! Terrapin."[53]

Over the course of the next few years, Burke and his team would come to rely heavily on the rapidly expanding capabilities of printers like Hoen, as they broke new ground in the development of custom-published pieces such as couriers, heralds (single-sheet handbills), and newspapers. These publications went by names such as the *Daily Scout*, the *Wild West Illustrated*, the *Frontier Express*, and the *Overland Trail*. Couriers were typically imprinted with the date and location of the upcoming show to give them currency and a local feel—for example, "Elgin, Thursday, August 20th." In 1898 the Wild West created a courier that was die-cut in the shape of a buffalo head. In 1899 they began publishing the *Rough Rider*, which was described as an "Illustrated Periodical Published by Cody & Salsbury" with a "guaranteed circulation of 500,000." The first edition featured an illustration of Cody, Custer, and Lieutenant General Sheridan galloping side by side through the plains toward some unspecified danger/destiny. The *Rough Rider* contained the usual Burke-generated Cody mythology ("It is but natural that one whose ideas take form and color from the tame environment and conventional influences of the effete East, or the bloodless pseudo-civilization of the Old World, should find it difficult to believe that the life of one man could really be so full of perilous vicissitudes, hazardous toils and romantic adventures") as well as advertising from outside companies like Cuticura

Soap & Ointment.[54] There was even a version published in French when the Wild West returned to Paris in 1905–1906.

By 1911, Burke had developed a new custom publication aimed at the local press called *From Desert Sands to Prairie Wilds,* which contained a series of "press notices"—prefabricated stories, illustrations, and photos that could be literally ripped out of the booklet and reprinted in toto. Since only one of these publications was brought to each market, any material not yet ripped out was guaranteed not to have previously run in the city in question. In the credits for this publication, John M. Burke was listed as "The Story Man" (see plates 12 and 13).[55]

But in 1894, all of that was still stewing around in Burke's lively mind. For now he had to try to fill seats to pay for the Wild West's huge investment in infrastructure and to recapture somehow the glory of the season in Chicago. And so, even without the fancy new publishing tools at his disposal, he engaged in some very sophisticated marketing tactics during the Ambrose Park season.

It began with a sneak preview and behind-the-scenes tour for journalists on May 10, and a blizzard of newspaper coverage followed as the voracious New York press looked for all kinds of new angles.

New York World, May 13: ONLY ONE BUFFALO BILL: He Shone Triumphant on the Occasion of the Opening of His Congress of Nomads, Wildness and Savages. A VERY FINE SIGHT IT ALL WAS, TOO.

Brooklyn Standard-Union, May 14: BUFFALO BILL And Congress of Rough Riders of the World TAKE THE TOWN BY STORM.

Brooklyn Standard-Union, May 19: AN OLD RELIC. The First Authentic History of the Deadwood Coach. BAPTIZED IN FIRE AND BLOOD.

New York Press, May 20: THEY THROW THE BOLA. Colonel Cody's Gauchos Are the Kings of Horsemen.

Morning Journal, May 20: OUR UNIQUE IDEA. ROUGH RIDERS' TALES.

Brooklyn Sunday Citizen, May 20: CITY CAMP LIFE. GOSSIP AND GOINGS ON AT AMBROSE PARK.

New York Sun, May 20: GIRLS SEE THE WILD WEST. COL. CODY'S SHOW AS IT STRIKES THE FEMININE MIND.

Sunday Mercury, May 20: TWO BIG SIOUX CHIEFS. Flat Iron, Orator of the Nation, and His Friend, Running Bear. MAJOR BURKE REVIEWS THEIR HISTORY.

Brooklyn Citizen, May 22: Rain and the Wild West.

New York Advertiser, May 28: A WILD WEST EXCURSION. Some of Buffalo Bill's Boys See the Only Coney Island.

New York Mail, May 31: HAPPY ENDING OF A ROMANCE. Two Sioux Indians Married at Buffalo Bill's Wild West Encampment To-Day. HIGH BEAR AND TASINA WAKAN.

Brooklyn Daily Eagle, June 4: Buffalo Bill's Indians Shopping.[56]

Throughout the season, Burke hosted several events and special groups at the Wild West, including a military contingent headed by Captain Edward Doherty, who led the group of soldiers that had killed Burke's old friend from theater days, John Wilkes Booth; members of the Women's Professional League of New York; and a group of two hundred scientists who came to Ambrose Park to inspect Edison's custom-built Wild West electrical plant, which now included four dynamos, eight hundred incandescent lights, and three movable search lights mounted on the roof—the press reported on all of it.

The Major also continued his long tradition of taking the Indians out on the town in an effort to create a "scene" and hence generate even more press coverage. On June 4, for example, he escorted several of them to meet with Mayor Thomas Gilroy of New York—and, according to the *New York Press*, delivered "one of the neat little speeches that are characteristic of him, telling the Mayor that as the Indians were the originators of Tammany Hall they wanted to see what progress had been made since the time their forefathers had sold out to the predecessors of the present incumbents."[57] On the same trip, they went to the famous dome of the *New York World* building, where Burke pulled another ironic (and in historical hindsight, painfully supercilious) tidbit out of his pocket by suggesting to reporters that this vantage point enabled the Indians to see the island that their forefathers had sold for twenty-four dollars.[58] The stories ran in the papers as news items, with no tinge of irony or exploitation. As with the manufactured news of Tody Hamilton, the coverage may well have been provided not because of its intrinsic merit but because the reporters found Burke's antics amusing.

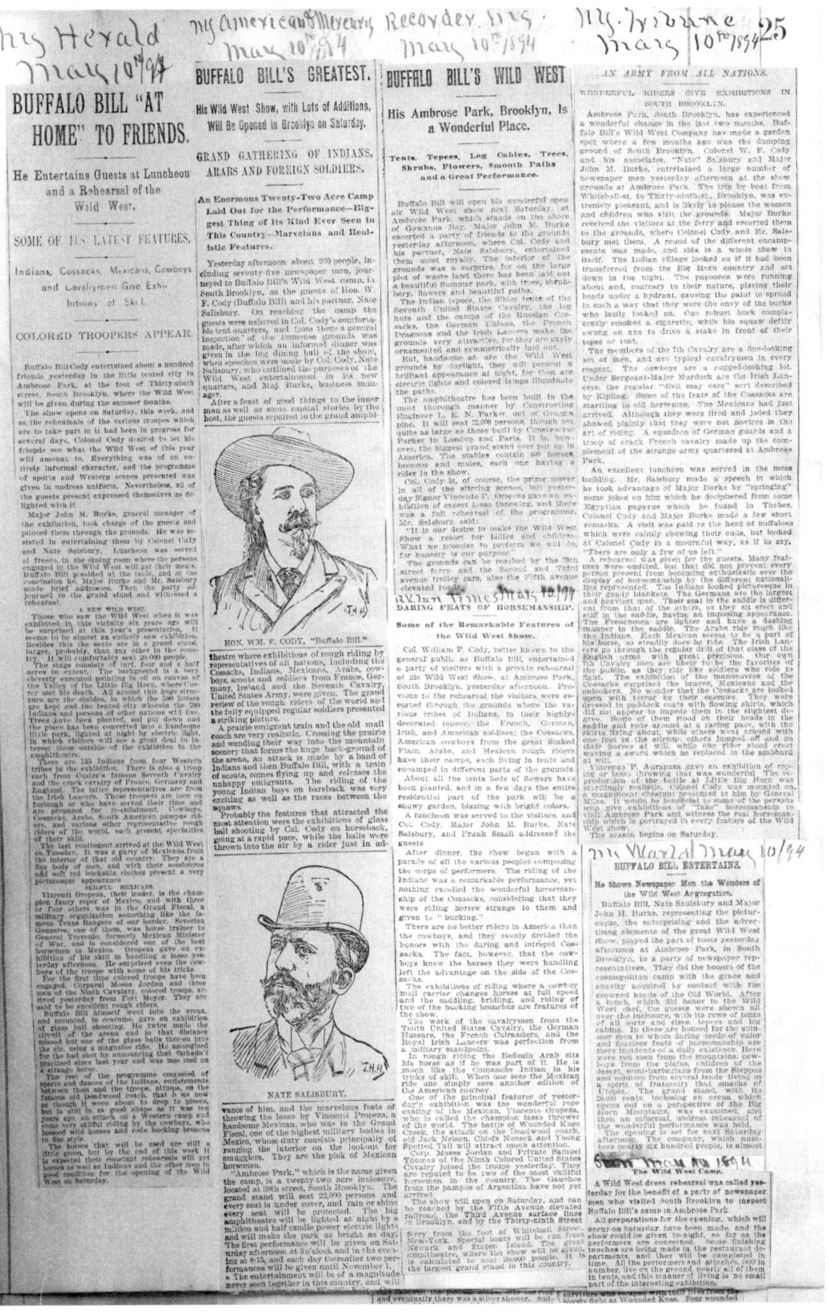

N.Y. Herald May 10th/94

BUFFALO BILL "AT HOME" TO FRIENDS.

He Entertains Guests at Luncheon and a Rehearsal of the Wild West.

SOME OF HIS LATEST FEATURES.

Indians, Cossacks, Mexicans, Cowboys and Cavalrymen Give Exhibitions of Skill.

COLORED TROOPERS APPEAR.

N.Y. American & Mercury May 10th/94

BUFFALO BILL'S GREATEST.

His Wild West Show, with Lots of Additions, Will Be Opened in Brooklyn on Saturday.

GRAND GATHERING OF INDIANS, ARABS AND FOREIGN SOLDIERS.

An Enormous Twenty-Two Acre Camp Laid Out for the Performance—Biggest Thing of Its Kind Ever Seen in This Country—Marvelous and Realistic Features.

HON. WM. F. CODY, "Buffalo Bill."

NATE SALISBURY.

Recorder N.Y. May 10th/1894

BUFFALO BILL'S WILD WEST

His Ambrose Park, Brooklyn, Is a Wonderful Place.

Tents, Tepees, Log Cabins, Trees, Shrubs, Flowers, Smooth Paths and a Great Performance.

N.Y. Times May 10/94

DARING FEATS OF HORSEMANSHIP.

Some of the Remarkable Features of the Wild West Show.

N.Y. Tribune May 10th 1894

AN ARMY FROM ALL NATIONS.

WONDERFUL RIDERS GIVE EXHIBITIONS IN SOUTH BROOKLYN.

N.Y. World May 10/94

BUFFALO BILL ENTERTAINS.

He Shows Newspaper Men the Wonders of the Wild West Aggregation.

Sun May 10 1894

The Wild West Camp.

25

SCRAPBOOKS from the 1894 season reveal the extent of newspaper coverage that Burke and his team generated for Cody and the Wild West. Buffalo Bill Center of the West, Cody, Wyoming; MS6.3781.025.

Later in the summer, there would also be a visit with the Indians to New Haven, Connecticut, to see Professor Othniel Charles Marsh, world-famous paleontologist at Yale College, and an appearance at the Rose Festival at St. Stephen's Church. Everything made the papers. Burke simply had great instincts for what would play well on Newspaper Row.

He also knew that Cody, who at age forty-eight had aged gracefully and now wore his fame like a comfortable pair of moccasins, would be a big drawing card for women reporters. Amy Leslie and Kate Field had made Cody seem like a divinity in Chicago, so Burke arranged for more feature stories to be written from the woman's point of view at Ambrose Park. He even hosted eighteen female reporters at the show on June 11, although they ended up more impressed by the way Burke tied his long hair up in a Psyche knot than by the shooting and showmanship down in the arena.[59]

Typical of this genre was the piece written by Daisy Miller of the *Commercial Advertiser* ("A Woman Sees the Wild West"), which read in part:

> There wasn't much of an affinity to start on, inasmuch as the only thing I ever killed was time, and that doesn't hold against a buffalo record. However, I immediately enshrined the hero of the plains in the recesses of my heart, and felt that the very atmosphere he breathed must necessarily bespeak romance. . . .
>
> Grim reality, one's sterner sense, dictates when one looks at the handsome but implacable countenance of Colonel Cody and realizes its history, though it is a hard thing to appreciate that this courtly and polished gentleman is actually the hero of so many deeds of desperate bravery.[60]

In another interview by an unnamed woman, for an article in the *New York Recorder*, Cody was asked if the life he led produced the kind of man who was a "pet" (favorite) with the women. Burke, who was there during the interview, objected to the question and advised Cody not to answer, saying it was too pointed and that "it would make a man look like an egotist to talk about a woman's attentions to him." But when the reporter persisted, Burke relented and said, "I'll leave you two to wrastle it out."[61] Cody then followed Burke's advice and dodged the question.

Perhaps the most interesting moment of the 1894 season occurred on September 24, when Burke and Cody led an excursion along with fifteen

Indians and Annie Oakley to West Orange, New Jersey, to be captured by Edison's motion picture camera, the Kinetograph.

More than just another Burke-juxtaposing-Indians-with-modernity publicity stunt, the visit to Edison's Black Maria studio was further evidence that the Major (and Cody) intuitively understood how technology was reshaping communications and might be used to revolutionize promotion. Both men had long embraced technological advancement. Burke, for example, was an early adopter and frequent user of telegraphy (in winter 1886–1887, after Cody and Salsbury chastised him for not sending letters to update them on his preparations for the London tour, he responded by touting the benefits of the telegraph: "The news [in a letter] is a week old before you get it, whereas on the other hand, if I telegraph you to-day from London, you get it yesterday in New York, don't you?").[62] At Ambrose Park, Cody's tent was equipped with a telephone and a refrigerator. A few years later, they incorporated automobiles into the Wild West. Cody was even photographed next to an airplane at the Panama Pacific Exposition in 1915.

Burke and Cody had first met Edison at the Exposition Universelle in Paris in 1889 (the inventor visited the show and took a ride in the Deadwood Stagecoach; Burke and some Indians had bumped into Edison on an elevator at the Eiffel Tower, and at the sight of him, the Indians had slapped their cheeks in a sign of respect). They met again at the World's Columbian Exposition. So now, in fall 1894, undoubtedly aware that the first commercial motion picture house had opened in New York, they made the trip to West Orange to see Edison on his home turf and experiment with the idea of using technology to capture their act. Cody performed an exhibition of rapid shooting for the camera. Oakley shot at glass balls tossed in the air. The Sioux demonstrated some of their ceremonial dances. And either on this visit or on a subsequent one, Cody recorded an off-the-cuff message on the phonograph in which he paid tribute to Edison: "He has made the dynamo that has changed the world. It seems almost uncanny that the voice in this place can be perpetuated and that he has set out to the world his phonograph, which have given [*sic*] more entertainment and pleasure than any invention in the history of the world."[63] Four years later, Cody would record his thoughts about intervention in Cuba on a Berliner gramophone. The recordings, much as Burke and Cody hoped, have survived.

But it was the advent of motion pictures, inaugurated with that first Kinetograph recording in 1894, that intrigued them most. Cody would return to be filmed by Edison in 1898 and appeared on film with Biograph in 1902 and with British Bioscope in 1903. Late in life, Cody would form two movie companies (Buffalo Bill/Pawnee Bill Film Company and Buffalo Bill Historical Picture Company) and participate in at least eight film projects. He had a little bit of success with his film *Life of Buffalo Bill* (1910), but then flopped with his much larger undertaking *The Indian Wars Refought* (1914), in which he employed thousands of former combatants to re-create four legendary Indian battles, including the Wounded Knee Massacre, in a two-and-a-half-hour "photo-play," as movies of this era were often called.[64]

Although *Indian Wars* was a commercial disaster, both Burke and Cody understood its greater significance, for if the arena version of the Wild West had educated millions of people about the history of the frontier, the film version could theoretically reach tens of millions more, including future generations. After all, the western had already begun to emerge as a popular genre: by 1912, American Mutoscope and Biograph had produced seventy western-themed films, and a new kind of western hero was beginning to emerge in Tom Mix, the Hollywood cowboy, who as a ten-year-old had visited the Wild West at Pennsylvania's Clearfield Fairgrounds and had come to idolize Cody.[65] Hence, the brochure produced for the *Indian Wars*

A NEW MEDIUM. Cody took his act from the arena to the big screen with the production of *The Indian Wars Refought* (1914), featuring actual participants from the Battles of Summit Springs, Warbonnet Creek, and Wounded Knee. Buffalo Bill Museum and Grave, Golden, Colorado.

premiere said the scenes they captured would be "as valuable a hundred years from now as they are today."

Cody screened the film for one thousand guests in Washington, D.C., on February 26, 1914. He told them, "My object and desire has been to preserve history by the aid of the camera with as many of the living participants in the closing Indian wars of North America as could be procured. It is something that has never been done before; that is, to preserve our old wars for future generations by living or motion pictures."[66] The program for the evening praised the "evolution of photography" which "through the marvelous movies worked wonders" and could now "aid in registering historic subjects."[67] And a few days later, before the film's opening at the Denver Tabor Grand Opera House, Burke told reporters that he had been stunned by the realism and that its power of storytelling had moved him to tears. "It is war itself; grim, unpitying and terrible; and it holds your heart still as you watch it and leaves you, in the end, amazed and spell bound at the courage and folly of mankind."[68] Reporters said, "It is hard to get the major to talk of anything else," and little wonder: he had discovered a storytelling tool that was more powerful than all of the grandiose words he had summoned throughout his long career.[69]

Burke and Cody had now effectively migrated their great moral and educational message from the stage to the arena to film, and had adapted and invented new methods of promotion each step of the way—establishing a path from the real West to the manufactured ones of Hollywood and Madison Avenue that would in time become well worn.

Burke's network of contacts and friends in newspaper offices was vast—a characteristic he shared with both Moses P. Handy and Tody Hamilton—and while this aided immeasurably in his ability to generate ink for the Wild West, it also increasingly landed him in the spotlight.

For example, a story circulated in newspapers in March 1894 that Burke was to be married. The woman in question was Corrine La Caeur, who had been in charge of the French exhibit in the Manufactures Building at the Columbian Exposition, and who had been charmed when Burke asked her a question in French. The stories indicated that they were to be married in the summer, and that Cody and Salsbury were giving her a half-section of a Nebraska farm as a wedding present.[70] It is heartwarming to think that Burke may have found love at age fifty-two, but what became of the engagement and La Caeur has been lost to history; after a brief burst of publicity, her name appeared in the paper no more, and Burke would die a bachelor.

In time there would be dozens of stories about Burke, as well as several pieces written by him. He knew that his messages—whether telegraphed to his friends in the newsroom, captured by a reporter during one of his many impromptu gatherings in a hotel lobby, or, increasingly, delivered in the form of biting letters to the editor—would earn a few column inches. This quickly became another one of his marketing innovations, very much akin to the modern-day op-ed.

The breadth of Burkean topics was astounding. *Burke is honored by his newspaper friends with a gold watch and a diamond locket. Burke urges closer relations with Mexico and Canada. Burke proclaims his support for trade relations with the Filipinos. Burke stands for women's suffrage. Burke tells the story of falling in a ditch in Louisville. Burke displays his knowledge of the restaurateurs in New York, and Chicago, and Billings, and Tucson. Burke proposes a $1 billion bond to finance an "innerline defense" of rivers and canals on the East Coast. Burke advises California winemakers to get philanthropists to fund a huge wine cave.* In one article, he suggested that St. Louis build an electric subway for its 1904 Louisiana Purchase Exposition, complete with underground restaurants and beer sellers ("The fact that I have attended every international exposition since the Philadelphia Centennial should keep me from being classed with the cranks who have schemes and propositions for filling the time of gentlemen in your position," he wrote to President David R. Francis of the Exposition).[71] In another article, he beat the drum for preparedness on the eve of World War I ("The sudden idiocy that has almost wrecked civilization, and wipes out Europe's 2,000 years of progress, shows the fallacy of too much pacific passiveness: to be on guard is to be respected in these days of hysteria and isms").[72] And in one especially odd instance, he told reporters gathered around him in the Rennert Hotel lobby in Baltimore that he would like to see the American people abandon the swearing habit, which he considered to be "a mark of vulgarity and ruffianism."

> Instead of ugly oaths when laboring under excitement, the coming generation should be taught to employ only near-swear words, such as "By the jumping Jehosaphat," "by Jingo Gee," "by the beard of the Prophet," and the like. The late Jim Hogg, governor of Texas, one of

> my best friends, used the innocent, but blood-curdling, cuss phrase "by goolings" whenever his hot Southern blood got inflamed.
>
> A great number of prominent Americans got on very well without using actual profanity. Col. Cody, though a frontiersman all his life and accustomed to the society of men who handle the mother tongue carelessly, is not given to blasphemous speech. The colonel, when worked up, has been known to say "dog-gone it," and "dad-blame it," and now and then "dod-gast it," but this is the limit of his impassioned vocabulary.[73]

Most poignantly, on at least two occasions, Burke professed his desire to be buried alone in the Big Horn Basin of Wyoming—which he had visited either right before or after the Ambrose Park season while on a trip with Cody to scout out interests in an irrigation project.[74]

Frequently, the headlines made him out to be nearly as big a celebrity as Cody himself.

MAJ. BURKE CORRALS THE INDIANS.
Kicking Bear and Other Wild West Heroes Secured for Col. Cody's Show.[75]

MAJOR BURKE, WHO KNOWS EVERYBODY.[76]

JOLLY COLONEL ADVANCE AGENT.
JOHN M. BURKE SPRINGS YARNS AND MAKES FRIENDS.[77]

Picturesque Burke Makes Way for Show; Old School Press Agent Is from "Cecil County, Befo' De Wah, Sir."[78]

IS DADDY OF ALL THE PRESS AGENTS
Seventy-Year Old Veteran Knows All Old Time Army Officers Who Campaigned Against Northern Indians.[79]

BUFFALO BILL'S BOSOM FRIEND.
Major John M. Burke, Participant in Stirring Events for Forty Years and the Chronicler of Them, in the City.[80]

The *Inter Ocean* observed, "Nearly every man and woman and certainly every child in Chicago knows Major Burke, and he has friends in every city of any importance in the land."[81] Sportswriter Macon McCormick's July 1, 1894, story about Sitting Bull was largely just a series of extended quotes from Burke so that his "delicious drawl and voice of vocal velvet" came through clearly. "When Major John Burke ('Arizona John') tells an Indian story," said McCormick, "he 'talks like a book,' and a very interesting book at that. . . . I wished in my heart that I had a phonograph with me that I might have preserved his manner of telling the tale as well as the tale itself."[82] The *Cleveland Plain Dealer* wrote about Burke's gift for gab: "Stories? Why, one can sit down in a social way with Major John M. Burke for days at a stretch and if he happens to get into a story telling mood there is no stopping him, and one tale is more interesting than the other."[83] The *San Bernardino Evening Transcript* observed: "Not all men are broad mentally in proportion to their physiques, but Major Burke is; and he is a very large man. Not all men are good natured in proportion to their avoirdupois, but Major Burke is; and he is a very heavy man."[84] A syndicated article that ran in several newspapers said, "He has never been known to forsake a friend, and is as courageous as he is good hearted. . . . The Major is the Major—unique, solitary, the only one of his kind. His huge form, all too small for his heart, casts as welcome a shadow as ever fell across the threshold of an editorial room."[85] The *Washington Post* branded him "Burke the philosopher and raconteur, the jovial, kindly man of the world, and Burke the friend of the red man and incidentally the general manager of Buffalo Bill's Wild West Show."[86] The *San Francisco Call* observed, "His stories are famous, his laugh is contagious. He is Colonel Cody's right hand man, and if he should quit smiling the warwhoop of the Indians would die away and the broncos would refuse to buck."[87] The *Atlanta Georgian and News* playfully described him as "hale, ruddy, of powerful physique and majestic port, witty and keen with the edge that comes from varied rubbing against the world at large, six feet by three of American man."[88]

The *Atlanta Constitution*, in particular, seemed to have great affection for Burke, referring to him as "the great big man" and "Jolly Major Burke" and "Major John M. Burke, the hale and hearty" (1895); Cody's "particular Pooh-Bah" and "adviser-in-extraordinary" (1901); "that genial, pleasant, ever smiling Irishman" (1907); "Major John M. Burke, of the world-at large . . . oh, such kindness" and "hot air and kind words dispenser" (1909); and "Dean of Boosters" (1911).[89]

And the *New York Times*, in a 1901 article otherwise filled with numerous factual errors about the Wild West, got it right when it called Burke "a cosmopolite."

> He can discourse in ever so many languages, and his English is something marvelous. It is his duty to exploit the show, and his stock of superlatives is inexhaustible.
>
> Major Burke is one of the most genial souls that ever lived. It is his duty to make friends for the show. He is a press agent and a diplomat all in one. He tries to keep everybody in a good humor, from the broken-down characters who seek tickets to the Indians who become disaffected toward Russian Cossacks. The Major is known from Dan to Beer-Sheba. He goes ahead of the show when it is on the road, and by liberal entertainment of everybody in sight and glorious pictures of the wonderful sights to come he excites an amount of eagerness which contributes very materially to the subsequent success.[90]

Given Burke's not infrequent star turns, it was not at all surprising that Nate Salsbury would say of him, "I do not believe there is another man in the world who could have covered as much space in the newspaper of the day as John Burke has done, and I do not believe there is another man in the world in his position, that would have had the gall to exploit himself at the expense of the show as much as John Burke."[91]

For his part, Cody occasionally grew irritated by Burke's self-aggrandizement, but generally seems to have been amused by him and to have tolerated his idolatry, almost as if he were some kind of inexplicably loyal and occasionally unruly Shetland sheepdog. Burke addressed Cody as "Colonel" or "Governor," and sometimes referred to him as "Bill" in the press; Cody called Burke "Arizona" or "Old Scarface" or "Burke." Cody mentioned Burke just three times in his 1879 autobiography, and then only in passing, although admittedly that was written fairly early in their relationship, before the start of the Wild West and before Burke's true genius emerged. It seems that Cody never said a great deal about Burke, but when he did it was usually to tease him about his claims to have been a brave scout and Indian fighter, or his loquaciousness. Perhaps Cody knew he could never match wits with Burke, or perhaps he never truly understood the depths of what Burke had done for him. (Louisa Cody, on the other hand, clearly did. She painted a very sympathetic portrait of Burke in her biography of Cody, often referring to him as "poor Major Burke" or "dear old faithful Major Burke." Far more than her husband ever did, she seemed to realize the amount of work the press agent put in and how underappreciated he was.)

The relationship between the two friends and partners sometimes turned testy, and in a couple of moments of exasperation, Cody threatened to fire Burke. One such occasion, according to press agent Lew Parker, occurred early in the show's history, when Burke did something to offend Cody and received a telegram that said, "If you want to remain with this show, you must obey my orders." Burke replied, "Who the hell ever told you that I wanted to remain with this Show. Bring out the band; let it play 'Hail to the Chief.' It's a matter of record that Columbus was put in chains after discovering America, and a matter of biblical history that the Jews crucified an awfully good man. Burke."[92] One can imagine Cody just shaking his head in wonderment.

On another occasion, according to Louisa, Cody fired Burke when they were in Italy, just long enough for Burke to send a telegram to Salsbury that said, "My scalp hangs in the tepee of Pahaska at the foot of Vesuvius. Please send me money to take me back to the Land of the Free and the Home of the Brave."[93] But all was remedied within five hours. Theirs was a partnership of unequals that would endure until the very end.

The long season at Ambrose Park should have been the high water mark for the Wild West. The promoters of the Wild West had created a popular product, a powerful mythology, and an impressive apparatus for delivering them both. But the crowds that turned out for that 1894 season were smaller than usual, causing the show to lose as much as five thousand dollars per day.[94] The slump was probably due to the ripple effects of the Panic of 1893, which had led to bank and railroad failures, sixteen thousand business closings, double-digit unemployment, widespread corporate consolidation, the worst economic depression the country had ever experienced, and the Pullman strike of July 1894, which crippled the nation's transportation system.

Because of the financial pressures encountered at Ambrose Park, James A. Bailey of Barnum & Bailey took a financial interest in the Wild West at the start of the 1895 season and became the business manager in an effort to restore the previous glory. Henceforth, there would be no more long stands such as those at the World's Columbian Exposition and Ambrose Park. That season, adopting Bailey's strategy for the Greatest Show on Earth, the Wild West became a traveling show again, making 131 stands in 190 days, covering 9,000 miles; in 1896 there would be 132 towns and 10,000 miles; by 1899, they were on the road for 200 days, performing 342 times in 132 stands across 11,111 miles. Their ability to pack up their portable stadium, along with six to eight hundred cast members and animals, move it all in a train that had as many as fifty-four railcars, and then set it all up again the next day in another town was a logistical miracle, but it was, according to Cody's sister Julia, "backbreaking."[95] Burke soon needed a staff of ten just to handle the promotional work, and his own hand in the marketing was less evident.

With Bailey's influence, the Wild West would begin to evolve into Burke's dreaded "show," and although he continued to insist there was no "sham or subterfuge about it" and no "familiar circus features," soon there were, including a side show.[96] In 1903, for example, a new feature called Buffalo Bill's Annex included such attractions as the eight-foot two-inch Egyptian Giant, Hassan Ali; Walters the Blue Man; Giovanni's Great Bird Circus; Griffin Necromancer and Sword Swallower; Alfonso, the Human Ostrich; and Mlle. Octavia, the Fearless Serpent Enchantress. The following year they added Carter, the Cowboy Cyclist, and not long after that Football on Horseback and Auto-Polo, in which two cars with open engines were driven around while a passenger with a mallet pursued a large white polo ball. "Without doubt the country's most thrilling sensation," Burke told the *Louisville Courier-Journal*, after shifting uncomfortably in the middle of his interview in the hotel lobby, supposedly to take advantage of the electric fan ("Zephyrs," he said with satisfaction).[97] The *Overland Trail* courier for the 1913 show touted Auto-Polo as "The New Game of a Thousand Thrills: Biff! Bang!! Smash!!! And then some more hair breadth curves and escapes."[98] The next year, Cody and Burke were now part of the Sells-Floto Circus, which the Major tried to pass off as "the last gasp in arenic marvels," but which contained even more extreme departures from the old Wild West formula, including the very circuslike Mlle. Lucia Zora's Herd of Performing Elephants.[99] The *New York Clipper* wrote,

> Can you imagine, in your wildest dreams, what would have happened to an individual who, fifteen years ago, had the temerity to suggest to Major John M. Burke that he (the Major), in our year of the Lord 1914, would be writing biographical sketches of the "varmints" with a circus.
>
> Fate plays funny pranks.[100]

A DIFFERENT KIND OF HORSEPOWER. Cody in the front passenger seat of a steam-powered Gardner-Serpollet car at London Olympia in 1903, giving a ride to Wild West treasurer Jule Keen (*rear left*) and John M. Burke (*rear right*). The National Archives of the UK, Motor Transport Collection, courtesy of Alan Gallop.

Meanwhile, for the first time since the Wild West had been founded, the United States entered a war, with navy armored cruisers and other warships steaming for ports in Cuba and the Philippines; the martial hysteria—much of it whipped up by William Randolph Hearst and other newspaper moguls—seemed to make the quaint bows-and-arrows Indian wars depicted in the Wild West seem like ancient history.

Cody, just shy of his fifty-second birthday on the date the Spanish sank the USS *Maine* in February 1898, made some statements both publicly and privately about wanting to go off and fight (and Burke told reporters it would take Cody "five minutes to lick 'em") but ultimately decided to stick with the show. When a reporter then questioned the star's change of mind, Burke struck back: "Damn it all! What we are doing is educating you people! I am not afraid to say, sir, that the Wild West symposium of equestrian ability has done more for this country than the Declaration of Independence, the Constitution of the United States, or the life of General George Washington. Its mission is to teach manhood and common sense. We are not traveling to make money, sir, but only to do good."[101]

Burke's seemingly endless supply of rationalizations about the value of the enterprise was running out, along with his patience. More importantly, the whole incident surely must have filled him with concerns about whether the gilding he had so painstakingly layered onto Buffalo Bill over the past quarter century was perhaps starting to lose its luster.

Burke himself would travel to Cuba after the fighting had ended—his penchant for skirting battle throughout his life was truly remarkable—to line up war participants for the Wild West's new act, which was called Color Guard of the Cuban Veterans. This performance, and the subsequent reenactment of the Battle of San Juan Hill in 1899 and the Battle of Tien-Tsin in 1901, marked another programmatic departure from the Wild West's roots, although the spirit of cowboy bravado that had been part of the manifest destiny epoch was equally recognizable in the new imperialistic one. To ensure this, Burke would again turn to celebrity endorsements in his ads: Lieutenant General John M. Schofield, for one, said the show would "arouse the patriotism of the people and inspire the military spirit in the youth of the land"; General William T. Sherman, for another, said "I thank you for this exhibition in the name of my children and grandchildren."[102] But not everyone approved: the Wild West's original backscratcher, Mark Twain, "clapped his hands feebly" at Cody's introduction of a 1901 show, and then walked out in protest over the martial representations.[103]

Cody's personal missteps exacerbated the show's problems. He periodically resumed his heavy drinking. He also invested in a number of speculative ventures, including real estate, the Cody Military College, the Campo Bonito (or Cody-Dyer Arizona) Mining and Milling operation near Tucson, and a massive irrigation project in Wyoming—all of which left him repeatedly asking Salsbury for loans or borrowing off the proceeds of the show.[104]

Even more damning, his marital indiscretions began to emerge from behind the tent flaps.

Back in Chicago, in 1893, he was rumored to have been keeping the company of another woman, and for this reason Louisa Cody had paid him a surprise visit there; their marriage was already in shambles, nearly ending in divorce in 1883, and this latest story of his attentions to another woman enraged her. By the end of the fair, it had come out into the open:

newspapers reported that Cody had spent forty thousand dollars promoting the career of an unnamed female protégé by sending her to Europe to study acting, providing her with elaborate scenery and beautiful costumes, and staging the show *Lady in Venice*.[105] The femme fatale turned out to be Katherine Clemmons, and Cody's interest turned out to be more than financial: she was later described as "the constant companion of Cody for several years." In total, he may have spent upwards of five hundred thousand dollars trying to support her.[106]

At first, Cody's (and Burke's) standing with the newspaper fraternity protected him from further innuendo; Burke also sought to deflect the rumors by frequently discussing the fact that Cody's daughter Irma was traveling with him at the Exposition.[107] But there would be other paramours—and with the power of the press now unleashed in a world in which celebrity was starting to become an aspiration, even the redoubtable Burke would not be able to contain the damage and protect Cody's reputation.[108]

Sometime between 1898 and 1900, a woman named Bess Isbell (or Bessie Isbelle) came onto the Wild West scene as a press agent. Born in 1872, Isbell was described in a 1902 newspaper article as "an exceedingly attractive girl—beautiful, many would call her. Her eyes are brown, with golden lights dancing in them, and her brown hair shows a strand of gold here and there." She recalled that when she began her work for the Wild West, "I could not do as other girls had done because there had been no other girl."[109] But her work soon extended beyond press agentry, and she and Cody apparently started an affair that went on for some time.[110]

Supposedly inspired by his feelings for Isbell, Cody would file for divorce from Louisa, even though he knew that the trial would be front-page news. "I was afraid and feared that it would, as I am a public man," he told the judge. "But I took every step and every means in my power to keep this family trouble out of the public press."[111] As the *New York Times* put it at the start of the trial, "'Buffalo Bill,' having come unscathed to the age of 50 years, through a thrilling succession of Indian fights, stage coach robberies, bison and bear hunts, bandit battles, and wild west shows, now is making one of his last stands."[112]

Nevertheless, an especially juicy trial ensued in 1905 that brought to light all sorts of salacious details of the Codys' lives. He accused Louisa of having tried to poison him, and the court heard testimony that she had beaten their daughter Arta with a horsewhip and frequently used language "so vulgar it's not fit for the presence of gentlemen, let alone ladies."[113]

She, in turn, documented his drunkenness, gambling, and philandering. As the *Chicago Tribune* recounted the story revealed during the trial, Isbell had lived with Cody and shared tents or adjoining hotel rooms with him in several locations. Cody claimed that their relationship was one of "business relations purely. She was connected with the show as lady press agent, and a mighty good one, too." But especially damning was a deposition by John W. Claire, valet and messenger for Cody for several years.

> I saw her in Chicago . . . at the show grounds at Wentworth avenue and Thirty-fifth street. Miss Isbelle was driven to the grounds in a closed carriage and I took her directly to the colonel's tent. While there a telegram came for Col. Cody. He was in a buckskin suit ready to go into the arena and told me to get some change out of his clothes in the dressing room. I couldn't find any change.
>
> "Wonder what I did with that hundred?" said Col. Cody.
>
> At that Miss Isbelle pulled a roll of bills out of her bosom and said: "Here it is—I took it out of your pocket in the hotel."
>
> [Claire] also testified that in a Sherman, Texas hotel, Isbelle was "In her room which adjoined the colonel's. I found the colonel in her room after dinner. . . ."
>
> "How was Miss Isbelle clothed?"
>
> "She had on a loose dressing gown—sort of kimono. The colonel asked her to step out of the room while I rubbed him down. Then the colonel told me to occupy his room that night, and if any persons called for him not to tell them where he was. If absolutely necessary I was to wake him without anyone knowing it."[114]

The judge would ultimately deny Cody's petition for divorce, and the Codys later reconciled. But irreparable damage had been done. The very same force that had enabled Cody to rise to national prominence had begun to erode his aura of invincibility. And John M. Burke was helpless to control the power that he had unleashed. Indeed, the press agent's influence was nowhere to be found during the trial. He had worked so hard to get Cody onto the front page, but now, when he needed to, he apparently couldn't get him off it.

Burke's "god," America's mythic western hero, had been rendered a mere mortal. As one newspaper reported, "It is unpleasant to see a national idol fall from its pedestal. But why worship at a shrine that has no illusion left or that has been desecrated by the idol itself?"[115]

By the time the trial ended, Cody's longtime business partner Nate Salsbury had passed away and hence never had to suffer through the indignity of his beloved enterprise being dragged through the mud. But in his final years Salsbury had grown infuriated with Cody's many problems outside the arena.

In 1899, when Cody asked for fifty thousand dollars to pay off debts plus one thousand dollars a week in salary, Salsbury was ready to end the partnership. "If you wish to avoid the scandal of a lawsuit, and consequent injury to the trademark we have worked so many years to build up, I will make you a proposition, that will separate our interests, and we will be well rid of each other," Salsbury wrote on October 5.[116] Cody responded that the money he owed Salsbury had been lost through speculation, but "I have . . . saved you money and made you money and not a whiff of thanks do I get."[117] Salsbury wrote back completely enraged at what he called Cody's "cowardly argument" and "vindictive nature," chiding him for acting in a "most childish, and unfair manner."[118]

The following year, when Cody accused Salsbury of planting a spy among the Wild West personnel to report back on his indiscretions, Salsbury again took a swipe at Cody: "You forget that when a man that has been advertised as much as you have been, goes on a drunk, all the world knows it and talks about it. I have long ago ceased to worry about it, and while I know that nature will be revenged some day, I also know that it is your affair so far as your health is concerned, so why should I worry?"[119]

The two would smooth over their differences, but things were never the same. Salsbury died on Christmas Eve, 1902, though not before he wrote several chapters of his scorched-earth autobiography—the one that would not be published until fifty years after his death. It included these zingers:

> "A partnership with W. F. Cody certainly is a picnic, as it is viewed in Hell."
>
> "John Burke . . . has been idolizing a hero any time these past thirty years. Poor Old John he still hugs his delusion, but perhaps it is for the salary, and I am doing him an injustice."[120]

> "For mind you, this Hero of the Plains, abused every man in our employ who ever showed that he did not regard the Hero as the head and front of the Showmans [*sic*] Universe."[121]
>
> "When the fever gets into his brain, he forgets honor, reputation, friend and obligation, in his made eagerness to fill his hide with rot gut of any kind. He becomes so utterly lost to all sense of decency, and shame, that he will break his plighted word, and sully his most solemn obligation."[122]
>
> "I am only giving those who are dear to me a club to pound him with if he ever attempts to blacken me in support of his overweening vanity that leads him to think he is a Tin Jesus on horseback. Make no mistake in thinking I have not said these things to him in person, or that he does not know how thoroughly I despise his character and habits, to say nothing of his morals and sense of honor."[123]

It was a bad ending for a good man who had grown frustrated and embittered, though it did not negate a great life and the considerable accomplishments that Salsbury, Cody, and Burke had enjoyed together.

The fact that Bess Isbell was a "lady press agent" was particularly ironic given the role that press agents had played in Cody's career—and the role that he and Burke were playing in the life of another "lady press agent" at the same time the Isbell affair was going on.

Mayme Jester was the daughter of Cody's sister Helen. She had grown up in Leavenworth, Kansas, and then moved to Duluth, Minnesota, where her mother and stepfather ran the *Duluth Press*, which had been purchased for them by William F. Cody. Mayme wrote for the paper, handling the traditional assignments of the female journalist (the Club and Woman's Departments), but some contemporary reports also listed her as city editor at the *Duluth News-Tribune*. In any event, she certainly showed great aptitude for journalism and was even assigned to cover the Democratic and Republican conventions during the 1896 presidential campaign.

Then, before the start of the Wild West's season in 1899, Mayme, who was in her early twenties, approached her uncle and asked if she could join the show as a press agent.[124] It was a bold request—there were virtually no women in the field, largely because the life of extensive travel, late night visits to newspaper rooms, and cigar-puffing, whiskey-swilling fraternization with old-boy editors was considered inappropriate for the fairer sex. Her family was against it: "My aunts and cousins and all the rest, think a girl should stay quietly under the shelter of the home roof and be ready to say 'I will' to the first man that asks her to share his lot in life," she told the *Boston Traveler*. "But I'm not built on that plan. I have my own ideas."[125]

Burke thought she would fail because she could not buy drinks. Cody himself felt she wouldn't last three weeks. But he was not one to capitulate to stereotypes, and besides, Mayme's mother, Helen Cody Wetmore, would also be traveling with the show to try to sell her new book, *Last of the Great Scouts*. So Mayme Jester became the Wild West's newest press agent.

Jester began her job in the spring, visiting newspaper offices in the Midwest—Cincinnati, Dayton, Columbus—and beyond. She was greeted warmly, if somewhat patronizingly. "She is a bright, intelligent young lady, and it is safe to say with her energy and tact she will experience no difficulty in accomplishing the mission on which she was sent by the show managers," wrote the *Cincinnati Times-Star*.[126] The *Williamsport Sun* called her "a young lady of exceptional literary qualifications, and a woman of practical newspaper experience."[127] The *Columbus Citizen* remarked, "The advance man of Buffalo Bill's Wild West show is a woman, and a most clever one at that. . . . She talked most entertainingly to The Citizen, and after long experience with crafty advance men who can talk of nothing but the merits of the production they represent, it was a refreshing novelty. She has a sort of suspicion of newspaper men and is surprised that so much she says is deemed worthy of reproduction."[128] The *Philadelphia Press* joked about her arrival that "there will be a general brushing up of last year's Spring suits by the newspaper workers and unusual attention to their general adornment in anticipation of the occasion so momentous."[129] The *Boston Traveler*'s "Matinee Girl" columnist "munched chocolate creams with her in schoolgirl fashion" and described her as "as sweet and unspoiled as when she did her horizontal exercise in the college gymnasium."[130]

At first it seemed that many of the newspapers were more interested in covering her than in writing about the Wild West or her mother's book. She tried to stay "on point"—providing multiple newspapers with the exact same 117-word description of the new Wild West act, featuring some of the heroes from the charge up San Juan Hill—but the headlines mostly trumpeted the novelty of her position ("MISS JESTER, Buffalo Bill's Niece, Calls on the Sun"; "CLEVER Is Young Lady Ahead of Buffalo Bill; Niece of Colonel Cody Visits the Newspaper Office"), and frequently the stories focused on her personal travails. The *Wilkes-Barre Times*, for example, quoted her at length in discussing her travel arrangements, and how she fought a "one-sided race" with her trunk, "as I invariably arrive at my destination first by a good many hours. . . . I rarely stop more than a day in a place and my work among the newspapers having to be done quickly, incidents of this kind are very annoying.[131]

A few weeks later she told the *Buffalo Times:*

> We think that we have one of the biggest shows in the country—in fact we know it, and we want the papers to say so. That is what I am here for. Just ask me anything about the show and I will tell you. But when you write it up please do not make a joke out of my name, will you? Every paper I have been to yet has done that and I am getting tired of it. It is so easy you know to say that 'Miss Jester is a joker' or something like that, and almost everybody yields to the temptation.

The paper ran a story, and her plea, under the headline "Young Woman's Name is a Good Joke."[132]

At one point, Jester was so concerned about the focus on her that she spent her entire visit with a newspaper asking them not to write about her and never did get around to mentioning the date that the Wild West would be in town.[133] It was a rookie mistake.

Jester was nothing if not earnest. She dressed in a necktie, just as her male counterparts did, and sometimes presented a card that said, "Miss Jester, Introducing The Last of the Great Scouts."[134] She worked hard to "boom" the Wild West and followed Burke's strategy to the letter—emphasizing its authenticity and educational merit, discussing her uncle's significance in western history, and of course refraining from use of the word "show." She even played to the locals, just as Burke did: visiting the offices of the *Worcester Telegram*, in between New Haven and Boston, she wore a Yale pin on her bosom and a Harvard pin on her hat.[135]

Eventually, she began to figure it all out. By July, she was delivering a much more personal pitch for the new performance of the charge up San Juan Hill. "It's great," she told the *Rochester Post Express.* "You know the man who fired the first shot was wounded eight times—Tom Isbel; well, we've got him and a number of the Rough Riders who were in the thick of the fight."[136]

These tactics paid off, as the Wild West attracted its usual share of media attention and large crowds—although many newspapers continued to focus on her, frequently commenting that her modern style stood in stark contrast to the traditional press agents. The *Wilkes-Barre Leader*, for example, wrote, "Miss Jester is not full of antiquated notions on how 'to work' the newspaper men. She does not announce that she is ahead of the greatest show on earth, does not invite the editor out for a drink, does not distribute bad cigars—or good ones either—around the office, and does not wear either big diamonds, big watch chains or big badges. . . . She is quiet, unassuming, [and] talks business."[137] The *Poughkeepsie News-Press* called her "a vast improvement over the familiar press agent," who was "heavily scented," wore "sparkling jewelry" and "flashy togs," and was "so loquacious as to stop a printing press." Instead, "Miss Jester calls on business and presents her material in a business way. She does not deliver stereotyped speeches."[138] Clearly, the role of the press agent was gaining acceptance and evolving; and this ambitious newcomer was advancing the cause—for her gender and for the profession as a whole.

Mayme Jester's career as a press agent only lasted that one season. Somewhere along the line, she met and fell in love with Robert Bruce Allen, and they were married in Duluth on June 27, 1901, or as one newspaper put it, "Miss Jester, in an evil moment, married and relinquished forever the joys of travel and the wild ki-yi of the Indians, for the more domestic delights of quiet housewifry [*sic*]."[139] The duties of publicity would fall back on Burke and the old guard.

But she was not done with her promotional work and would ultimately take Burke's vision to an entirely new level. A quarter century later, in 1927, the woman then known as Mary Jester Allen would create a museum to honor her uncle and his legacy. It is today the Buffalo Bill Center of the West in Cody, Wyoming, a popular tourist attraction and one of the foremost centers for research of the American West.

She died in 1960.

In their final years, Cody and his show went through a series of transformations.

Forced to confront middle age with eyeglasses and a roomier set of buckskins, Cody also acceded to Burke's request and started wearing a wig in 1900 ("The curls flowed down to his shoulders," reported the *Atlanta Constitution*. "They were immensely becoming if you like your heroes fluffy. Burke has said that the public does."[140]) Burke eventually worked up a storyline that essentially cast the Grim Reaper in the traditional role of Cody's enemy, with the scout living in fear that, as Burke put it, "the insidious emissary of the old scythe-bearer is liable to approach him with the same cunning and strategy as his Indian foes of old—in other words, that it has come to be a question whether he has to dismount or whether he will fall from the saddle."[141]

After a devastating head-on train accident in 1901, in which more than one hundred performing horses were killed and Annie Oakley was badly injured, the Wild West suffered significant financial losses, and the sharpshooting star left the show for good.

The Wild West returned to Britain in 1902 through 1904, and to the Continent in 1905–1906, but "the brilliance of that first [European] trip was sadly lacking," said press agent Dexter Fellows.[142] Much of Burke's effort was simply to convey to patrons, through the press, that the Wild West was coming, that it would be the full show and not some scaled-down version, that it would be instructive and not "partaking of a circus," and that Cody himself would be appearing.

Then, while the Wild West was in Europe, James Bailey died—forcing Cody back into a managerial role for which he had always been ill suited.

From 1907 on, Cody's story was that of a "faltering giant," said the western artist Dan Muller (who claimed to have been raised as a sort of foster son by Cody and wrote a 1948 book entitled *My Life with Buffalo Bill*). "There were many of the old flashes of warmth—there was even magnificence—but essentially from that point on his story was that of a strong man's reluctant descent to the grave."[143]

The debt continued to mount, and Cody opted to partner with Major Gordon Lillie to create a new combination called Buffalo Bill's Wild West and Pawnee Bill's Great Far East Show, known colloquially as the Two Bills Show. This ran for five seasons, but then went bankrupt. To stay afloat, Cody sold the rights to his name and his show, and was then hired as the featured performer with the Sells-Floto Circus for 1914 and 1915. His final year of performing was with another outfit, the Miller Brothers 101 Ranch

BURKE IN ROME, during the Wild West's final European tour (1906), holding up one of the tools of his trade. Buffalo Bill Center of the West, Cody, Wyoming; P.6.1726.

Wild West. It was a gradual denouement, a slow bleeding out of what had been the liveliest and most original form of entertainment the country had ever known.

John M. Burke was there for the entire ride. His role diminished over time, and in the final years, forced out by owners who refused to acknowledge his contributions, he served as Cody's personal publicist—a role not all that different from just being the friend he had been for more than forty years.

But even in this period of decline, Burke always had a twinkle in his eye and a trick or two up his sleeve. For example, after a group of eleven Indians was photographed at Land's End, the most southerly point in Britain, looking out over the ocean toward their home, Burke organized an ironic excursion and photograph at the most *northerly* village of John O'Groat's, almost nine hundred miles away in the far northern Scottish Highlands. Enjoying every minute of it, Burke managed to get himself invited to the wedding of a Highland soldier, and he also sent a postcard to fellow press agent Frank Small, signing it "From John O'Groat's, John M. Greets."[144] In 1906, during a week-long stand in Rome, Burke posed for a photograph (along with two Indians) and apparently sat for a portrait and sculpted bust while visiting the Caffè Greco. It is not known whether he ever found out about, or perhaps just played along with, the delicious mistaken identity that was printed in the caption under the photo: "Buffalo Bill coi suoi pellirosse al Caffè Greco" (Buffalo Bill with his redskins at Caffè Greco). All three items sit in the restaurant to this day, and the caption has never been corrected.[145]

Burke had always tried to get the public to view the West through a lens of nostalgia, and now that same lens was trained on the Wild West itself. By 1907, the introduction to the program, written in telltale Burke language, acknowledged that the show was now "admittedly more antique" but said it was "like old relics enhanced in priceless value; like old wine improved with age, veritably a nectar for those who thirst for the untinselled."[146] And as usual, the thoughts went right from Burke's pen to the newspapers' galleys—as for example on May 21, 1907, when the *Hartford Courant* wrote:

> There is absent the glamor of the footlights, the cunning use of electricity, the lavish display of tinsel. It is simplicity and reality. No effort is made to improve on the one hand or the other: on the contrary you are carried back to the day that tried the souls of men and women, before railroads opened up the wide territory between the Mississippi and the Rocky Mountains. Life among the Indian natives, pioneers, and the national armed forces is here presented in the most commonplace manner, yet with a sincerity and directness which give this wonderful exhibition a permanent and ever pleasing delight to the American and the foreigner.[147]

When Cody and Lillie came together to create the Two Bills Show in 1909, Burke and his team seamlessly shifted his Old West routine to help generate press coverage for the "Far East" portion of the show—camel caravans, elephants, boomerang-throwing Australian Bushmen, and more. He deemed it the "greatest educational show on earth" and "a veritable kindergarten of ethnology." The ads declared "The Orient Meets the Occident."[148] The 1911 printed program noted that there were "more varied types of different nationalities and races from around the world than any governmental or private enterprise has heretofore collected" and that the exhibition was now "a school of human kinship, in which the public at large can study their fellow-man by comparison."[149]

As usual, the press responded. The *New York Clipper* wrote, "Adjectives serve not, and panegyric is limp, to describe this year's exhibition, for the creative genius of the 'Two Bills' is inexhaustible."[150] The *Cincinnati Enquirer* said, "The combination of the Wild West and Far East is so novel that there is nothing under the sun like it. . . . [Its] education and patriotic value . . . is something which the children should see."[151] The *Atlanta Georgian and News* quoted Burke as saying, "Morse has made the two worlds touch the tips of their fingers together. Cody has made the warriors of all nations join hands. Who but this man has conceived so fantastic a play?"[152] *Show World Magazine* concluded:

> Among advertising people it has been common talk for the past week or ten days that not in years have the Chicago newspapers carried as much interesting press stuff for an amusement attraction as they have for the Two Bills' show. Each comment of this kind has been a new laurel for the veteran Major John M. Burke, Col. Cody's personal representative and associate for years, and Frank Winch, the clever young purveyor of 'tories' who is this season officiating as general press representative for the show.[153]

Outside the show, Burke continued to work relentlessly to rebuild and defend Cody's reputation. When any newspaper dared to evince the slightest disrespect—for example, printing a story about a Kansas man who claimed to be the original holder of the nickname Buffalo Bill—Burke would immediately weigh in with a telegram-cum-history-lesson that might run six hundred words.[154] He devised a slightly more heroic version of the story about why Cody had been unable to save Sitting Bull back in 1890.[155] Burke also succeeded in generating a good deal of speculation that Cody might be a candidate for senator in Arizona when that territory achieved statehood in 1912 ("Incidentally," wrote the *New York Times*, "Major Burke . . . is looking forward to cutting off his curly locks and setting down in Washington as the Senator's secretary").[156]

Around this time, too, Burke appears to have engineered a licensing deal of sorts. This in itself was not unusual: the Wild West had been featured on many products, including The Game of Buffalo Bill, by Parker Brothers (1898), a Candyland-like board game with squares such as "Stampede of Buffalo—8 spaces back"; and Buffalo Bill's Wild West Songster (1899), with music for songs like "My Gal is a High Born Lady," "The Blow Almost Killed Father," and "Who Threw the Overalls in Mistress Murphy's Chowder?"

But this one was different. The American Caramel Company—which had been founded by Milton Hershey and sold when he opted to keep his chocolate company instead—decided to capitalize on the growing nostalgia for the West by creating a product called Wild West Caramels. To promote these, the company created trading cards featuring legends of the Old West, one of which was inserted into each package. Cards like these, usually featuring baseball stars but sometimes entertainers, were commonly included in cigarette and candy packages during this era. In this case, the set featured twenty iconic figures of the West—including Buffalo Bill, Daniel Boone, Kit Carson, Davy Crockett, General Custer, Yellow Hair, Sitting Bull . . . and John M. Burke (see plate 14).

Had he convinced the manufacturer of his western bona fides? Burke *did* have a legitimate claim to having been a western scout, and based on the number of newspaper articles throughout his career describing him as a participant in Indian skirmishes, possibly even the massacre at Wounded Knee, he had clearly enjoyed and participated in the propagation of that myth. Even his obituary writers would make matter-of-fact references to "his renown as an Indian scout" and his "experiences in the old frontier days [that] were thrilling."[157] But as Cody had once complained, "Look at those [newspaper clippings]. . . . All about Burke the Indian fighter. Why, damn it, Burke never even saw an Indian until he came with me, much less kill one."[158]

Certainly, others were more deserving of inclusion in this set of cards, such as Wyatt Earp, Wild Bill Hickok, or even Teddy Roosevelt, General Miles, and General Carr—the latter three of whom *were* included in an American Caramel Company gum set in the same year. So why was Burke included?

The answer can be found in the presence of one other card in the set: Pawnee Bill, aka Gordon Lillie, the tinhorn showman who was then Cody's partner and hence Burke's other promotional charge—a clear indication that this was all about marketing, not mettle. So perhaps it was all just Burke having fun, a wink to the future historian, much as he had done a few years earlier when, in the middle of the 1895 season, he had quietly replaced the longstanding image of the cowboy on the front of the printed program with a similar-looking image of himself. In any event, he was certainly the first publicist to find his way onto a "baseball card," and probably the last (see plates 15 and 16).

John M. Burke's last significant promotional innovation was the farewell tour he engineered, beginning with the 1910 season.

This was not a new tactic—Barnum had often advertised a performance as being in its final night, even though it was not. "Let the public conceive that a performance announced for one night can never be played again, and it is a sure attraction," he wrote.[159] Similarly, the great actress Sarah Bernhardt had launched her American farewell tour in 1905–1906—although, as it turned out, she would conduct two more such tours. But Burke executed Cody's valediction masterfully.

It was intended to last two years, under the premise that the show would not visit any city twice during that time, and thus could legitimately claim that this was, indeed, good-bye. Burke probably did not plan this as a deception, for Cody had grown weary of performing and had often talked about retirement: the exact same headline "Buffalo Bill to Retire" ran in different newspaper articles in 1896, 1898, 1901, 1902, 1903, and 1906, and Cody told press agent Dexter Fellows, "As a fellow gets old he doesn't feel like tearing around the country forever. I do not want to die a showman. I grow very tired of this sort of sham worship sometimes."[160] Nevertheless, Burke squeezed every drop of publicity out of it by incorporating sentimental farewell messages into the printed programs and ads, often accompanied by an official-looking "seal." He also created Cody's "Farewell Proclamation to the Public!," which emphasized in block letters and underlining that this would be his "last, sole and only professional appearance" in the city at hand. It read in part:

> AND NOW that I have reached this unalterable conclusion, I want to thank my numerous friends and the public for the full measure of success and applause that they have bestowed upon me, and I know

> of no honor that I shall cherish more than their good wishes, while the silent years are lurking in ambush for "The Old Scout," and at the conclusion of each and every performance I shall bid my numerous friends a fond farewell.[161]

A press release entitled "He Will Appear to Bid Adieu," in the *From Desert Sands to Prairie Wilds* press kit, ran verbatim in papers such as the *Bismarck Daily Tribune* (August 10, 1910) and *Arizona Republican* (October 24, 1910). The 1911 program also contained more of this self-aware pabulum about the significance of Cody's retirement, in Burke's characteristically florid language: "A shining light in any realm that disappears from public view is missed, its brightness since measuring the after gloom. Thus a little farewell cloud gilded with friendly wishes will cast its shadow over our city when Buffalo Bill says good-bye."[162]

And of course Burke managed to work it into all his interviews with newspapers—for example, telling the people of Detroit in 1910, courtesy of the *Free Press*, that this was Cody's "last visit to your city on the closing tour of his career as an exhibitor, one he can point to with pride as he bids you at the same time from the saddle a regretful farewell."[163] In 1911, he somehow persuaded the *Altoona (Pa.) Tribune* to run a story entitled "Farewell of Buffalo Bill," which consisted of exactly 34 words from the newspaper itself, followed by a 668-word quote from Burke full of bombast about Cody's role in fulfilling the country's manifest destiny: the "celerity and breadth of the wave of conquest," the "danger-defying pertinacity of the pioneers," the "self-sacrificing dash and daring of the army," and, ever so modestly, the suggestion that Cody's "present retirement from public life . . . is deserving of more than passing notice."[164] And that was just Altoona—a one-day stop on the tour of Buffalo Bill's Wild West and Pawnee Bill's Far East.

The promotion worked well at first: the 1910 Farewell Tour generated income of $1 million and a profit of $400,000.[165] But the crowds faded, and the bills mounted, and when the idea that Buffalo Bill was hanging up his spurs became, according to Dan Muller, "a recurrent joke that elicited only guffaws," the farewell theme was dropped after the 1911 season.[166]

Cody appeared in Detroit again in 1912, 1914, 1915, and 1916.

Burke and Cody still occasionally managed to summon some of the old promotional magic, but by now they were old men, the world was hurtling toward war, and the Old West was a relic. Cody often needed to be helped into and out of the saddle in his final years of performing and sometimes consented to be carried around the arena in a phaeton, centurion-like. After three hundred thousand dollars of losses on the last European tour, he had mortgaged his ranches in North Platte and Cody, as well as the Irma Hotel.[167] He continued to invest unwisely in his Arizona mine (up to five thousand dollars per month), and in the Big Horn Basin, and saw his assets dwindle down to one hundred thousand dollars. Gordon Lillie said Cody "had no business or executive ability . . . never had any thought of tomorrow, or of laying up for a rainy day. Money to him was only made to spend or aid and make others happy, not for himself."[168]

In January 1913 Cody had to borrow twenty thousand dollars from Harry Tammen, owner of the *Denver Post* and the Sells-Floto Circus. When he couldn't repay it, Tammen and other creditors closed down the Two Bills Show and forced it to be auctioned off, piece by piece. To make amends, Cody would go to work for Sells-Floto as an employee and would eventually have to pay Tammen five thousand dollars to recover the use of his own name.[169]

Burke had been well paid during his heyday but apparently never managed to put any money away. He retained a position as press agent during Cody's two-year run with Sells-Floto but was pushed off the payroll and seems to have fallen on hard times. Muller described him as "a seedy remnant of his old dominant self."[170] He spent winter 1914 in Denver helping Cody with the promotion of the film *Indian Wars*, and one cold morning he was spotted by press agent Courtney Ryley Cooper (who would later collaborate with Louisa Cody on her biography of Buffalo Bill, and with Annie Oakley on her autobiography), who described a touching scene:

> I watched him, whiskers flying, threadbare coat pulled tight around his rotund form, set forth to what I knew by experience would be a meager breakfast. But in ten minutes he was back in the [Sells-Floto] circus offices, a copy of the New York Times tucked under his arm. "You didn't take long for breakfast, Major," I said. He grew red-faced. "Well, I just decided I didn't want any," came at last. "I noticed this New York Times and I just thought I'd see whether it had anything to say about the Colonel . . ." I bought the Major's breakfast that morning. The ten cents with which he had started for his coffee and rolls had gone upon the altar of his devotion.[171]

"Time," as Cody had written during his Farewell Tour, "beats us all at last."[172]

12

LEGACIES

"Like a masterpiece by a weaver wrought"

All the past we leave behind;
We debouch upon a newer, mightier world, varied world,
Fresh and strong the world we seize, world of labor and the march,
Pioneers! O pioneers!

Walt Whitman, *Pioneers! O Pioneers!* (1900)

The days of the great spectacle are over.

There are still some regional rodeos, such as the Frontier Days celebrations in Prescott, Arizona, and Cheyenne, Wyoming, but the Wild West shows are no more. Expositions are still held every few years, but the last time the international community paid much attention to a world's fair was in 1964. In fact, alone among the great entertainment exhibitions that were so prevalent in the late nineteenth century, and which paved the way for the development of the modern marketing industry, the circus survived relatively unscathed all the way to the twenty-first century. But along the way it lost the street cavalcades and bill-posting operations, then it lost the elephants, and finally it lost the battle altogether—folding up its tents for good in 2017.

Of course, Tody Hamilton's role in establishing the promotional tone of that circus and fixing it forever in the American mind was long ago forgotten.

He had remained a highly influential and much-imitated force right through the 1905 season, his twenty-fifth with Barnum & Bailey, and this period marked the pinnacle of his notoriety. He was, as one newspaper commented, "as much a part of [the circus] as the main tent."[1] The *New York Sun* remarked, "The Barnum & Bailey Circus is in town; also Tody Hamilton, press agent. Perhaps it would be more nearly correct to reverse the order of statements."[2] The *Sun* would later say, "His name is known from one end of this country to the other—and then some. . . . It may be asserted without fear of contradiction that the outpourings of Mr. Hamilton's muse have been more widely perused than any other literary efforts of the age."[3]

But when James Bailey died in spring 1906, the last connection to Barnum was severed, and Hamilton soon announced he would be leaving the circus, which he did the following March. Days later, four hundred people (including John M. Burke) gathered at the Waldorf-Astoria in New York to pay tribute to a beloved man and his brilliant career. The event was so large and the scope so grand, it was effectively a coming out party for the new marketing industry itself. The *New York Times* called it "as odd a collection of men as could be gathered together, the list embracing, in addition to the newspaper men (who predominated in point of numbers), press agents, theatrical men and managers, all of whom, at some time or other, had been reporters and editors, and as such had come under the spell of Mr. Hamilton's truthful, earnest, and whole-hearted nature."[4] The *New York Sun* described "the glitteringly glorious gastronomic gyrations" at the dinner and noted that the printed program distributed at every plate referred to the guest of honor as "the Foremost Florid, Fluorescent, Forever Fresh and Fair, Fervid, Fast and Furious, Fosforescent Father of Freely Flowing Fancy, Florentine Frazes and Far Flung Fame in captivity."[5] Tody Hamilton had made his mark.

Hamilton then moved to the suburbs of Baltimore, but he never truly retired. He tinkered with inventions, such as his duplex safety see-saw and his railroad brake. In 1910, he started a new business called the International Publicity Company, through which he began publishing a monthly magazine called *International Inventor*. Inevitably, though, he got pulled back into novelty entertainment, and worked for short stretches promoting the Moisant Flying Circus and then both Luna Park and Dreamland at Coney Island—the spiritual successor to the Columbian Exposition's Midway Plaisance. He died of heart disease on August 16, 1916, at the age of sixty-nine, and was laid to rest on August 19—giving newspaper editors all around the country three days to work up the cleverest and most alliterative obituaries of their lives.

* * *

After the death of Moses P. Handy, Sarah retreated to Berlin, Maryland, and built a home known as Anchuka, which would become the family compound for the next several generations. She resumed her career in journalism, contributing a number of domestic features, historical perspectives, and short stories until about 1908. She lived the last quarter century of her life quietly, surrounded by children and grandchildren, until she passed away just shy of her eighty-eighth birthday—right in the midst of the 1933 Chicago World's Fair.

The oldest and youngest of Moses and Sarah's children, William Matthews Handy and Henry Jamison "Jam" Handy, both followed their parents into the newspaper business. Will died fairly young, at age fifty-four in 1925, but Jam, who had accompanied Moses to the Department of Publicity and Promotion office each day instead of going to school, would go on to a long and fascinating career.

First, he fulfilled an ostensible mandate of his upbringing by heading off to the 1904 World's Fair (which unsurprisingly had an enormous Press and Publicity Department housed within the charmingly named Division of Exploitation). There, Handy competed in the Olympic Games, which were being held in conjunction with the fair, and won a bronze medal in the 440-yard breaststroke (he would win another one with the U.S. water polo team at the 1924 games in Paris). Later, Jam Handy went to work for the *Chicago Tribune* and spent time, among other places, with the Advertising Department, where he became interested in how to motivate the sales staff. He eventually combined the flair for persuasion that was in his blood with his training in writing, advertising, and sales, as well as the newest communications technology—motion pictures—and ultimately became perhaps *the* premier promotional filmmaker of the twentieth century. The Jam Handy Organization produced thousands of promotional, training, and advertising films for the likes of Chevrolet, General Motors, AT&T, Alcoa, U.S. Steel, and Coca-Cola; educational films; stop-motion and animated TV commercials, as well as the 1953 ads featuring Dinah Shore singing "See the U.S.A. in Your Chevrolet"; plus an estimated seven thousand propaganda films for the government during World War II. The

Jam Handy name still has resonance in the advertising community and in recent years was elevated to pop culture icon status when several of its films were used in the cult parody TV show *Mystery Science Theater 3000.*

Throughout John M. Burke's long career, his indefatigable spirit worked like the coupling rod between locomotive wheels, keeping his romantic heart and innovative mind in lockstep as they raced ahead of the rest of the world, through the western frontier and into the future. He was one of those rare individuals who was always aware of the significance of the current moment, and where it stood in the long arc of history, and so he managed to produce—usually with laughable construction aforethought, but occasionally with brilliant spontaneity—a hundred insightful lines that could have served as his epitaph, if only a grave marker could be found that were large enough to accommodate all the words.

But there would be no epitaph. There would be no grave marker at all.

Burke was of course present for Cody's final arena appearance, on November 11, 1916 (which happened to be in Moses P. Handy's old hometown of Portsmouth, Virginia). He knew it was the end of the long trail they had ridden together. According to Julia Cody Goodman, Burke "walked to the center of the arena, and with tears pouring down his cheeks made the announcement that this marked Buffalo Bill's closing performance."[6]

Days later, Cody headed West, and Burke returned to Washington, D.C. It was there, in January 1917, that he learned that Cody was extremely weak (from what turned out to be kidney failure) and that doctors had issued a dire prognosis. On January 9, Burke sent a telegram:

> Dear friend Bill am appealing to the Celestial court to revise the medical jury's decision hoping nerve will and constitution may steer you off the trail over Great Divide and let you camp for years yet on the banks of the rippling Shoshone. Stay with them. How Koolah old pal.[7]

Cody passed quietly into history the next day.

John M. Burke remained subdued for some weeks thereafter, feeling that his "proper tribute should be in hidden tears and golden silence."[8] He was also dismayed about the war, "the present sanguinary maelstrom of universal strife in Europe, when hordes of personally uninterested humans mostly entirely ignorant of its reason or innocent of its cause are being sacrificed wholesale," and may have felt that public grieving over the loss of one man, however great, was inappropriate.[9]

Then, on the day before his seventy-fifth birthday, Burke came down with pneumonia and was soon admitted to Providence Hospital in Washington, D.C. He passed away there on April 12, 1917, having outlived Cody by ninety-two days. He had no heirs. He had no money. His fellow members of the Benevolent and Protective Order of Elks, Lodge 15, took charge of the funeral arrangements. Perhaps none of them knew about his desire to be laid to rest on "Burke's Bluff" near McCullough Peak in Wyoming, or perhaps there were no funds to make it happen. Tribute was paid to him in a "lodge of sorrow" ceremony and a mass at St. Aloysius Church, and in many newspaper articles around the country; but then he was buried in an otherwise anonymous plot, in a nondescript section of the Mount Olivet Cemetery, with no headstone.

John M. Burke's role in creating Buffalo Bill and the Wild West would be acknowledged and debated by Cody's many biographers, but his more profound contributions in developing an industry that reshaped American society would be overlooked, and then forgotten completely. Today, Burke's name almost never appears in histories or discussions of the founding fathers of the marketing, advertising, or PR industries. And like Tody Hamilton and Moses P. Handy, John M. Burke does not even have an entry in Wikipedia—despite the distinct possibility that the Internet, as a marketing-based medium, would never have come into being without the work that these men did.

Yet in another sense, Burke's epitaph was writ large because of the marketing industry he had done so much to create. He certainly was not the first person to labor in this field, nor to recognize the inherent power of harnessing communications for commercial purposes. Advertising and promotion, in one form or another, had been around for centuries, and it could be argued they are instinctual and eternal human impulses. But the mechanism of using them for persuasion, something more profound than just a transaction—perhaps best captured in Goethe's couplet from *Faust* (1832): "Frankly, to manufacture thought/Is like a masterpiece by a weaver wrought"—had never truly been understood until John M. Burke came along.

Burke was among the first of the professional class of promoters, and he was certainly the most successful. The techniques he helped develop in publicity, promotion, and advertising—celebrity endorsements, press junkets and press kits, publicity stunts, op-ed pieces and letters to the editor, mobile billboards, custom publishing, product licensing deals, and much more—were truly groundbreaking and paved the way for the development and professionalization of the field of promotion, which became the marketing industry. By turning William F. Cody into an icon, building and protecting his reputation and that of the Wild West, turning the nation's westering gaze backward to a nostalgic and more salable past, and attracting an estimated 50 million people to the show, Burke helped prove the efficacy of marketing.

It had been a remarkable transformation. The motley mix of promotions from early in Burke's career—Barnum and his humbugs, dowdy theatrical press agents, and the fanatical skullduggery of patent medicine ads and western boosters—had by this time evolved into a legitimate industry that was infiltrating and integrating into nearly every sector of American society.

The most prominent of the marketing "tent poles" was, of course, advertising, which alone had become a $500 million business by around 1900.[10] By then there were dozens of advertising agencies; the largest, N. W. Ayer, had 160 employees by the turn of the century. A 1,016-page encyclopedia of advertising was published, called *Fowler's Publicity*, and universities began to offer courses on marketing topics like "principles of advertising." The number of daily and weekly newspapers continued to rise, so that by 1900 more than half of all the newspapers in the world were being published in the United States, with an average of two copies per capita.[11] Several magazines now had circulations exceeding 1 million, and many were accepting advertisements. One publication in 1907 observed, "To market many a car it costs almost twice as much as it does to manufacture it."[12]

But by this time, thanks to Burke and the other pioneers of promotion, there were also far more sophisticated tools and techniques. Publicity bureaus, for example, were set up inside many of the big trusts and other companies (despite the outcry of muckraking journalists), and outside public relations counselors were available as hired guns. Just after the turn of the century, Guglielmo Marconi had used a press agent to build brand awareness for his wireless telegraph (radio) system, and then set up the Marconi Press Agency to create a sophisticated publicity campaign that would outdistance all rival technologies.[13]

By 1904, the *Saturday Evening Post* declared that publicity was "the science of free advertising, a science as fascinating as astronomy and far more intricate," for to master it "one must go direct to the human heart and soul."[14]

Against this backdrop of the increased sophistication and commercialization of promotion, a man named Ivy Lee emerged as the new face of the industry.

Lee had worked as a journalist for many years before setting up his first publicity shop in 1904, and in his capacity as a newspaperman, he had become friendly with John M. Burke and his team at the Wild West. Indeed, Dexter Fellows later reflected, "Not one of us ever dreamed at that time that [Lee] would make a fortune as America's greatest propagandist . . . [and] would lift the lowly trade of press agentry to the euphonious heights of counselor in public relations."[15]

Lee felt there had been an evolution from the press agent who tried to fool the public to the publicist who tried to inform it, and corporations were the new frontier for this kind of work. His motto was "Accuracy, Authenticity, Interest." In his view, the work on behalf of corporations was all about "shaping their affairs so that when placed before the public they will be approved" because many of them already operated with an "enlightened self-interest." Lee was hired by International Harvester to head off antitrust action, and by John D. Rockefeller Jr. in the wake of the Ludlow Massacre of 1913, when forty of Rockefeller's striking coal miners were killed. Some described Lee's philosophy as "situational ethics."[16] Others thought of his work as nothing more than manipulation. The writer Carl Sandburg called Lee a "paid liar," and the muckraker Upton Sinclair nicknamed him "Poison Ivy."[17]

But there was no going back.

Indeed, by the last years of John M. Burke's life, the services of advertisers and publicists in one form or another had become indispensable in nearly every sector of society. The Mutual Life Insurance Company, Westinghouse Electric, the American Medical Association, presidential campaigns, the Union Pacific and Illinois Central Railroads, universities, the American Red Cross—all of them and many more had marketing disciples in their employ.

Soon, so would the White House. Because six days before John M.

Burke died, the United States declared war on the German Empire, and two days after Burke died, President Woodrow Wilson signed Executive Order 2594 establishing the Committee on Public Information (CPI), the federal government's first publicity bureau.

Wilson had been contemplating forming some sort of publicity arm for three years, but now that the country was at war, he could wait no longer. Secretary of State Robert Lansing, Secretary of War Newton Baker, and Secretary of the Navy Josephus Daniels sent him a letter urging him to act, declaring that "America's great needs are confidence, enthusiasm, and service," and "our opinion [is] that the two functions—censorship and publicity—can be joined in honesty and with profit."[18] Wilson intended the committee to be "intimately associated with the policy of the administration," and to help coordinate the distribution of news from across the federal government. There was no overt discussion about the suppression or manipulation of news, although it was well known by this time that European governments were using the power of publicity to shape public opinion by exaggerating minor victories or trumping up enemy atrocities.[19]

To head the committee, Wilson selected the acerbic and opinionated writer George Creel, who years earlier had decried corporate press bureaus but was now put in charge of the largest one in the world. Creel quickly set about building a vast publicity machine that, according to historian David Greenberg in his book *Republic of Spin*, "produced literally millions of press releases, news bulletins, syndicated feature articles, advertisements, movies, political cartoons, classroom lesson plans, songs, museum exhibits, Chautauqua-circuit speeches, talking points, and overseas radio broadcasts . . . all designed to inform the public, explain the administration's views, and stoke popular support for the war."[20]

The CPI used and improved on virtually every tool that the earlier promotional geniuses had developed: emotional imagery (including James Montgomery Flagg's "I Want You" Uncle Sam poster, photographs, and murals plastered on trolley cars and barn doors); films (such as the eight-reel documentary called *Pershing's Crusaders*); persuasive writing (ten press releases a day that yielded, by Creel's estimate, twenty thousand columns of material in American newspapers each week); special events (a traveling War Exposition); and even theatrical performances (a platoon of "Four-Minute Men," who stood up and delivered prowar speeches in between reels at movie theaters, something they did 755,190 times over two years). The CPI also took advantage of the latest technological advancements by, for example, sending out all of Wilson's official speeches via wireless so that "within twenty-four hours [they] were in every language in every country in the world."[21]

The combined effects of these efforts were huge increases in enlistments, war bond sales, donations to the Red Cross, and support for Woodrow Wilson—as well as denunciations of the CPI's work as propaganda, censorship, news fabrication, and hyperbole. Depending on one's political orientation, Creel and his committee were guilty of either pacifism or giving comfort to the enemy. Indeed, "propaganda" became almost as closely associated with Creel's name as "humbug" had with Barnum's.

In 1920, Creel would pen a book, appropriately titled *How We Advertised America*, in which he rode to his own defense. His committee had "a record of stainless patriotism and unspotted Americanism," he said, one that "stands unparalleled for honesty, accuracy and high purpose." The CPI had displayed "American unity, resolve, and invincibility" through the foreign press, and as a result, in phrasing the sounded eerily like Moses P. Handy before the World's Columbian Exposition, "[a] world that was either inimical, contemptuous, or indifferent was changed into a world of friends and well-wishers." The total tab for taxpayers, according to Creel, was only about $5 million, because they had managed to secure "a bit of press-agenting . . . done out of patriotism by men and women whose services no money could have bought."[22]

In Creel's view—and he was probably right—his was a whole new kind of promotion, and it had been highly effective. But his irascibility stood in such stark contrast to the conviviality of the Gilded Age press agents that even his successes were assailed. It did not help his cause when he turned on some of his critics in the newspaper industry and accused them of being unpatriotic. In his book, he acknowledged that he sometimes built up "savage contempt" for them, realizing that the journalists were all "husky, healthy, and within the military age . . . holding down their peace-time jobs, while others sailed across the sea to offer their lives on the altar of American ideals."[23]

Regardless of its motives or merits, the CPI became the next logical (if surprisingly expansive) step in the evolutionary development of the field, which had originally taken root with Barnum and then blossomed with Buffalo Bill's Wild West, the World's Columbian Exposition, and the Barnum & Bailey Circus. But the CPI had done something they never had: laid bare the threat of marketing for all the world to see, right alongside the promise.

And the committee had one other legacy as well. The CPI seeded the field for the *next* iteration of the marketing industry, a period of professionalization, codification, and legitimization—because among those who worked for the committee were two young journalists who would become PR luminaries: Carl Byoir, who in 1930 would form one of the best-known public relations agencies in the country, Carl Byoir & Associates; and Edward Bernays, who would become known as the "father of public relations" through his brilliant work over the course of more than seventy years.

Many decades have now passed since the deaths of P. T. Barnum, Tody Hamilton, Moses P. Handy, William F. Cody, John M. Burke, and even the members of the CPI. And here in twenty-first-century America, we are *all* marketing experts.

Of course, we have no choice in the matter. The average American is said to be exposed to as many as five thousand marketing messages a day. Television commercials have penetrated into elevators and taxis, gas station pumps and doctors' waiting rooms. Coupons spit out of supermarket cash registers for products we have just bought, or for competitors of products we have just bought. Digital billboards allow us to see three ads instead of just one while we cruise by at 60 miles per hour. Our cell phones buzz with text messages triggered by a satellite in geostationary orbit twenty-two thousand miles away, which has determined that we are within a few feet of a store whose mailing list we joined (perhaps unwittingly) that is running a promotion *right now.* "Retargeting" enables digital marketers to record the content that we clicked on or searched for online, and then follow us all around the web with highly specific ads that seem to know our very thoughts. The bins in airport security checkpoints, the front pages of daily newspapers, the urinals in restaurants, the websites of nonprofit organizations, the floors of supermarkets, the programs on commercial-free National Public Radio, the evening newscast itself—*all* have been overtaken by zealous or ingenious marketing campaigns in an effort to position a brand, burnish an image, restore a reputation, or attract a crowd to an event or product.

In turn, we consumers think we have become highly sensitized to marketers' efforts to reach us, prod us, and persuade us, no matter how clever or insidious those efforts may be. We pride ourselves on our ability to tune out much of it, filter it, pay attention only when we want to, and, as rational beings, resist its many temptations. But the marketing is often one step ahead of us, crafted in exquisitely subtle ways to reach even those who don't want to be marketed to. Welcome to the post-information age, in which companies don't just market but anticipate and manipulate our desires, intentions, and motivations.

It is a world of fierce competition for the consumer dollar. A world of press manipulation and carefully crafted celebrity pitchmen. A world in which marketing has infiltrated seemingly every square inch, every moment we once held sacred.

It is a world, in other words, not all that much unlike the one of Hamilton, Handy, and Burke.

EPILOGUE

Stone. It is surely the proper metaphorical medium for the telling of this tale.

It was the original means for conveying the written word. It was the original material used to create the plates with which the press agents' lithographs were printed (*lithos* means "stone" in Greek). It is the substance and symbol of the western landscape. And in the concrete sidewalk outside my house in Arizona, engraved with a stick in an instinctive moment of neighborhood immortality some years before I moved there, is the signature of a child named for a western legend created by a pioneer of promotion—a name that stares up at me every time I walk by, like a beacon, like a reminder, like a calling card, like a request: "Cody." Ultimately, I could not ignore it any longer.

But in the course of writing this book, I realized there was another stone that required my attention.

At my behest, a crowd of thirty people, including five descendants of the Burke family, gathered at the Mount Olivet Cemetery in Washington, D.C., on April 12, 2017—the one hundredth anniversary of the Major's death—to mount a stone over his grave. Historians came from the Buffalo Bill Center of the West, the Buffalo Bill Museum and Grave, and the Smithsonian Institution. According to the *Washington Post*, I had "beseeched (repeatedly) reporters to come see Western scholars and a Catholic deacon pay homage to this forgotten Svengali." I also live-streamed the ceremony on Facebook, which Burke would surely have liked. It was a publicity stunt to honor the man who more or less invented the publicity stunt.

At precisely 11:00 A.M., as the ceremony began, the clouds broke, the drizzle lifted, and the sun shone down on section 53 of the cemetery. Minutes later, we unveiled the marker. John M. Burke's legacy had finally been written in stone.

The next day, on my way out of town, I stopped at the Western Cemetery in Baltimore to pay my respects to Tody Hamilton, who had died eight months before Burke, in August 1916 (much as I had done the previous September by visiting Moses P. Handy's grave in Berlin, Maryland). I navigated my way over narrow pathways, past many fallen stones, along the edge of the cemetery. A dog barked behind a chain-link fence.

I finally reached section Y, plot 243.

There is no gravestone.

NOTES

CHAPTER 1. BURYING A LEGEND

1. Russell, *The Wild West*, 100. Russell said that as many as 557 original stories were written about Buffalo Bill, with perhaps another 1,200 reprints, but the estimates vary wildly from source to source.
2. Interview with Don Perez, January 8, 2015.
3. Burke, "Reminiscences of Col. Cody."
4. Cutlip, *Public Relations History*, 177.
5. Big Horn is sometimes spelled Bighorn.
6. "A Tomb Among the Clouds," *New York Times*, May 4, 1902.
7. "Maj. Burke's Bluff," *St. Louis Post-Dispatch*, October 4, 1899. Moreover, as early as 1888 Burke may have been thinking about making the West his final resting place: one newspaper reported, "His present hope and ambition is that he will be able to settle on some pretty far west spot, and end his days in that peaceful contentment that characterises the life of the aboriginal." See "Major John M. Burke ('Arizona John')," *Black and White*, January 20, 1888.
8. Although Cody's funeral on Lookout Mountain was not held until June 3, 1917, he passed away on January 10 and his body was kept in a morgue until the site and facilities for his final resting place could be prepared.
9. Athearn, *The Mythic West*, 183, 188.
10. Interview with Jim Fuqua, September 24, 2015.
11. "Wild West Getting Home," *New York Sun*, October 2, 1906.

CHAPTER 2. THE BIG TENT OF P. T. BARNUM AND TODY HAMILTON

1. Bellamy, *Looking Backward: 2000–1887*, 175.
2. Carl J. Guarneri, "An American Utopia and Its Global Audiences: Transnational Perspectives on Edward Bellamy's *Looking Backward*," accessed April 2, 2015, http://ftp.stmarys-ca.edu/cguarner/documents/Bellamyarticle-UtopianStudies.pdf.
3. Scudo et al., *Life of Henriette Sontag*, 53; and "Miscellaneous," *Perth Sunday Times*, Nov. 24, 1912, on Trove, National Library of Australia, accessed April 2, 2015, http://trove.nla.gov.au/ndp/del/article/57742270.
4. Joseph Ator, "Classified Ad History Long, Fascinating," *Chicago Tribune*, January 26, 1964.
5. See "Ad Age Advertising Century: Timeline," *Advertising Age*, March 29, 1999, accessed April 4, 2015, http://adage.com/article/special-report-the-advertising-century/ad-age-advertising-century-timeline/143661; and M. C. Barrès-Baker, *An Introduction to the Early History of Newspaper Advertising*, Brent Museum and Archive Occasional Publications, no. 2, accessed April 4, 2015, http://brent.gov.uk/media/387509/Newspaper_advertising_article_2011.pdf. For Franklin ad items, see *Advertising Society & Review* 11, no. 1 (2010), https://muse.jhu.edu/article/377516.
6. *Burlington Free Press*, September 16, 1836.

7. Hutchinson, "Periodical Distribution," in *A Publisher's History*, chap. 3, p. 35, citing Groner et al., *The American Heritage History*, 83.
8. See "Historical Timeline—Farmers & the Land," *Growing a Nation: The Story of American Agriculture*, accessed April 6, 2015, https://www.agclassroom.org/gan/timeline/farmers_land.htm.
9. Hutchinson, *A Publisher's History*, chap. 3, p. 9. Since literacy was not measured until the 1840 census, Hutchinson relied on work from Soltow and Stevens, *Rise of Literacy*, which used literacy rates of U.S. Army inductees as a surrogate for the greater population.
10. Hutchinson, *A Publisher's History*, chap. 3, p. 1, and chap. 1, p. 24, citing Mott, *A History of American Magazines*, 1:113, and Thomas, *The History of Printing in America*, 17.
11. Weeks, *A History of Paper Manufacturing*, 212, 220; and "Egyptian Mummies as Source of Paper Stock," *Paper*, March 12, 1913.
12. See "Roads and Travel in New England 1790-1840," TeachUSHistory.org, accessed April 6, 2015, http://www.teachushistory.org/detocqueville-visit-united-states/articles/roads-travel-new-england-1790-1840.
13. Atack and Passell, *A New Economic View of American History*, 36.
14. Resseguie, "Alexander Turney Stewart," 317.
15. *Vermont Phoenix* (Brattleboro), January 7, 1847.
16. Historian LeRoy Ashby says that the *New York Sun* was producing forty thousand sheets an hour by 1840. Ashby, *With Amusement for All*, 22.
17. Ibid., 23.
18. Hutchinson, *A Publisher's History*, chap. 3, p. 35, citing Presbrey, *History and Development of Advertising*, 188, 195.
19. David A. Copeland, "19th Century U.S. Newspapers: Setting the Agenda in the Antebellum Era," Gale Group, accessed June 2, 2016, http://www.galegroup.com/pdf/whitepapers/gdc/NCUSN_Antebellum_whtppr.pdf.
20. De Tocqueville, *Democracy in America*, 185.
21. Hutchinson, *A Publisher's History*, chap. 3, p. 35, citing Presbrey, *History and Development of Advertising*, 210.
22. Cited in Pope, *The Making of Modern Advertising*, 115.
23. Cited in Applegate, *The Rise of Advertising*, 47.
24. Adams, *E Pluribus Barnum*, 83. A review of newspapers from that era now available online reveals that Barnumism was used to refer both to a marketing stunt and to a humbug. For example, the *Fayetteville (N.C.) Weekly Observer*, July 16, 1855, ran the headline "The Latest Barnumism" over a story of Barnum's plan to stage a photo submission contest to find the most beautiful women in North America. But a few weeks earlier, on April 11, 1855, the *Raleigh Weekly Register* ran the headline "The Coolest Barnum-ism Yet" to describe a letter Barnum had written to counter the criticisms of Beta, a correspondent who had attacked Barnum's autobiography—though the implication is that Beta was actually Barnum himself.
25. *Burlington Free Press*, August 18, 1837.
26. Ibid.
27. Ober, *Mark Twain and Medicine*, 62, 66.
28. Cited in Werner, *Barnum*, 15.

29. Goodrum and Dalrymple, *Advertising in America*, 20.
30. Barnum, *Struggles and Triumphs*, 71.
31. Ibid., 74.
32. *The Greatest Show on Earth*, chap. 1, n. p.
33. *New York Evening Journal*, August 20, 1835.
34. Cited in Rowsome, *They Laughed When I Sat Down*, 30.
35. Quoted in "'Barnaby Diddleum' on Joice Heth, *New York Atlas*, 1841," The Lost Museum Archive, accessed April 21, 2015, http://chnm.gmu.edu/lostmuseum/lm/265.
36. Cited in Cook, *The Colossal P. T. Barnum Reader*, 25.
37. *The Greatest Show on Earth*, chap. 2, n. p.
38. Ashby, *With Amusement for All*, 35.
39. Barnum, *Struggles and Triumphs*, 142.
40. Ibid., 132; and *Barnum's American Museum Illustrated*, 1850, Library of Congress, https://www.loc.gov/item/10034181/.
41. *The Greatest Show on Earth*; and Barnum, *Struggles and Triumphs*, 356. Remarkably, no sign or plaque today commemorates the spot where Barnum's American Museum stood—but, perhaps fittingly, it is occupied by a Citibank branch.
42. Barnum, *Struggles and Triumphs*, 130.
43. Cook, *The Colossal P. T. Barnum Reader*, 103.
44. Barnum, *Struggles and Triumphs*, 131.
45. Applegate, *The Rise of Advertising*, 50.
46. Barnum, *Struggles and Triumphs*, 281.
47. *Evansville (Ind.) Daily Journal*, August 23, 1850.
48. Applegate, *The Rise of Advertising*, 52.
49. *New York Daily Tribune*, September 2, 1850.
50. Barnum, "The First Jenny Lind Ticket," 107.
51. Kunhardt, Kunhardt, and Kunhardt, *P. T. Barnum*, 224.
52. Davis, *The Circus Age*, 7.
53. A few years later, the Adam Forepaugh circus would actually "mummify" an entire building in Philadelphia with 4,938 lithographs.
54. Kunhardt, Kunhardt, and Kunhardt, *P. T. Barnum*, 252.
55. Parkinson and Fox, *The Circus Moves by Rail*, 75.
56. Ibid., 76.
57. Quoted in Albrecht, *From Barnum & Bailey to Feld*, 7.
58. "War to the Death," *Pittsburg [sic] Dispatch*, November 30, 1890.
59. Cited in many places, including "'Tody' Hamilton Dead," *Topeka State Journal*, August 17, 1916.
60. "Tody Hamilton's Own Story," *New York Sun*, April 1, 1906.
61. Ibid.
62. "A Press Agent to Be Remembered," *Christian Science Monitor*, August 19, 1916, cited in "A Wizard in Weirdly Wonder-Working Words."
63. "City Characters: The Theatrical Press Agent," *National Police Gazette*, December 20, 1879.
64. Quoted in Wallace, *Notes from the Fabulous Showman*, 289.
65. "'Tody' Hamilton Dead," *Topeka State Journal*, August 17, 1916; "Tody Hamilton's Own Story," *New York Sun*, April 1, 1906.

66. Currie, "The Backbone of America," *Country Gentleman*, March 13, 1915.
67. "'Tody' Hamilton Ends His Career," *New York Tribune*, August 17, 1916; and "Circus Stories Now on Tap," *New York Sun*, March 20, 1905.
68. "Circus Stories Now on Tap," *New York Sun*, March 20, 1905; and *New York Clipper*, March 31, 1906.
69. Currie, "The Backbone of America."
70. "Circus Stories Now on Tap," *New York Sun*, March 20, 1905.
71. "The Yankee Press Agent Abroad," 196.
72. Program from P. T. Barnum's Greatest Show on Earth, November 11, 1889, folder 3, MS 6 oversize, box 7, Buffalo Bill Center of the West, Cody, Wyoming.
73. "Rehearsal of the Circus," *New York Times*, March 18, 1903.
74. "'Tody' Hamilton and Caesar," *Washington Times*, August 18, 1916.
75. "Histrionic Hustlers," 494.
76. *London Daily Mail*, unknown date, cited in "The Yankee Press Agent Abroad."
77. "Mr. Barnum at the Circus," *New York Sun*, April 10, 1887.
78. "The Yankee Press Agent Abroad."
79. Cobb, *Roughing It Deluxe*, 15–16.
80. Press agent Whiting Allen in 1902, as quoted in Fellows and Freeman, *This Way to the Big Show*, 195.
81. "The Circus Placard," *Puck*, April 12, 1905, 3.
82. *Cincinnati Enquirer*, May 25, 1884.
83. John Walker Harrington, "Tody Hamilton Remembered as Advance Agent of Happiness," *New York Sun*, September 17, 1917.
84. "Col. R. F. Hamilton," *Arizona Republican*, September 9, 1905.
85. "Original Press Agent," *Salt Lake Tribune*, August 7, 1910.
86. See, for example, "'Tody' Hamilton Ends His Career," *New York Tribune*, August 17, 1916. On the other hand, a detailed and credible account of the origins of the purchase, run in *Billboard* in 1906, tells a different story. See "Real Story of Jumbo," *Walla Walla Evening Statesman*, December 5, 1906.
87. See, for example, "Barnum and His Elephant Jumba [*sic*]," *New York Times*, February 24, 1882.
88. Cited in Ashby, *With Amusement for All*, 75.
89. From undated ad reproduced in Parkinson and Fox, *Billers, Banners and Bombast*, 227.
90. "Jumbo to Cross the Bridge," *Delaware County (Pa.) Times*, April 21, 1883.
91. "Elephants on Brooklyn Bridge," *National Republican* (Washington, D.C.), May 19, 1884.
92. "Advent of the Circus," *Brooklyn Daily Eagle*, May 18, 1884.
93. "Miscellaneous City News: Barnum's Invading Hosts," *New York Times*, March 25, 1883.
94. Davis, *The Circus Age*, 2.
95. Barnum to Secretary of the Interior William F. Vilas, September 25, 1888, cited in Saxon, *Notes from Selected Letters of P. T. Barnum*, 306.
96. "'Tody' Hamilton Ends His Career," *New York Tribune*, August 17, 1916.
97. *Washington Evening Star*, September 17, 1885.

98. Gwen Langdon, "'Tody' Hamilton and Hall Caine," *Cameron County (Pa.) Press*, December 11, 1902.
99. "Arrival of Jumbo's Widow," *New York Times*, April 18, 1886.
100. *New York Times*, April 10, 1905; "'Tody' Hamilton Ends His Career," *New York Tribune*, August 17, 1916.
101. "Tody Hamilton's Own Story," *New York Sun*, April 1, 1906.
102. "'Tody' Hamilton Defends the Press Agent," 11.
103. "'Tody' Hamilton's Reminiscences," 164.

CHAPTER 3. BOOM OR BOOST

1. Quoted in Cook, *The Colossal P. T. Barnum Reader*, 115.
2. *Grand River (Mich.) Times*, August 15, 1855; *Wilmington (N.C.) Journal*, October 23, 1857.
3. Quoted in "Barnum the Charlatan," *Spirit of the Times* (Ironton, Ohio), January 9, 1855.
4. *The Greatest Show on Earth*, chap. 2, n. p.
5. "P. T. Barnum and Humbugs," *Green-Mountain (Vt.) Freeman*, April 28, 1859.
6. Quoted in Cook, *The Colossal P. T. Barnum Reader*, 211.
7. "Barnum and Advertising," 193.
8. DeVoto, *The Year of Decision*, 38–39.
9. "The Half Was Never Told," *Omaha World-Herald*, July 15, 1896.
10. Cronon, "Telling Tales on Canvas," 44.
11. Cited in Dye, *All Aboard for Santa Fe*, 17.
12. "Western Careers for Eastern Young Men," 301–2.
13. Gilpin, *The Cosmopolitan Railway*, 350.
14. DeVoto, "Geopolitics with the Dew on It," 313.
15. Quoted in ibid., 320.
16. Stegner, *Beyond the Hundredth Meridian*, 2.
17. Gilpin, *The Central Gold Region*, 14, 18, 20, 22.
18. Goddard, *Where to Emigrate, and Why*, 13, 15.
19. Ibid., 22, 135–36, 178–79.
20. Crofutt, *Crofutt's Trans-Continental Tourist*, title page.
21. Strahorn, *To the Rockies and Beyond*, 15.
22. Strahorn, *Fifteen Thousand Miles by Stage*, 20.
23. Knight, "Robert E. Strahorn," 33–45.
24. Knott, *Duluth!* 3–7.
25. Quoted in Athearn, *The Mythic West*, 12, 14.
26. Turner, "Significance of the Frontier."

CHAPTER 4. THE HERO CODY AND THE MYTHMAKER BURKE

1. Wetmore, *Last of the Great Scouts*, 265.
2. Warren, *Buffalo Bill's America*, 19–20.
3. Friesen, *Buffalo Bill*, 7.
4. Cody, *The Life of Hon. William F. Cody*, 153.

5. Quoted in Russell, *Lives and Legends*, 90.
6. Both quotations ibid., 102–3.
7. Cody, *The Life of Hon. William F. Cody*, 197.
8. At the time, this was the only medal conferred by the army, and it was bestowed on many men (three enlisted men serving with Cody at Loupe Fork also won it). In the years to come, the army tightened the criteria for the Medal of Honor and, one month after Cody died in 1917, rescinded his medal and nine hundred others. His was restored in 1989. See Barnes, *The Great Plains Guide to Buffalo Bill*, 66–67.
9. "Buffalo Bill: What His Old Friend Thinks of Him," *Cincinnati Enquirer*, September 11, 1881.
10. Cody, *The Life of Hon. William F. Cody*, 299.
11. Wetmore, *Last of the Great Scouts*, 178.
12. See "The Grand Duke," *Chicago Tribune*, January 21, 1872.
13. Sell and Weybright, *Buffalo Bill and the Wild West*, 81.
14. Cody, *The Life of Hon. William F. Cody*, 307.
15. Ibid., 311.
16. Marshall Fishwick says that Ingraham wrote one thousand novels, of which two hundred featured Buffalo Bill. Fishwick, *American Heroes, Myth and Reality*, 108.
17. Quoted in Wilson and Martin, *Buffalo Bill's Wild West*, 21.
18. Sell and Weybright, *Buffalo Bill and the Wild West*, 102.
19. As reported in Leonard and Goodman, *Buffalo Bill*, 219.
20. Quoted in Monaghan, "How Buffalo Bill Captured Chicago."
21. Quoted in Sagala, *Buffalo Bill on Stage*, 68.
22. Quoted in Sell and Weybright, *Buffalo Bill and the Wild West*, 103.
23. *Boston Journal*, March 4, 1873, quoted in Logan, *Buckskin and Satin*, 80.
24. *New York Herald*, no date but likely April 1–2, 1873, quoted in Logan, *Buckskin and Satin*, 80–81.
25. Walsh, *The Making of Buffalo Bill*, 203–5.
26. Warren, *Buffalo Bill's America*, 518.
27. The scant accounts of Burke's early life usually suggest he had only one brother, Thomas. A recently digitized article, however, "Meeting After Many Years," *Wilmington Daily Republican*, June 9, 1879, suggests that there was a third brother named James. Regarding Burke's heritage, some newspaper articles about Burke listed his place of birth as New York, which also had an "Old Seventh Ward." Philadelphia seems the more likely of the two given that he had family connections, and later lived, in nearby Wilmington, Delaware. In "Marylander from the Plains," *Baltimore Sun*, April 7, 1911, it was stated that he was born in Cecil County, Maryland.
28. Burke, "Reminiscences of Col. Cody."
29. Stegner, *Recapitulation*, 182.
30. *Atlanta Constitution*, October 14, 1909; *Richmond Times Dispatch*, October 30, 1909; *Arizona Republican*, September 24, 1902; and *Washington Post*, May 28, 1909.
31. Hal Schindler, "Buffalo Bill Cody: Ever the Showman," *Salt Lake Tribune*, September 26, 1993.
32. "John M. Burke," *San Antonio Light*, December 1, 1882; and *Texas Siftings*, August 21, 1886.

33. Burke, "Reminiscences of the Show Business." Cody scholar Chris Dixon, who has studied enlistment records and found more than one John M. Burke from Wilmington, believes it is possible that this Burke was an enlisted man, at least for a short while.
34. One of the accounts is from Oliver Wendell Holmes, the future Supreme Court Justice. Legend has it that Holmes yelled, "Get down, you damn fool!" although he refused to take credit for that memorable line. See "Oliver Wendell Holmes Recalls the Incident at Fort Stevens When Abraham Lincoln Was Forced to Duck from Enemy Fire," Shapell Manuscript Foundation, accessed July 3, 2016, http://www.shapell.org/manuscript.aspx?get-down-you-damn-fool-abraham-lincoln-battle-of-fort-stevens.
35. "Major Burke, Who Knows Everybody," *Hartford Courant*, May 18, 1907. For information on Burke's relationship with Lincoln and Booth, see "See Saw," *Leadville (Colo.) Daily Herald*, September 21, 1882.
36. See, for example, "Maj. Burke, Friend of Col. Cody, Dead," *Washington Post*, April 13, 1917; and "Scout, But Not Soldier," *Washington Times*, April 14, 1917.
37. Burke, "Reminiscences of Col. Cody."
38. Ibid.
39. Ibid.
40. Dixon, *Buffalo Bill*, xiv. But the listing also had the last name as "Burk."
41. Walsh, *The Making of Buffalo Bill*, 182; the quotation is likely a reference to his time as general business manager of the Second Royal Japanese and Arab Troupe that toured the country, cited in "Two Popular Managers."
42. *Arizona Republican*, September 24, 1902.
43. "John M. Burke," *San Antonio Light*, December 1, 1882.
44. Mystery surrounds the origins of the nickname. Some believe it was an affectation Burke created in his quest to become more like Cody and more of a credible westerner. Cody biographer Don Russell wrote, "It is doubtful that [Burke] had ever been west of the Missouri" prior to 1872, but newspaper articles from late in Burke's life give an accounting of his early travels through Colorado, New Mexico, Arizona, Utah, Nevada, and California with his theatrical troupe, likely as early as 1868. One of those articles attributes the nickname to Wild Bill Hickok: "He was thus christened by Wild Bill when he [Burke] came west as a curly haired boy, by reason of his resemblance to a former associate of Wild Bill who was known by that appellation." Another article cites the name as early as 1883, before the start of the Wild West. See Russell, *Lives and Legends*, 202; *Arizona Republican*, September 24, 1902; *Salt Lake Tribune*, July 22, 1913; and *Music and Drama*, August 5, 1882.
45. *New York Times*, September 3, 1873.
46. Certainly by that fall he was already her manager. See *Pittsburgh Daily Post*, September 12, 1868. Herschel Logan stated that John DePol, the man who brought her to the United States, was still her manager in January 1868. See Logan, *Buckskin and Satin*, 101–3.
47. *Texas Siftings*, August 21, 1886.
48. Rosa and May, *Buffalo Bill and His Wild West*, 46.
49. *Pittsburgh Commercial*, February 2, 1872.
50. "Opera House—The French Spy," *Rochester Democrat and Chronicle*, August 27, 1873.

51. "Morlacchi," *Louisville Courier-Journal*, February 26, 1870.
52. "Amusements," *Atlanta Constitution*, November 12, 1875.
53. Fellows and Freeman, *This Way to the Big Show*, 18.
54. *Memphis Public Ledger*, August 6, 1870.
55. Cody and Cooper, *Memories of Buffalo Bill*, 252–53.
56. See Dixon, *Buffalo Bill*, xiv; Russell, *Lives and Legends*, 202; and Kasson, *Buffalo Bill's Wild West*, 46–47.
57. *Albany (N.Y.) Argus*, February 24, 1874; and *Rochester Daily Union and Advertiser*, March 11, 1874, both cited in Logan, *Buckskin and Satin*, 90, 92. "Amusements," *Atlanta Constitution*, November 12, 1875.
58. Cody and Cooper, *Memories of Buffalo Bill*, 257–59.
59. Quoted in Burke, *The Noblest Whiteskin*, 107.
60. *Ottawa (Ill.) Free Trader*, April 4, 1874.
61. *Nashville Union and American*, September 14, 1873.
62. It also went on the road with the Combination, and was promoted in, for example, the program for *Life on the Border*, June 14–16, 1877.
63. See, for example, *Hartford Courant*, May 21, 1907; and *Washington Post*, May 30, 1907.
64. Smith, *Virgin Land*, 106–7.
65. From photograph of contract dated February 12, 1884, in Rosa and May, *Buffalo Bill and His Wild West*, 60.
66. Burke, *The Noblest Whiteskin*, 126–28.
67. In the book, Cody (or Burke) referred to previous biographies of Boone, Crockett, and Carson, noting, "Idle stories thus incorporated in their work being left so long uncontradicted have become an almost inseparable part of frontier history." This is, of course, precisely what happened to Cody himself. See Frank Christianson's introduction to Cody, *The Wild West in England*, xxvi, xl.
68. Cunningham, *"Your Fathers the Ghosts,"* 292; and Havighurst, *Annie Oakley of the Wild West*, 38.
69. Carter, *Buffalo Bill Cody*, 218.
70. "Buffalo Bill: What His Old Friend Thinks of Him," *Cincinnati Enquirer*, September 11, 1881.
71. Burke, *From Prairie to Palace*, 192.
72. Warren, *Buffalo Bill's America*, 79.
73. *Washington Post*, August 8, 1894.
74. "When the West Was Still Unsettled," *El Paso Herald*, November 2, 1915.
75. *St. Louis Globe Democrat*, May 12, 1877, cited in Logan, *Buckskin and Satin*, 97.
76. "Texas Jack's Troubles," *Brooklyn Daily Eagle*, March 18, 1878.
77. *New Orleans Times-Picayune*, December 6, 1882.
78. Russell, *Lives and Legends*, 296.
79. Sell and Weybright said that Cody and Burke had daily discussions about this and had been planning it since 1877. *Buffalo Bill and the Wild West*, 125, 133.

CHAPTER 5. THE NEWSMAKER, MOSES P. HANDY

1. "Some Noted Women," *Harrisburg Daily Telegraph*, December 19, 1873. The article was reprinted from the *Rochester Democrat and Chronicle*, likely December 4, 1873.

2. *Harrisburg Daily Telegraph*, December 19, 1873.
3. Quotation and details of *Virginius* are from Handy, "Special Correspondent's Story," 757–65.
4. Moses P. Handy, "The Spanish Surrender," *New-York Tribune*, December 18, 1873.
5. *Petersburg (Va.) Index & Appeal* and *Charleston (S.C.) News* are undated clips from scrapbook, box 37, Handy Family Papers, William L. Clements Library, University of Michigan, Ann Arbor. The *Norfolk (Va.) Landmark* quotation is from *Richmond Enquirer*, June 18, 1874.
6. See "Handy Coat of Arms," Our Family Legacy, accessed May 14, 2015, http://www.ourfamilylegacy.info/files/handy0000crest.html.
7. See ibid. and "Capt George Handy," Find A Grave, accessed May 14, 2015, http://www.findagrave.com/cgi-bin/fg.cgi?page=gr&GRid=116719932.
8. See Bryant, *The Epidemic of Yellow Fever*, also available online, accessed May 16, 2015, http://www.usgwarchives.net/va/yellow-fever/yfbryant.html.
9. Galen Wilson, the Handy Papers, 1678–1945, finding guide, 2.
10. "The General Assembly of 1857," *Presbyterian Quarterly Review*, September 1857, 242.
11. Wilson, Handy Papers finding guide, 2–3.
12. Moses P. Handy, diary, 1857, box 36, Handy Family Papers.
13. Moses P. Handy, notebooks, 1859, box 36, Handy Family Papers. Perhaps Webster was a bit ahead of his time. In 1859, only fifty-eight elements had yet been added to the periodic table. Cesium would be next, in 1860, but the number wouldn't hit sixty-two until the 1863 discovery of Indium. See "Periodic Table of Elements Sorted by Year of Discovery," Environmental Chemistry, accessed May 16, 2015, http://environmentalchemistry.com/yogi/periodic/year.html.
14. Handy, notebooks, 1859.
15. *Report of the Committees of the Senate*, 122.
16. From the Brown University commencement of 1861. See Guild, *History of Brown University*, 419.
17. Quoted in Burrage, *Brown University in the Civil War*, 23.
18. Bronson, *History of Brown University*, 352.
19. Burrage, *Brown University in the Civil War*, 32–34.
20. Handy's comings and goings during these weeks are reconstructed as best as possible here using his diary (box 36, Handy Family Papers); his 1866 article "A Courier's Experience During the Great Retreat," 9–10; and Galen Wilson's finding guide to the Handy Papers.
21. Handy may well have gotten the instruction to head for Johnston in Greensboro from the troops under General FitzHugh Lee, who had refused to surrender with Robert E. Lee at Appomattox and intended to join Johnston. FitzHugh Lee was in the area at this time and stopped for lunch at the home of William Matthews—whose daughter, Sarah, Moses Handy would marry. She wrote about the lunch in an 1877 article entitled "Home Life in the Confederacy," in the *Philadelphia Times*, n.d.
22. Scrapbook, 1866, box 37, Handy Family Papers.
23. Handy, "A Courier's Experience During the Great Retreat," 9–10.
24. Ibid., 13–15.
25. Ibid., 17.

26. Diary, 1863, box 36, Handy Family Papers.
27. Scrapbook, box 37, Handy Family Papers.
28. Unidentified clip, circa 1869, scrapbook, Handy Family Papers.
29. Occasionally spelled Sara and sometimes referred to by the nickname Sadie.
30. *Richmond Journal*, April 15, 1869; clip in box 37, Handy Family Papers.
31. Handy and Pleasants, *Visitor's Guide to Richmond and Vicinity*.
32. Unidentified clip, scrapbook, box 37, Handy Family Papers.
33. *Wilmington (N.C.) Morning Star*, November 17, 1874.
34. "Punch in the Presence of the Passinjare," *Saline County (Kans.) Journal*, July 20, 1876; and Mark Twain, "A Literary Nightmare," *Atlantic Monthly*, February 1876, 167–69.
35. *Cincinnati Enquirer*, September 13, 1876.
36. "Gunpowder and Glory," *Philadelphia Times*, July 5, 1876; "An Indian Massacre," *Philadelphia Times*, July 6, 1876.
37. Quoted in *Cincinnati Enquirer*, September 13, 1876.
38. Cited in Deacon, *The Clover Club*, 286.
39. *Raleigh Observer*, April 25, 1878; and *Boston Globe*, September 9, 1880.
40. Handy diary, 1881, box 36, Handy Family Papers.
41. Uncited clip from typewritten page, temporary box 23, Handy Family Papers.
42. Quotation attributed to the *New York Times*, undated, in DeFerrari, *Historic Restaurants of Washington*, 30.
43. Deacon, *The Clover Club*, 234–35.
44. Mrs. M. P. Handy, "A Talk With Young Wives," *Christian Union*, March 31, 1875; and "A Talk About Babies," *Christian Union*, July 29, 1874.
45. Mrs. M. P. Handy, "Under Which Flag?"
46. See Goodman, *Eighty Days*, 8.
47. Sarah Handy diaries, 1890 and 1891, box 36, Handy Family Papers.
48. "A Grand, Good Time," *Salt Lake Herald*, September 17, 1887. Also see Hillary S. Kativa, "Constitution Commemorations," *Encyclopedia of Greater Philadelphia*, accessed May 19, 2015, http://philadelphiaencyclopedia.org/archive/constitution-commemorations.

CHAPTER 6. BIRTH AND GROWTH OF THE WILD WEST

1. Barnum, *Struggles and Triumphs*, 543.
2. Salsbury, "The Origin of the Wild West Show," 208.
3. Catlin, *The Manner, Customs, and Conditions*, 156.
4. George Catlin to Putnam Catlin, August 31, 1840, Catlin Papers, Missouri Historical Society, St. Louis, as quoted in Lewis, "Wild American Savages," 3.
5. Reddin, *Wild West Shows*, 12.
6. W. F. "Doc" Carver was a renowned marksman who had toured the country putting on various exhibitions. In July 1878, at Brooklyn's Driving Park, he broke five thousand glass balls within five hundred minutes. One of the special guests in attendance was none other than John M. Burke. See "A Human Mitrailleuse," *Ohio Democrat* (New Philadelphia), July 25, 1878.
7. Leonard and Goodman, *Buffalo Bill*, 239.
8. Ibid., 235.

9. See “Omaha, Nebraska Population History,” Biggest U.S. Cities, accessed July 14, 2015, https://www.biggestuscities.com/city/omaha-nebraska.
10. “A Show from the Plains,” *Belvidere (Ill.) Weekly Standard*, April 24, 1883.
11. Carter, *Buffalo Bill Cody*, 248.
12. Wild West ad in *Bloomington (Ill.) Pantagraph*, May 10, 1884.
13. Sell and Weybright, *Buffalo Bill and the Wild West*, 137.
14. Deahl, “History of Buffalo Bill’s Wild West Show,” 15.
15. This was the original Polo Grounds, at 110th Street and Fifth Avenue, which had been built in 1876 and was demolished in 1889. The more famous stadium of the same name, the third iteration, which was the longtime home of baseball’s New York Giants, was built farther north, at 155th Street and Harlem River Drive, in 1890.
16. As reported in *Omaha Daily Bee*, June 20, 1884; see also Fellows and Freeman, *This Way to the Big Show*, 69–70.
17. Quoted in Sell and Weybright, *Buffalo Bill and the Wild West*, 135; and Johnston, “Passing of the ‘Wild West,’” 38-39, although the article does not show up on a search of the *Hartford Courant* online archives.
18. “Buffalo Bill’s Wild West,” *Philadelphia Times*, July 15, 1884.
19. “Wild West,” *New Haven Morning Journal and Courier*, July 28, 1883.
20. Fellows and Freeman, *This Way to the Big Show*, 83.
21. “Col. Cody is Reminiscent,” *Duluth (Minn.) Evening Herald*, May 20, 1910.
22. “Major John M. Burke (‘Arizona John’),” *Black and White*, January 20, 1888.
23. “The Two Portsmouths,” *Portsmouth (UK) Evening News*, August 5, 1903.
24. “Burke,” *Rock Island (Ill.) Argus*, June 16, 1896.
25. Sell and Weybright, *Buffalo Bill and the Wild West*, 135.
26. “Maj. J.M. Burke,” *Lexington (Ky.) Morning Herald*, August 25, 1897.
27. “The Man Who Made Frontier Life Famous,” *Rocky Mountain News*, September 6, 1898.
28. Kasson, *Buffalo Bill’s Wild West*, 44. In 1885, Burke, on behalf of Cody, also ended up filing a libel suit against Carver, which resulted in the disbandment of Carver’s show and the arrest of the sharpshooter himself. See “The Dr. Carver and Buffalo Bill Law Case,” *New Haven Morning Journal and Courier*, July 7, 1885.
29. *Inter Ocean*, May 18, 1884; see also May 19; and *Philadelphia Times*, July 15, 1884.
30. Twain to Cody, September 10, 1884, reprinted in “Buffalo Bill’s Wild West,” *Wheeling Daily Intelligencer*, October 1, 1884.
31. One early example of a celebrity endorsement that might have inspired Burke was the “Lindmania” product-licensing frenzy that had erupted during the soprano’s tour of the United States with Barnum in the early 1850s. Most of this was the work of profiteers unconnected to Barnum or Lind, but a few products, such as a riding hat, were actually endorsed by Lind. Another type of endorsement was that of the sultry actress Lillie Langtry, whose image and name began appearing in ads for Pears’ soap by at least 1883. Nevertheless, Burke’s rendering of the Twain testimonial letter as news was truly novel.
32. Today, the telltale sign of a wire service story is usually the absence of a byline, but in Burke’s era, there were almost never any bylines, so we can’t be sure of an article’s provenance.

33. Cameron Blevins, "Making Numbers Legible," *Cameron Blevins* (blog), accessed July 3, 2016, http://www.cameronblevins.org/posts/making-numbers-legible.
34. See "A 19th-century Hectograph Advertisement," *Wikipedia*, accessed July 3, 2016, http://en.wikipedia.org/wiki/Hectograph#mediaviewer/File:1876_Transfer-Tablet-Hektograph-Holcomb_1.jpg.
35. Quoted in Burke, *From Prairie to Palace*, 85–98.
36. Warren, *Buffalo Bill's America*, 291.
37. Burke, *The Noblest Whiteskin*, 163.
38. "Major Burke Hale and Hearty at 69," *Bridgeport (Conn.) Evening Farmer*, May 6, 1912; and Walsh, *The Making of Buffalo Bill*, 261.
39. Kasson, *Buffalo Bill's Wild West*, 69.
40. Russell, *Lives and Legends*, 326. Cody had already been using the title "Hon." by virtue of his election to the Nebraska state legislature in 1872. In 1889, he would receive a commission in the Nebraska State Guard as a brigadier general.
41. Daisy Miller, "A Woman Sees Wild West," *New York Commercial Advertiser*, June 9, 1894; "Buffalo Bill's Camp," *Chicago Times*, July 9, 1893; and "The Wild West in Sheffield," *Sheffield and Rotherham (UK) Independent*, August 10, 1891.
42. Burke, *From Prairie to Palace*, 197.
43. See Berger, "Buffalo Bill's Wild West and John M. Burke," 242, citing Jack Rennert, *100 Posters of Buffalo Bill's Wild West* (New York: Darien House, 1976).
44. Sagala, *Buffalo Bill on Stage*, 201. It is worth noting that most of the billboard and barn-door-style posters featured the dates and locations of performances, and less of the color imagery.
45. Wilson and Martin, *Buffalo Bill's Wild West*, 45.
46. Cody to Nate Salsbury, February 14, 1885, in Nathan Salsbury Papers, Beinecke Library, Yale University. "Joner" is an archaic term meaning loner, or someone without friends.
47. Wilson and Martin, *Buffalo Bill's Wild West*, 124.
48. In an article from the *Buffalo Courier* reprinted in the 1885 Wild West program, the scene of Sitting Bull's meeting with Cody is described thus: "Buffalo Bill and Sitting Bull vigorously grasped hands, and both seemed to say to the other, 'I can trust you.' Major Burke, pointing to Mr. Cody, said: 'Ea ton sha Wee-chasta To kia' (This is the white chief). With a gesture toward the sturdy redskin, Major Burke said: 'Dakota Wee-chasta ya tape' (The great Dakota Sioux king). A grim smile passed over the dusky face of the sturdy Indian, and he glanced unconcernedly around at the vast multitude of people about him."
49. *Omaha World-Herald*, June 15, 1895.
50. Sell and Weybright, *Buffalo Bill and the Wild West*, 223; also "Observations of the Stroller," *Billboard*, August 29, 1908.
51. "Greek Meets Greek," *Buffalo Courier* article reprinted in the 1885 Wild West program.
52. Burke, *The Noblest Whiteskin*, 157.
53. As reported in Kasper, *Annie Oakley*, 54.
54. "Nate Salsbury an Indian Chief," *Inter Ocean*, July 28, 1885.
55. Sell and Weybright, *Buffalo Bill and the Wild West*, 148. The authors said that Burke happened to witness the event and told reporters about it, and that Sitting Bull

refused to shake Carr's hand; Kasper, in *Annie Oakley*, 53, however, tells a different story and quotes the *St. Louis Republican* talking about a handshake. (He likely meant the *Republic*, as the *Republican* ceased publication in 1876.)

56. Leonard and Goodman, *Buffalo Bill*, 243.
57. *New York Herald*, November 25, 1886, as quoted in Sell and Weybright, *Buffalo Bill and the Wild West*, 155.
58. MacKaye to Nate Salsbury, November 8, 1886, in Nathan Salsbury Papers.
59. Reddin, *Wild West Shows*, 82.
60. Berger, "Buffalo Bill's Wild West and John M. Burke," 245.
61. Bridger, *Buffalo Bill and Sitting Bull*, 336.
62. Quoted in Gallop, *Buffalo Bill's British Wild West*, 63.
63. Both quotations in ibid., 48.
64. "The American Exhibition," *London Observer*, March 27, 1887.
65. Quoted in Gallop, *Buffalo Bill's British Wild West*, 45.
66. Burke, *From Prairie to Palace*, 201.
67. Gallop, *Buffalo Bill's British Wild West*, 51.
68. Sell and Weybright, *Buffalo Bill and the Wild West*, 166.
69. Quoted in Gallop, *Buffalo Bill's British Wild West*, 106.
70. *Bloomsburg (Pa.) Columbian*, June 10, 1887.
71. Gallop, *Buffalo Bill's British Wild West*, 45.
72. Henry Irving, "'Buffalo Bill' from the Wild West," *Pall Mall Gazette* (UK), October 12, 1886.
73. Bridger, *Buffalo Bill and Sitting Bull*, 337.
74. Blackstone, *Buckskins, Bullets and Business*, 22.
75. June 18, 1887, folder 5, box 1, Nathan Salsbury Papers.
76. Quoted in Sell and Weybright, *Buffalo Bill and the Wild West*, 170.
77. Quoted in Friesen, *Buffalo Bill*, 70.
78. As told in Russell, *Lives and Legends*, 331.
79. He also had the prudence to keep certain celebrity stories out of the press. Many years after that first London tour, Burke confessed to a reporter at the *Baltimore Sun* that he drank sherry cobblers with the future Queen Victoria when she, as the Princess of Wales, had visited the Wild West incognito. "The Princess insisted that I should join them and—suppressing a shudder, because my preference is the beverage produced in Kentucky—I acquiesced. . . . No word of this visit was permitted to get into the London papers." See "Says He Drank with Queen," *Baltimore Sun*, July 6, 1902.
80. The Wild West would return to London later that season; Salsbury estimated that total attendance for all the shows in Great Britain was 2.5 million—see "American Exhibition" chapter of his unpublished manuscript, Nathan Salsbury Papers.
81. "A Wild, Western Passage," *New York Sun*, January 23, 1888.
82. "The American Exhibition," *London Magnet*, May 9, 1887.
83. Quoted in Cody, *The Wild West in England*, 73.
84. *Puck*, November 6, 1887, 192–93.
85. "The Wild West Show," *Manchester Courier and Lancashire General Advertiser* (UK), January 5, 1888.
86. "Buffalo Bill in London," *Accomac (Va.) Peninsula Enterprise*, reprinted note from T. C. Crawford of the *New York World*, November 5, 1887.

87. "Buffalo Bill Happy," *New York Times*, July 15, 1887.
88. Sherman to Cody, May 8, 1887, and June 28, 1887, quoted in Burke, *From Prairie to Palace*, 216–17.
89. "An American View of 'Buffalo Bill,'" *Pall Mall Gazette* (UK), July 8, 1887.
90. "The Arrival of Buffalo Bill in America," *Manchester Courier and Lancashire General Advertiser* (UK), June 2, 1888, quoting from the *New York Herald*, May 21, 1888; *New York World*, quoted in Leonard and Goodman, *Buffalo Bill*, 253. The steamer had an enormous hold capable of transporting all the Wild West animals; indeed, this very ship had originally been designated to transport Jumbo the elephant across the Atlantic for P. T. Barnum, although delays had ultimately forced the use of its sister ship, the *Assyrian Monarch*. "They're Seasick by Now," *New York Sun*, April 28, 1889.

CHAPTER 7. EVOLUTION OF A MARKETING VIRTUOSO

1. Leonard and Goodman, *Buffalo Bill*, 254; and "How the Wild West Show Has Developed," *New York Times*, April 7, 1901.
2. "Buffalo Bill's Dazzler," *New York Herald*, May 31, 1888.
3. *Lincoln County Tribune*, June 23, 1888.
4. Walsh, *The Making of Buffalo Bill*, 274.
5. Rosa and May, *Buffalo Bill and His Wild West*, 140.
6. Salsbury, "The Origin of the Wild West Show," 209.
7. "Burke's Whiskers Are Truly Grand," *Richmond Times Dispatch*, October 30, 1909.
8. "How the Wild West Show Has Developed," *New York Times*, April 7, 1901.
9. Fellows and Freeman, *This Way to the Big Show*, 18.
10. Ibid., 18–19, 103.
11. For example, he commended Atlanta for its "prosperous conditions . . . it is well known that Atlanta is going some." When he arrived in Idaho Falls in September 1908 ahead of the show, he commented, "Do you know that you people have better . . . cement streets than they have in New York?" See "Major Burke Here; Oh, Such Kindness!," *Atlanta Constitution*, October 14, 1909; "Major Burke Congratulates Idaho Falls on Activity," unknown Idaho Falls paper, September 1908, from record 720148–43_1, Johnnie Baker's scrapbook, Buffalo Bill Museum and Grave, Golden, Colorado.
12. Fellows and Freeman, *This Way to the Big Show*, 18.
13. David Curtis, "The Union Square that Was," *New York Tribune*, December 16, 1922.
14. Cited in Mitchell, *Liberty's Torch*, 261.
15. "Major Burke Learned French," *New York Times*, September 7, 1894.
16. Emma Bullet, "Our Show," *Brooklyn Daily Eagle*, May 3, 1889. Bullet also noted that the Parisians were astonished at the exaggerations in other American advertising at the Exposition. "Everything on each card and bill is represented as the best in the world. How do the venders [*sic*] know it is the best in the world? Here, by such self laudation, estimation is lowered and people immediately ask, 'What Barnum is that?'"
17. Quoted in Kasson, *Buffalo Bill's Wild West*, 84.
18. Burke, *Prairie to Palace*, 234.

19. "They're Seasick by Now," *New York Sun*, April 28, 1889.
20. "Good-By, Buffalo Bill," *Chicago Tribune*, April 28, 1889.
21. *New York Herald*, August 10, 1889, as quoted in Moses, *Wild West Shows*, 82.
22. Burke, *Prairie to Palace*, 239.
23. Burke, *The Noblest Whiteskin*, 194.
24. Ibid., 192.
25. Deahl, "History of Buffalo Bill's Wild West Show," 83.
26. "Advance Agent," folder 63, box 2, Nathan Salsbury Papers.
27. Salsbury, "The Origin of the Wild West Show," 212.
28. "The Imperial Rescripts," *Salt Lake Herald*, March 4, 1890; "The Pope and the Cavalier," *Richmond Dispatch*, April 20, 1890; *Sacramento Daily Record-Union*, March 5, 1890.
29. Burke, *Prairie to Palace*, 239. For one especially good later reference to the event, see "Visited the Pope," *Cleveland Plain Dealer*, August 25, 1895.
30. *Arizona Weekly Journal-Miner* (Prescott), November 16, 1892. There was a Private John Burk involved in the battle, and the agent at the Standing Rock Agency was named John Burke. But it is unlikely that a paper as small as this one would have known about them or had access to any records. The information almost certainly came from John M. Burke himself.
31. "Sitting Bull and Braves," *Boston Globe*, July 26, 1885.
32. "For Object Lessons," *St. Paul Daily Globe*, June 16, 1888.
33. "The Indian's Future," *Columbian and Democrat* (Bloomsburg, Pa.), August 17, 1888, reprinting an article from the *Philadelphia Times*.
34. "Wild West Getting Home," *New York Sun*, October 2, 1906.
35. "Sitting Bull and Braves," *Boston Globe*, July 26, 1885.
36. Ibid.
37. "Noble Reds Here for Battle," *New York Sun*, April 15, 1907.
38. "Sitting Bull and Braves," *Boston Globe*, July 26, 1885.
39. Macon McCormick, "Man-in-the-Dark," *New York Sunday Advertiser*, July 1, 1894.
40. Burke, *Prairie to Palace*, 157, 192.
41. "Favors Shaft to Red Men," *Baltimore Sun*, May 27, 1909.
42. "The Indian's Future," *Columbian and Democrat* (Bloomsburg, Pa.), August 17, 1888.
43. Quoted in Bridger, *Buffalo Bill and Sitting Bull*, 361.
44. Quoted in Gallop, *Buffalo Bill's British Wild West*, 158.
45. "Our William in Germany," *Omaha Daily Bee*, October 15, 1890; and "Tolstoy; 'The Kreutzer Sonata,'" Intercommunication Center, accessed April 29, 2017, http://www.ntticc.or.jp/en/feature/1995/The_Museum_Inside_The_Network/fileroom/documents/Cases/259tolstoy.html.
46. Burke, *The Noblest Whiteskin*, 199.
47. Quoted in Sagala, *Buffalo Bill on Stage*, 107.
48. "Major J. M. Burke's Picturesque Career," *Guthrie (Okla.) Leader*, October 2, 1902.
49. "What Maj. Burke Says," *Washington Evening Star*, November 25, 1890.
50. "Major Burke, Peacemaker," *Washington Times*, April 13, 1917.
51. "Buffalo Bill's Associate Dead," *Harrisburg Telegraph*, April 13, 1917. More than one newspaper article would later refer to Burke's presence at, and role after, Wounded

Knee. The *Telegraph* obituary stated, "Burke was a scout under Colonel Charles Taylor and was with him when he captured Red Cloud and Sitting Bull was killed in the campaign of 1890–91." A more interesting reference is "Indian Fighters Meet in Capital," *Deseret News* (Salt Lake City, Utah), January 6, 1910, in which the story is told about Burke and Taylor meeting up at Harvey's in Washington, D.C., on the nineteenth anniversary of the surrender of Red Cloud in 1891.

52. "Major John M. Burke, Well Known Here, Dies," *Scranton Republican*, April 13, 1917.
53. "Big Chief Makes a Speech," *New York Times*, December 9, 1906.
54. Fellows and Freeman, *This Way to the Big Show*, 18–19. In 1902, a mellowing Burke told one newspaper reporter that he "took a turn at playing target for the infuriated redskins" at Wounded Knee, but also admitted that much of his "frontier record" was "simply reflected glory." See *Arizona Republican*, September 24, 1902.
55. Details of the Indian boy's upbringing remain unclear. Many articles of the time said that Burke adopted him, but there is no documented evidence of that. One unidentified newspaper account from May 1894 says that the boy was found on the third day after the battle by No Neck, chief of Indian scouts under General Miles and a performer in the Wild West, and then presented to Burke, who gave him clothes and comfort, and that No Neck then adopted him. See 1894 scrapbook, Buffalo Bill Center of the West, Cody, Wyoming.
56. McCormick, "Man-in-the-Dark," *New York Sunday Advertiser*, July 1, 1894.
57. "He Was a Wild Westerner," *St. Albans (Vt.) Messenger*, July 19, 1895.
58. "Major J. M. Burke's Picturesque Career," *Guthrie (Okla.) Leader*, October 2, 1902.
59. "Oratory for a Crisis," *Washington Post*, February 5, 1891.
60. Burke, *Prairie to Palace*, 264.
61. Stetler, "Buffalo Bill's Wild West in Germany," 189, citing *Tageblatt und Anzeiger*, June 21, 1890.
62. Ibid.
63. *Hamburger Nachrichten*, August 22, 1890; *Bremer Nachrichten*, September 5, 1890; and *Anzeiger Dresden*, June 15, 1890, cited in Stetler, "Buffalo Bill's Wild West in Germany," 193.
64. Cited in Reddin, *Wild West Shows*, 112.
65. "Buffalo Bill's Show in Germany," *Grand Forks (N.Dak.) Herald*, September 19, 1890.
66. "Visited the Pope," *Cleveland Plain Dealer*, August 25, 1895.
67. See "Life of Plain Pulsates in Wild West," *San Francisco Call*, September 11, 1902; and "He Was a Wild Westerner," *St. Albans (Vt.) Messenger*, July 19, 1895.
68. *Birmingham Daily Press* (UK), *Birmingham and Aston Chronicle* (UK), and uncited source from Cunningham, *"Your Fathers the Ghosts,"* 147.
69. Gallop, *Buffalo Bill's British Wild West*, 191.
70. Wilson and Martin, *Buffalo Bill's Wild West*, 80.
71. Stetler, "Buffalo Bill's Wild West in Germany," 161. Also see Bridger, *Buffalo Bill and Sitting Bull*, 356.
72. "How the Wild West Show Has Developed," *New York Times*, April 7, 1901.
73. Remington, "Buffalo Bill in London," 847.
74. Cody, *The Wild West in England*, 44.
75. Burke, *Prairie to Palace*, 157.
76. Ibid., 156–57.

CHAPTER 8. THE BATTLE FOR THE WORLD'S FAIR

1. Mike Sunnucks, "Super Bowl XLIX Generated $295M in Direct Spending, $719M in Overall Impact," *Phoenix Business Journal*, June 23, 2015, accessed July 3, 2016, http://www.bizjournals.com/phoenix/news/2015/06/23/super-bowl-xlix-generated-719m-in-direct-ripple.html.
2. "Super Bowl Commercials: How Much Does a Spot Cost in 2017?" *Sports Illustrated*, January 16, 2017, https://www.si.com/nfl/2017/01/26/super-bowl-commercial-cost-2017.
3. Badger, *The Great American Fair*, 131. For a good discussion of the competition for world's fairs, also see Curti, *Probing Our Past*, 246,
4. De Young, "The Columbia World's Fair," 597.
5. "Not Spoiled by Honors," *New York World*, October 7, 1889.
6. Quoted in Curti, *Probing Our Past*, 266.
7. Bancroft, *The Book of the Fair*, 37.
8. *The Chicago Record's History of the World's Fair*, 3.
9. *Dedicatory and Opening Ceremonies*, 53.
10. In *The Official Directory of the World's Columbian Exposition*, 26, Handy cleared up this arcane mess. Dr. Charles W. Zaremba, he wrote, was a native of Prussia who studied in Germany, came to live in Chicago, and did some work in Mexico.
11. *Dedicatory and Opening Ceremonies*, 54; and 13. *New York Times*, December 9, 1886.
12. Barnum, "What the Fair Should Be," 400.
13. *Harper's Weekly*, August 3, 1889, 614.
14. "Edison Back from Paris," *New York Times*, October 7, 1889.
15. *The Chicago Record's History of the World's Fair*, 3.
16. Cameron, *The World's Fair*, 8.
17. *Report of the President to the Board of Directors*, 10.
18. "Every quarter of the globe" is an interesting turn of phrase, considering that Columbus was the one who proved the earth to be round.
19. Quoted in Cameron, *The World's Fair*, 8.
20. Cameron, *The World's Fair*, 17.
21. "Chicago Is a Candidate," *Chicago Tribune*, July 26, 1889.
22. Barnum, "What the Fair Should Be," 401.
23. *New York Times*, August 3, 1889.
24. Astor, "New York's Candidacy for the World's Fair of 1892," 166.
25. *New York Times*, September 23, 1889.
26. *New York Times*, September 25, 1889.
27. "Chicago and the Fair," *New York Times*, October 7, 1889.
28. Applebaum, *The Chicago World's Fair of 1893*, 1.
29. "The Scheme Won't Work," *New York Times*, November 11, 1889. For its part, the *Chicago Tribune* came up with "the Young Giant of the West"—again typical of the sectional mentality. See *Chicago Tribune*, July 30, 1889.
30. *Times of London*, October 24, 1887, as quoted in Pierce, *As Others See Chicago*, 230.
31. Giuseppe Giacosa, "Chicago and Her Italian Colony," as quoted in Pierce, *As Others See Chicago*, 276, 278.
32. Ibid., 282.

33. Quoted in Burg, *Chicago's White City of 1893*, 47.
34. Quoted in Pierce, *As Others See Chicago*, 283.
35. Quoted in Ralph, *Our Great West*, 18.
36. Kipling, *From Sea to Sea*, 139–41.
37. "Chicago Fills the Bill," *Chicago Tribune*, July 26, 1889.
38. "Out of the Swim," *Inter Ocean*, August 5, 1889.
39. *Chicago Tribune*, July 31, 1889.
40. See "Chicago and the Fair," *New York Times*, October 7, 1889.
41. *Critic* 326 (March 29, 1890), 156.
42. Quoted in Badger, *The Great American Fair*, 48; see also *Chicago Tribune*, July 26, 1889.
43. On July 29, 1889, the *Tribune* commented, "They never had a more appropriate opportunity of showing a patriotic sentiment, and they never displayed a greater lack of that article—not even in their Tory sympathies during the Revolution or in their draft-riots during the Rebellion—than in connection with the alleged attempt to erect a monument over the grave of America's greatest General."
44. *Chicago Tribune*, August 2, 1889.
45. "Editor's Easy Chair," 796.
46. Newspaper quotations all taken from "Tips on the World's Fair," *Chicago Tribune*, August 3, 1889.
47. *Chicago Tribune*, August 17, 1889.
48. *New York Times*, November 16, 1889.
49. "Both Are in the Soup," *St. Louis Post-Dispatch*, November 25, 1889.
50. Brunner, "The Making of the White City," 402–3.
51. Pierce, *As Others See Chicago*, 255.
52. "Presenting Chicago's Claims," *Chicago Tribune*, January 12, 1890.
53. A vote in the Senate and a presidential proclamation would follow in April, but the House vote was the important one.
54. Bancroft, *The Book of the Fair*, 40.
55. "Congress' Choice, Chicago," *Inter Ocean*, February 25, 1890.
56. *Chicago Tribune*, February 25, 1890.
57. Cameron, *The World's Fair*, 22. Politics were very much a part of the struggle on both sides. At one point the *Chicago Tribune* had threatened local congressmen: "If they wish to be reelected next fall they must be up and doing. If they come back from Washington next spring with the fair they will be welcomed with music and song. If they do not get it they might as well pull up stakes and go to New York and vegetate. Their fellow citizens will banish them to that remote and desolate region." Indeed, the final balloting showed a strong preference among Republicans for Chicago and Democrats for New York. See *Chicago Tribune*, July 26, 1889; and *New York Times*, February 25, 1890, for voting.
58. "Chicago It Is," *New York Evening World*, February 25, 1890.
59. Quoted in the *Chicago Tribune*, February 25, 1890.
60. "Platt the Great," *Brooklyn Daily Eagle*, February 25, 1890.
61. *Chicago Tribune*, February 25, 1890.

CHAPTER 9. THE DEPARTMENT OF PUBLICITY AND PROMOTION

1. Handy, "How to Move Easily and Well," 6.
2. Sarah Handy diary, 1890, box 36, Handy Family Papers.
3. "The President's Family at Cape May," *Pittsburgh Press*, July 20, 1890.
4. Manuscript in temporary box 13, Handy Family Papers.
5. "Moses Is Pretty Well Backed," *Alton (Ill.) Evening Telegraph*, December 8, 1890.
6. Correspondent Frank G. Carpenter reported, "Colonel Moses P. Handy has refused the consul generalship to Cairo, and he is happy in his newspaper duties in connection with the world's fair. He tells me he got the two appointments on the same day and preferred the world's fair position because it enabled him to remain at home." *Salt Lake Herald*, December 28, 1890; see also Sarah Handy diary, 1890, Handy Family Papers.
7. Moses P. Handy, report on the history of the department, temporary box 13, Handy Family Papers.
8. Quotations from an ad reprinted on "Hotel Richelieu," Chicagology, accessed May 26, 2016, https://chicagology.com/goldenage/goldenage013.
9. "Sudden Attack," *Kansas City (Kans.) Gazette*, December 30, 1890.
10. Ibid.
11. "P. T. Barnum is Dangerously Ill," *Chicago Tribune*, November 16, 1890; and *Philadelphia Times*, March 2, 1891.
12. As originally reported in Werner, *Barnum*, 371.
13. Quoted in Sell and Weybright, *Buffalo Bill and the Wild West*, 136.
14. Barnum, "What the Fair Should Be," 400.
15. Ibid.
16. Hutchinson, *A Publisher's History*, chap. 3, pp. 12, 14.
17. Steve Myers, "U.S. Has the Same Number of Newspapers Now as in 1890s," *Poynter*, accessed June 2, 2016, http://www.poynter.org/2011/u-s-has-same-number-of-newspapers-now-as-in-1890s/138940.
18. "The Gulf Dock Site," *Wichita Daily Eagle*, March 8, 1891.
19. *Journalist*, October 18, 1884, quoted in Lee, *The Daily Newspaper in America*, 434.
20. Quoted in Jonnes, *Empires of Light*, 207.
21. Quoted in Baldwin, *Edison*, 202.
22. Handy, report on the history of the department, Handy Family Papers.
23. See Burrelle to Handy, June 12, 1893, temporary box 23, Handy Family Papers. Other information about the department's use of clipping services is mentioned by Handy in his report on the history of the department.
24. All quotations in this section are from Handy's report on the history of the department.
25. William Rice, "A Tradition of Restaurant Bounty," *Chicago Tribune*, July 16, 1997.
26. Henry M. Hunt, "World's Fair Gossip," *Olean (N.Y.) Democrat*, January 8, 1891.
27. Weston died shortly after taking the job.
28. Campbell to Handy, January 4, 1893, box 25, Handy Family Papers; see also Handy, report on the history of the department.
29. Handy, report on the history of the department.
30. Ibid.
31. Dorr to Handy, June 22, 1891, box 25, Handy Family Papers.

32. Handy to Davis, September 29, 1891, box 25, Handy Family Papers.
33. Handy, report on the history of the department.
34. Various documents, box 25, Handy Family Papers.
35. Dorr to Handy, July 7, 1891, temporary box 23, Handy Family Papers.
36. Ayme to Handy, June 22, 1891, box 25, Handy Family Papers.
37. Dorr to Handy, July 7, 1891, temporary box 23, Handy Family Papers.
38. Dorr to Handy, July 9, 1891, temporary box 23, Handy Family Papers.
39. Handy, report on the history of the department.
40. Handy testimony, *The Reports of Committees of the House of Representatives for the First Session of the Fifty-Second Congress*, vol. 6, report 1454 (Washington, D.C.: Government Printing Office, 1892), 190.
41. For an excellent description of railroad opulence, see Goodman, *Eighty Days*, 93.
42. "The Chicago Special," *Cambridge Chronicle*, June 6, 1891, accessed May 28, 2016, http://cambridge.dlconsulting.com/cgi-bin/cambridge?a=d&d=Chronicle18910606-01.2.43#.
43. Sarah Handy diary, 1891, box 36, Handy Family Papers.
44. "Construction News," *Inter Ocean*, May 28, 1891; and Hales, *Constructing the Fair*, 1.
45. "Awed by Its Majesty," *Chicago Herald*, May 2, 1893.
46. "Will the World's Fair Be a Failure?" *Oracle*, June 27, 1893.
47. *Birmingham Daily Post*, July 3, 1891.
48. See, for example, *Colonies and India*, July 4, 1891.
49. Letter from Lewis H. Davis of Davis & Requa Underwriters, Chicago, introducing Handy to Sir Henry Knight, July 2, 1891, temporary box 23, Handy Family Papers.
50. "Europe and the Fair," *New York Times*, September 13, 1891.
51. Quoted in Dorr to Handy, July 31, 1891, temporary box 23, Handy Family Papers.
52. Dorr to Handy, July 15, 1891, temporary box 13, Handy Family Papers.
53. M. Handy to S. Handy, August 3, 1891, box 16, Handy Family Papers.
54. Dorr to Handy, July 15, 1891, temporary box 13, Handy Family Papers.
55. Dorr to Handy, August 24, 1891, temporary box 23, Handy Family Papers.
56. Sarah Handy diary, 1891.
57. Sarah Handy, "Chicago," unknown publication, 1892, box 30, Handy Family Papers.
58. Sarah Handy, "The Folly of Fretting," undated, box 30, Handy Family Papers.
59. M. Handy to S. Handy, May 29, 1892; S. Handy to Will Handy, September 1, 1892; William Pinkerton to M. Handy, September 30, 1892; and Fred Handy to M. Handy, May 10, 1892, all box 16, Handy Family Papers.
60. MacKaye to Handy, February 15, 1892, box 16, Handy Family Papers. Handy wrote a touching tribute when MacKaye passed away twenty-four months later. See "Major Handy's Letter," *Inter Ocean*, February 27, 1894.
61. Dole to Handy, May 25, 1892, box 16, Handy Family Papers.
62. "Preparing to Open the Fair," *Hamilton Daily Democrat*, January 14, 1893; "New-York's Great Bee Exhibit," *New York Times*, May 15, 1893; and Deacon, *The Clover Club*, 234–35.
63. Dorr to Handy, October 13, 1896, box 25, Handy Family Papers.
64. Handy to Davis, September 29, 1891, box 25, Handy Family Papers.
65. "Major Handy Is Safe," *Chicago Post*, October 15, 1891. It is interesting to note that Handy saved this clip, which was highly critical of him.

66. He was also well aware of his own word count; at one point in the manuscript of his report on the history of the department, he wrote by hand, "9045 words so far."
67. Dorr to Handy, June 22, 1891, box 25, Handy Family Papers.
68. Handy, report on the history of the department.
69. Ayme to Dorr, September 30, 1891, box 25, Handy Family Papers.
70. Handy, report on the history of the department.
71. Ibid.
72. Handy, outline for report on the history of the department, box 25, Handy Family Papers.
73. *Reports of Committees*, 77.
74. Handy, report on the history of the department.
75. *Atchison (Kans.) Daily Patriot*, April 11, 1892.
76. Handy, "Local Press Work," the dedication section of report on the history of the department.
77. Handy, report on the history of the department.
78. Handy testimony, *Reports of Committees*, 190.
79. Staunch to Handy, January 23, 1893, box 25, Handy Family Papers.
80. Handy, report on the history of the department.
81. Ibid.
82. See *Inter Ocean*, August 10, 1892, box 25, in Handy Family Papers.
83. "Cut Off Major Handy," *Chicago Tribune*, August 7, 1892.
84. Handy, "Local Press Work."
85. Ibid. Handy's initial assessment in the report for the period ending October 31, 1892, was that the number of press attendees had been three times that of any other event in history. See Department of Publicity and Promotion report for the period ending October 31, 1892, box 25, Handy Family Papers.
86. "Buffalo Bill and Royalty," *Kate Field's Washington*, July 19, 1893.
87. Now spelled Stony Island Avenue.

CHAPTER 10. 1893

1. Handy, report on the history of the department; and "Unique Newspaper Exhibit," *New York Times*, May 6, 1893.
2. "J. Frost in Command," syndicated story in *Harrisburg Star-Independent*, February 2, 1893; and "The First Building," *Bismarck Tribune*, February 14, 1893.
3. "J. Frost in Command," *Harrisburg Star-Independent*, February 2, 1893.
4. Department of Publicity and Promotion report for the period ending July 31, 1893, box 25, Handy Family Papers.
5. Handy, report on the history of the department.
6. Burke, *The Noblest Whiteskin*, 219.
7. "All Fight for Space," *Chicago Evening Journal*, May 29, 1893.
8. Wild West ad in *Chicago Daily News*, May 5, 1893.
9. Wild West courier, 1893, folder 12, oversize 2, Wojtowicz Collection, Buffalo Bill Center of the West, Cody, Wyoming.
10. "How It Was Done," *Inter Ocean*, August 14, 1892.
11. *The Columbian Exposition and World's Fair Illustrated.*

12. *Chicago Dispatch*, April 18, 1893.
13. "Sioux Chiefs Arrive," *Chicago Record*, April 20, 1893.
14. "World's Fair Doings," *Inter Ocean*, April 20, 1893.
15. *Inter Ocean*, March 26, 1893.
16. Burke, *Prairie to Palace*, 194–95, 250, 264.
17. Ibid., 121–22.
18. "Books and Authors," *Chicago Globe*, July 22, 1893.
19. "Buffalo Bill's Camp," *Chicago Times*, July 9, 1893.
20. "Is a Great Show," *Chicago Dispatch*, April 26, 1893.
21. "Buffalo Bill's Show Opens," *Chicago Tribune*, April 27, 1893.
22. *Chicago Post*, August 26, 1893.
23. "Tribunes Sold $3.50," *Chicago Tribune*, May 1, 1893.
24. *Chicago Herald*, May 2, 1893.
25. "Achieved Is the Glorious Work," *Chicago Tribune*, May 1, 1893.
26. "Awed by Its Majesty," *Chicago Herald*, May 2, 1893.
27. Quotations cited in *Chicago Herald*, May 2, 1893; and "Second Day of the Fair," *New York Times*, May 3, 1893.
28. "In a Frame of Light," *Chicago Tribune*, May 9, 1893.
29. "World's Fair Grounds," *Galveston (Tex.) Daily News*, May 14, 1893.
30. "The World's Fair, An Illuminated Night," *Otago Daily Times* (New Zealand), August 24, 1893.
31. "Illuminated," *Louisville Courier-Journal*, May 9, 1893.
32. Handy, report on the history of the department.
33. Igleheart, "What the Publicity Department Did," 478.
34. Abbot, "The Makers of the Fair," 885.
35. "Week of Declines," *Chicago Tribune*, May 8, 1893.
36. Amy Leslie at the Fair, *Chicago Daily News*, May 2, 1893.
37. Amy Leslie at the Fair, *Chicago Daily News*, unknown date, 1893, from Pony Bob Haslam scrapbook, Buffalo Bill Museum and Grave, Golden, Colorado; Kasper, *Annie Oakley*, 125; and Amy Leslie at the Fair, *Chicago Daily News*, May 5, 1893.
38. Amy Leslie at the Fair, *Chicago Daily News*, May 5, 1893.
39. Ibid.
40. Barnum & Bailey ad, *New York World*, April 17, 1893.
41. Barnum & Bailey herald, June 20, 1893, accessed July 3, 2016, http://fsu.digital.flvc.org/islandora/object/fsu%3A197844.
42. "Ghost of P. T. Barnum," *Chicago Herald*, July 1, 1893.
43. "Gates Closed Tight," *Chicago Journal*, May 8, 1893.
44. "Money for the Big Fair," *New York Times*, August 14, 1892.
45. "Forty Thousand Are Kept Out," *Chicago Mail*, May 22, 1893.
46. "Hurt the Side Show," *Chicago Tribune*, May 29, 1893.
47. See *Chicago Evening Journal*, May 29, 1893; and Wild West ad, *Chicago Tribune*, May 1, 1893.
48. "Arena—'Wild West,'" *Chicago Post*, July 2, 1893. He would reuse this the following season in Brooklyn, with the headline "The Coolest Place on the Bay." See ad in *Brooklyn Daily Eagle*, September 10, 1894.

49. "Waifs to See the Fair," *Inter Ocean*, August 19, 1893.
50. "Illinois Fair Commissioners in a Row Over Somebody's Blunder," *Chicago Record*, August 23[?], 1893.
51. "Injustice to 'Wild West,'" *Chicago* [*Daily*] *News*, August 25, 1893.
52. Kasson, *Buffalo Bill's Wild West*, 103–4.
53. Buffalo Bill's Wild West advertisement in *Inter Ocean*, June 27, 1893; and "Cowboy Race Over," *Chicago Post*, June 27, 1893.
54. *Chicago Herald*, September 16, 1893.
55. "The Wild West," *Inter Ocean*, May 28, 1893.
56. "Buffalo Bill's Wild West," *Chicago Herald*, July 2, 1893.
57. "Buffalo Bill and Royalty," *Kate Field's Washington*, July 19, 1893.
58. See, for example, "Buffalo Bill Coming," *Detroit Free Press*, July 19, 1906.
59. "The Wild West," *Inter Ocean*, June 11, 1893.
60. Turner, "Significance of the Frontier."
61. See "Mark Twain, James W. Paige and the Paige Typesetter," *TwainQuotes.com*, accessed June 16, 2016, http://www.twainquotes.com/paige.html.
62. "Banquet of Publishers," *Chicago Times*, May 27, 1893.
63. "Men Who Have Made the Fair," *New York Times*, April 30, 1893.
64. "Deadheads at the Fair," *New York Times*, June 1, 1893; and Department of Publicity and Promotion reports for the periods ending June 30, 1893, and July 31, 1893, box 25, Handy Family Papers.
65. Burnham to Handy, May 6 and 7, 1893, box 16, Handy Family Papers.
66. Davis to Handy, September 12, 1893, temporary box 23, Handy Family Papers.
67. William M. Handy to Moses P. Handy, April 14, 1893; Will to Moses, June 5, 1893; and Moses to Will, August 18, 1893, box 17, Handy Family Papers.
68. Cameron, *The World's Fair*, 247.
69. *New York Times*, October 30, 1893.
70. "Two Pictures," *Albany Journal*, August 4, 1893.
71. Harrison, a cousin of President William Henry Harrison, was in his fifth term as mayor and had served two terms as a congressman. He had also been editor of the *Chicago Times* during the two years prior to the fair. He was shot in his home by Eugene Prendergast, who had been turned down in his bid to be appointed as the city's corporation counsel.
72. Chatfield-Taylor, "Chicago's Entertainment of Distinguished Visitors," 600–601.
73. Ingalls, "Lessons of the Fair," 142–43.
74. Quoted in Patrick T. Reardon, "The World's Columbian Exposition at the 'White City,'" *Chicago Tribune*, accessed June 16, 2016, http://www.chicagotribune.com/news/nationworld/politics/chi-chicagodays-columbianexposition-story-story.html.

CHAPTER 11. DENOUEMENT

1. Group to Handy, November 22, 1893, box 26, Handy Family Papers. A driving force of this dinner was R. E. A. Dorr, erstwhile second-in-command at Department O, and now an editor with the *New York Mail and Express*.
2. See "Dinner to Major Handy," *New York World*, December 8, 1893; *Reading (Pa.) Times*, December 9, 1893.

3. "The Great Fair Over," *Advance*, November 2, 1893. For some of the suggestions about what to do with the buildings, see "Now the Buildings," *Inter Ocean*, November 19, 1893.
4. "Fair is Fire Swept," *Chicago Tribune*, January 9, 1894.
5. McKinley to Handy, November 14, 1893, box 17, Handy Family Papers. Handy's original letter to McKinley is absent from the archives.
6. "Where is Moses P. Handy?" *Washington Post*, February 14, 1897.
7. "Moses P. Handy Appointed," *Philadelphia Times*, July 28, 1897.
8. "As Advance Agent," *Inter Ocean*, July 28, 1897.
9. "Major M. P. Handy Dead," *New York Times*, January 9, 1898.
10. Sarah to Handy children, October 23, 1897, temporary box 13, Handy Family Papers.
11. Sarah Handy, untitled, box 30, Handy Family Papers.
12. Mrs. M. P. Handy, "The Great French Exposition," *New York Mail and Express*, March 12, 1898.
13. G. W. Weippiert, in A. N. Kellogg Syndicate Letter.
14. Davis, *The Circus Age*, 7.
15. See, for example, *Richmond Dispatch*, October 21, 1903. One *New York Sun* story said that forty advance agents sailed to London ahead of the circus in 1889—see "Showman Barnum," *New York Sun*, printed in *Indianapolis Journal*, October 14, 1889. Barnum and Bailey actually split in 1885, then reunited in 1888.
16. Davis, *The Circus Age*, 44.
17. "Col. R. F. Hamilton," *Arizona Republican*, September 9, 1905.
18. "Under the Tents," *New York Clipper*, December 21, 1895.
19. "Billboards Abandoned," 511.
20. Blanchard, "Tody Hamilton," 685.
21. "Price of the Rare Beast Is Sure to Satisfy the Zoological Hunger," *Washington Post*, April 8, 1906; and "Circus Stories Now on Tap," *New York Sun*, March 20, 1905.
22. "The Greatest Show on Earth," *Illustrated Police News*, December 19, 1897.
23. See "City Characters: The Theatrical Press Agent," *National Police Gazette*, December 20, 1879; and "Gratitude of Oysters," *Holton (Kans.) Recorder-Tribune*, April 5, 1877.
24. "In the Matter of Free Reading Notices," *Printers' Ink*, December 3, 1902.
25. "Press Agents Ponder Truth," *New York Sun*, April 26, 1903.
26. "Maypole Dance by Riders," *New York Times*, March 11, 1894.
27. "Tody Hamilton's Latest Scheme," *Fourth Estate*, March 14, 1895.
28. "Circus Stories Now on Tap," *New York Sun*, March 20, 1905.
29. Watkins, *Four Years in Europe*, 21.
30. As reported in Latzke, "Fortunes and Freaks in Advertising."
31. Root, *The Ways of the Circus*, 271.
32. See "The Revolt of the Freaks," *London Standard*, January 16, 1899. In his book, Harvey Watkins maintained a straightforward tone in describing the revolt, as if the whole thing were indeed a news event and not a publicity stunt. See Watkins, *Four Years in Europe*, 22.
33. "A Substitute for 'Freak," *Chicago Journal*, as reprinted in *Anaconda (Mont.) Standard*, March 19, 1899.

34. "Press Agents Ponder Truth," *New York Sun*, April 26, 1903.
35. "Joanna's Jealousy," *Yorkshire Evening Post* (UK), March 25, 1899.
36. *London Daily Mail*, unknown date, cited in "The Yankee Press Agent Abroad."
37. Walter Emanuel, "Those Freaks," *To-Day*, January 7, 1899.
38. Watkins, *Four Years in Europe*, 8.
39. *New York Clipper*, February 1, 1902.
40. *New York Sun*, unknown date, cited in "'Tody' Hamilton in Germany," 41.
41. "'Tody' Hamilton and His Vocabulary Back," *New York Times*, October 29, 1902.
42. "Bomben Erfolg Von Barnum & Bailey," *New York Clipper*, March 2, 1901.
43. "Barnum & Bailey Jottings," *New York Clipper*, December 22, 1900.
44. "B&B's Valentine to the Old Reliable," *New York Clipper*, March 9, 1901.
45. *New York Sun*, unknown date, cited in "The Circus Poster in Europe," 389.
46. "A Famous Press Agent," *Minneapolis Journal*, August 1, 1904.
47. "Tody Hamilton's Own Story," *New York Sun*, April 1, 1906.
48. "A Testimonial Dinner to Tody," *Grand Forks (N.Dak.) Evening Times*, March 2, 1907.
49. "'Tody' Hamilton and Caesar," *Washington Times*, August 18, 1916.
50. "Buffalo Bill Ready to Take the Trail to Camp," *Hawaiian Star*, September 2, 1911.
51. Cody received praise for his fair pay to Annie Oakley and as early as 1894 came out in support of women's suffrage. See "Colonel Cody Talks," *New York Recorder*, May 22, 1894.
52. Reddin, *Wild West Shows*, 142.
53. Burke to Hoen, February 7, 1894, folder 21, Wojtowicz Collection, Buffalo Bill Center of the West, Cody, Wyoming.
54. *Rough Rider*, 1902, folder 4, oversize box 4, MS6, Buffalo Bill Center of the West, Cody, Wyoming.
55. *From Desert Sands to Prairie Wilds*, August 1, 1911, folder 11, box 2, MS6, Buffalo Bill Center of the West, Cody, Wyoming.
56. These and previous headlines from 1894 scrapbook on microfilm, Buffalo Bill Center of the West, Cody, Wyoming; and "Buffalo Bill's Indians Shopping," *Brooklyn Daily Eagle*, June 4, 1894.
57. "Chiefs Visit Chief Gilroy," *New York Press*, June 5, 1894.
58. "Indians See 'The World,'" *New York Evening World*, June 4, 1894.
59. See "Fired at by Indians in Brooklyn," *New York Times*, June 12, 1894.
60. Miller, "A Woman Sees Wild West," *New York Commercial Advertiser*, June 9, 1894.
61. "Colonel Cody Talks," *New York Recorder*, May 22, 1894.
62. Parker, *Odd People I Have Met*, 87.
63. Transcription at "Cody's Tribute to Edison," the William F. Cody Archive, accessed June 30, 2016, http://codyarchive.org/multimedia/wfc.aud00002.html.
64. The film was released under several different titles, including *Wars of Civilization* and *The Last Indian Battles, or From the Warpath to the Peace Pipe*.
65. Kasson, *Buffalo Bill's Wild West*, 256; see also Reddin, *Wild West Shows*, xv.
66. "Historic Indian Fights Are Filmed," *Ogden (Utah) Standard*, March 27, 1914.
67. Program/ad for the first public presentation at the Columbia Theatre, February 27, 1914, folder 37, box 2, Wojtowicz Collection, Buffalo Bill Center of the West, Cody, Wyoming.
68. Moses, *Wild West Shows*, 245–46.

69. "Is Daddy of All the Press Agents," *El Paso Morning Times*, March 19, 1914.
70. "Major Burke, of the Buffalo Bill Show, to Wed a Girl Met at the Fair," *Inter Ocean*, March 17, 1894.
71. "President Francis Leaves the City," *St. Louis Republic*, June 9, 1901.
72. "Wake Up! Says Maj. Burke," *Boston Globe*, July 16, 1916.
73. "The Profanity Habit," *Washington Post*, May 15, 1908.
74. See "Maj. Burke's Bluff," *St. Louis Post-Dispatch*, October 4, 1899; and "A Tomb Among the Clouds," *New York Times*, May 4, 1902.
75. "Maj. Burke Corrals the Indians," *Washington Post*, March 15, 1896.
76. "Major Burke, Who Knows Everybody," *Hartford Courant*, May 18, 1907.
77. "Jolly Colonel Advance Agent," *Austin Statesman*, September 21, 1912.
78. "Picturesque Burke Makes Way for Show," *Baltimore Sun*, May 10, 1913.
79. "Is Daddy of All the Press Agents," *El Paso Morning Times*, March 19, 1914.
80. "Buffalo Bill's Bosom Friend," *Arizona Republican*, March 28, 1914.
81. "Major Burke, of the Buffalo Bill Show, To Wed a Girl Met at the Fair," *Inter Ocean*, March 17, 1894.
82. McCormick, "Man-in-the-Dark," *New York Sunday Advertiser*, July 1, 1894.
83. "Visited the Pope," *Cleveland Plain Dealer*, August 25, 1895.
84. "Major J. M. Burke in Town," *San Bernardino Evening Transcript*, September 20, 1902.
85. "Major John M. Burke," *Bryan (Tex.) Eagle*, June 16, 1897.
86. "Our Border Friends," *Washington Post*, April 22, 1901.
87. "Life of Plain Pulsates in the Wild West," *San Francisco Call*, September 11, 1902.
88. "Prince of Press Agents Hits Atlanta for a Day," *Atlanta Georgian and News*, October 14, 1909.
89. "A Council of Three," July 30, 1895; "Jolly Major Burke," October 25, 1895; "'Cold?' Says Major Burke," October 31, 1895; "A Story Told of Buffalo Bill's Wig," March 27, 1901; "Major Burke Here to Boom Wild West Show," October 2, 1907; "Maj. Burke Here; Oh, Such Kindness!" October 14, 1909; "Maj. Burke, Dean of Boosters, Heralding Cody's 'Goodbye,'" October 12, 1911—all *Atlanta Constitution*.
90. "How the Wild West Show Has Developed," *New York Times*, April 7, 1901.
91. Nate Salsbury, unlabeled chapter in his unpublished manuscript, Nathan Salsbury Papers.
92. Parker, *Odd People I Have Met*, 85–86.
93. Cody and Cooper, *Memories of Buffalo Bill*, 295.
94. McMurtry, *The Colonel and Little Missie*, 188.
95. Leonard and Goodman, *Buffalo Bill*, 264.
96. Wild West "Roll of Honor" ad from Beloit, Wisconsin, August 23, 1900, folder 14, box 1, Wojtowicz Collection, Buffalo Bill Center of the West, Cody, Wyoming; and "The Man Who Made Frontier Life Famous," *Rocky Mountain News*, September 6, 1898.
97. "Major Burke Breezes in to Say That Colonel Cody's on the Way," *Louisville Courier-Journal*, June 17, 1913.
98. The *Overland Trail* (courier), week ending May 24, 1913, vol. 27, no. 33, folder 15, oversize 2, Wojtowicz Collection, Buffalo Bill Center of the West, Cody, Wyoming. The show in 1913 was no longer Buffalo Bill's Wild West but the new combination,

Buffalo Bill's Wild West and Pawnee Bill's Great Far East Show, otherwise known as the Two Bills Show.

99. "Circus News," *New York Clipper*, May 9, 1914.
100. "Burke with Sells-Floto," *New York Clipper*, September 13, 1913.
101. Quoted in Burke, *The Noblest Whiteskin*, 230–31.
102. Wild West ad in *Duluth Herald*, August 4, 1898, from folder 13, box 1, Wojtowicz Collection, Buffalo Bill Center of the West, Cody, Wyoming.
103. Reddin, *Wild West Shows*, 135–36.
104. Having by this time learned a great deal about the art of promotion, Cody put his knowledge to use in trying to promote his plan to settle three hundred thousand acres he had leased from the government in Wyoming's Big Horn Basin. He created what we would now think of as newspaper advertorials and distributed promotional literature at the entrance to the Wild West. See "The Half Was Never Told," *Omaha World-Herald*, July 15, 1896; and Reddin, *Wild West Shows*, 137.
105. "Cody's Hospitality," *North American* (Philadelphia), November 1, 1893.
106. "She Cost Cody His All," *Washington Post*, November 17, 1907.
107. One interesting example may be a fight that occurred at Chamberlin's in Washington, D.C., on February 16, 1894, in which Cody knocked down a man named Fred May. Some historians report that the fight was about Katherine Clemmons, and that Burke simply told the press it was over a bottle of wine. See Burke, *The Noblest Whiteskin*, 220, 235; and Warren, *Buffalo Bill's America*, 512. A contemporary newspaper account, however—while understandably not mentioning Clemmons—provides sufficient detail about the fight, including affidavits from John Chamberlin and Major Barber (formerly of the World's Columbian Exposition administrative staff), to indicate that it may very well have been about an old bottle of wine and May's provocative behavior and insistence upon an apology. See "Fred May and Buffalo Bill," *Alexandria (Va.) Gazette*, February 19, 1894.
108. One measure of Cody's own celebrity: an ad that ran in the 1910 Wild West program from "Stubb's [*sic*] the Piano Man," which boasted, "I Sold and Delivered to 'BUFFALO BILL' A Piano Sept. 19th 1874 36 years ago. For which he paid me $1,000.00 in GOLD." See Wild West "Buffalo Bill Bids You Goodbye" program, 1910, Newberry Library.
109. "Miss Bess Isbell, Ahead of Buffalo Bill Show," *St. Paul Globe*, August 10, 1902.
110. Testimony at Cody's divorce trial would indicate that she started her work at the Wild West in 1900, but an earlier profile of her in the *St. Paul Globe* quoted her as saying that she began in 1898. See ibid.
111. *Cripple Creek (Colo.) Times*, February 14, 1905, quoted in Enss, *The Many Loves of Buffalo Bill*, 91. Burke apparently also tried to keep the news out of the press, as indicated in the report by Dan Muller of a meeting between Cody, Burke, and Harry Tammen of the *Denver Post*, in which Burke tried to get Tammen to stop publishing details about the trial. "But the stories are damaging the Colonel's reputation," Muller quoted Burke. "It'll hurt the show." See Muller, *My Life with Buffalo Bill*, 146–47.
112. "'Buffalo Bill' at Last Stand," *New York Times*, February 17, 1905.
113. Ibid.
114. "Cody's Heart Won by Press Agent?" *Chicago Tribune*, February 20, 1905.

115. From unidentified clipping in March 1905, part of William F. Cody scrapbook, Robinson Locke Collection, New York Public Library, quoted in Kasson, *Buffalo Bill's Wild West*, 140.
116. Salsbury to Cody, October 5, 1899, Nathan Salsbury Papers.
117. Cody to Salsbury, October 6, 1899, Nathan Salsbury Papers.
118. Salsbury to Cody, October 10, 1899, Nathan Salsbury Papers.
119. Salsbury to Cody, September 27, 1900, Nathan Salsbury Papers.
120. Salsbury, "Cody, Manager," in unpublished manuscript, Nathan Salsbury Papers.
121. Salsbury, "Cody's Personal Representatives," in unpublished manuscript, Nathan Salsbury Papers.
122. Salsbury, "Secret Service," in unpublished manuscript, Nathan Salsbury Papers.
123. Salsbury, "Long Hair and a Plug Hat," in unpublished manuscript, Nathan Salsbury Papers.
124. Various newspaper accounts pegged her age at eighteen or nineteen, but her father, A. C. Jester, had died in 1877, so the youngest she could have been in 1899 was twenty-one. Another account, in the *Paducah (Ky.) Sun* (August 10, 1899), listed her age as twenty-four.
125. "Matinee Girl," *Boston Traveler*, June 1, 1899.
126. "An 'Advance Woman,'" *Cincinnati Times-Star*, April 29, 1899.
127. "Miss Jester, Buffalo Bill's Niece, Calls on the Sun," *Williamsport Sun*, May 11, 1899.
128. "Clever Is Young Lady Ahead of Buffalo Bill," *Columbus (Ohio) Citizen*, May 6, 1899.
129. *Philadelphia Press*, May 14–15, 1899.
130. "Matinee Girl," *Boston Traveler*, June 1, 1899.
131. "Woman Press Agent," *Wilkes-Barre Times*, May 12, 1899.
132. "Young Woman's Name is a Good Joke," *Buffalo Times*, July 8, 1899.
133. *Bridgeport (Conn.) Post*, June 13, 1899.
134. The *Columbus (Ohio) Dispatch*, May 6, 1899, included an illustration of her wearing a tie; also see *Dayton Times*, May 4, 1899.
135. *Worcester (Mass.) Telegram*, June 18, 1899.
136. "Unique Occupation," *Rochester Post Express*, July 6, 1899. There was apparently no relation between Tom Isbel and Bess Isbell, even though they were part of the Wild West at the same time.
137. "A Novel Position," *Wilkes-Barre Leader*, May 16, 1899.
138. "The Woman Advance Agent," *Poughkeepsie News-Press*, May 24, 1899.
139. Unknown newspaper and date, from Mary Jester Allen scrapbook on microfilm, Buffalo Bill Center of the West, Cody, Wyoming.
140. "A Story Told of Buffalo Bill's Wig," *Atlanta Constitution*, March 27, 1901.
141. "Marylander from the Plains," *Baltimore Sun*, April 7, 1911.
142. Fellows and Freeman, *This Way to the Big Show*, 143.
143. Muller, *My Life with Buffalo Bill*, 156. Muller's claims to his relationship with Cody have never been verified.
144. Cunningham, *"Your Fathers the Ghosts,"* 266–67. This was a fitting bookend to the inscription Burke had made on an 1889 photograph of him standing in front of the statue of Joan of Arc at the Rheims Cathedral in France: "Joan et Jean."
145. The photograph appears to show a model, perhaps made of plaster of Paris, and the partially completed sculpted bust of Burke sitting on the table. The misidentification

of Burke as Cody was all the more inexplicable because it seems that on the same trip, Cody presented the caffè with a framed and signed photo of himself. The plaque on that one correctly identifies Cody and states the year as 1906.

146. Shirley, *Pawnee Bill*, 199.
147. "Wild West to Be Here Tomorrow," *Hartford Courant*, May 21, 1907.
148. Ad for Buffalo Bill's Wild West and Pawnee Bill's Far East, *Des Moines Register*, August 15, 1909.
149. Buffalo Bill's Wild West and Pawnee Bill's Far East program, 1911, Buffalo Bill Center of the West, Cody, Wyoming.
150. F. C. Cooper, "Two Bills' Show Notes," *New York Clipper*, May 11, 1912.
151. "Buffalo Bill's Farewell," *Cincinnati Enquirer*, July 3, 1910.
152. "Prince of Press Agents Hits Atlanta for a Day," *Atlanta Georgian and News*, October 14, 1909.
153. *Show World Magazine*, June 24 or July 22, 1911, cited in Yost, *Buffalo Bill*, 478.
154. See, for example, "The Only Buffalo Bill," *Arizona Republican*, May 7, 1911. The claims of Bill Matthewson of Wichita had been dogging Burke and Cody for years. As early as 1894, Burke had dispatched fellow press agent Frank Small to send correspondence to the newspapers refuting Matthewson and his supporter, Jack Crawford, and comparing them—unfavorably—to a skunk and a rattlesnake. See "Buffalo Bill," *Louisville Courier-Journal*, August 20, 1894.
155. See, for example, "Meeting of Old Comrades," *Austin Statesman*, October 31, 1910.
156. "Cody Arrives in New York," *New York Times*, as reprinted in *North Platte (Neb.) Semi-Weekly Tribune*, March 31, 1911.
157. "Maj. Burke, Friend and Press Agent of Colonel Cody, Dies," *Detroit Free Press*, April 13, 1917.
158. Fellows and Freeman, *This Way to the Big Show*, 18–19.
159. P. T. Barnum, *Adventures of An Adventurer*, as quoted in Cook, *The Colossal P. T. Barnum Reader*, 18.
160. "Buffalo Bill to Retire," *Boston Post*, April 12, 1896; "Buffalo Bill to Retire," *Salt Lake Herald*, August 21, 1898; "Buffalo Bill to Retire," *Inter Ocean*, December 30, 1901; "Buffalo Bill to Retire," *Salina (Kans.) Daily Republican-Journal*, November 13, 1902; "Buffalo Bill to Retire," *Indianapolis Star*, October 31, 1903; "Buffalo Bill to Retire," *Salt Lake Tribune*, September 22, 1906. Cody to Fellows quotation in Burke, *The Noblest Whiteskin*, 225.
161. "Buffalo Bill's Farewell Proclamation to the Public!," Buffalo Bill Collection, Denver Public Library.
162. Buffalo Bill's Wild West and Pawnee Bill's Far East program, 1911.
163. "'Buffalo Bill' on Final Tour: Show of Unusual Magnitude," *Detroit Free Press*, July 7, 1910.
164. "Farewell of Buffalo Bill," *Altoona (Pa.) Tribune*, June 24, 1911.
165. "Buffalo Bill's Wild West Historical Sketches and Daily Review," Buffalo Bill's Wild West and Pawnee Bill's Far East program (version 1), 1911.
166. Muller, *My Life with Buffalo Bill*, 256.
167. Shirley, *Pawnee Bill*, 189.
168. Quoted in Wilson and Martin, *Buffalo Bill's Wild West*, 209, referencing manuscript held by Glenn Shirley.

169. See Friesen, *Buffalo Bill*, 132–38.
170. Muller, *My Life with Buffalo Bill*, 290.
171. Cooper, *Annie Oakley*, 278.
172. Shirley, *Pawnee Bill*, 189.

CHAPTER 12. LEGACIES

1. "Col. R. F. Hamilton," *Arizona Republican*, September 9, 1905.
2. "Circus Stories Now on Tap," *New York Sun*, March 20, 1905.
3. "Tody Hamilton's Own Story," *New York Sun*, April 1, 1906.
4. "400 Entertain Tody Hamilton," *New York Times*, March 3, 1907.
5. "Hughes Still for Recount," *New York Sun*, March 3, 1907.
6. Leonard and Goodman, *Buffalo Bill*, 283.
7. Quoted in Blackstone, *The Business of Being Buffalo Bill*, 82–83.
8. Burke, "Reminiscences of Col. Cody."
9. Ibid.
10. Fox, *The Mirror Makers*, 38–39.
11. Schlesinger, *Rise of the City*, 185.
12. "The Auto Publicity Man."
13. In 1907, one magazine referred to Abraham White's efforts to promote the rival DeForest Wireless as "a publicity campaign worthy of 'Tody' Hamilton." See *Success*, June 1907.
14. Hale, "The Gentle Art of the Publicist," 4–5.
15. Fellows and Freeman, *This Way to the Big Show*, 22.
16. Olasky, *Corporate Public Relations*, 4–5.
17. Quotations from Greenberg, *Republic of Spin*, 76.
18. "Committee on Publicity Named," *Charlotte (N.C.) Observer*, April 15, 1917.
19. See Greenberg, *Republic of Spin*, 107–8.
20. Ibid., 110.
21. Creel, *How We Advertised America*, 10.
22. Ibid., 12, 13, 14, 50.
23. Ibid., 34.

BIBLIOGRAPHY

Abbot, Willis John. "The Makers of the Fair." *Outlook* 48, no. 21 (November 18, 1893): 884–85.

Adams, Bluford. *E Pluribus Barnum: The Great Showman and the Making of U.S. Popular Culture.* Minneapolis: University of Minnesota Press, 1997.

Albrecht, Ernest. *From Barnum & Bailey to Feld: The Creative Evolution of the Greatest Show on Earth.* Jefferson, N.C.: McFarland, 2014.

A. N. Kellogg Syndicate Letter. *Printers' Ink*, March 16, 1898: 49.

Applebaum, Stanley. *The Chicago World's Fair of 1893.* New York: Dover, 1980.

Applegate, Edd. *The Rise of Advertising in the United States: A History of Innovation to 1960.* Lanham, Md.: Scarecrow Press, 2012.

Ashby, LeRoy. *With Amusement for All: A History of American Popular Culture Since 1830.* Lexington: University Press of Kentucky, 2006.

Astor, William Waldorf. "New York's Candidacy for the World's Fair of 1892." *Cosmopolitan* 8 (December 1889): 165–67.

Atack, Jeremy, and Peter Passell. *A New Economic View of American History.* New York: Norton, 1994.

Athearn, Robert G. *The Mythic West.* Lawrence: University of Kansas Press, 1986.

"The Auto Publicity Man." *Horseless Age* 20, no. 5 (July 31, 1907): 142.

Badger, R. Reid. *The Great American Fair.* Chicago: Nelson-Hall, 1979.

Baldwin, Neil. *Edison: Inventing the Century.* Reprint, Chicago: University of Chicago Press, 2011.

Bancroft, Hubert Howe. *The Book of the Fair.* Chicago: Bancroft Company, 1893.

Barnes, Jeff. *The Great Plains Guide to Buffalo Bill.* Mechanicsburg, Pa.: Stackpole Books, 2014.

Barnum, P. T. "The First Jenny Lind Ticket." *Cosmopolitan* 4 (October 1887): 107–9.

———. *Struggles and Triumphs: Or, Forty Years' Recollections of P. T. Barnum.* London: Sampson, Low, Son, and Marston, 1869.

———. "What the Fair Should Be." *North American Review* 150 (March 1890): 400.

"Barnum and Advertising." *Printers' Ink*, July 14, 1910, 193.

Bellamy, Edward. *Looking Backward: 2000–1887.* New York: Grosset and Dunlap, 1898.

Berger, Jason. "Buffalo Bill's Wild West and John M. Burke." *Journal of Promotion Management*, January 16, 2009, 225–52.

"Billboards Abandoned." *AD Sense*, December 1904, 511.

Blackstone, Sarah J. *Buckskins, Bullets and Business.* Santa Barbara, Calif.: Greenwood Press, 1986.

———. *The Business of Being Buffalo Bill: Selected Letters of William F. Cody, 1879–1917.* Santa Barbara, Calif.: Greenwood Press, 1988.

Blanchard, Frank Leroy. "Tody Hamilton, for Many Years with the Barnum & Bailey Show." *Editor and Publisher and Journalist*, February 6, 1915, 695.

Bridger, Bobby. *Buffalo Bill and Sitting Bull: Inventing the Wild West.* Austin: University of Texas Press, 2009.

Bronson, Walter C. *History of Brown University.* Providence, R.I.: Brown University, 1914.

Brunner, H. C. "The Making of the White City." *Scribner's*, October 1892, 399–418.

Bryant, J. D. *The Epidemic of Yellow Fever in Norfolk and Portsmouth, Virginia During the Summer and Fall of 1855.* Philadelphia, Pa.: T. K. and P. G. Collins, 1856.

Burg, David F. *Chicago's White City of 1893.* Lexington: University of Kentucky Press, 1976.

Burke, John. *Buffalo Bill: The Noblest Whiteskin.* New York: Putnam, 1973.

Burke, John M. *"Buffalo Bill" from Prairie to Palace: An Authentic History of the Wild West, with Sketches, Stories of Adventure, and Anecdotes of "Buffalo Bill," the Hero of the Plains.* Chicago: Rand McNally, 1893.

———. "Reminiscences of Col. Cody." *Billboard*, March 24, 1917, 20–21, 209–10.

Burrage, Henry Sweetser. *Brown University in the Civil War.* Providence, R.I.: Brown University, 1868.

Cameron William E. *The World's Fair—Being a Pictorial History of the Columbian Exposition.* Grand Rapids, Mich.: P. D. Farrell, 1893.

Carter, Robert A. *Buffalo Bill Cody: The Man Behind the Legend.* New York: Wiley and Sons, 2000.

Catlin, George. *The Manner, Customs, and Conditions of the North American Indians.* Vol. 2. London: Printed by the author, 1841.

Chatfield-Taylor, Hobart C. "Chicago's Entertainment of Distinguished Visitors." *Cosmopolitan* 15 (September 1893): 600–602.

The Chicago Record's History of the World's Fair. Chicago: Chicago Daily News, 1893.

"The Circus Placard." *Puck*, April 12, 1905, 3.

"The Circus Poster in Europe." *Fame* 11 (1902): 389.

Cobb, Irwin S. *Roughing It Deluxe.* New York: George H. Doran, 1914.

Cody, Louisa Frederici, and Courtney Ryley Cooper. *Memories of Buffalo Bill.* New York: D. Appleton, 1920.

Cody, William F. *The Life of Hon. William F. Cody.* Hartford, Conn.: Frank E. Bliss, 1879.

———. *The Wild West in England.* Lincoln: University of Nebraska Press, 2012.

The Columbian Exposition and World's Fair Illustrated. Philadelphia, Pa.: Columbian Engraving and Publishing, 1893.

Cook, James. *The Colossal P. T. Barnum Reader: Nothing Else Like It in the Universe.* Urbana: University of Illinois Press, 2005.

Cooper, Courtney Ryley. *Annie Oakley, Woman at Arms.* New York: Duffield, 1927.

Creel, George. *How We Advertised America.* New York: Harper and Brothers, 1920.

Crofutt, George A. *Crofutt's Trans-Continental Tourist.* New York: G. W. Carleton, 1875.

Cronon, William. "Telling Tales on Canvas: Landscapes of Frontier Change." In Jules David Prown, Nancy K. Anderson, William Cronon, Brian W. Dippie, Martha A. Sandweiss, Susan Prendergast Schoelwer, and Howard R. Lamar, *Discovered Lands, Invented Pasts,* 37–88. New Haven, Conn.: Yale University Press, 1992.

Cunningham, Tom F. *"Your Fathers the Ghosts": Buffalo Bill's Wild West in Scotland.* Edinburgh: Black and White, 2007.

Currie, Barton W. "The Backbone of America." *Country Gentleman*, March 13, 1915, 492, 520.

Curti, Merle. *Probing Our Past.* New York: Harper and Brothers, 1955.

Cutlip, Scott M. *Public Relations History from the 17th to the 20th Century.* Hillside, N.J.: Lawrence Erlbaum, 1995.

Davis, Janet M. *The Circus Age: Culture and Society Under the American Big Top.* Chapel Hill: University of North Carolina Press, 2002.

Deacon, Mary R. *The Clover Club.* Philadelphia, Pa.: Avil, 1897.

Deahl, William E. "A History of Buffalo Bill's Wild West Show, 1883–1913." Ph.D. diss., Southern Illinois University, 1974.

Dedicatory and Opening Ceremonies of the World's Columbian Exposition. Chicago: Stone, Kastler and Painter, 1893.

DeFerrari, John. *Historic Restaurants of Washington, D.C.: Capital Eats.* Washington, D.C.: History Press, 2013.

de Tocqueville, Alexis. *Democracy in America.* Vol. 1. Translated by Henry Reeve. New York: Colonial Press, 1900.

DeVoto, Bernard. "Geopolitics with the Dew on It." *Harper's,* March 1, 1944, 313–23.

———. *The Year of Decision: 1846.* Boston: Little, Brown, 1943.

De Young, M. H. "The Columbian World's Fair." *Cosmopolitan* 12 (March 1892): 599–605.

Dixon, Chris, ed. *Buffalo Bill: From Prairie to Palace.* Lincoln: University of Nebraska Press, 2012.

Dye, Victoria E. *All Aboard for Santa Fe.* Albuquerque: University of New Mexico Press, 2005.

"Editor's Easy Chair." *Harper's New Monthly,* October 1889, 795–800.

Enss, Chris. *The Many Loves of Buffalo Bill.* Guilford, Conn.: Two Dot, 2010.

Fellows, Dexter W., and Andrew A. Freeman. *This Way to the Big Show—The Life of Dexter Fellows.* New York: Viking, 1936.

Fishwick, Marshall. *American Heroes, Myth and Reality.* Washington, D.C.: Public Affairs Press, 1954.

Fox, Stephen. *The Mirror Makers: A History of American Advertising and Its Creators.* Urbana: University of Illinois Press, 1984.

Friesen, Steve. *Buffalo Bill: Scout, Showman, Visionary.* Golden, Colo.: Fulcrum, 2010.

Gallop, Alan. *Buffalo Bill's British Wild West.* Gloucestershire: Sutton, 2001.

"The General Assembly of 1857." *Presbyterian Quarterly Review* (September 1857): 226–54.

Gilpin, William. *The Central Gold Region: The Grain, Pastoral and Gold Regions of North America.* Philadelphia, Pa.: Sower, Barnes, 1860.

———. *The Cosmopolitan Railway.* San Francisco, Calif.: History Company, 1890.

Goddard, Frederick B. *Where to Emigrate, and Why.* New York: Printed by the author, 1869.

Goodman, Matthew. *Eighty Days: Nellie Bly and Elizabeth Bisland's History-Making Race Around the World.* New York: Ballantine, 2013.

Goodrum, Charles, and Helen Dalrymple. *Advertising in America: The First 200 Years.* New York: Harry N. Abrams, 1990.

The Greatest Show on Earth. Cambridge: Charles River Editors, n.d.

Greenberg, David. *Republic of Spin.* New York: Norton, 2016.

Groner, Alex, and the editors of *American Heritage* and *Business Week. The American Heritage History of American Business and Industry.* New York: American Heritage, 1972.

Guild, Reuben A. *History of Brown University.* Providence, R.I.: Providence Press, 1867.

Hale, David. "The Gentle Art of the Publicist." *Saturday Evening Post,* December 24, 1904, 4–5.

Hales, Peter B. *Constructing the Fair.* Chicago: Art Institute of Chicago, 1993.

Handy, Moses P. "A Courier's Experience During the Great Retreat." *American Magazine and Historical Chronicle,* 1, no. 2 (1985–86): 9–10. Originally published in the *Watchman* (1866).

———. "Special Correspondent's Story: The Surrender of the Virginius." *Lippincott's Monthly Magazine*, December 1892, 757–65.

Handy, Moses P., and William H. Pleasants. *Visitor's Guide to Richmond and Vicinity*. Richmond, Va.: Benjamin Bates, 1871.

Handy, Mrs. M. P. "How to Move Easily and Well." *Ladies' Home Journal*, April 1890, 6.

———. "Under Which Flag?" *Harper's Bazaar*, June 7, 1884, 359.

Havighurst, Walter. *Annie Oakley of the Wild West*. Lincoln: University of Nebraska Press, 1992.

"Histrionic Hustlers." *Theatre* 5, no. 23 (October 5, 1889): 494.

Hutchinson, Peter. *A Publisher's History of American Magazines*. The Magazinist, 2008–2012. http://themagazinist.com/Magazine_History.html.

Igleheart, William. "What the Publicity Department Did for the Columbian Exposition." *Lippincott's Monthly Magazine*, April 1893, 478.

Ingalls, John J. "Lessons of the Fair." *Cosmopolitan* 16 (December 1893): 141–49.

"In the Matter of Free Reading Notices." *Printers' Ink*, December 3, 1902, 19.

Johnston, Winifred. "Passing of the 'Wild West': A Chapter in the History of American Entertainment." *Southwest Review* 21, no. 1 (October 1935): 33–51.

Jonnes, Jill. *Empires of Light*. New York: Random House, 2003.

Kasper, Shirl. *Annie Oakley*. Norman: University of Oklahoma Press, 2000.

Kasson, Joy S. *Buffalo Bill's Wild West*. New York: Hill and Wang, 2000.

Kipling, Rudyard. *From Sea to Sea: Letters of Travel, Part II*. Norwood, Mass.: Norwood Press, 1899.

Knight, Oliver. "Robert E. Strahorn: Propagandist for the West." *Pacific Northwest Quarterly* 59, no. 1 (January 1968): 33–45.

Knott, J. Proctor. *Duluth! Speech of Hon. J. Proctor Knott, of Kentucky, Delivered in the House of Representatives, on the St. Croix and Superior Land Grant*. Washington, D.C.: F. and J. Rives and Geo. A. Bailey, 1871.

Kunhardt, Jr., Philip B., Philip B. Kunhardt III, and Peter W. Kunhardt. *P. T. Barnum, America's Greatest Showman*. New York: Knopf, 1995.

Latzke, Paul. "Fortunes and Freaks in Advertising." *Saturday Evening Post*, August 22, 1903, 4–5, 19.

Lee, Alfred McClung. *The Daily Newspaper in America: The Evolution of a Social Instrument*. New York: Macmillan, 1947.

Leonard, E. J., and J. C. Goodman. *Buffalo Bill—King of the Old West*. New York: Library Publishers, 1955.

Lewis, Robert M. "Wild American Savages and the Civilized English: Catlin's Indian Gallery and the Shows of London." *European Journal of American Studies* 3, no. 1 (Spring 2008): 1–20.

Logan, Herschel C. *Buckskin and Satin: The Life of Texas Jack and His Wife Mlle. Morlacchi*. Harrisburg, Pa.: Stackpole, 1954.

McMurtry, Larry. *The Colonel and Little Missie: Buffalo Bill, Annie Oakley, and the Beginnings of Superstardom in America*. New York: Simon and Schuster, 2006.

Mitchell, Elizabeth. *Liberty's Torch: The Great Adventure to Build the Statue of Liberty*. New York: Grove Press, 2014.

Monaghan, Jay. "How Buffalo Bill Captured Chicago." *Chicago Tribune Grafic Magazine*, January 6, 1952, 3, 10.

Moses, L. G. *Wild West Shows.* Albuquerque: University of New Mexico Press, 1996.
Mott, Frank Luther. *A History of American Magazines, 1850–1865.* Vols. 1 and 2. Cambridge, Mass.: Harvard University Press, 1938.
Muller, Dan. *My Life with Buffalo Bill.* Chicago: Reilly and Lee, 1948.
Ober, K. Patrick. *Mark Twain and Medicine: Any Mummery Will Cure.* Columbia: University of Missouri Press, 2003.
The Official Directory of the World's Columbian Exposition. Chicago: W. B. Conkey, 1893.
"Observations of the Stroller." *Billboard,* August 29, 1908, n.p.
Olasky, Marvin N. *Corporate Public Relations: A New Historical Perspective.* Hillsdale, N.J.: Lawrence Erlbaum, 1987.
Parker, Lew. *Odd People I Have Met.* N. p.: n.p., 191[?].
Parkinson, Tom, and Charles Philip Fox. *Billers, Banners and Bombast: The Story of Circus Advertising.* Boulder, Colo.: Pruett, 1985.
———. *The Circus Moves by Rail.* Boulder, Colo.: Pruett, 1978.
Pierce, Bessie Louise. *As Others See Chicago.* Chicago: University of Chicago Press, 1933.
Pope, Daniel. *The Making of Modern Advertising.* New York: Basic Books, 1983.
Presbrey, Frank. *The History and Development of Advertising.* Garden City, N.Y.: Double, Doran, 1929.
Ralph, Julian. *Our Great West, A Study of the Present Conditions and Future Possibilities of the New Commonwealths and Capitals of the United States.* New York: Harper and Brothers, 1893.
Reddin, Paul. *Wild West Shows.* Urbana: University of Illinois Press, 1999.
Remington, Frederic. "Buffalo Bill in London." *Harper's Weekly,* September 3, 1892, 847.
Rennert, Jack. *100 Posters of Buffalo Bill's Wild West.* New York: Darien House, 1976.
Report of the Committees of the Senate of the United States for the Second Session of the Thirty-Seventh Congress, 1861–62. Washington, D.C.: Government Printing Office, 1862.
Report of the President to the Board of Directors of the World's Columbian Exposition. Chicago: Rand McNally, 1898.
Resseguie, Harry E. "Alexander Turney Stewart and the Development of the Department Store, 1823–1876." *Business History Review* 39, no. 3 (Autumn 1965): 301–22.
Root, Harvey W. *The Ways of the Circus: Being the Memories and Adventures of George Conklin, Tamer of Lions.* New York: Harper and Brothers, 1921.
Rosa, Joseph G., and Robin May. *Buffalo Bill and His Wild West.* Lawrence: University of Kansas Press, 1989.
Rowsome, Frank. *They Laughed When I Sat Down: An Informal History of Advertising in Words and Pictures.* New York: McGraw-Hill, 1959.
Russell, Don. *The Lives and Legends of Buffalo Bill.* Norman: University of Oklahoma Press, 1961.
———. *The Wild West: A History of the Wild West Shows.* Fort Worth, Tex.: Amon Carter Museum, 1970.
Sagala, Sandra K. *Buffalo Bill on Stage.* Albuquerque: University of New Mexico Press, 2008.
Salsbury, Nate. "The Origin of the Wild West Show." *Colorado Magazine,* July 1, 1955, 204–14.
Saxon, A. H., ed. *Notes from Selected Letters of P. T. Barnum.* New York: Columbia University Press, 1983.

Schlesinger, Arthur M., Sr. *Rise of the City: 1878–1898*. Columbus: Ohio State University Press, 1933.

Scudo, [Paul], Hector Berlioz, Louis Boerne, Adolphe Adam, Marie Aycard, Julie de Margueritte, Prince Puckler-Muskau, and Theophile Gautier. *Life of Henriette Sontag, Countess de Rossi*. New York: Stringer and Townsend, 1852.

Sell, Harry Blackman, and Victor Weybright. *Buffalo Bill and the Wild West*. New York: Oxford University Press, 1955.

Shirley, Glenn. *Pawnee Bill: A Biography of Major Gordon W. Lillie*. Albuquerque: University of New Mexico Press, 1958.

Smith, Henry Nash. *Virgin Land: The American West as Symbol and Myth*. Reprint, Cambridge, Mass.: Harvard University Press, 1978.

Soltow, Lee, and Edward Stevens. *The Rise of Literacy and the Common School*. Chicago: University of Chicago Press, 1981.

Stegner, Wallace. *Beyond the Hundredth Meridian*. New York: Penguin, 1992.

———. *Recapitulation*. New York: Penguin, 1979.

Stetler, Julia Simone. "Buffalo Bill's Wild West in Germany: A Transnational History." Ph.D. diss., University of Nevada, Las Vegas, 2006.

Strahorn, Carrie Adell. *Fifteen Thousand Miles by Stage*. New York: Putnam, 1911.

Strahorn, Robert E. *The Hand-Book of Wyoming and Guide to the Black Hills and Big Horn Regions for Citizen, Emigrant and Tourist*. N.p.: privately printed, 1877.

———. *To the Rockies and Beyond*. Omaha, Neb.: Omaha Republican Print, 1878.

Sunnucks, Mike. "Super Bowl XLIX Generated $295M in Direct Spending, $719M in Overall Impact." *Phoenix Business Journal*, June 23, 2015, accessed July 3, 2016, http://www.bizjournals.com/phoenix/news/2015/06/23/super-bowl-xlix-generated-719m-in-direct-ripple.html.

"Super Bowl Commercials: How Much Does a Spot Cost in 2017?" *Sports Illustrated*, January 16, 2017. https://www.si.com/nfl/2017/01/26/super-bowl-commercial-cost-2017.

Thomas, Isaiah. *The History of Printing in America*. 2nd ed. New York: Weathervane Books, 1970.

"'Tody' Hamilton Defends the Press Agent." *Fourth Estate*, September 10, 1904, 11.

"'Tody' Hamilton in Germany." *Printers' Ink*, January 3, 1900, 41.

"Tody Hamilton's Latest Scheme." *Fourth Estate*, March 14, 1895, 3.

"'Tody' Hamilton's Reminiscences." *American Printer*, April 1907, 164.

Turner, Frederick Jackson, "The Significance of the Frontier in American History." Address delivered at the Forty-First Annual Meeting of the State Historical Society of Wisconsin, Madison, December 14, 1893.

Twain, Mark, "A Literary Nightmare," *Atlantic Monthly*, February 1876, 167–69.

"Two Popular Managers." *Journalist*, August 14, 1886, n.p.

Wallace, Irving. *Notes from the Fabulous Showman*. New York: Knopf, 1959.

Walsh, Richard J. *The Making of Buffalo Bill—A Study in Heroics*. Indianapolis, Ind.: Bobbs-Merrill, 1928.

Warren, Louis S. *Buffalo Bill's America: William Cody and the Wild West Show*. New York: Knopf, 2005.

Watkins, Harvey L. *Four Years in Europe: The Barnum & Bailey Greatest Show on Earth in the Old World*. Paris: P. Dupont, 1901[?].

Weeks, Horace Lyman. *A History of Paper Manufacturing in the United States, 1690–1916.* New York: Lockwood Trade Journal, 1916.
Werner, M. R. *Barnum.* New York: Harcourt, Brace, 1923.
"Western Careers for Eastern Young Men." *Century,* December 1882, 301–2.
Wetmore, Helen Cody. *Last of the Great Scouts.* Duluth, Minn.: Duluth Press, 1899.
Wilson, R. L., and Greg Martin. *Buffalo Bill's Wild West—An American Legend.* New York: Random House, 1998.
"A Wizard in Weirdly Wonder-Working Words." *Literary Digest,* September 23, 1916, 770–74.
"The Yankee Press Agent Abroad." *Current Literature* 23, no. 3 (March 1898): 196.
Yost, Nellie Snyder. *Buffalo Bill: His Family, Friends, Fame, Failures, and Fortunes.* Chicago: Snyder Press, 1979.

ACKNOWLEDGMENTS

A tip of the Stetson to the many people who inexplicably believed in the merits of this project and provided assistance and encouragement along the way—including Gil Fuchsberg, Marc Handelman, Jennifer Schwed, Kathy Sklar and Paul Love, Carol Cone, Nancy Kopans, Phil Calian, Larry Vale, Mira Vale, Aaron Vale, Chad Jordan, Chris Berry, Alan and Vicki Dobrow, and my incredibly supportive siblings, Marty and Julie, whose brilliant writing always leaves me feeling inadequate.

On the research front, thanks to Janet Bloom and the great staff at the University of Michigan's Clements Library, repository of all things Handy; the always colorful and helpful Steve Friesen, former director of the Buffalo Bill Museum and Grave in Golden, Colorado; the entire team at the McCracken Research Library, Buffalo Bill Center of the West, in Cody, Wyoming, especially Sam Hanna, Sean Campbell, Mary Robinson, and Jeremy Johnston, who has been a friend and staunch supporter, and may not even have the word "no" in his vocabulary; the other editors of the William F. Cody Series on the History and Culture of the American West, Frank Christianson and Doug Seefeldt; Pete Shrake at Circus World Baraboo; Jan Boles at the College of Idaho; and Alan Gallop.

Jay Gitlin of Yale University and the Bales-Gitlin Band offered guidance not once but twice, adding notes to make the melody soar and producing harmonies that I had not heard; and so did our mutual inspiration, Howard Lamar, who long ago told me I didn't need a Ph.D. to be a writer of history.

Heartfelt thanks also to Kent Calder of the University of Oklahoma Press, who calmly and patiently guided me through the long publishing process; Emily Schuster, who capably managed the project in its precarious latter stages; and Melanie Mallon, a capital copyeditor if ever there was one.

The Burke ceremony described in the epilogue would never have happened without the ingenious detective work of Dennis Haynes, the warm response from Jim Fuqua and his family, and the logistical support of Keena Terry at Mount Olivet Cemetery.

Most important of all is Julie Zagars, who has redefined love by always encouraging me to pursue my passions, even when that has meant investing a great deal of time pursuing indulgent and expensive hobbies, like authoring books.

INDEX

References to illustrations appear in italics. Names of individuals not preceded by a title in subentries are alphabetized by last name.